QUEEN ELIZABETH
AND THE MAKING OF POLICY,
1572-1588

Queen Elizabeth
AND THE MAKING
OF POLICY,
1572-1588

By Wallace T. MacCaffrey

PRINCETON UNIVERSITY PRESS
PRINCETON, NEW JERSEY

1981

TO MY WIFE

ACKNOWLEDGMENTS

I HAVE MANY DEBTS of gratitude for assistance in the writing of this book. A year free from teaching responsibilities in which I did most of the actual writing was made possible by a fellowship from the National Endowment for the Humanities. A particularly happy environment for my work was provided by the generous hospitality of the Master and Fellows of Churchill College, Cambridge, and the kindness of the Faculty of History at that university who made available a study in their Faculty Building. The staffs of Harvard College Library, the Houghton Library, the British Library, and the Cambridge University Library were all most helpful. The History of Parliament Trust made available a transcript of the Cromwell Parliamentary diary. My ideas were formed and re-formed in many discussions, particularly those which took place in Professor Geoffrey Elton's seminar and many others with Professor Elton himself. The manuscript was read and very helpfully criticized by my colleague, Professor Bernard Bailyn. Professor and Mrs. Samuel Thorne gave me their expert assistance in deciphering particularly difficult manuscript passages. Mrs. Madeleine Rowse Gleason provided expert advice and assistance in the editorial preparation of the manuscript and Mrs. Patricia Denault was an efficient and accurate typist.

CONTENTS

QUEEN ELIZABETH
AND THE MAKING OF POLICY,
1572-1588

INTRODUCTION

IT IS FITTING that a book open with a statement of intent: some explanation of the intended scope and purpose of the work. This book is a continuation of an earlier study which dealt with the making of the Elizabethan regime down to about 1572. In shape and in themes it is quite different. What it does share with the earlier volume is a concern with short-term history. In both cases the historian's lens is brought to bear upon a brief era in English history—some fourteen years in the first volume and in this about twenty, so that the time limits of this study are at one end St. Bartholomew and, at the other, the Armada. This book also shares with its predecessor an effort to keep one's range of vision within the same limits as that of contemporaries—to avoid so far as possible the fallacies created by our hindsight. For us, who know of the Armada's dispersal, of the achievement of Dutch independence, or the victory of Henry IV, it is easy to forget that all these providential dispensations were veiled from the Elizabethans. They lived for decades in an atmosphere of dread which was worsened by a long series of setbacks, particularly after 1578, and at the end of the 1580's England stood almost alone against the might of Spain, her sole allies the two battered provinces of Holland and Zealand.

By focussing on short-term history one is necessarily restricted as to the topics which can be usefully considered. The rhythms of history are very uneven and in many instances the cycle is too long to be neatly contained within the limits of two decades. In this particular volume there are several necessary omissions. There is no attempt to deal with the tangled relationship between government and the socio-economic order which consumed so much of the time and thought of Elizabethan statesmen. Nor is there opportunity to explore the interplay between central government and the numerous complex local societies which were only loosely held together by the authority of the Crown. The book is not intended to be a

3

general history of England during these decades; it is limited to a study of selected themes.

What is dealt with is a range of problems which rose to the surface of events in the 1570's with alarming suddenness and forced themselves upon the reluctant attention of England's rulers. In the next decade the ever more intense pressure of events drove the government willy-nilly to the making of important and, for the most part, irreversible decisions. What the outcome of these decisions would be was still veiled in the mists of the future at the end of the 1580's, but the fork in the road had been taken in each case and there was no turning back. In another volume I hope to explore the working out of these decisions through the remaining years of Elizabeth's reign.

What were these problems? One can make a rough-and-ready division between those which were set in motion by actions outside the realm and those which took their rise from impulses of domestic origin. Hence the first two of the book's three parts deal respectively with domestic problems and foreign relations. Such a division, while artificial, is, I think, useful. The section on domestic affairs is devoted to the central problem of religious dissidence, both Protestant and Catholic. The pace of events is irregular, marked by intervals of inactivity punctuated by sudden, often unpredictable, bursts of activity. Hence the organization of these chapters, while roughly chronological, makes no effort to recapitulate the whole sequence of events. Foreign affairs, on the other hand, offer a very crowded canvas. Events move at a rapid pace, crowding upon one another in bewildering complexity. Here I have undertaken to provide a fuller, although by no means exhaustive, narrative of England's external relations—with the continental monarchies and Scotland. The last, briefer, section is straightforwardly analytic in character and deals with the two foci of decision-making—the court and Parliament.

All of these problems have of course been explored by earlier historians of the Elizabethan epoch. The structure of this book very much reflects the work of my predecessors. In the chapters on religious dissent I have relied very heavily on recent work, particularly the magisterial study of Puritanism contained in Patrick Collinson's *The Elizabethan Puritan Movement* and on other studies, published and unpublished, including those of William P. Haugaard, Francis X. Walker, and Thomas H. Clancy.[1] The most important recent general study of Tudor foreign policy is that of R. B. Wernham;[2] its scale enforces a relatively brief treatment of the two decades dealt with in this book. Charles Wilson's *Queen Elizabeth and the Revolt of the Netherlands*[3] focusses on a particular theme. The older studies of Conyers Read, his two massive biographies of Walsingham and Burghley,[4] necessarily have a biographical form. Hence I have thought it best to go back to the sources in the Public Record Office and the British Library since the scale and the intent of this study is quite different from any of those mentioned above. The study of Parliament in Part III necessarily depends on the exhaustive studies of J. E. Neale,[5] but I have sought to go back to the manuscript sources for the more important and detailed episodes dealt with in this book.

SEVERAL THREADS connect all the chapters of this book. One is formed by the simple fact that the Elizabethans lived in the aftermath of revolution. The newly emerging issues of the 1570's and 1580's had their origins in decisions made thirty years earlier when Henry and his ministers had deliberately

---

[1] William P. Haugaard, *Elizabeth and the English Reformation* (1968); Francis X. Walker, "The Implementation of the Elizabethan Statutes against Recusants, 1581-1603" (Ph.D. thesis, University of London, 1961), cited henceforth as Walker, "Recusants"; and Thomas H. Clancy, *Papist Pamphleteers* (Chicago, 1964).

[2] Richard B. Wernham, *Before the Armada: The Growth of English Foreign Policy, 1485-1588* (1971).

[3] Charles Wilson, *Queen Elizabeth and the Revolt of the Netherlands* (1970).

[4] Conyers Read, *Mr Secretary Walsingham and the Policy of Queen Elizabeth* (3 vols., Cambridge, Mass., 1925) and *Lord Burghley and Queen Elizabeth* (1960).

[5] J. E. Neale, *Elizabeth I and Her Parliaments, 1559-1581* (1953) and *Elizabeth I and Her Parliaments, 1584-1601* (1957), cited henceforth as Neale I and Neale II, respectively.

severed the immemorial link with Rome and had then proceeded to restructure radically the national religious life. The consequences—the implications—of these mighty acts began to surface only in the next generation, that of Elizabeth and her councillors. It was they who had to deal with the awkward and unforeseen problems which now emerged. How was a national church built on the principles enunciated by Thomas Cromwell and his Edwardian successors to be infused with the life of a vital social organism? How was England to live in an international community split, not merely by the rivalries of dynasties, but by the far more venomous enmities engendered by ideological division?

What strikes the historical observer is the compelling novelty of these problems. Religious dissidence within the framework of an Erastian state was a different matter from heresy in the matrix of medieval Catholicism. And foreign enemies who were not merely fellow combatants in the same European tourney but the protagonists of a perverse and abhorrent creed, with whom coexistence seemed impossible, also posed difficulties which could not be dealt with by the simple application of past experience or the formulae of received wisdom. English leaders would have to grope their way cautiously and fearfully along a dark and unmarked path.

Quite obviously all these phenomena are bound up with the nature and functioning of the royal government itself. The post-Reformation English monarchy labored under new burdens to which it had to make painful adaptation. Most of this book is taken up with a close examination of the way in which these challenges were met. It is not a tidy history; the very novelty of the situation begot all kinds of confusions and uncertainties. Past experience often clouded rather than illuminated the present. And the very reluctance of the principal actors to make painful decisions delayed action and hindered solutions.

In ENGLAND the years between 1529 and 1553 had been a time when the nation's leaders had quite deliberately broken with the past by rupturing the ancient ecclesiastical polity of the realm—in the first instance by ripping apart the constitutional and legal fabric and then later by introducing radical doctrinal and liturgical innovation. In part this had been a response to deep-rooted impulses for religious and moral reform which had been fermenting, especially among the clergy, since early in the century, but the actual shaping of events, once the Crown began to act, was dictated by many other considerations as well, less idealistic in character. Henry's restless and ever-widening ambitions could be realized only by exploiting the profound anti-clericalism of the English ruling classes. Some of it was quite primitive greed for clerical possessions; some equally primitive jealousy of clerical privilege; a third and more sophisticated element was a revolutionary rejection of the clergy's domination in the whole realm of value. The earliest stage of the revolution was skillfully managed by Thomas Cromwell, who orchestrated cooperation among the monarchy, the lay aristocracy, and the clerical reformers. In its later untidier stages a loose alliance between the "regents" Somerset and Northumberland and the religious leaders was linked to a glorious plundering of church (and Crown) land by piratical aristocrats. When the death of the boy-king in 1553 halted this process, the work of destruction was largely complete, but the necessary tasks of reconstructing the Church and of ordering its relations with the new Supreme Head were far from finished. For five years the clock was turned backward under a monarch of the most conservative bent, but the reversal of direction was as short-lived as the reign of Queen Mary. The arrival on the throne of a Protestant princess (a certain sign of Divine intervention in reformers' eyes) gave them a second chance; the rapid consolidation of their power and the demoralization of organized Catholicism, ecclesiastical or political, was a central theme of the first decade of the new reign.

The final triumph of the Protestant party gave the realm a breathing space. Elizabeth herself ensured that this would be more than a mere interlude between bouts of innovation by firmly braking the engines of state. She had committed herself unequivocally to a reformed regime but she was determined that its final shape should be that so hastily molded at the opening of her reign; there were to be no more acts in the drama of reformation. The ensuing struggle between a strong-willed conservative monarch and an equally determined body of single-minded evangelicals, pressing on to that perfect restoration of the primitive church, blueprinted in the pages of the New Testament, was to be a long and bitter one.

The Puritan controversialists re-awakened ancient disputes within the Christian Church, which had slumbered since the high Middle Ages, as to the rival claims to supreme authority of the secular and the spiritual powers. In the context of the Reformation they took on new and confusing shapes. The reformers had rejected the old Petrine myth with its far-reaching implications and in its stead set up the claim of the Scriptures *in toto* as the touchstone of final authority. So far so good—but they now were brought face to face with the problem of fleshing out the doctrine of the Book in acceptable institutional forms. In the earlier stages of the English Reformation its clerical leaders had accepted and indeed expounded the claims of the King to a wide authority over the Church. But there had not been an agreed definition of the functions or the bounds of that authority. The specific questions raised by the Elizabethan critics—and, more particularly, their formulation of what they believed to be Scriptural injunctions as to the right government of the Church—forced the English government and the leaders of the established Church to contend with their critics on the most fundamental and delicate questions. In the longer run some considered answer had to be given to the comprehensive presbyterian schema for ecclesiastical organization; this would require intellectual efforts of high-level quality and a careful re-thinking of the whole theory of right social order. More immediately the authorities civil and ecclesiastical had to deal with disobedience in the ranks—with the uncomfortable social (and political) fact of dissent from the order of public worship established by law.

But the Puritan leaders were not the only authors of religious nonconformity in the country. From the very beginning of the reign there had been a body of unreconciled Catholic opinion which clung obstinately to the old faith. Passive and unorganized in character—manifest merely in abstention from the parish church—it seemed to be a solely residual phenomenon which could be counted on to disappear in the fullness of time. But the government woefully underestimated the regenerative capacities of the Catholic faith. The intense spirituality of Catholic reform which now revivified the Papal Church proved to be a powerful magnet for some of the ablest and most devoted of young Englishmen. By 1580 the English government was faced with a second community of dissidents, who, like the Puritans, presented immediate problems of civil disobedience as well as the larger challenge made by English Catholic controversialists at the highest levels of theory. The same disputes about ultimate spiritual authority which were propounded in one form by the Puritans were stoutly maintained in quite another setting by the Catholic writers. But there was an additional, and ominous, dimension to the Catholic problem, since from as early as 1570 Catholic exiles were in close contact with England's continental rivals, seeking to win their support for an armed assault on the reformed regime and its replacement by a restored Catholic government, probably under Mary Stuart.

The political aspects of the Catholic problem were perhaps the easiest to face; once Roman priests could be identified as political agents of a foreign enemy, they could be dealt with accordingly, as traitors. At least that was the government's formulation of policy, although it proved singularly difficult in execution. Religious nonconformists, of both persuasions, who refused to accept the settlement of 1559 by coming to church but who insisted on their devoted loyalty to the Queen's sovereignty while rejecting her plain commands baffled and confused the government. The very notions which formed the ideological underpinning of the regime were not consistent with the traditional response to such dissidents—prosecution for heresy, the ruthless rooting out of dangerous infection within the body politic. The clerical apologists of the new religious regime had sought to persuade rather than to compel assent by an appeal to a Scripture open to all readers, by reasoned argument and by the examples of history. The more fervent of the reformers, supremely confident, like John Knox, of the absolute rightness of their convictions, would not have hesitated to use compulsion, but such power was withheld from them. The lay wing of the reform movement was as resolutely opposed to a Protestant clerical authoritarianism as they had been to that of the old faith. Coolly secular in outlook, they sought to limit, indeed to prohibit, compulsory acceptance of any doctrinal or theological norms. Under these conditions it was very hard for the government to find the right road to take in its search for outward religious conformity. Only very slowly were patterns of response evolved and they were to prove of limited success. The simple aim of a nation united in political loyalty and religious faith, a fact which was taken for granted at the opening of the reign, was gradually to fade in the ensuing decades but without being replaced by any new vision.

For the Elizabethan generation, life was to be much grimmer than it had been for that of their parents. The preceding age had at least the freedom and the exhilaration of a revolutionary epoch. The very repudiation of the past left them free to strike out in new directions, bold in their convictions and hopeful of an as yet unshaped future. But their children had to live with decisions already made and so hardened by the passage of time and the pressure of events as to be irreversible. They were forced into roles which were not always to their liking, often uncomfortable and not seldom dangerous. Elizabeth herself abhorred the role which so many of her subjects would have thrust upon her—that of active patroness of zealous evangelical reform within the realm. Equally she rejected the championship of international Protestantism, a female St. George setting out to slay the Papist dragon. Yet she would spend much of her life in repelling the obstinate persuasions of her Puritan subjects while, on the international scene, she found herself, willy-nilly, pushed into active, costly, and dangerous intervention in the affairs of her neighbors.

The conduct of England's foreign relations was to prove as demanding as the management of the new national Church.

The old familiar international scene of Henry VIII's time, dominated by dynastic rivalries, regulated by a loose but generally accepted set of rules, and safeguarded by a tacit commitment to limited wars, in which the ultimate survival of the regime was never at risk, had been replaced by a new and forbidding landscape, glacially grim in its main features. Europe was increasingly split apart by the unbridgeable gulf of profound ideological difference, so painfully familiar to the twentieth century. By the early 1560's Rome and Geneva faced each other, two citadels of irreconcilable principles. For zealots on either side the very existence of the rival faith was a threat to the salvation of souls, an intolerable evil, with which there could be no compromise. The English leadership numbered a minority of such enthusiasts among its ranks, although most of Elizabeth's councillors, while swayed by such considerations, took a much less simplistic view. But even though they were more disposed to see the Dutch revolt or the French civil wars as political events, they were by no means immune from ideological predispositions. The religious dimension of these events sharpened antagonisms and polarized differences in a dangerous way. Elizabeth and her ministers would struggle with these thorny problems, divided among themselves as to the best strategy to be followed and even as to ultimate goals. They would find themselves at the end of the 1580's involved in a war in which the very existence of the Elizabethan order in Church and State would be at issue.

THESE WERE the central and abiding problems which faced the Elizabethan leadership in the decades from 1570 to the end of the reign. But what about the habits of thought, the preconceived ideas, the general underlying assumptions these men—and their sovereign—brought to bear on them? They were for the most part men of at least some formal education and some acquaintance with the high culture of the world in which they lived. They were also men of extensive and varied political experience and all shared the amalgam of received wisdom which was the common property of the elite. Its formal constituents were necessarily classical or Christian in character;

its more pragmatic elements sprang from English political experience over several centuries, but particularly from the previous century and a half.

It is not possible to single out any formal or "official" pronouncement as to the nature of right political order nor was there any work of abstract political thought which defined it. Most of the basic political conceptions were to be found afloat in the consciousness of educated Englishmen but well below the level of self-conscious articulation. They emerge obliquely as agreed points of reference in such formulations of official viewpoints as the Homily on Obedience. More formal attempts at expressing conventional views of right order are to be found in such works of edification as Edmund Dudley's *Tree of Commonwealth* (1509), Thomas Elyot's *Book of the Governour* (1531), or Thomas Smith's *De Republica Anglorum* (1583). All three of these authors were servants of the Crown, two of them within the highest level of confidence and intimacy. But none of them wrote a truly "political" work; and all these writers assume that political power is one aspect of a providentially ordered moral universe. The two earlier writers are determinedly moralistic in aim; Smith is narrowly descriptive in his purposes but he too is careful to place his English commonwealth within a timeless, Aristotelian frame of reference. For all these writers it is *society* rather than the realm (that is, some merely political organization) which is fundamental to their discussion. And society is a natural organism, a subordinate part of a larger and over-arching cosmos —not in any sense a temporal, human, and expedient creation. Power is bestowed by Divine authority for moral purposes—the doing of justice, the protection of the weak against the strong, the maintenance of a Christian-classical social morality. In this framework rulers are enjoined, indeed required, to eschew any pursuit of mere personal glory or advancement and to subordinate themselves entirely to the prescriptions of transcendent moral law. Conversely, subjects are required to submit themselves with unquestioning obedience to the hierarchy of "higher powers" ordained for their benefit. What perhaps strikes the modern observer most forcibly in the work of so practical and experienced a civil servant as Smith is the ahistorical and apolitical character of his approach. The business of the Crown and, under it, of the aristocracy is very simply the maintenance of an unchanging and timeless social structure, which in spite of its awesome credentials is—given the unstable characteristics of fallen nature—always dangerously vulnerable to the hazards of individual ambition and greed. The role of the ruler and the ruling classes is that of a physician, guarding the health of the social organism, or, to vary the analogy, that of an engineer, hastening to repair any symptoms of breakdown in the social machine. But any notion that such a machine might one day have to be replaced by a new and improved model was wholly lacking.

There was in such a view no place whatsoever for the pursuit of personal, dynastic, or, more important, ideological goals. The power of the state cannot legitimately be used as a means to any other end than the maintenance of a social order, providentially designed to secure social justice. The Tudor age was not one which found it necessary to refine or to challenge the ancestral wisdom. During the earlier sixteenth century there appeared a considerable body of social criticism, oriented largely around orthodox Christian and humanist conceptions of social justice. It faded out in the decade before Elizabeth's accession, not to revive for nearly a century. The Marian exiles produced a tiny corpus of political theory centering on the problem of obedience to the ungodly ruler which gave some promise of the rich theoretical developments later seen in France, but the advent of a Protestant queen ended the need for such speculation and it was not developed—interestingly enough—by English Catholic writers.

These abstract high level ideals fitted reasonably well into the pragmatic circumstances of English historical development, especially since the early fifteenth century. Earlier medieval experience, hewn out in the thirteenth-century struggles between Crown and baronage, had given rise to a body of legal doctrine which laid some emphasis on the limitations of royal power and the rights of the free-born subject. But a rival tradition which laid stress on the far-reaching power and responsibilities of an anointed king had also respectable medieval precedents and it was the latter which, tacitly, had come to the fore since the middle of the fifteenth century.

The disastrous breakdown of public order under the hapless Henry VI had brought home, particularly to the middling landed aristocracy and to the urban upper classes, the importance of strong and effective royal leadership. The noble dynasts of the Wars of the Roses had, unlike their medieval predecessors, been unable to dignify their private ambitions with the consequence of a public cause. Therefore the whole drift of sentiment for a century or more had been in favor of the Crown, although the rival theme of subjects' rights had by no means become extinct. The events of the Reformation—and much of the rationale used to justify the royal supremacy—had gone far to strengthen this tendency in men's minds. Certainly the notion that the high public obligations of the Crown and the arcane knowledge of matters of state which belonged to the monarch and his chosen advisors alone gave special privilege and freedom to the sovereign was firmly grounded in contemporary thought. In a grand sense the Crown was responsible for its actions but not answerable to any earthly body. Subjects must be content to bow to the superior wisdom and experience of their governors and to give unquestioning obedience to their orders. The result was a regime of authority and deference which rested not upon any very explicit absolutist doctrine but on a generally diffused acceptance of its leadership.

The pragmatic experience of English politics since the late fifteenth century added another strand to the political inheritance of the Elizabethan generation. From the 1470's down well into Henry VIII's reign the kings or their ministers had devoted a major part of their energies to the work, first of rehabilitating the monarchy and then of bringing its institutions to the highest possible degree of efficiency. Such activity was necessarily restorative—conservative in character; the goal was always to improve existing practice—as in the administration of the royal demesne, or further to exploit hitherto unused potential—as in the case of wards and liveries. Royal activity had also meant re-emphasizing the traditional functions of medieval monarchy, that is, the preservation of social order, mainly through the effective use of highly developed judicial institutions. Thus the most noteworthy achievement of early Tudor monarchy was the erection of such courts as Star Chamber and Requests, and the steady extension of the JP's functions. All this had made the English monarchy appreciably more efficient and more responsive to the needs of its subjects and had done much to strengthen national loyalty to the dynasty. The ancient machinery of the monarchy had been tuned to the highest possible pitch of performance.

Yet these very successes placed the English monarchy in sharp contrast with its continental contemporaries. Indeed, it might be said to be distinctly old-fashioned, if not anachronistic, by their standards. The attention of the continental rulers had, since at least the 1490's, been focussed on the problems of large-scale and continuous warfare and on the building of the requisite fiscal and military structures necessary to support such enterprise. And later in the new century the progress of religious revolution drove them, particularly the Hapsburgs, to elaborate measures for the supervision and control of their subjects' beliefs and conduct. The resulting increase in the power of the central authority turned them into reasonably efficient war-making machines and, in Spain and Italy, into effective police states. The gap between them and England, where the king lacked army, bureaucracy, and taxing power, was all the more startling.

When the French kings were embarking on their Italian adventure, Henry VII, like his predecessor, Edward IV, was following a policy at once conciliatory and defensive. His son hankered after a revival of Lancastrian or Plantagenet military exploits, but Henry VIII lacked the steadiness of purpose to turn these aspirations into serious national enterprises until the very last years of his reign. The struggle for Scotland began as an offensive in Henry's time but was transformed in the next dozen years into a desperately defensive action.

War remained for the English government a spasmodic enterprise, conducted with *ad hoc* machinery which was mostly dismantled at the conclusion of hostilities. And the fiscal resources of the English government, although capable of expansion under pressure and for brief intervals, remained no more than adequate for a modest peace-time establishment. Financially English monarchy was tightly corseted within the inflexible binding of custom. Elizabeth and her servants inherited a structure of government largely adapted to the ancient tasks of medieval government. It was still largely oriented to a peace-keeping role, to mediating and arbitrating the endless frictions of a land-holding society, and to the "punishment of wickedness and vice," i.e., the chastisement of offenders against the public peace. Its character is revealed in detail for us in Thomas Smith's commonwealth; it is hardly surprising that he thought it needed to be carefully described to continentals. It was by their standards a curiously archaic realm.

Elizabeth herself found nothing to quarrel with in these general notions; they chimed in harmoniously with her own temperamental predispositions. If she inherited her father's character, she chose to imitate her grandfather's policy. Like him she was forced by circumstances to stand always on the defensive; in her earlier years the menace to her security was at home; later on it was abroad. But beyond those compulsions of circumstance, she was quite innocent of those conventional ambitions for glory or for augmented dominions which had consumed the large but diffuse energies of her father. And she was quite free of the strong sense of purpose or mission which had driven her half-sister. It may well be that the very task of asserting and maintaining by sheer force of will and personality her ascendancy over a violent, masculine political and social order exhausted all her energies and left nothing over for other enterprises. Be this as it may, it was quite clear that she intended to be a queen Log and not a queen Stork. In a quieter age Elizabeth's passive stance might have served very well, but she reigned in a strife-torn era in which one new event after another, like successive waves on a stormy day, broke over her. The consequence was a constant tension between royal inertia and the importunities of her restless

16

councillors which shaped much of the political history of the reign.

But what about her councillors? They were free from the personal constraints which bore upon their mistress and more open to the currents of social and political thought flowing so vigorously about them. The older of them had begun their careers in the courts of her father or her brother; a few had travelled abroad; some among the younger were products of the universities and influenced by the fashionable humanism of the age. But probably the deepest and most lasting influence upon them was that of the religious revolution through which they had lived. By the 1570's the initial break with Rome was more than a generation in the past and the self-conscious promulgation of an evangelical faith reached back almost as far. The first phase of indecision and uncertainty was now well past; the men who surrounded Elizabeth had encountered the new religion as young men, had made their choice, and were now the defenders of an existing, indeed an established, order. For them the questions in debate between the old and the new faiths were settled. What counted now was the preservation of the reformed order. A decade earlier, when the Queen was new on the throne, there had been an optimistic mood; offense rather than defense was in the air in the aftermath of the reformed victory in Scotland and the rising expectations of the French and Netherlandish Protestants. But now Alva's successful suppression of the new religion in the Low Countries, the successive checks to an advance in France, and after August 1572 the staggering catastrophe of St. Bartholomew had altered the balance. Protestants everywhere looked fearfully to an uncertain future, quailing before the massive forces of renascent Catholicism, so imposing beside the meager and divided resources of the evangelicals.

These circumstances served to alter the balance of forces and the thrust of their objectives within the reformed ranks in England. A decade or two earlier the central foci of attention had been the demolition of the institutions of the Catholic order and the definition of the new reformed faith; the former had been mainly the business of lay leaders, the latter of the clerics. Now the laity, firmly in control of the machinery of the English state, were much more concerned about protecting the secular power base on which the new religion rested from internal and external enemies than in the continuing problems of defining the doctrine and the institutions of a rightly ordered Protestant polity. That latter task was left to the attentions of the divines. And they, in turn, relatively secure within the framework of the established ecclesiastical order, became more and more engrossed in internal issues, largely theological or ecclesiastical in their character. To put it in other terms, the two groups whose uneasy coalition had carried the Protestant cause to victory in England—the "politique Machiavels" and the "hot Gospellers"—were drifting apart to some degree, at least in the focus of their attention. The former were increasingly distracted, first, by England's international situation, on which, as they saw it, the future of their religion depended and, to a lesser degree, by the need for suppressing the politically dangerous dissidence of the recusants at home. The clerics, on the other hand, were ever more deeply preoccupied with specifically religious issues, such as the right nature of public worship and the legitimate forms of church government. These divergences within the ranks of the reformed would not lead to an open break but they did produce a sense of confusion and a loss of common purpose as the two groups moved in differing directions.

Hence, religion, although a common factor in the experience and the predispositions of the Elizabethan councillors, affected them in uncertainly differing ways. None of the principal lay leaders were to be won over to the dogmatic and systematic view of right social order which the radical clerics worked out after 1570, and which offered a plausible alternative model to that entertained by the Elizabethan court establishment. But neither would they accept wholeheartedly the counter-propositions of Whitgift which sought to validate the establishment of 1559. The politicians remained obstinately pragmatic in their approach, consistent in their commitment to the reformed religion but increasingly politicized in their approach, guiding themselves by the landmarks of power politics rather than by the beacons of the undefiled Gospel. International Protestantism which in 1560 still had about it the aura of a true *corpus evangelicum* was becoming more and more a loose alliance of states sharing a common religion but not necessarily enjoying any identity of their other interests.

Loyalty to the Protestant faith formed a large element in the assumptions of many of the leading Elizabethan statesmen. But discussion of the character of that loyalty has led to another, less definable, strand in the fabric of their preconceptions. Much has been written of the "politiques" and the term is an important one although it defines an attitude rather than a party or even a movement. Characteristically one adopts a foreign rather than an English word—or at least a French word in the process of being naturalized. The official English doctrines of right political behavior, lay or ecclesiastical in origin, placed great emphasis on the moral ends of all public institutions and condemned any notion of self-serving or self-interested behavior by any public officer, from the Crown downwards. An abhorrent and contrary doctrine was popularly supposed to be embodied in the writings of Machiavelli and by the mid-century his name had become a byword for a totally perverted and malign view of public order. Nevertheless there is visible in the conduct and the utterances of English politicians a growing sense if not of an enlightened self-interest at least of a morally neutral public interest. Burghley's state papers, for instance, with their endless balancing of pro and contra propositions pose the problems of English policy, foreign and domestic, in just such terms. Taking for granted the survival of the regime, the dynasty, and the commonwealth as given desiderata, he calculates what is the best balance of possible actions to achieve the goal desired. The increasing preoccupation, discussed above, with the preservation of the existing English regime above all other considerations naturally tended to accentuate thinking along such lines. Plans for mobilization of means steadily displaced the consideration of ends. There was, of course, nothing new in the pursuit of means, but it was becoming a more self-conscious enterprise as the reign wore on, and the gap grew between idealists, particularly those of left-wing evangelical persuasion, and the practitioners of politics at the highest level. The existence led to the angry reproaches of the zealots and to the growing disillusionment of the younger generation—that of Philip Sidney and Fulke Greville, for instance—as they themselves came to have a firsthand acquaintance with the world of high politics. Thus another ingredient was added to that ill-mixed blend— tags of received wisdom, a rather muddied piety, and now a dash of worldly wisdom—which served as a nutrient for the Elizabethan political mind.

PART I

THE DOMESTIC SCENE
1572-1588

CHAPTER 1

THE PROBLEM OF

DISSENT

IN THE 1560's domestic politics had been troubled by faction within the Council which rippled out into wider circles and helped to beget conspiracy and eventually open insurrection. These disturbances had been quieted by firm royal leadership, and the decades which followed were notable by the very absence of factious disagreement within the higher ranks of government. Councillors and sovereign worked together, a harmonious and effective team. In one area alone was there divergence between Crown and councillors and that reflected a new kind of discontent which troubled the country at large. This was the reaction to the uniformity of worship required by the acts of 1559.

The notion of national religious uniformity in worship had been accepted first by the Edwardian and then by the Elizabethan authorities as a necessity of public policy as much as a fulfillment of religious conviction, and the decision had been made without much conscious reflection about its implications. Public worship was taken for granted as a social function, essential to the well-being of the commonwealth, rather than as the outward expression of carefully defined theological doctrine. It was also taken for granted that all right-minded subjects would obey the precepts laid down by constituted authority. The legally required acceptance of the Prayer Book liturgy had been aimed at the adherents of the old faith who might prove recalcitrant in coming to church; these laws had certainly not provided for dissidents within the Reformed ranks. Consequently, the very fact of radical criticism by men of the Reformed faith of the worship established by law was both repellent and baffling to the rulers of the Elizabethan state. Nothing in their past experience prepared them for such a contingency, and they were left uncertain how to deal with it. It was easier to evade the problem than to confront it and, as we shall see, the Elizabethan leaders fumbled gingerly and half-heartedly with it, spurred on to fitful action by outbursts of royal ill-temper. But any serious attempt to come to terms with the problem of Protestant dissent was very slow to emerge.

Catholic recusancy presented the same problem in a different guise. Although a formed Catholic position was slow to appear, when it was formulated in the 1570's, it took direct issue with the government's view that public worship was essentially a social rather than a theological act. The Catholics insisted that attendance at the Anglican service would in fact endanger their own hopes of salvation. For them the Book of Common Prayer was not merely defective but positively pernicious, pregnant with false and wicked doctrine. Here again the response of the Elizabethan regime was to prove slow, halting, and uncertain.

(In the chapters which follow I have chosen to use the term "dissent" and sometimes "nonconformity" to describe the phenomena under discussion. I apply the terms to both Puritans and Catholics. It is of course meant to be distinguished from the common usages of later times when Dissent and Nonconformity had very well understood meanings. But I think these terms, in lower case, are useful and illuminating in a discussion of sixteenth-century problems.)

THE ROOTS OF THE PROBLEM

AT THE BEGINNING of the 1570's the English leadership could count among its other achievements the satisfactory development of its religious policy. At the opening of the reign the main threat to religious peace seemed to come from the Roman Catholics. That threat now seemed much overestimated. While a substantial number of Englishmen were reluctant to attend regularly at the services of the established church, it was clear that no considerable body of them were prepared to risk life or property by overt action in behalf of the old faith. The putative leader of a Catholic revolt, the Queen of Scots, was now badly discredited in the eyes of all but a small minority, labelled as a conspirator caught in intrigue to bring in foreign forces. As yet the renascent forces of Catholic spirituality, which would pose such problems by the end of the decade, were still invisible. The most that seemed necessary was continuing vigilance against another version of the Ridolfi plot.

But the leaders of Church and State were already aware of a cloud appearing in quite another quarter of the horizon— the opposition to important aspects of the 1559 settlement being mounted within Protestant ranks themselves. The problem was not a new one in 1570; it had first begun to smoulder in the controversy over vestments and over conformity in public worship in 1565-1566; but in 1572 it burst into a dangerous blaze with the publication of the two *Admonitions to Parliament*.

The roots of the problem lay forty years back, at the very beginnings of the English Reformation. Since it was the royal will of Henry VIII which set in motion the changes of the 1530's, the predominant note sounded in justifying those changes had been the restoration of authority to its rightful possessor—the new Supreme Head. Great emphasis was laid by the apologists for the Henrician regime on the comprehensive power of the King over all his subjects, clerical or lay, and over all questions bearing upon right religious order.[1] Tyndale, Gardiner, and many lesser writers had all proclaimed the Caesaro-Papal nature of Henry's office, and there is no doubt

---

[1] The views set out here strongly reflect recent scholarship, particularly the work of G. R. Elton, summarized in *Reform and Reformation: England 1509-1558* (Cambridge, Mass., 1978) and J. J. Scarisbrick, *Henry VIII* (Berkeley and Los Angeles, 1968).

the King thought of himself as truly a lay Pope, vested with all the powers the Popes had exercised—powers usurped from his royal predecessors. Most of the legislation of these years had been devoted to spelling out in detail the firm control of the sovereign over every aspect of the Church's life. But the situation was in fact much less clear than the King may have assumed; even in his lifetime it was possible to argue that the kingship and supreme headship were so blended as to be indistinguishable and that consequently the regulation of religion was as much a part of Parliament's business as straightforwardly secular matters. Time and circumstance would not diminish this ambiguity.

A more muted, almost minor, note of Henry's reign had been that of religious reformation. A modest installment of religious change of a mildly Erasmian character was introduced, but the change which most affected the religious life of the country—the dissolution of the monasteries—was ultimately carried out without any serious effort to represent it as a measure of religious reform. The religious radicals who were recruited by Cromwell played only secondary roles during the lifetime of the old King.

Their opportunity came with his death. Many of them had been placed in highly strategic posts within the Church in the former reign when their support was useful to Henry and when they had a sympathetic patron in Cromwell. Henry had also courted the lay anti-clericals among his subjects, men who rejected the clergy's claim to overriding moral authority and many of whom, at a different level, hungered after the Church's broad acres. The King had used both groups for his purposes and held both firmly within his grasp, but, when it loosened, they found it an easy matter to form a coalition for the total destruction of the old religious order—a Reformation on the same sweeping principles as those of continental Protestants.

The lay element—what we may term the *politiques*—was, as suggested above, primarily anti-clerical in its motivations. These men resented all forms of clerical privilege, above all the clergy's claim to monopolize the whole realm of value judgments, to be sole arbiters of all moral actions. And once their belief in the basic *raison d'être* of the clerical estate weakened, it was altogether natural that they should look with coldly appraising eyes on its great landed endowment. Henry had found them receptive collaborators in carrying through his program of destruction.

The other element in the Reformation alliance was predominantly clerical in composition. Deeply idealistic, full of zeal, these evangelicals sought nothing less than a profound spiritual revival in which the reordering of ecclesiastical institutions was only a means to a divinely ordered end. "Seek ye first the kingdom of God. . ." was their heartfelt motto.

It was probably in the very nature of things that these somewhat ill-consorted allies would sooner or later fall out over fundamental issues—the true direction and the ultimate goals of the whole Reformation movement. But for a time they worked in tandem; King Henry's imperious will subordinated men and events to his purposes; in King Edward's time there was just enough common ground to provide a footing for a viable coalition between zealous evangelicals and worldly, indeed unscrupulous, politicians. Before the end of the reign the strains in this uncomfortable partnership began to show.

The politiques' goals were the easier to achieve. Under the talented direction of Thomas Cromwell, the destruction of the Church's ancient privileges had proceeded apace. Skillfully and economically adapting the existing framework, Cromwell had brought the episcopate, the parish clergy, the clerical endowment, and the ecclesiastical courts all firmly under royal, and lay, control.

The task of the reformers had been more difficult. It required first a large work of destruction and then a reconstruction for which there were no helpful blueprints; they had to be both architects and builders as they went. The dismantling of the old order of worship was accomplished with relative ease; the rebuilding process proved difficult, yet much was done. The two Books of Common Prayer, the Ordinal, and the Forty-Two Articles were considered but still tentative achievements. It was clear even before King Edward's death that for many reformers these were experimental efforts and by no means definitive or final. Moreover, some vital topics had not yet really been broached. On the central questions of church government there had been little discussion; the episcopal order had been maintained intact, an instrument now of royal rather than Papal authority, but still compactly authoritarian. So long as lay and clerical leaders were in reasonable harmony it served well enough. But the corollary question of right relations between the temporal and spiritual authorities remained discreetly untouched. It had more than one aspect. The issue discussed above—the very nature of the Supreme Headship within the domestic constitution—remained unresolved. But there was also the larger problem of the whole balance between the two social institutions, the church and the commonwealth, now that the universal Papal organization, with all its ancient rationale, had been rejected. The new structure of English religious life was still very much unfinished in the summer of 1553.

The experiences of Mary's reign would serve in the long run to split apart politiques and evangelicals; they would also initiate a rift within the ranks of the latter party. The lay reform leaders were initially scattered; many of them—those less deeply committed to the new faith—took service under Mary without much difficulty. Others, more ardent in their beliefs, found themselves excluded from the political world. Among them were the backers of Wyatt's rebellion. Most of them survived that tempest without too much damage, and by the end of the reign the Edwardian circle was regrouping itself quite systematically around the Lady Elizabeth and proved more than ready to return to the political arena upon her succession. Their commitment to a reformed polity was if anything strengthened by their five years in the wilderness; they had learned to think of themselves as a political faction and of the Catholics as political rivals. But their general ideas about the nature of a reformed church were not much altered.

Those religious reformers who fled abroad had, on the other hand, been deeply influenced by what they saw and learned in exile. First-hand acquaintance with the Reformed communities in the Rhineland and in Switzerland had at once widened their general horizons while focussing their ideas on specific problems. They brought back models of religious organization and patterns of public worship which they were eager to experiment with on their native soil. More important still, they were filled with an exalted sense of mission and soaring expectations of the great work about to be accomplished in England.

But Protestant divines and politicians alike, hastening back to the seats of power in the winter of 1558-1559, would have to reckon with a third element, a force lacking since the death of Henry VIII—a strong-minded and strong-willed sovereign of the reformed persuasion, with her own views of right religious order. They would find these views both novel and seemingly contradictory. While fully committed to a renewed break with Rome and a Protestant form of worship, she differed from her Protestant contemporaries in her determination that there should be no more acts in the drama of reformation. To understand her views one needs again to turn back to the preceding reigns.

Under Henry, and more particularly under Edward, the Crown had boldly used its powers as an instrument to bring about radical change. This in itself was a great novelty in a society in which the traditional role of the sovereign was entirely a conserving and defensive one, shoring up a static but ever vulnerable social order against violence and disorder. That the Crown should move from a conservative to a radical —even revolutionary—stance was a risky venture. Henry VIII had made the uncomfortable discovery that royal encouragement of change might leave him in the awkward position of the sorcerer's apprentice, unable to check the flow of new ideas which he had set in motion. And it was only with some difficulty that, in the last years of the reign, the pressures for more change were bottled up, at least for the time being.

In his successor's time the Crown's power had been used unstintingly to forward radical religious reform; lay and clerical reformers had worked together fairly comfortably. But even before the end of this brief reign they were slipping out of phase with one another; the more austere divines began to have doubts about collaboration with the secular power—in this case the unscrupulous Northumberland. At the same time a gap began to show within the divines' own ranks between those who saw the end of their work in sight and those who still looked to a whole series of undone tasks of reform stretching ahead. For them the break with the Roman past was only a preliminary victory; the war was yet to be fought and won. Only the death of Edward VI checked both of these widening cracks.

The experience in exile opened up more widely still the gap within the clerics' ranks, and in the quarrels at Frankfort the nature of the disagreements was spelled out for the first time. Men whose whole experience had been within the framework of an established and hierarchical institution were faced by the problems of organizing private and autonomous religious communities with no authoritative superior to give direction. Some reacted by seeking to reproduce, as far as possible, the familiar setting they had left behind at home—"the face of an English church." Others, bolder and more flexible, embraced with enthusiasm the very different models which they found in the German and Swiss city-states of their refuge. Two parties grew up, one, theologically moderate, liturgically conservative, and "nationalist" in its view; the other, radical, experimental, and "ecumenical." The former still thought of themselves as a temporarily displaced fragment of the Church of England; their opponents conceived themselves as a branch of an international reformed communion. These differences were far from resolved when Elizabeth's accession summoned the exiles home again. The euphoria of that event—which all Protestants agreed in seeing as a providential intervention in their favor—veiled for the time being all differences, both within the evangelicals' ranks and between them and their politique allies.

In fact in the very moment of triumph there were disquieting signs visible to those who had eyes keen enough to see them. The events of Elizabeth's first Parliament are dismayingly difficult to disentangle; but the House of Commons was already showing signs of an impatience to move along the road of radical reform which outdistanced the Queen's desires. In the excitements of the new reign these differences perhaps seemed minimal. It is pretty clear from later events that the radicals thought the settlement still subject to further reform and quite failed to understand that for the Queen it was a conclusive and final enactment.

Certainly the settlement itself was a scissors-and-paste affair, glued together out of the remains of the unfinished, and outdated, Edwardian structure. A liturgy which some of the exiles already set aside as too full of Popish relics was restored with slight but theologically blurred changes. An ordinal and a confession of faith were both omitted altogether, although Edwardian models for each existed. As for the internal government of the Church and the legal code by which it would be ordered, the complete silence of statute presumably meant implicit acceptance of the existing structure. In regard to relations with the temporal power there was the simple re-enactment of the Act of Supremacy with the single alteration in the royal style. In short, the making of the settlement was dominated by the circumstances of the renewed break with Rome, with disengagement from the Papal connection; the vacuum thus created had to be filled with hastily built structures thrown together out of available materials. Such a ramshackle construction might be expected to show signs of strain once it was put to use.

Yet, however many shortcomings it might reveal, it had much to recommend it to the new Supreme Governor. For all its apparent clumsiness the new establishment fitted neatly into the conceptions of right order entertained by the Queen. Elizabeth's private religious convictions were, like so much of her private persona, so discreetly veiled that it is not possible to give any satisfactory account of them. But her view of public religious order was made explicit by the record, although contemporaries were perhaps slow to read it. Many of them were reluctant to recognize how far she differed from their expectations of a princess miraculously raised to the throne by the direct hand of Providence. What were her views on the right order of the established Church?

Elizabeth was more than willing to resume the place her father had laid hold on as temporal ruler of the English Church, but she rejected *in toto* the role of religious reformer into which her brother had entered with so much enthusiasm. The machinery of state power which for twenty years between 1533 and 1553 drove England along the road of radical religious change was now to shift into neutral gear, to be used in a merely static operation. For the Queen the active phase of the Reformation was over; destruction of the old order and reconstruction of a new were tasks accomplished. The Papal authority had been overturned; the deformed Roman liturgy had been replaced by a purified, English version; idolatry was crushed; what else remained to do? The time had come for consolidation, for the sober, humdrum tasks of maintaining an established order. What was required now was the steady, routine celebration of a decorous and uniform public worship and the regular, unvarying inculcation of simple principles of public and private morality into the laity. The duty of the clergy was essentially that of moral policemen, acting under orders; they needed only to enforce the rules already on the statute book, by the repetition of the prescribed services of worship while the laity—obedient subjects—did their part by regular attendance. What the Queen totally excluded from the duties of her clergy was evangelical fervor, the stirring up of religious excitement or of spiritual aspirations. Such activity could only lead to a restless itch for novelty and to disturbing, possibly dangerous, contention. Conservative as she was in so many respects, Elizabeth was in one sense well ahead of her age. Her view of public religion was more akin to that of a Walpolian Whig than to the feelings of most of her contemporaries. How wide the gulf that separated her from those who would have had her play Solomon to her predecessors' Moses hardly needs explication.

This gap of sensibility was to create one of the major problems of the reign. For her evangelically minded subjects, the royal antipathy to their zeal posed almost intolerable choices for men who were at once ardent reformers and deeply loyal subjects. The history of their aspirations and of their responses to the painful dilemma they faced has been well written elsewhere and does not require repetition here. But the other side of the coin—the government's slow, fumbling response to a problem for which past experience offered no useful or certain guide—deserves more consideration.

How were they to deal with the distasteful, and indigestible, fact of religious dissent? The precedents were abundant and familiar but not altogether useful. The problem of dissent first reared its head in Henry's time, in the late 1530's; his characteristically simple response had been *The Act to end diversity of religious opinions* (1539), laying down statutory requirements as to men's beliefs. It had not in fact been much used in the remaining years of the reign and was promptly repealed under his son. Edward's government had not had to face either major Catholic resistance (except the rising in Devon) or full-fledged divisions within the Protestant ranks, and could afford to follow an open and lenient line. Mary, of course, had restored the medieval machinery for the suppression of heresy, under which temporal and spiritual authority cooperated in its extermination.

Elizabeth's government faced a new kind of problem. The earliest dissent from the new established order was of course that of the Roman Catholics. Early on it became clear that there was a core of recalcitrants who would not accept the requirement of the law that they attend the services prescribed in the Prayer Book. But it was also clear that theirs was a passive resistance, resting on a traditional and nostalgic loyalty. There was no disposition to raise active opposition to the new order; it seemed probable that once death removed the ministrations of the disaffected Marian clergy, the remnants of Roman Catholicism would quietly fade away. Hence the wisest strategy was to leave the strict letter of the law unenforced until time itself solved the problem. As we shall see, by the mid-1570's this policy was no longer tenable and a new strategy had to be worked out.

Dissidence within the Protestants' own ranks presented another and baffling problem, one painfully novel to the Elizabethan authorities. There were some slight precedents from

33

the last months of Edward's reign, particularly the case of Bishop Hooper, who scrupled at the use of episcopal vestments required by law. But this had been dealt with in an *ad hoc* fashion and really offered no useful guidance. The statutes of 1559 were, of course, designed to smoke out Catholic objectors to the new order. The oaths required in these laws struck at those who could not conscientiously accept the restored royal supremacy; this was hardly applicable to Anglican clergy who balked at wearing the surplice. But, in any case, the problems of Protestant dissent emerged more slowly than those of Catholic recusancy and did not become a major concern until about 1570. From that time on the problem of Protestant dissent was to make heavier demands on the time, energy, and political imagination of the English leadership than any other domestic issue of the reign. Only the looming crisis in foreign relations equalled it in importance.

Overt Protestant opposition to the regime established by law did not emerge until the late 1560's. In the Convocation of 1563 and again in the Parliament of 1566 the proponents of further reform brought forward relatively modest proposals for change. They assumed these could be achieved with the approval, and the collaboration, of the new ecclesiastical leadership, but after the failure of 1566 there began to develop a new antagonism towards the episcopate in particular and towards the existing regime in general. This would eventuate in the early 1570's in far-reaching proposals for a total restructuring of the Church's government. Puritanism was to emerge as a critique of the 1559 establishment. To understand that reaction we need to look at developments in the first years of the new reign, above all at the Queen's role.

The Origins of Elizabethan Dissent

The Queen had hoped that some significant number of the Marian bishops would follow in the footsteps of their Henrician and Edwardian predecessors and agree to conform to the new regime. Such a continuity of ranking personnel would bridge over the gap between the old and new orders. But this hope faded quickly during the meeting of Parliament and in the following summer. All but one of the episcopate refused the oaths to the new regime and in this were joined by a large proportion of the upper clerical echelons, the cathedral clergy and the archdeacons. Thus the first task which faced the new Supreme Governor was the wholesale replacement of the leadership of the national Church. She had no choice, if she were to find men of requisite qualifications and experience, but to turn to the reformed divines. These were, of course, the dispossessed Edwardian clergy. Their leaders in the young king's reign were largely gone, many of them victims of the Marian persecution. The few remaining Edwardian bishops were negligible figures. The pool from which the Queen had to draw therefore consisted largely of younger men who had held second-string posts—cathedral prebends or archdeaconries—before 1553. Most of them had entered the universities when the Reformation was already underway and had their faith from their teachers; they were not men who had themselves gone through the experience of conversion. Many had been in exile; others, like Parker, had gone underground. Very few had conformed under Mary; they were men wholly committed to the cause of the Reformation. They were wholehearted partisans, devoted to a transcendent cause. This generation of clergy, Protestant and Catholic alike, stands in sharp contrast to the traditional careerists of the early century or the new ecclesiastical courtier-bureaucrats of late Elizabethan times. Enthusiasts all, they were servants of an ideal rather than of an institution. The visible Church was but the earthly vehicle for the realization of spiritual ends.

The Queen's vision of their role was poles away from theirs. The very process by which she selected her bench of bishops was an early clue to this difference. In choosing her civil councillors the Queen had taken great care to surround herself with men she trusted and, after her fashion, respected. Most of them were well known to her before her accession. But in choosing her chief ecclesiastical servants the Supreme Governor demonstrated much less interest or concern. Cox apart, none of them were men with whom she had had much past association;

none seems to represent a personal preference. There is little doubt the she was powerfully influenced by the persuasions of her councillors—of Cecil and (in Parker's case) Bacon—and of that unofficial but already influential advisor, Robert Dudley. Bishops Grindal, Horne, Sandys, Pilkington, Scambler, and Young all owed something to his patronage.[2] Others, like May of Carlisle, had the backing of a regional magnate, in his case, Shrewsbury. The Queen's relative indifference to these choices is of a piece with her whole attitude towards the new episcopate. So were her relations with them once they were in office. Her actions speak for themselves in telling us how she thought about the government of the Church established by law.

At the very opening of her reign she quite deliberately diminished episcopal incomes by compelling the exchange of landed endowment, often the richest manors belonging to the see, for spiritual revenues, i.e., impropriated livings, a source of income notoriously difficult to collect. The anguished protests of the first episcopal appointees and their attempts at compromise were brusquely repelled and it was made painfully clear that surrenders of this kind were a condition of appointment.[3] The queen protected the bishops against the wholesale expropriation of episcopal lands which courtiers sometimes urged on her, but she regarded their properties as meadows in which her servants might nibble in their incessant hunger for land.

Even more important was the deliberate exclusion—for the first time in centuries—of any bishop from a seat on the Privy Council or a major administrative post under the Crown. This meant that the inner circle of power around the Crown was firmly closed to them and they were denied any share in decision-making at the highest level, even in ecclesiastical causes.

[2] Patrick Collinson, *The Elizabethan Puritan Movement* (Berkeley and Los Angeles, 1967) (cited henceforth as Collinson, *Movement*), 62-63.

[3] John Strype, *Annals of the Reformation* (4 vols., Oxford, 1820-40), pt. I, 142-43, and *Correspondence of Matthew Parker*, ed. John Bruce and T. T. Perowne (Parker Society, 1853; reprint, 1968), 97-102. See also Haugaard, *Elizabeth*, 155, and F. Heal, "The Bishops and the Act of Exchange of 1559," *Historical Journal* 17 (1974), 227-46.

It also meant that even the Archbishop of Canterbury had limited access to the Queen herself; he was constantly driven to use Cecil or some other councillor as a means to engage the royal attention. And, indeed, in her personal relations with the bishops, the Queen seems often to manifest a barely veiled contempt for their persons. To her they were manifestly not Reverend Fathers in God but second-level royal servants.

However, exclusion from the Council did not mean a release from major secular responsibilities. Elizabeth had gone to considerable pains to use all the traditional legal formulae which went to the making of a bishop.[4] These emphasized their role as functionaries, another generation in a line of official succession, assigned for their lives to carry out long-defined tasks in an ancient institution. There could be no doubt that their formal legal status as prelates was identical with that of their medieval predecessors. But it was the secular functions of the episcopacy which concerned the Queen, not their spiritual authority. They were to be lords of Parliament and in their own dioceses they were expected to assume a leading place in local government, as members of the justices' bench and of other local commissions.[5] They were required to play a major role in the detailed and burdensome tasks of governing the counties. This, of course, required that they should maintain the splendid style of living appropriate to such status. In this sense they were very directly the successors of the lordly Catholic prelates of preceding ages. The secular—baronial—side of their office was defined for them: But what of their spiritual character?

It is hardly surprising that the first Elizabethan bishops underwent a severe identity crisis, for the role of a lord bishop hardly squared with their own reformed conceptions of their pastoral role. While these conceptions were certainly not fully worked out, they firmly rejected any notion of themselves as

---

[4] See the proceedings in the election, confirmation and enthronement of Parker in Strype, *Parker*, I, 101-25.

[5] For a discussion of an Elizabethan bishop's duties, see F. Heal, "The Bishops of Ely and Their Diocese during the Reformation Period: c. 1515-1600" (Ph.D. thesis, Cambridge University, 1972).

hierarchs on the Roman model. They would have preferred a simpler life style and one much more focussed on immediate pastoral tasks. Beyond these general notions, all was unclear. The guidelines offered by the reformed churches with which they were most familiar were not helpful. Practice varied, but, more important, the churches of the Rhineland and Switzerland, situated in small city-states, were in geographic size, political constitution, and social composition entirely different from England. The Protestant ecclesiastical order in Scotland was, in the 1560's, still incoherent; while in France the Huguenots were an underground community, struggling for existence. But for the time being the definition of the episcopal office had to be put aside while the bishops gathered up the reins of power from their Marian predecessors.

The first step in the setting up of the new order was the tendering of the oath of supremacy and the consequent culling out of recalcitrant clergy, particularly in the cathedrals and among the archdiaconate. Significantly this was left to the ecclesiastical commissioners (mostly laymen) whose appointments predated those of the new bishops. Replacements at the higher levels presented no particular difficulties since the pool of evangelical clergy was large enough to meet the need. The greater problem of the parish clergy was in one sense made simple by their general willingness to conform to the new order without a murmur. But the conscientious bishop could not shut his eyes to their shortcomings; many of these all too docile shepherds had shifted their obedience as many as four different times and could hardly be fit instruments for the great work of spiritual regeneration which lay ahead. Some program of retraining, of "further education," had to be devised for incumbents and additional measures taken to insure that new appointees were of the quality which new spiritual standards demanded.

But the episcopal "identity crisis" was only one manifestation of a deeper lying problem. What was the "identity" of the new Church established by law? What were its sources of authority; what were the contents of its doctrine; what justified its rejection of past custom and belief? These questions were already being pressed by English Roman Catholic controversialists and Bishop Jewel, in his *Apology*, was already defending the new order.[6] He took pains to repel the specific Roman charges against it, but this was a defensive work and by its very nature precluded much more than a bare sketch, a tentative outline, for a more positive statement about the new establishment.

These large issues were certainly not of interest to the Supreme Governor, who, at a very pragmatic level, was moving to assert her authority over the Church. In 1559, acting under the authority of statute, she set up a new commission—the earliest form of the body later to be known as the Court of High Commission.[7] Among its members clerics were in a minority; the Primate, Grindal of London, Cox of Ely (and from 1562 Guest of Rochester) plus a few deans were outnumbered by fourteen lay members, a majority of them lawyers. Their first task was the tendering of the oath of supremacy; that done, the commission remained in being, its duration indefinite, its functions undefined.

In this same year the Queen, following precedents set by her father and brother, issued a set of Injunctions,[8] which laid down the working rules for the new regime. Issued by the Queen after consultation with the Privy Council, they regulated carefully the ritual practices to be observed in public worship and prescribed norms of clerical conduct. Modelled closely on King Edward's Injunctions, they were closer in spirit to those of 1547 than to the more radically Protestant program of 1552. These initial acts of the new ecclesiastical governor made plain her intentions. The Church was to be governed as another department of the State, although with its own separate bureaucracy. Central authority was vested partly in a hybrid High Commission, partly in the episco-

[6] John Jewel, *An Apology or Answer in Defence of the Church of England* (1562).

[7] See Roland Usher, *The Rise and Fall of the High Commission* (Oxford, 1913), 27-30.

[8] For the injunctions of 1559, see Henry Gee and W. J. Hardy, *Documents Illustrative of English Church History* (1896), 417-41, and Haugaard, *Elizabeth*, 139-44.

pacy, acting under the direction of the Primate. He and his fellow bishops were officers of the Queen, as Supreme Governor, and expected to execute her will. A comparison of the ecclesiastical bureaucracy with its civil counterpart is illuminating. In the latter instance the Queen was assisted by a Privy Council which was at once an executive and a consultative body. Most of its members had departmental responsibilities; all of them shared in its meetings as a central executive committee; and all shared in its collective advisory capacity. The most important of them were in almost daily association with the Queen herself.

The government of the Church was much more incoherent. The High Commission, a hybrid body of clerics and laity, had uncertain powers and as yet indeterminate functions. The bishops, rarely meeting as a single body, were the ranking bureaucrats of ecclesiastical government, executing in their various sees the orders given by the Queen and transmitted by the archbishops, but they had no advisory function. Even the Primate was simply the recipient of orders passed on by the Secretary, often without previous discussion.

These developments made fairly clear several things. One was the royal conviction that what we have come to call the "settlement of religion" was now complete. The passing of the statutes, the issue of the Injunctions, the activities of the commissioners, the appointment of the new hierarchy and their subordinates accomplished all that was necessary to set the ecclesiastical machinery in motion. What remained now was to keep the machinery turning over in good order, fulfilling its role within the larger structure of society. They also suggested that the Queen gave religious affairs a relatively low priority in her scheme of things. She was prepared to play no more than a clock-maker role. The machinery was now wound up; it ought not to demand much future attention.

This might have been a workable program if two necessary conditions had been met. The first was that the men responsible for carrying it out—the bishops and their senior colleagues among the clergy—should wholeheartedly believe in it. That this was not so, we already know. The bishops were uneasy and confused about their authority and their functions while their conceptions of their pastoral task took them a good deal closer in their sympathies to their reforming brethren than to the Supreme Governor. And even had they been enthusiastic about the Queen's Erastian program, they lacked the necessary royal countenance to quicken the dry abstractions of their merely legal authority.

The second necessary condition would have been the more or less willing obedience of the rank and file clergy in the royal program. In fact it was opposed by a small but determined and very articulate body of divines, who were fervently devoted to a far-reaching work of further Reformation. The vision of the evangelicals was eloquently voiced by Cartwright. The Queen's task as he saw it, was nothing less than "the full and whole deliverance of the people." More fortunate than Moses, she shared with David and Solomon the opportunity of building the temple—of fulfilling the Lord's will. Surely she and her councillors would "not make themselves guilty of so great unthankfulness as will follow the forsaking of so incomparable a benefit."[9] Support for the royal program was, on the other hand, largely passive, the mere acquiescence of docile functionaries; there was certainly lacking in the early years of the reign any formulation of the establishment position which had the force or persuasiveness of the Puritan call.

The first inkling that not all her ecclesiastical servants shared the Queen's complacent views came in the Convocation which met, as usual, at the same time as Parliament, in 1563.[10] In that body a strong nucleus of clergy in the Lower House (the representative element) brought forward detailed proposals for changes in the Prayer Book ceremonial and for the abolition of clerical vestments. They were able to obtain a majority among those present but lost (by one vote) when proxies were counted. Later in the session they managed to obtain support for a somewhat amended version of their previous program.

[9] Cartwright quoted in John Whitgift, *Works*, ed. John Ayre (3 vols., Parker Society, 1851-1853), I, 26.

[10] For a full account of this convocation, see Haugaard, *Elizabeth*, chap. 2.

But the Lower House could do no more than petition; its powers, as against those of the Upper House (the bishops), were very limited. Here the reformers met no response at all; there is no direct evidence, but there can be little doubt that the episcopate was acting under royal pressure. The program that had been rejected was a modest one and much of it reflected issues which had agitated critics since the beginning of the century—absenteeism, pluralism, and an unlearned clergy. But even such modest changes were too much for the Supreme Governor, who had firmly closed the door on any alterations of the order now established by statute and injunction.

This marked the first rift between the new episcopate and their evangelical colleagues in the rank and file of the clergy. The latter were astute enough to shift their tactics, and in 1566 it was the House of Commons, rather than Convocation, to which they directed their efforts. They were no more successful there, and this time royal displeasure was quite overt. The consequences of these two failures will engage our attention below.

The first open collision between the activists and constituted authority came in 1565 over what came to be called the vestiarian issue. There was in fact more than the immediate question of vestments at stake. Many clergymen had taken matters into their own hands and amended the liturgy of the Book, mandated by statute, to suit their own judgments. As early as 1561 during the royal progress in Suffolk the Queen's (and Cecil's) attention had been drawn to the variety of forms of worship, each tailored according to the local clergyman's preferences and usually characterized by a radical simplicity which quite ignored the Prayer Book and the Injunctions. There is in Burghley's papers an undated paper (possibly of 1564) which lists the array of variants obtaining in individual parishes. In the Parliament of 1563 Lord Keeper Bacon, in his opening speech, had deplored the lack of discipline in the Church, particularly the lax regard for ceremonies and ornaments.[11] These evangelical clergy were not consciously in re-

[11] Parker, *Correspondence*, 148-49; Strype, *Parker*, I, 301-2; Strype, *Annals*, I, pt. 1, 436.

volt against authority, but they were ignoring both the requirements of statute (and injunction) and the approval of their clerical superiors. Boldly outpacing the bishops, they were cheerfully carrying forward reform at the grass-roots level, quite on their own initiative without any serious regard to the Injunctions which were supposed to regulate public worship. Such a situation was bound to arouse royal wrath, but the Queen's intervention, when it came, was sudden and, so far as we know, unexpected.

Just what, or who, moved the Queen to action in January 1565 is hidden from us. The first sign of her displeasure was conveyed to Parker in a draft which Cecil had prepared at the royal command.[12] The last clause of the Secretary's covering letter (which alone survives) in which he worries "whether the Queen's Majesty will not be provoked to some offense that there is such cause of reformation and whether she will not have more added than I shall allow" suggests a royal rather than a Cecilian initiative. The royal letter when it reached the Archbishop on 25 January was a pithy exposition of the Queen's ecclesiastical policy. Nothing, she said, more profited her own ease of government and the universal weal of her people than "unity, quietness, and concord as well among the public ministers having charge under us as in the multitude of people by us and by them ruled." Diversity, contention, "and vain love of singularity" could only offend Almighty God and be to his earthly lieutenant "discomfortable, heavy, and troublesome." Novelties both of ceremonies and opinions "by persons abounding more in their own senses than wisdom and delighting with singularities and changes" would lead to schism and deformity in the Church; the Queen's authority under Almighty God would be violated and she might well be thought to bear the sword in vain. The bishops, who had plainly failed in their duties, were to censure all dissident clergy and see that no person holding such unsound opinions should remain in authority within the Church.

The tone and the substance of the royal letter were unmistakable, and the Primate had no choice but to proceed to ac-

[12] Parker, *Correspondence*, 223-27.

tion. This took the initial form of a set of articles—prepared by the Primate and several episcopal colleagues—put together partly out of earlier formulations and partly newly devised; they were designed for royal promulgation and covered a wide range of subjects, preaching, ceremonial, and vestments among them. The articles, submitted by the Archbishop to the Secretary, came back amended in some details, but most important with explicit royal authorization excised. Without such royal backing the timid Archbishop feared to proceed on his own; it was more than a year before the articles were published and then under the ambiguous title of "Advertisements," a species of public enactment of curious and uncertain status.[13]

But even before the royal letter the Primate had moved to action in regard to one particular aspect of its complaints— vestments. The statute laid down that the full traditional vestments used in the first year of King Edward were the required norm, a norm that was highly conservative and, in many men's eyes, Papistical. In practice it had been modified to the wearing, by parish clergy, solely of the surplice. But for many even this was too much. Already in 1564 the Archbishop had been hard at work trying to persuade the two most conspicuous recalcitrants, Sampson, Dean of Christ Church, and Humphrey, President of Magdalen, to conform. These dignitaries, after much discussion, had rejected a proposed compromise. After the royal command Parker took a stronger line and summoned them to London, demanding obedience to the vestments requirements (and communion in wafer-bread), on threat of deprivation. Even then he was uncertain about his legal powers to act; in the end he deprived Sampson (probably acting as ordinary of Oxford in the vacancy of the see) but left Humphrey, at Magdalen, where the visitor, Bishop Horne of Winchester, did not act.[14]

There was another confrontation in the capital, the most conspicuous center of dissident activity. The reluctant Bishop

[13] Gee and Hardy, *Documents*, 467-75; Haugaard, *Elizabeth*, 213-17.
[14] Richard W. Dixon, *History of the Church of England* (6 vols., Oxford, 1878-1902), VI, 39-43; Strype, *Parker*, I, 329-45; Haugaard, *Elizabeth*, 222.

of London, Grindal, was finally brought to act by the Primate. The city clergy were summoned by their bishop and those who refused conformity were deprived of their livings by archiepiscopal authority. Some then gave in; the militant core who still refused were eventually packed off to confinement with various provincial bishops by the action of the Privy Council. Thus immediate resistance to the vestment requirement was broken in London; although how far the new orders were enforced outside the sees of London and Canterbury is hard to know. The most prominent of the resisters soon reappeared in new posts provided for them by sympathetic lay patrons—Sampson, for instance, as master of Wigston Hospital in Leicester (thanks to Huntingdon) and also as a prebendary of St. Paul's and rector of Brightlingsea, Essex. Humphrey remained in his college until he died in 1590 (later, conforming, he was also appointed to the deanery of Gloucester).[15]

The whole episode had far-reaching effects. First of all it opened a painful fissure in the ranks of the reform-minded clergy. Their discords did not arise from the issue itself; all, including the bishops, were pretty well agreed that those relics of Papist practice, "these Judaical and heathenish rites," as Bishop Sandys called them in a sermon to Parliament, should be abolished. At the most they might be borne temporarily as a concession to an unenlightened populace. The pain which the episode inflicted arose from the difficult choice which all alike, bishops and conscientious parish priests, had to make between an action which offended their consciences and the commands of the Supreme Governor. Many of the bishops were uneasy; Pilkington protested vehemently; Sandys and Parkhurst dragged their feet; and Grindal had to be pushed into reluctant cooperation.[16]

Elizabeth's command forced many of her clergy upon the horns of a dilemma which had long been inherent in English Protestant tradition. For forty years reforming divines had with varying emphases rested their arguments on Biblical au-

[15] Haugaard, *Elizabeth*, 226-27; Dixon, *History*, VI, 64.

[16] Strype, *Parker*, I, 308, 311; Parker, *Correspondence*, 278; Collinson, *Movement*, 73.

thority, giving particular emphasis to those New Testament passages which enjoined obedience to God's earthly lieutenant, the sovereign. Now they found themselves compelled to choose between the revealed Word and the Supreme Governor's commands. Some had already found their way to the comfortable doctrine of "things indifferent" but others could not so view the matter. The spate of angry pamphlets which the occasion produced marked the first engagement in the long and painful warfare within English Protestant ranks which was to rend the Church for generations to come.

The Archbishop, after much hesitation, was forced to fall back on the uncertain authority of the "Advertisements." This document began by citing the Queen's letter of January 1565, making clear her view on the question of uniformity but then the enacting clause—if it can be said to have one—which followed, struck a wavering and very uncertain note. Speaking in the name of the metropolitan and "other bishops . . . namely such as be in commission for causes ecclesiastical" the preface goes on to say that "by assent and consent of the persons aforesaid, these orders and rules ensuing have been thought meet and convenient to be used and followed." But then, backing away, the Archbishop and his colleagues take pains to deny that these rules in any way bound the consciences of Englishmen or added "any efficacy or more holiness to the virtue of public prayer." They were to be seen as "temporal orders mere ecclesiastical" and "as rules in some part of discipline concerning decency, distinction, and order for the time."[17] Their legal nature remains mysteriously uncertain. The "Advertisements" are clearly not an enactment of the Commissioners Ecclesiastical since only the clerical members of that board are even mentioned. The Archbishop makes no claim to any powers of his own—or to collegial episcopal authority. The Queen's name is brought in to explain the purpose of issuing the document and her approval of its general thrust is expressed, but it is also clear that this is not a royal decree. The contrast with the Injunctions of 1559 could not be more obvious; these begin

[17] Gee and Hardy, *Documents,* 468.

with the traditional phrase of royal command, "The Queen's most royal majesty, by the advice of her most honorable council . . . doth minister unto her loving subjects godly Injunctions hereafter following. All which Injunctions her highness willeth and comandeth her loving subjects . . ." to receive, observe, and keep, under stated penalties.[18] Various arguments have been brought forward to explain the Queen's refusal to give her direct backing to the Archbishop and his episcopal colleagues. Leicester is known to have intervened in favor of the dissidents and against the vestiarian requirement, and some have ascribed her apparent volte-face to his influence. This seems unlikely; on lesser matters the Queen was prepared to listen to the favorite; he certainly influenced ecclesiastical appointments in the early years of the reign. But on a matter of principle—and that principle one of overriding importance, to which the Queen was immovably attached—she would be little disposed to yield.

A more serious argument has been put forward by a recent authority on the 1559 settlement.[19] Dr. Haugaard's argument is that the Queen would not sign the Advertisements because they altered the legal standard of the 1559 settlement. As she saw it, assent to the new articles would supersede the requirements of the ornaments rubric in the Statute of Uniformity, because they reduced the vestments solely to the surplice. The rather subtle legal argument is that the bishops on their own authority could lower these standards—could compromise— but that the Queen would not allow her Supreme Governorship to be used, then or later, to support any variance from the 1559 settlement. In addition, Haugaard argues that Elizabeth would not allow the kind of royal (or conciliar) interventions to back up his authority which Parker sought during the strains of 1565-1566. She wished to keep her ecclesiastical supremacy in a water-tight compartment separate from her secular sovereignty.

There is force in both arguments; the Queen did not and would not alter one jot or title of the 1559 arrangements and

---

[18] *Ibid.*, 418.   [19] Haugaard, *Elizabeth*, 217.

she was certainly unwilling to mingle her ecclesiastical prerogatives with her civil, lest Parliament encroach on the former. But the argument ascribes a consistency and an intellectual rigor which are hardly characteristic of the Queen. It presupposes that the Queen was more concerned in the legal and constitutional niceties of the problem than she was in effective suppression of the diversities of practice which had excited the royal anger initially. And in fact the Privy Council had intervened to exile from London the most obstreperous of the anti-vestiarian clergy in 1566.[20]

Although the Queen had fixed and unchangeable ideas about her ecclesiastical authority and about the settlement of 1559, they were not matched by any sustained interest in religious affairs—of the kind, for instance, which she always displayed in foreign relations. From time to time, when some flagrant example of clerical indiscipline was brought to her attention, her anger flared up, as it had done in January 1565. She expected Parker, once instructed, to proceed under his own steam; she did not wish to be bothered by the details of enforcement. What she would not face was the realization that if the settlement was to be enforced in every detail, she needed much stronger machinery to accomplish it than yet existed. The whole progress of the controversy had served to illustrate the narrow and ill-defined limits of episcopal authority. It had been possible to dislodge Sampson from Oxford (only to see him reappear on the scene at Leicester); a handful of London clergy had been deprived and a nucleus of dissidence they had formed broken up. But individually they were not silenced, merely dispersed to other theaters of action. And across the country individual incumbents continued to ignore the vestments requirement and to alter the liturgy as they saw fit. The goals of uniformity in public worship which the Queen had so forcibly expounded in her letter to Archbishop Parker were as far from fulfillment as ever.

And the position of the bishops had perceptibly worsened. It was not only that they were now under attack from within the reformers' ranks for having betrayed the cause, but the

[20] *Ibid.*, 227.

very nature of their coercive authority was unsettled. Whatever powers the Queen believed them to have in theory, they certainly did not possess in fact. The uncertainties as to their legal powers made them all the more vulnerable to their critics' assertion that they were prelatical tyrants, mini-Popes, and hastened the fast-approaching day when the very nature of their office would be called into question. What the Queen did not recognize was the fragility of the new episcopal order on which she laid so heavy a burden. Its lack of a basic rationale and the absence of adequate legal definitions were serious impediments in the performance of her commands. Even more frustrating—as time would show—was the difficulty the new prelates faced in finding an acknowledged place in the traditional socio-political framework. Neither the aristocracy nor the commons were ready to accord them the unfeigned deference and unquestioned status as great magnates which their predecessors had enjoyed. To overcome these barriers they desperately needed the public and wholehearted countenance of the Crown; what they had in fact to endure from the sovereign was a barely veiled contempt or at the best cold indifference.

The net effect of the vestiarian episode was at once to clarify and to confuse. The Queen's intentions were made clear at least to her councillors and bishops; the latter were forced to act as royal agents to enforce an ecclesiastical program in which few of them wholeheartedly believed. Evangelical clergy were driven to acts of overt resistance and to suffer penalties accordingly. Their resentment against the bishops, whom they perceived as the active agents, and their growing contempt for the latters' authority were now all too evident. But if this much was clear, much else was not. The Queen's failure to give public backing to the bishops left the impression that it was all their doing rather than hers; the nature of the authority which Parker and his colleagues exerted seemed more questionable than ever; while the backstairs influence of the dissidents' friends at court gave strong hope that conformity would not be insisted on. But the lines of division were now drawn, the issue of episcopal authority brought into the open, and the polarization of parties within the Protestant fold had begun.

The Archbishop, on the other hand, had learned a good deal from the experience. Goaded by the Secretary, he had tried flying with his own wings, first in the Sampson affair and later in the episode of the London clergy. He gained confidence in his powers; he also began to adopt a more strongly authoritarian conception of his office and to show a growing irritability towards his opponents.[21] A decade as archbishop had imperceptibly worked on the timid scholar who had resisted appointment in 1559. The bearing of responsibilities and the making of decisions had made him irritably sensitive to criticism and intolerant of those who flouted established authority. A certain taste for the office and for the status which it entailed had grown on him, as his extensive rebuilding of the episcopal residences bore witness. He had come to take pride in the lavish hospitality with which he entertained the sovereign at Canterbury or in his country houses. Consciously or unconsciously he had come to resemble, at least in external appearances, his Catholic predecessors. These changed attitudes would have a good deal to do with his response to the next round of reformist effort in the early 1570's.

[21] See Parker, *Correspondence*, 272.

CHAPTER 2

THE PURITANS IN PARLIAMENT,

1566-1572

IN THE PERSPECTIVE of four hundred years the struggle between the Puritans and their adversaries takes on a certain grand simplicity in which the issues and the protagonists are dramatically highlighted. But a closer examination of events, as recent scholarship[1] has made abundantly evident, reveals a confused and ragged warfare—guerrilla engagements for the most part, although interspersed with short, sharp, full-scale campaigns when Parliament met. The confusions arose in no small part from the very circumstances of conflict. The dissidents were, of course, a private and unofficial grouping within an authoritarian official establishment; the strategies open to them, dictated by these circumstances, were necessarily half-clandestine and imperfectly coordinated. In official eyes their disobedience was equated with illegality and even disloyalty. Moreover, although they were all critical in some measure of the existing Church order, they varied widely in their objections to that order—from the relatively moderate who would have been content with minor liturgical changes to "root-and-branch" radicals who wanted a whole new order of Church government.

[1] Throughout the whole discussion of Protestant dissent, I have relied heavily on the authoritative study of Elizabethan Puritanism by Professor Collinson.

Nor were their opponents, although representatives of an established institution, by any means an integrated or coherent body. Their presumptive leaders, the bishops, were in many cases more or less openly sympathizers with many of the critics' causes. Hence the establishment, until the 1580's, lacked effective leadership, indeed any leadership at all. The Queen had to dragoon the reluctant prelates into half-hearted enforcement of policies which, at heart, they did not accept. Not until the 1580's was there a clerical leader drawn from their own ranks. Whitgift had spelled out, in the previous decade, an effective rationale for the establishment, but until he came to power there was little chance of fleshing it out in action. Up until then, even with all the advantages of institutional organization at their disposal, the representatives of the established Church were not able to make effective use of them. They endured all the disadvantages of a stodgy, badly led, and dispirited regular army faced by nimble, purposeful, and unorthodox guerrillas.

It is necessary first of all to sort out the various parties to this untidy quarrel. The first to be considered, the key figure in the whole struggle, is the Queen. It was her views about right Church order which set in motion the rush of events; without her rock-like opposition, the advocates of further change after 1559 would almost certainly have had their way, supported, if not led, by a sympathetic episcopal bench and a warmly approving House of Commons. Indeed without royal obstinacy there might have been no Puritans—no party of critics and, ultimately, of dissenters.

Elizabeth's views about the Church were part of her whole, highly conservative and in some respects archaic conception of her own role and office. They were anything but self-conscious; they seemed to her self-evident and needing little defense. They are expounded from time to time in her infrequent but unequivocal pronouncements on religion addressed either to the bishops or to Parliament.

To her, the society over which she presided was a natural and self-sustaining organism. It functioned as spontaneously as the other orders of nature, biological or physical, and like

them fulfilled some basic human requirements. Its structure—
the socio-political hierarchy—was thus a given, no more a matter of speculation or of debate than the succession of the sea-
sons. It was, however, subject to continual pressures, arising
from the very instability of individual human behavior, which
threatened its good health and at times its very existence. The
Queen's duties were those of continual and vigilant conserva-
tion; her subjects' necessary duty, to obey without demur. It
hardly needs to be said that such a view was profoundly anti-
historical since it viewed the social organism as entirely static,
virtually immobile, subject only to surface fluctuations, mere
flurries of weather in a climate of Mediterranean equability.

In this light Elizabeth saw the recent change in religion as a
passing storm or, to put it another way, as a spell of social bad
health, an indisposition in the body politic. There had been a
derangement occasioned by the usurpation and consequent
abuses of Papal authority, but this had now been corrected; the
organism was once again healthy and could return to normal
uneventful functioning. Hence the settlement of 1559, far from
being a temporary stage in a grand *restauratio* of pure and undefiled religion, a cosmic transformation and perhaps even
eschatological fulfillment, was merely a return to healthy routine.

That settlement was shaped, not by long-term, self-conscious
goals of universal reform, but merely by commonsensical considerations of immediate utility. They were dictated by the
need to set a piece of social machinery in good working order
again and to ensure that it would continue without further in-
terruption. The decisions as to what that order should be were,
as the Queen saw it, entirely her own. That responsibility was
given to her ultimately by God and was inherent in the very
nature of the social organism. It could not, therefore, be shared
with anyone else.

These convictions were quite unshakeable, and no amount
of argument would move the Queen from them. They were
held by her as self-evident assumptions, shared by all reasonable men. She therefore took for granted that the ordinary social machinery would provide for their realization. That ma-

53

chinery was, in this case, the bishops and their subordinate diocesan officers. They were supplemented by the ecclesiastical commission set up in 1559, largely staffed by the Primate and a number of his episcopal colleagues, plus a contingent of civil lawyers. The Queen, so far as she thought about the matter, expected these men to carry on the routine administration of the Church as her privy councillors and their agents managed that of the realm.

The bishops, for their part, began with a rather different conception than that of their sovereign. While no doubt sharing her premises about the ultimate nature of the social order, they were each to some extent imbued with a sense of an immediate God-given task; the great work of reform, of manifesting in the Church of England the clearly expressed will of the Deity, was yet to be completed. Within their own sees many of them worked, with varying degrees of enthusiasm, to forward these ends in the parishes within their charge, although none came forward as an active leader in any national effort at continuing reform. And with the passage of time the contradictions between their own inclinations and the royal will became evident. The demands imposed by office were too strong to be altogether resisted. Consciously or unconsciously they were becoming servants of the Tudor Crown, inextricably involved in its purposes, gradually bending to the will of the Supreme Governor. The full extent of their involvement in this role became apparent towards the end of the 1560's. One of its consequences was the withering away of any effort to define the episcopal office, or, in a larger sense, the very polity of the English reformed Church. When a rival formulation emerged among the dissident clergy in the early 1570's it found the establishment without a prepared response.

A third force at play within the establishment was that of the eminent laity, particularly in the Privy Council but also at large within the governing orders. This of course contradicted the simplicities of royal orthodoxy according to which the Queen's lay servants had no role to play in her ecclesiastical establishment. But facts contradicted theory, and their interventions, formal and informal, were numerous and effective. The councillors, by the 1570's, were almost all men warmly attached to the Protestant faith. Some of them had close ties with the evangelical clergy and shared the hopes and expectations of the eager reformers. They could be counted on to cushion the effects of official disapproval upon individual dissident clergy. If they could not prevent deprivation from a living, they could often in their private capacities as patrons provide an alternative benefice. But they too were servants of the Crown, habituated to obedience to their sovereign, and practical politicians, acutely aware of the multiple strains within English society. They also shared with the Queen something of the anti-clerical feeling so potent a strain in the English Reformation tradition. While they in general respected the prelates of the Reformed Church, they were by no means free of a certain suspicion and sometimes even contempt towards their clerical colleagues. They were wary of any clerical pretensions which might tend to restore the privileges and wealth lost in the preceding decades. All this was to lead to an ambivalence which aroused hopes among the dissident clergy and fears among the prelates —neither of which were to be fully realized.

The divergencies among those in power were matched by the varieties of dissidence. These divergencies were apparent even in the days of the Marian exile, as the famous troubles at Frankfort revealed. They continued at the opening of the new reign when the more austere and extreme core of the exile clergy refused to accept posts in what they regarded as a very imperfectly reformed Church. Some of them would take service under Warwick at Newhaven in 1562-1563.[2] Among those who did accept office, another sorting out came in the vestiarian controversy. And the differences between moderates who continued to struggle for reform within the ranks of the beneficed clergy and the more radical who were prepared to risk, and to lose, their benefices continued to display themselves across the succeeding decades. What contemporaries would begin to call

[2] *Letters of Thomas Wood, Puritan, 1566-1577*, ed. Patrick Collinson (*Bull. Inst. Hist. Res.*, special suppl. 5, London, 1960), ix.

Puritanism soon spread itself across a spectrum of ever-increasing width marked by disagreements on matters of substance and on those of tactics.

But dissidence would have been a short-lived phenomenon had it been limited to clerical ranks. Just who the lay supporters were and how many of them there were would—as among the Catholics—reveal itself only with time and circumstance. The most immediately conspicuous were those high-placed patrons at court who intervened in behalf of the clerical recalcitrants during the vestiarian episode. Leicester was the most eminent of these; he was backed by Sir Francis Knollys and after 1572 by Sir Francis Walsingham. Sir Walter Mildmay was a less outspoken patron who would prove his loyalty to the cause in the foundation of Emmanuel College. Burghley, while less wholehearted than these men, was cautiously sympathetic to moderate reform. But in addition to these great court patrons there was, as events would soon prove, a solid and substantial core of squires who would give active help within Parliament and without.

The leaders and spokesmen of the nonconformists were, of course, clergy. And it was in the clerical body, Convocation, that they made their first concerted move for further change. In the 1563 meeting a well-conceived and quite modest program failed very narrowly of actual adoption in the Lower House, and a second more watered-down program did win approval there.[3] It was in the Upper House (the bishops) where it failed completely. The reformers were inclined to blame the prelates for this, little appreciating the brute fact of royal pressure. But they drew an obvious tactical lesson from their defeat. In 1566 it was not in Convocation but in Parliament that they made their move. These new tactics necessarily involved the initiative of laymen. The response of their lay backers must have been gratifying to the clerical leaders; it proved easy to find Parliamentary collaborators to put forward bills in the House and the ease with which most of these measures gained Commons approval was cheering evidence of wide backing in the country at large.

[3] Haugaard, *Elizabeth*, 64-65, 68-72.

This first attempt to mobilize lay support for further reform was undertaken under somewhat unfavorable circumstances since the overriding preoccupation of that session was the succession, and Lords and Commons labored mightily, although in vain, to press the Queen to marriage. But at the very end of the session someone—we do not know who—brought in a whole budget of bills, six in all, each proposing a measure of ecclesiastical reform. Five of them dealt with long-standing grievances which had concerned earnest Christians of all persuasions for decades—pluralism, absenteeism, simony, corrupt presentations, and so on. Bill A (as it was labelled) was more topical since it proposed to give statutory authority to the Thirty-Nine Articles of Religion, agreed on in Convocation in 1563 (and which with minor revisions were the Forty-Two Articles of Archbishop Cranmer). It was only Bill A which the backers seriously sought to pass; the others were left to sleep.[4]

The sponsorship of the bills was of course unofficial and undoubtedly had the backing of the clergy who had pressed their program of reform in 1563. Burghley favored the bill on the articles and so did the bishops, although they were not, as the Queen angrily suspected, its authors.[5] Her own views were emphatic and and consistent; she wanted it killed and after it had passed the Commons and received its first reading in the Lords, she commanded the Lord Keeper to stop its progress. Even then the Houses dragged their feet to save the bill on the Articles by delaying routine legislation (particularly the renewal of statutes about to lapse). But the Queen would not yield and the Parliament ended with no acts on religion and no renewal of the eleven statutes which the government was anxious to continue. The Queen sent the MP's home with an irritable scolding for their behavior, aimed, however, primarily at their demands on the succession.

It was to be five years before Parliament met again and then in the aftermath of the Northern Rebellion and the publication of the Papal bull of deposition. It was a highly excited body of men who came together with more than one topic of concern

[4] Neale I, 166-70.

[5] PRO, SP 12/41/36; Parker, *Correspondence*, 290-94.

in their minds. They might have moved in several different directions, but with the curious inconsequence of an assembly which lacked continuity of agenda or leadership, it was carried away by the first members to get the floor. In this case it was the cause of religion which caught the attention of the House. What eventuated was the first full-scale effort of the reformers to use Parliament as an instrument to realize their purposes. It was to produce a complex interplay of all the forces at work within the English political system—sovereign, Council, Commons, bishops.

The preliminary speeches which always opened a Parliament carried more than one hint of what was to come. Bishop Sandys, preaching in the Abbey, called for a purging of the Church of all idolatry and superstition, a return to the simplicity of the primitive church, "casting away Judaical and heathenish rites," thus displaying his sympathies on the vestiarian controversy and on the larger issue of ceremonies. Lord Keeper Bacon, speaking for the Queen,[6] indicated the causes for the meeting and explicitly told them that they were "to consider first whether the ecclesiastical laws concerning the discipline of the Church be sufficient or no; and if any want shall be found to supply the same." Finally, Bacon, again speaking in the Queen's voice, responded to the Speaker's usual petition for privileges. In an unaccustomed gloss on the Speaker's petition he warned the House not to meddle with any matters of state except those "proponed" to them and otherwise to limit themselves to matters of the commonwealth. Certainly this admonition harked back to the disorderly scenes about the succession in the preceding Parliament; it may also have warned them off any discussion of Church affairs. This would have been consistent with the Queen's general view that ecclesiastical matters were subsumed under her supremacy and not Parliamentary business. But Bacon's earlier injunction, quite emphatic, that they should consider the discipline of the Church makes the supposition less certain. The House was

---

[6] Edwin Sandys, *Sermons* (Parker Society, 1842) 43; BL, Cotton, Titus, F 1, ff. 123-25.

quick to respond to the first and content to ignore the second of these conflicting signals.

Whatever the Queen's intent, the reformers were quite certain about what they intended to do. Very early in the session Strickland, member for Scarborough,[7] and a prominent member of the "choir" of 1566, opened up the subject of religion in a long speech which criticized the Book of Common Prayer as "very near to the sincerity of the truth" but needing further purification from Papist superstitions. Secondly, he called for the production of Cranmer's *Reformatio Legum*, the revised (and Protestant) code of canon law. He proposed that these matters be discussed by a Commons committee with the bishops. In later sessions the bills of 1566 for reforming clerical abuses were reintroduced, including now two measures dealing with the Articles of Religion. One would probably have confirmed most but not all the Articles (omitting those on the homilies, consecration of bishops and others not agreeable to precisians' consciences) and would have established a religious test for the laity. The second dealt with clerical subscription to the Articles.

All this went well beyond the modest reforms proposed in 1566. The Articles were turned into a weapon against the Papists, lay or clerical; but at the same time they offered a relaxation of those requirements of the 1559 settlement which most galled the left wing and opened the door for major changes in liturgy and discipline. The attempt to rewrite the Articles of Religion by this oblique method drew the fire of the bishops, who were also indisposed to pursue the question of the *Reformatio Legum* or any changes in the Book of Common Prayer.

At this point what seems to have been the original scheme of the reformers—a bold program but one pursued by moderate tactics, bringing the bishops along—fell apart. Whether it was because of disappointment at the prelates' negative response or simply the exasperated impulse of the excitable Strickland we cannot tell. But the latter gave a new and radical turn to the

[7] For this Parliament, see Neale I, 192-207.

proceedings by bringing in a bill for wholesale alterations in the Book of Common Prayer, abolishing vestments, kneeling at Communion, private baptism or private communion, and including other alterations in rites to wipe out what the Puritans regarded as Popish remnants. Earlier measures had called for additions to the settlement of 1559; this very explicitly demanded revision of the settlement and directly assaulted those provisions for conformity of dress and ritual which the Queen explicitly backed. It was a confrontation with royal authority and an implicit condemnation of the bishops.

The warnings of the councillors, led by the Puritan Knollys, that the Queen would regard this measure as an intrusion on the prerogative, had no effect. There followed a passionate outburst of Puritan oratory by Tristram Pistor in which he lamented the worldliness of their proceedings. They had dealt with mere trifles—subsidies, crown, kingdoms—when their attention should be riveted on God's kingdom. Nevertheless, the House was sober enough to decide on a petition to the Queen asking for her license to proceed in this bill. They then adjourned for Easter; during the interval Strickland was sent to the Tower, by conciliar command, no doubt at the Queen's bidding. The Commons reassembled in a state of high excitement to be treated to indignant speeches about liberty of speech and warned, again by Knollys, of trespassing on prerogative. The councillors sensed the degree of irritability in the House; next day Strickland was released. No more was heard of his bill for the alteration of the Prayer Book.

The final struggle of the session was over the two bills dealing with the Articles of Religion. The more ambitious passed the Commons but was halted in the Lords by the Queen. The Lower House revenged itself by altering the other bill—on clerical subscription—so as to limit it to those articles "which only concern the confession of the true Christian faith and the doctrine of the sacraments." The Queen signed this bill although she took occasion through Lord Keeper Bacon to declare that it should have been debated in the Convocation and by the bishops and not by them. Moreover, "the prerogative touched her Majesty and her authority, which, without her favour, ought not to be had in question. Those, therefore, that so audaciously and arrogantly have dealt in such matters may not look to receive further favor than by the statutes of this realm is ordained."[8]

The interval between this Parliament and its successor was to be unusually brief; the revelations of the Ridolfi plot, with its involvement of the Duke of Norfolk and the Queen of Scots, were the occasion for summoning a new Parliament in the spring of 1572. The chief cause for this new assembly,[9] so the Lord Keeper told them, was to devise laws for the safety of the Queen's Majesty, the existing ones being inadequate for such great treasons as had just been revealed. The assembly was warned to avoid other topics and to keep the session as short as possible.

This admonition had as little effect as those of earlier meetings. The religious reformers were as determined as ever to have their way, although perhaps not so well prepared as they had been a year earlier. Certainly the interval since the last Parliament had given them cause for grievance. In June 1571 the Ecclesiastical Commissioners, under Parker's chairmanship, had, immediately after the dissolution of Parliament, summoned a group of the protesting clergy for examination and in the same month had sent out a circular to all parish churches with strict orders that no one was to minister sacraments or to conduct any religious service except as the Book of Common Prayer and the royal Injunctions provided; this was in pursuance of a canon of the recent convocation demanding subscription to the Articles (all of them), the Prayer Book, and the surplice. The Commission was busy throughout the summer, implementing a policy which also had royal approval. Later there were negotiations with the dissident leaders, some of whom offered a limited subscription to the Articles and the Book although refusing the surplice altogether. At least one of these clergymen, John Field, was deprived by early 1572.[10]

[8] *Ibid.*, 238.　　　　　[9] Strype, *Annals*, II, pt. 1, 183-86.
[10] Strype, *Parker*, II, 65-66; Parker, *Correspondence*, 381-83, 386-87; Edmund Grindal, *Remains* (Parker Society, 1843), 326.

It may have been these ministers who counselled the measure Robert Snagge and Tristram Pistor presented to the House on 17 May.[11] It began with a long preface which, although very tendentious, is nevertheless a fair statement of the way in which the evangelicals viewed developments since 1559. The Book then enacted was substantially sound but it had retained certain rites and ceremonies out of consideration for the "great weakness of the people then blinded with superstition." Now, through the work of zealous clergy, the congregations were better informed and ready for a purer worship. Already individual preachers had (with the approval of "some godlie bishops") ventured to omit the offending clauses and conformed more nearly to the apostolic church and the best reformed European models. Many, it was alleged, had been accused at assizes for the most trivial omissions by "malicious adversaries of the truth." They sought therefore to end this abuse and to regularize a godly practice by giving each pastor (with the consent of his bishop) the right to omit whatever he chose from the Prayer Book rite and to make such additions as seemed appropriate. Furthermore, he could make use of the liturgy of the French or Dutch exile congregations in London and elsewhere.[12]

This summed up quite neatly the reformers' conviction that the liturgy of 1559 was provisional and that the conditions which had justified it then had now passed. It was a logical extension of the pattern of King Edward's reign—stage-by-stage reform adapted to improved instruction and a better prepared laity. In the light of hindsight this seems to be a singularly naive move, foredoomed to failure. Yet one must remember, first of all, that it did little more than regularize widespread existing practice in many areas; this was probably reflected by the ease with which the main purpose of the measure won approval by the Commons. The willingness of the House to accept it may not suggest a majority filled with passionate Puritan conviction so much as the lack of any opposi-

[11] Neale I, 297-304.
[12] W. H. Frere and C. E. Douglas, eds., *Puritan Manifestoes* (1954), 149-51.

tion to what may have seemed commonplace and common-sense changes. In other words, the movers of the motion may have felt they were speaking for a generally received body of opinion. Secondly, even more important, they were probably not aware of the true state of the Queen's opinions. These had been expressed so far as we know largely in directives to the bishops or to the councillors but the public face of the policy was wholly an episcopal one. And even here the reformers had good reason to believe that at least some of the bishops were on their side. Still, one cannot underestimate the daring of these MP's in pushing forward on private initiative a major change in the public ecclesiastical polity.

The reaction of Knollys, the most reform-minded of the Privy Councillors but a loyal and responsible servant of the Queen, was significant. Instead of killing it, as the Speaker expected him to do, the Treasurer of the Household took advantage of his membership on the committee to vet the bill of its most provocative features.[13] In its amended form the preface, with its statement of reform intentions, was pruned while in the main body of the bill permission to vary from the Book was committed to the whole body of bishops collectively and any permission to use alternate forms withdrawn. A more moderate measure by far, it would still have attained the main goals of the reformers. But once again the Queen intervened by commanding that no more bills of religion were to be dealt with unless they had the prior approval of the bishops. She also asked to see the bill in both its versions. The Queen's comments delivered by Knollys, while disapproving, were moderate in tone. The bill, of course, vanished and even at the conclusion of Parliament the Queen had no more to say about it. Rather surprisingly, this measure, more radical than its predecessors of 1566, ruffled the royal temper a good deal less and occasioned much less discussion in the House. The overriding preoccupation with the fate of Mary Queen of Scots no doubt had something to do with this.

Nevertheless, the rebuff the reformers suffered in this session triggered a violent reaction in reforming circles which

[13] *Ibid.,* 152.

ended the first, and most moderate, phase of their agitation. Hitherto they had explored "constitutional" strategies, first in Convocation and then in Parliament. It is true that implicit in their moves was a novel, not to say radical, stance; they were assuming that religion was a "commonwealth" rather than a "state" matter, open to private initiatives and public discussion. But they had sought to draw the bishops with them and to present their proposals as logical and desirable extensions of the reforms already accomplished, a natural evolution towards a generally accepted goal. The new phase now opening up was to be much less gentlemanly and would see the replacement of evolutionary argument by revolutionary concepts.

CHAPTER 3

THE RADICAL ASSAULT,

1572-1575

THE NEW PHASE began with the famous manifestoes known as the *First and Second Admonitions to Parliament*, the first, issued probably before the body had ceased to sit, in June 1572; its companion followed before the end of the year.[1] The first pamphlet was the work of two clergymen, already notable among the reformers, John Field and Thomas Wilcox; the second may have come from the hand of Christopher Goodman.

The two *Admonitions* are a landmark in the history of English Protestantism since they mark both an attack on the existing polity and the liturgy of the Church of England as well as the elaboration of an alternative platform of Church government and worship. But they need to be seen in the context of their immediate circumstances. The first *Admonition* was the work of young, disappointed, and angry clergymen, who threw discretion to the winds and, particularly in the part of the *First Admonition* written by Field, manifested their contempt not only for the details of ceremonial but for the whole spirit and system of the establishment. However, it must not be read as a political manifesto, calling for immediate action; it was

[1] These are most conveniently available in Frere and Douglas, *Puritan Manifestoes*, 1-39 and 79-134.

65

their very despair of any effective action which spurred them to take up pen. The proposals which are made, especially those in the *Second Admonition*, where the outlines of a presbyterian polity are sketched out, were of a quite different order from the bill brought into the recent Parliament. That was a practical proposal, based on contemporary experience and moving forward only a stage from present practice. What the *Admonitions* displayed was the aspirations of idealists, indeed, of would-be prophets; it was with the Old Testament worthies and with John the Baptist that Field and Wilcox chose to compare themselves. "It is no time to blanch nor to sew cushions under men's elbows or to flatter them in their sins."[2] And the *Second Admonition*, more sober in tone, offered not a platform for continued action along traditional lines—pressure in Parliament and in court, specific and pragmatic measures—but a new grand-scale vision of what a truly reformed polity would contain. It is certain that this new program offended many of the older generation of reformers—Humphrey, Sampson, Crowley, John Foxe, and among the laity Norton, one of the most articulate spokesmen of the Protestant left.[3]

It was of course a highly provocative action, and Field and Wilcox, who had made no secret of their authorship, cannot have been surprised to find themselves in Newgate very shortly after the book's publication. It was not until October—and after an appeal against imprisonment without trial—that their case was heard, probably before a commission of oyer and terminer for causes ecclesiastical for London, certainly by a court including the Lord Mayor and his aldermanic colleagues. They were sentenced to a year in prison. They were hardly abashed by their fate, however, since in September they were penning an apology for Lord Burghley's edification and preparing petitions to Leicester and the Council for their release. They could congratulate themselves on the appearance of three more printings of the *First Admonition* during the course of the summer and on the appearance of the *Second*

[2] *The Seconde Parte of a Register*, ed. A. Peel (2 vols., Cambridge, 1915), I, 87-90.
[3] Collinson, *Movement*, 121.

Admonition before the end of the year. Parker was grumbling to Burghley about the laxness of the city authorities in searching out the printers; he had little confidence in their good will. By March of 1573 the Privy Council was writing to Bishop Sandys about the "late prisoners in Newgate" who were now to remain in the custody of the Archdeacon of Middlesex or of some other person until the Privy Council might have more occasion to obtain the Queen's pardon. In August Bishop Sandys finally got his hands on the printing press. But by then the controversy was much enlarged; in April, Cartwright, the Cambridge divine, had entered the fray with a pamphlet answering Whitgift's response to the *Admonitions*. By December a warrant was out for Cartwright's arrest and he was on his way to foreign exile.[4]

The episode had strong reverberations since the open challenge thrown down by the Young Turks set the whole ecclesiastical machinery in motion against all manner of nonconformity. The bishops set out to drive all dissidents out of official posts within the Church. The means for accomplishing this were already at hand. A standard of conformity for clerics had been set up as early as 1565 when the Advertisements required clergy newly ordained to use "such order and uniformity in all external policy rites and ceremonies of the Church as by the laws good usages and orders are already well provided and established." In 1571 a royal letter to the Archbishop as head of the Ecclesiastical Commissioners declared the Queen's command for reformation of all abuses "attempted to deform the uniformity prescribed by our laws and injunctions." No one was to be "suffered to decline either on the left or on the right hand from the direct line limited by authority." In the same year the Canons of Convocation decreed that licensed preachers were to subscribe to the Articles. Grindal, commenting on this book of canons (and possibly on the Queen's letter), doubted that without the Queen's written consent or else a statute, they had *vigorem legis*, and he feared the

[4] Strype, *Annals*, II, pt. 1, 275, 418; pt. 2, 482-83; *Seconde Parte of a Register*, I, 91; Parker, *Correspondence*, 397; *APC*, VIII, 93; Frere and Douglas, *Puritan Manifestoes*, 155.

bishops might bring a *praemunire* on their heads by acting on them.[5]

However, in 1573 the bishops were given a little additional leverage by two royal proclamations occasioned by recent developments. The first of these, issued 11 June, denounced those who, "unquietly disposed, desirous to change and therefore ready to find fault with all well established orders," refrained from coming to church and used rites of their own. The Queen commanded her subjects to keep the uniform order of the Prayer Book upon pain of punishment set out in the Act of Uniformity. She also denounced the *Admonitions* and ordered all copies to be turned in to the authorities under penalty of imprisonment.[6]

In October another salvo of the royal guns was fired off. This was probably occasioned by the attempt on Christopher Hatton's life which occurred six days earlier. The assailant mistook Sir John Hawkins for the intended victim; the Queen's alarm may well have persuaded her to the second proclamation. She asserted straightforwardly that the Book of Common Prayer contained nothing but the Word of God although some "bold and vain curious men" had spoken and written against it and devised rites of their own with resulting contentions and sects among her subjects. The cause, she went on to add, was the negligence of bishops *and other magistrates* [italics mine] who were now to see that these laws were enforced. All bishops, justices of oyer and terminer, and mayors were to put in execution the Act of Uniformity; any one who spoke or wrote against the Book of Common Prayer was to be imprisoned. Ecclesiastical officers—bishops, deans and archdeacons—were to proceed against clergy who offended, depriving them of office.[7]

This was followed up by a letter to the bishops from the

---

[5] Gee and Hardy, *Documents*, 475; E. Cardwell, *Documentary Annals of the Reformed Church of England* (2 vols., Oxford, 1839, 1844), I, 332-33; Grindal, *Remains*, 327.

[6] *Tudor Royal Proclamations*, ed. Paul L. Hughes and James F. Larkin (3 vols., New Haven and London, 1964-1969), II, 375-76.

[7] *Ibid.*, 379-81.

Council which roundly stated that the reason for so much non-conformity is that ecclesiastical supervision is only used "as is commonly said, (the more the pity) . . . of you and your officers to get money." If the bishops were only diligent there would be no need for new proclamations; their existing authority was quite sufficient without calling upon "extraordinary and temporal (as it is termed) jurisdiction and judgment."[8]

In 1572 the Ecclesiastical Commission was renewed; in the process its numbers were more than doubled (71 as against 27). There was a large access of lay members (51 as against 20), including such formidable patrons of reform as Sir Francis Knollys and Sir Walter Mildmay. How many of these new appointees actually participated is a question we cannot answer. Presumably the new commission was meant to strengthen the hands of the ecclesiastical establishment faced by challenge, but it looks as though some of the reformers' friends at court may have taken a hand in the selection of the new members.[9]

From all this it is clear that the Queen's response to the new agitation was a continued determination not to budge an inch. The Statutes and Injunctions of 1559 were to be taken as final; any further change was simply not a discussable matter; the recalcitrant clergy were to conform or be driven from the Church. All available machinery was to be used to achieve this end. Deprived of any official standing, they would presumably be rendered innocuous.

It is worth standing back at this point, when Protestant dissent had gained so much ground, to gain some perspective on the problem of dissidence as it was seen in the Elizabethan generation. A contrast with their fathers' era is instructive. Thirty years earlier, criticism of the established religious order was a dangerous business for it was tainted with the suspicion of heresy. The latter was, of course, a legally defined offense and included only those opinions which endangered the salva-

[8] Cardwell, *Documentary Annals*, I, 352-53; BL, Add. Ms. 22,473, f. 1; BL, Add. Ms. 48,064, f. 205.

[9] Usher, *High Commission*, 90.

tion of souls. But particularly after 1517 the threatened *ancien regime* had become so sensitive that the distinction between permissible criticism of existing abuses and outright heresy had dangerously narrowed. Disagreement was no longer a matter of degree, but of kind. What separated the contending parties was not disagreements over the need for possible reform within the Church but profound differences as to the terms on which salvation could be found. Each party saw its opponents as mired in the most dangerous kind of error, totally abhorrent to the truth necessary for salvation. Their quarrel had become a very deadly business indeed.

To this grim death-struggle the short-lived English reform regime of 1547-1553 offered a refreshing contrast. The reasons for its relative lenity towards opponents were complex. Perhaps most simply it did not have to face an organized Catholic resistance within the realm. At any rate those of the bishops who balked (and they were virtually the sole resisters) were treated as delinquents rather than as criminals and the worst they had to suffer was imprisonment. (The Devon and Cornwall countrymen who rose in 1549 were in open revolt and were treated as rebels.) Under Mary the old rules again obtained and every weapon available was pressed into service to crush heresy. But when the Protestant regime was restored in 1559 a profound shift in underlying attitudes became visible. Its origins and its development are not easy to perceive but its manifestations are quite apparent. One of the most obvious was the clause in the Statute of Supremacy dealing with heresy.[10] It prohibited any ecclesiastical official from judging a cause to be matter of heresy except under stringent conditions. Heresy had to be so defined either by one of the first General Councils or another Council "wherein the same was declared heresy by the express and plain words of the said canonical Scriptures" or else by act of Parliament assented to by Convocation. Whether this clause was inserted by royal command or by action from the floor of the House we do not know, but it clearly expresses the powerful thrust of lay opinion, deter-

[10] *Statutes of the Realm*, ed. A. Luders *et al.*, V (1819), 1 Eliz. c.1, 20.

mined to wrest from the clerics this dangerous weapon. Nor was there any disposition among the Parliament-men to use it themselves. Neither in this nor in later Parliaments was there any move to place a heresy statute upon the books.

The presence of the clause in the act signals an important movement in the whole history of the English Reformation. One way of putting it would be to say that the politique element was firmly in the saddle. At the crucial moment of Elizabeth's accession there was no effective clerical voice to speak for any of their concerns, so the settlement of 1559 bears a strongly laic imprint. However, the politique impulses behind it were by no means of a single kind; the Queen, for instance, interpreted the settlement as a victory for untrammeled royal control over the Church and the national religious life. Many of the ruling classes, as we shall see, viewed the new order as one in which the aristocracy, as legislators in Parliament and as patrons in their own parishes, would dominate religious institutions. But there was general agreement that there was to be no more bloody extremism over matters of doctrine and faith. For the politiques the Reformation movement had always been primarily anti-clerical in purpose; they were determined to wrest power from the priestly elite, but they had no interest in coercing men into the acceptance of a new orthodoxy; there was in the lay backers of the Reform an underlying strain of skepticism, a harbinger of the Enlightenment. They were quite prepared to repress their Catholic enemies, if they showed their heads, but the terms of the struggle were to be political rather than religious. The Catholics were to be struck down for their refusal to accept civil ordinances laid down by the legitimate sovereign, not for religious heterodoxy.

Here they found common ground with the Queen; one may surmise that she shared their general views but her overriding concern was an irenic approach to the great inert mass of traditional Catholics, whose latent loyalties to the old faith might be stirred into a blaze by persecution but who were likely, given enough leeway, to subside imperceptibly into an establishment which laid minimum requirements upon them. Hence sovereign and aristocracy alike—for somewhat differing reasons—joined in eschewing any policy of doctrinal compulsion.

On this subject the clerical reformers were for the most part not in deep disagreement with their lay allies—although their reasoning on the matter was somewhat different. They certainly did not feel that doctrinal issues were of secondary importance, they were anxious for a confessional statement and for the active propagation of the new religion. But they were not, for the most part, would-be persecutors of their religious opponents. The earlier Protestant tradition in England had been marked by a strong Erasmian element, resting on argument and persuasion, confident in the intrinsic, self-demonstrable truths of their position. As we have seen, no strong coercive policy developed under Edward, and one of the strongest reproaches levelled against Mary was that she needed the terrors of Smithfield to bring men to her faith. The Marian persecution did not last quite long enough to fuse fear and hatred into a determination to exterminate the Catholic opposition. Hence most of the leaders of the Elizabethan Church were initially disposed to use instruments of persuasion against the Papist remnant. And towards the dissidents within their own ranks there was a deep ambiguity which arose from many shared sympathies, personal and ideological. There was to be real pain in the widening rift within Protestant ranks, especially for the older men, and it would take some years of bitter controversy to create lasting hostility and deep partisanship.

The one element among the Protestants which would have used coercion against the Roman Catholics was the very left-wing group which was itself suffering at the hands of the establishment. They sought in the Parliament of 1566 to establish a doctrinal test based on the Articles of Religion which would have sifted out lay Catholics. The triumph of politique elements in 1559 was to give much occasion of grief to the evangelicals in the years to come, but one uncovenanted blessing was their freedom from the threat of death. They found that they could level their attacks against the establishment, pillory the bishops, and unleash the very considerable resources of sixteenth-century polemic without fear of their lives until the rise of articulate separatists in the 1580's. What they risked was office and livelihood, no inconsiderable stake, but at least the quarrel within Protestant ranks did not reach the level of rancor which led Protestants and Catholics to such deadly strife.

Indeed it was this very "indifferentism" of the Church authorities which so infuriated the Puritans and which marked out the sharp angle of difference between them and the establishment. For them its inadequacies came to be seen as more than mere blemishes susceptible of improvement; they were fundamental flaws which did indeed hinder the very process of salvation. For the most outraged among them there would eventually be no road except that of separation.

Elizabeth's strategy was not an unreasonable one within the historical context. She refused to acknowledge the malcontents' right to protest; as subordinate clerical officers it was their business to obey; they must either conform to regulations laid down from above or suffer dismissal from office and forfeit livelihood for unacceptable conduct. That done, they were at least in theory deprived of a *locus standi*; they had no place from which to speak, no audience to hear them, no footing from which to continue the struggle. Unlike the Catholic dissident they could not seek institutional housing abroad; they would simply be cast into a limbo of silence. Dissidence could be extinguished simply by depriving the dissidents of their forum. But such a theory did not square with fact. The loose and porous structure of the English Church, and particularly the large role which laymen played in its affairs, made such a tidy elimination of dissent impossible.

The work of suppression was to be centered in the Ecclesiastical Commissioners, a body which in practice consisted of the Primate, three or four episcopal colleagues, and a staff of civil lawyers.[11] The Queen had insisted that this body as set up in 1559 (and renewed at later intervals) plus the normal ecclesiastical administrative and judicial machinery was quite adequate for the task in hand and she firmly declined to add any weapons to their existing arsenal. She took little cogni-

[11] Parker, *Correspondence*, 382-83, 386-87.

zance of the facts of the situation. The machinery of the commissioners was new and untried; its powers undefined. Like
other *ad hoc* creations of the Tudor Crown it would require
the strongminded—and singleminded—exertions of a forceful
personality to shape it into a workable instrument for the control of nonconformity. The querulous scholar-archbishop,
Parker, was not the man to achieve this task. Secondly, the
effectiveness of the establishment's control over the lower
clergy depended very much on the action of the twenty-six
diocesans. These men, governing sees of widely divergent size
and population, were anything but a coherent collegial body.
The whole bench of bishops met only when Parliament or
Convocation sat. Most of the time they were isolated from one
another, each in his own diocese, deeply involved in the affairs
of his own region. It was here that they had to meet the
test of efficiency. In the 1570's this was a very rigorous trial.

Although in a legal sense the bishops stepped into the shoes
of their Romanist predecessors, their inheritance was a diminished and a troubled one. They had now sunk from being
great court magnates to a merely local preeminence. But even
this was not easy to attain; it was not automatically conceded
by their independent, contentious, and opinionated lay neighbors, the county aristocracies. Each bishop had to strive with
whatever native abilities he had for acceptance in this proud
society. Some succeeded; Whitgift at Worcester was briskly effective and apparently generally popular. But the history of
the great East Anglian see of Norwich was throughout Elizabeth's reign one of repeated disaster.[12] There, either indifference towards the royal objectives or sheer ineptitude marred
each successive episcopal reign. The success or failure of the
ecclesiastical polity laid down at the center was directly pro-
portional to the effectiveness of the local diocesan.

His chances of success were conditioned very much by the
cooperation which he could secure from the local magistracy.
As we have seen, the justices of the peace were specifically en-

[12] See A. Hassell Smith, *County and Court* (Oxford, 1974), 210-28
for details of Freake's career at Norwich.

joined by the Crown to discipline those lay men and women who refused attendance at the parish church. But in a more than merely legal sense, their cooperation was essential because of the role they played within the structure of the Church itself. As owners of advowsons, as lay impropriators, and above all as the squires in their respective parishes, their collaboration would make or break any effort to carry out the royal program of uniformity. Elizabethan history was to be replete with instances of lay intervention in the choice and in the protection of the local incumbent[13] and in ordering the character of worship; they were to show little hesitation in crossing the episcopal policy when it suited them.

But even where there was an efficient and determined bishop (like Whitgift at Worcester, who had the respect of his lay neighbors), the task was rendered nearly impossible by the clumsiness of the administrative machinery at his disposal. He had inherited a structure set up in another age to deal with other problems, least of all with the recalcitrance of inferior clergy who were neither heretical nor quite schismatical but certainly not biddable. The process of visitation, the prime instrument at the bishop's disposal, was slow and cumbersome and lacked effective follow-up procedures. The bishop's subordinates were often more concerned with the privileges and profits of their office than with the carrying out of grand policy. More than one Elizabethan bishop found himself grappling with a fiercely resistant dean and chapter (Chichester) or a recalcitrant chancellor (Norwich).[14] And yet these were all subordinate issues to the central task of raising pastoral standards in the diocese to the level of zeal and piety posited by a reformed Church. As we shall see shortly, this herculean task was more often and more effectively tackled by local clergy than by the bishop, who was likely to be mired in the struggle to maintain his own position and to fulfill the multi-

[13] For such an instance, see Paul Seaver, "Community Control and Puritan Politics in Elizabethan Suffolk," *Albion* 9 (1977), 316-36.

[14] Roger B. Manning, *Religion and Society in Elizabethan Sussex* (Leicester, 1969), 72-76, 108-9; Smith, *County and Court*, 210 ff.

ple demands of a central government which often regarded him as just another rather more potent justice of the peace.[15]

But for the ranking clerics of the Ecclesiastical Commission, charged with the prime responsibility for the Queen's religious policy, there was yet another problem. They were expected to act as a kind of ecclesiastical Privy Council, the central agents of the royal supremacy as their lay counterparts were of the civil prerogative. However persuasive this analogue was in theory, in brutal fact they were signally lacking in the necessary political consequence, what modern Americans call "clout." They did not have the access to the Queen nor the tokens of her approval which were the prerequisites for effective authority under the Crown. Even Parker saw the sovereign only irregularly and, if his correspondence is a good witness, had to deal with her largely through the intermediary of Cecil.

Behind the Queen's indifference to ecclesiastical affairs lay a deeper antipathy. It is a paradox of Elizabeth's character that on the one hand she believed most profoundly in her Supreme Governorship and required the strictest obedience to her commands in that capacity, yet treated her ecclesiastical servants rudely, almost contemptuously. In truth she shared the prevailing anti-clericalism so common among the English upper classes. At times it led her almost full circle, to an attitude towards her prelacy not much more respectful—although for different reasons—than that of the Puritans. Not until she found a bishop who shared at least some of her highly Erastian views about the nature of the Church was she willing to lend the prestige of her great office to support the efforts of the ecclesiastical leaders to enforce her policy. In the meantime they had to labor on as best they could under the burdens of royal neglect, punctuated by fitful explosions of bad temper.

All this was bad enough, but the situation was made much worse by the fact that the radicals on their side had easy and

[15] For discussion of these problems, see *Continuity and Change*, ed. Rosemary O'Day and Felicity Heal (Leicester, 1976), and *Church and Society in England*, ed. Felicity Heal and Rosemary Heal (London and Hamden, Conn., 1977).

ample access to great court patrons, whose prestige far outdistanced that of the bishops. The most notable of these was, of course, the favorite, Leicester; there was also that outspoken cousin of the Queen, her Treasurer of the Household, Sir Francis Knollys, and after 1572 the prime Protestant politique, Secretary Walsingham. The Earls of Bedford and of Warwick were other spokesmen within the Council; away from Court, in the great office of Lord President of the North, was the most Puritan of all the nobles, the Earl of Huntingdon. Over against this formidable array of patrons, there was, at least until the 1580's, no comparable figure to back up the bishops. Cecil was courteous and attentive to Parker and a steady supporter of the Primate but not disposed, one feels, to risk his prestige or to pledge his influence with the Queen for the sake of the bishops.[16]

The Archbishop's sense of insecurity deepened into a fixed grievance as the 1570's moved on. As early as November 1572 he complained bitterly that the Puritans were everywhere justified while the bishops were "judged to be extreme persecutors." "The more they [the Puritans] write, the more they shame our religion; the more they be applauded too; the more they be comforted." In the following March he repeated the refrain. "The comfort that these Puritans have and their continuance is marvellous." Two months later he was predicting the coming of Munzer's commenwealth if they were not checked. Sandys was at the same time complaining that the Puritans' fancies were favored "by some of great calling who seek to gain by other men's losses." And Grindal, in the North, was hopeful of carrying out the Queen's intentions only if the nonconformists "be not countenanced (as they have been) by those that are no bishops."[17]

Parker's complaints rose to a shrill pitch as he grew older and they reached a climax in the last year of his life. He came to believe that there was a conspiracy against him and his col-

[16] Note his speech in the Star Chamber, 28 Nov. 1573, supporting the Ecclesiastical Commission, Strype, *Parker*, II, 350-355.

[17] Parker, *Correspondence*, 407-11, 418-19, 426, 434-35; Grindal, *Remains*, 347-48.

leagues, directed by the Earl of Leicester. As early as 1572 he had been at odds with the Earl; by 1574 he wrote to Burghley of the existence of the conspiracy. Burghley seems to have thought the Primate's suspicions justified and in 1575 the Archbishop's metropolitan visitation of Winchester diocese brought complaints to Leicester, and through him the Queen's rebuke to the Archbishop. The quarrel with the favorite reached such a point that Parker would not attend the Queen when she was staying at Leicester's house. Parker's credit was very badly damaged when he and Burghley became the dupes of an intriguer who purported to hold the threads of a Puritan plot against the leading councillors. He incriminated both the Earl of Bedford and the Duchess of Suffolk. The disclosure of the informer's fraudulence was humiliating to the Primate and to his enemies a sure proof of his malice towards them.[18]

One of Parker's final letters—written after the Winchester affair—summed up the Primate's views of his position in the very last months of his life. "Does Your Lordship think that I care either for a cap, tippet, surplice, or wafer-bread or any such? But for the laws so established I esteem them and not more for exercise of contempt against law and authority which I see will be the end of it nor for any other respect." But how was he to fulfill his office? "Her Majesty told me that I had supreme government ecclesiastical but what is it to govern cumbered with such subtlety?" The Queen herself listens to others rather than the pastors of her dioceses. The Queen is more moved "by some mortal man's request" in granting benefices and neglectful of "the principal pastor of a great diocese wherein peradventure her authority is utterly contemned." Indeed, Parker has come to assert that "whatsoever the ecclesiastical prerogative is, I fear it is not so great as your pen [Cecil's] hath given her in the Injunction."[19] On this very doubtful note Elizabeth's first archbishop ended his career.

And yet it would be quite inaccurate to suggest that victory in the struggle had gone—or was going—to the radicals. As

[18] Strype, *Parker*, II, 160, 368-71, 393, 422-23, 489-90.
[19] Parker, *Correspondence*, 477-79.

we have seen, Cartwright had to flee overseas; Field may have done the same. Edward Dering, the reader in divinity at St. Paul's and one of the most articulate of the evangelical preachers, was silenced, then allowed to resume, but finally silenced again by the Privy Council at the Queen's order. An inquisition on the London clergy, conducted in December 1573, led to the imprisonment of the most eminent reformers among the city churches and to the death of one from prison conditions. In Northamptonshire Bishop Scambler of Peterborough, one of the most insecure of the Elizabethan prelacy, pounced on the reform leaders in a diocese peculiarly rich in dissent and deprived five of the leaders even though they offered to use the Book of Common Prayer and not to preach against it until the next Parliament.[20]

But the record, so far as it goes, suggests a very spotty enforcement of the conformity decrees in the areas where reforming clergy were at their strongest. They were being harried sufficiently to raise the temperature of debate again and to increase their acrimony against the bishops. But they were far from being crushed. Continuing support at Court gave them hope, and many looked forward to another meeting of the oft-prorogued Parliament of 1572. Certainly the Queen's commands of 1573 were far from being fulfilled.

[20] Collinson, *Movement*, 151.

CHAPTER 4

THE FAILURE OF GRINDAL

IN THE MIDDLE 1570's the forces of dissent seemed to be growing stronger in fact and in hope. The establishment had acquired some sense of identity by the very act of self-defense, but the effectiveness of such efforts as it made was hamstrung by the Queen's fitful interest in religious matters and by the strength of the "fellow-travellers" at Court. Moreover, the problem to be dealt with was taking on a new complexity. The volley of pamphlets discharged by the Young Turks of the Puritan movement was a visible and embarrassing assault on the establishment; such polemics against the existing order were an obvious strategy of the militants. Less dramatic and less obvious but more effective was the strategy of those moderate reformers who labored as pastors. Evangelically minded incumbents were able, in their particular cures, to affect very directly the spiritual tone of their congregations. An emphasis on sermons, instruction outside the hours of service, home visitations, and adaptation of the services of worship were all means by which the conception of a truly reformed religious life could be implanted among the laity. Such activity—often carried on by cooperating groups of local clergymen—presented a much more difficult problem to the authorities than the fulminations of angry polemicists. Much of this grass-roots evangelism enjoyed the cooperation of the bishops and the sympathetic backing of devout middle-of-the-road Protestant laity. It was hard to quarrel with programs of spiritual education which aimed at transforming the religious aspirations of the English people and winning them to a positive and committed acceptance of the reformed religion.

This activity grew steadily from the beginning of the reign down into the 1570's and had become a matter of royal concern in the very last years of Archbishop Parker. That tired and disillusioned prelate died in May 1575. The appointment of a new Primate was obviously a matter of first importance for the future of the English Church. It was not until December of the same year that Edmund Grindal was translated from York to Canterbury. The choice of Grindal seems hardly to have surprised contemporaries, but it leaves a puzzle for the historian. Why did the Queen assent to his appointment? On past record he seemed an unlikely choice to put into effect the aims so emphatically asserted by her. His record as a bishop was one of temperance, mildness, and evangelical fervor. His translation from London to York in 1570 was pressed by both Parker and Cecil, who agreed that his temper was too soft for the turbulent urban see, notoriously the most difficult in the realm to manage. He had to be pushed hard to take action in the vestiarian controversy and had dealt mercifully with the separatist congregations—Anabaptists in the eyes of contemporaries—which had been discovered in London in 1567.[1]

In the North where Catholicism rather than Puritanism was the central problem facing the Church Grindal had worked well with the ardently evangelical Lord President, Huntingdon. He had expressed his distaste for Cartwright's views as early as 1570, urging the latter's expulsion from the pulpit. He summoned Dean Whittingham of Durham, one of the more radical of the exilic generation, to conform in 1571 and he had taken his part in the efforts to implement the royal commands in 1573, expressing his dislike for the younger radicals who had livings in the Church and yet affirmed it to be no church. To him as to Parker these men seemed little better than schismatics. The generational difference showed with him, as with his predecessor at Canterbury; nevertheless his sympathies for

[1] John Strype, *The History of the Life and Acts of . . . Edmund Grindal* (Oxford, 1821), 200, 234.

the evangelical pastors who labored to animate the spiritual lives of their flocks were well known.[2]

Certainly Grindal was Burghley's choice; before the death of Parker had actually occurred, the Treasurer was declaring his voice in favor of the Archbishop of York for "both his knowledge of government and good proof of the same in the North and also for the place he holdeth next to this place by degree."[3] It was certainly a popular choice among the older generation of reformers and aroused the most favorable expectations in Protestant lay circles. But we shall never know what induced the Queen to assent to this choice. There were of course few real alternatives. Cox was old and had made a second marriage, an act which the Queen abhorred; of Sandys, then Bishop of London, and soon to succeed Grindal at York, nothing was heard. He was closely identified with Parker's policy and possibly not popular in left-wing circles. Cox was the only voice to mention the name of Whitgift as a candidate for promotion —but not to Canterbury. The latter had made a name as a disciplinarian at Cambridge and as a polemicist in his controversy with Cartwright, but he was as yet only a dean. There is no hint of a Dudley candidate. In any case, given Burghley's powerful backing and the absence of any other candidate— either of the "right" or of the "left"—the Queen may have felt she had no other choice. It is clear that she herself had no favorite in the matter; one suspects a certain indifference, or at least a lack of any warm interest.

Professor Collinson has argued persuasively that Grindal was seriously concerned to redress abuses within the Church and that he had a modest but wisely chosen program of specific reforms, particularly in the Court of Faculty, the source of so many abuses, and of considerable profit to the archbishop.[4] He patronized the Geneva Bible, the favorite version of the left, which Parker had effectively suppressed. He might well by a policy of modest reform and by lifting the pressure for conformity upon evangelical clergy have brought a consid-

[2] Grindal, *Remains*, 323-24, 326-27.

[3] PRO, SP 12/103/48; CSPF, xi, 468-69.

[4] Collinson, *Movement*, pt. 4, chap. 1.

erable measure of peace to the Elizabethan Church. But he, like his predecessor, was not master of the situation. Hardly was he seated at Canterbury, when once again, as in 1565, Juno descended from her throne to make another sweeping intervention in the affairs of the Church.

The occasion for this renewed royal intervention was the "prophesyings" or exercises which had become a common feature of local religious life throughout many English sees. They were a very pragmatic response to the gravest problem of the reformed Church. It inherited a body of clergy of indifferent quality, many of whom had conformed without hesitation to at least three religious regimes. They certainly lacked the zeal; in most cases they lacked the training to meet the requirements of a reformed and revived faith. The exercises were in effect educational programs for clergy, where they had to expound publicly some chosen and prepared portion of Scripture, in the presence of their peers and of their professional superiors, who gave them the benefit of criticism. The details varied from diocese to diocese and from one rural jurisdiction to another, but the intent was the same everywhere. In some instances local laity were allowed to attend as listeners, a logical extension for an exercise designed to raise the spiritual level of both clergy and congregations. Characteristically the initiative in almost every case had been taken locally by interested clergy, rather than by their constituted superiors, the bishops, the presumed directors of the spiritual life of the Church. The latter had, in most cases, given their *post hoc* approval to the local arrangements. In some sees the exercises dated back to the beginning of the reign and they were patently not a sudden innovation of the mid-1570's.

What drew the Queen's attention to these programs of education? We do not know with certainty; it was not the initiative of an anti-Puritan faction in the Church, so far as we can tell, although it is true that in some cases the prophesyings provided arenas for the preaching of reformist, and deprived, clergy. It may well be that mere local animosities—one of the endless struggles for power and place among the squirearchy —led someone to carry a tale to the Court. Someone was shrewd enough to appreciate that reports of nonconformity were a sure-fire way of unleashing an almost automatic burst of royal displeasure. How better to embarrass one's local rivals?

The Queen's attention was first drawn to these practices in 1574 in Parker's lifetime when Sandys of London was ordered by the Archbishop, acting on royal instructions—in a postscript—that "the exercises in your diocese called prophesyings should stay."[5] Sandys protested vigorously, defending the exercises as a practice of many years' standing and predicting that their cessation would unsettle men's minds and disturb a quiet regime; he asked the Council for further direction. What ensued is not clear.

Again in 1575 during her summer progress the Queen was made aware through some unknown agent, of the exercises held at Welwyn in Hertfordshire. She ordered Secretary Smith to write to Bishop Cooper of Lincoln to dissolve them immediately. The bishop however temporized, consulted the local JP's (who gave the exercises a clean bill of health), and referred the matter back to Smith. But Smith told the bishop he must dissolve the exercise "in such sort as I might conveniently" and Cooper terminated all the exercises in the southern counties of his vast diocese except one at Aylesbury.[6]

In the same year Parker sent—through an intermediary—the same order to Bishop Parkhurst, the ordinary of that most Puritan of sees, Norwich. Parkhurst apparently made inquiries to London and was told by "certain of good place and great credit" (Knollys, Smith, and Mildmay) that the intention was to suppress only schismatical and seditious meetings. Baffled by these contradictory instructions, he wrote again to his metropolitan, who rather enigmatically reaffirmed his earlier instructions. The Bishop of Rochester, consulted by Norwich, denied any instructions from the Primate but said that he and Sandys had taken order "that no controversial matter should be moved in the exercises." The bewildered Bishop of Nor-

[5] BL, Add. Ms. 29,546, f. 56ʳ.
[6] S. E. Lehmberg, "Archbishop Grindal and the Prophesyings," *Historical Magazine of the Protestant Episcopal Church* 34 (1965), 122.

wich took what seemed the safest road and dissolved all the exercises in his see on 7 June 1574.[7]

These confused episodes suggest that the royal intervention was casual and sudden, sparked off by some bit of tittle-tattle conveyed to the Queen. One has the impression of a hasty flare-up of royal bad temper and an imperious command to act, but certainly not a considered or sustained policy.

However, the matter became more serious in the summer of 1576 when the Queen queried Leicester about the prophesying at Southam, Warwickshire, where two notorious reformers, Oxenbridge and Paget, were moderators. Before the summer was out, Bishop Bentham of Lichfield and Coventry had suppressed the exercise altogether. But this time the Queen's interest and attention was more sustained and she now sought a far wider measure of suppression.[8]

In an oral communication to the Archbishop, Elizabeth ordered the suppression of the exercises and the restriction of the number of preachers—about three or four per shire would suffice, she thought. Grindal may already have begun to reform the prophesyings by laying strict regulations as to supervision, careful choice of speakers, exclusion of laymen and of deprived ministers, and a rigorous vetting of the topics discussed. He also circularized the bishops of his province and leading clergy for their views on the value of prophesyings. The extant answers are interesting since ten of the fifteen bishops responding gave their qualified approval, in tones which suggested that the exercises had been very much taken for granted and were not seen by them or others as cells of embryonic dissent. The Archdeacon of Lincoln, Aylmer (soon to be Bishop of London) was the one strong dissentient to this view; his experience led him to see the exercises as centers for pushing the extreme views of those who sought not merely reform but a whole new polity in the Church.[9]

But the Queen was not to be shifted in her opinions, and

---

[7] Parker, *Correspondence*, 457-59.

[8] Strype, *Grindal*, 320.

[9] Strype, *Grindal*, 327; Lehmberg, "Grindal," 84-145.

Grindal had to nerve himself up to an unaccustomed stance of resistance. He fortified himself with a careful study of sources, from the Bible itself and from all the generations of learned commentators. The resulting document[10] was a courageous and dignified protest by the Archbishop against the Queen's new orders; it was also a very effective statement of the whole position of the moderate reformers. The Archbishop paid full and honest tribute to the many benefits lavished on the Church by the Queen—freedom of conscience, suppression of idolatry, the sincere preaching of the Gospel amidst public peace and tranquillity. Even in the present case he did not doubt her zeal and good meaning. Yet his duty was clear; he was appointed to be a watchman, not a flatterer (Ezekiel 33) and kings, even David, could err.

And on two points Grindal's conscience compelled him to disagree with the royal command and to seek to change the royal mind. One was the furnishing of adequate numbers of preachers in every diocese, the second the question of the prophesyings. Both preaching and the exercises were defended with ample Biblical citation as well as with reference to recent experience, "the most certain seal of sure knowledge." He drew on the testimony of his colleagues to confirm his own observation. He continued, "I trust when Your Majesty hath considered and well weighed the premises, you will rest satisfield and judge that no such inconveniences can grow of these exercises, as you have been informed, but rather the clean contrary."[11]

Moreover, the Queen should turn in such matters to the appropriate counsellors. "They are things to be judged . . . *in ecclesia, seu synodo, non in palatio,*"[12] he said, quoting Ambrose to Theodosius. Matters touching religion, doctrine, or discipline should be referred to the bishops or other head ministers. The Queen must not "pronounce too resolutely and peremptorily *quasi ex authoritate* as you may do in civil and extern matters but always remember that in God's causes the will of God (and not the will of any earthly creature) is to

---

[10] Strype, *Grindal*, 558-74. [11] *Ibid.*, 569.
[12] *Ibid.*, 572.

take place." And if this were not enough, Grindal warned her that though she was a mighty prince "He which dwelleth in heaven is mightier."[13] The Archbishop ended by citing the example of King Ozeas (Joash), who prospered so long as he was mindful of God; when he turned away from that obedience, he suffered accordingly. The felicity the Queen had enjoyed so far came from the goodness of the cause (true religion) and from the prayers of the godly, which had preserved her from the many plagues which God might—in all justice —have poured on her and her people.[14]

The Archbishop made his own position crystal-clear. "I am forced with all humility and yet plainly to profess that I cannot with safe conscience and without the offence of the majesty of God give my assent to the suppressing of the said exercises, much less can I send out any injunction for the utter and universal subversion of the same."[15] If she wished, he was prepared to give up his office.

The consequence of Grindal's letter to the Queen was his suspension from his archiepiscopal functions. He was never again to be restored to them, but he remained nominally in office until his death in 1583. The record of these years in his life is tantalizingly incomplete. We know that as late as 1580 he sought restoration to office and release from the house arrest which (at least for a time) he had to endure. In two extant documents he makes his submission. In both he emphasizes that it was his conscience and not stubbornness which motivated his action; he insists that he does not condemn those who have obeyed the royal orders; in such matters there may be diversity of opinion without prejudice to salvation. While he promises obedience for the future, he continues to defend his past action as a matter of conscience.[16]

In another, undated, document there is an account of Grindal's summons before the Council for what was intended as a

---

[13] *Idem.*   [14] *Ibid.*, 573.

[15] *Ibid.*, 569-70.

[16] Grindal, *Remains*, 392-94; Grindal, *Life*, 403-4; Harris Nicolas, *Memoirs of the Life and Times of Sir Christopher Hatton*, etc. (1847), cited henceforth as Hatton, *Memoirs*, 52-53, 98-99, 118-19; BL, Lansdowne MS. 25, 163-64.

formal hearing. He was charged with direct disobedience to the royal orders; in addition, it was stated that the Queen had later sent councillors to persuade him to obedience, and the document lays out in some detail the arguments they used (which contains the royal view of her own actions).[17]

Elizabeth had learned, not from private advertisements but from some bishops and justices of the circuit who appealed for her help, of "great divisions and sects grown by reason of the exercises." Indeed "it was like that religion, which of his own nature should be uniform would against his nature have proved milliform, yea, in continuance nulliform, especially in rites and ceremonies and sometimes also in matters of doctrine." The councillors who saw Grindal not only urged these considerations but also argued that the exercises were new-fangled (and therefore easily suppressed) and merely local, not used by the reformed Churches elsewhere. Nevertheless, the Archbishop had not yielded to their arguments and so compounded his first disobedience by a second act. It is not clear when this hearing actually took place; we know that at least once Grindal's health forced a postponement of a Star Chamber hearing. He was not without his friends at Court, even Hatton, often reputed his enemy. The bishops apparently nerved themselves to the composition of a petition for his restoration; there may even have been a proposal for a kind of ecclesiastical strike in Convocation to force the Archbishop's return to office. It does not seem that any of these efforts actually reached the stage of confrontation with the Supreme Governor. By 1583 Grindal, an old, sick, and blind man, had given up any hope of restoration and hoped only to be allowed a decent retirement. But that too was denied him before death caught up with him.[18]

This episode reveals with unflattering clarity the disarray of English religious affairs in the latter 1570's. The direction of the national Church, already wavering and uncertain in the

[17] Grindal, *Remains*, 471-73.

[18] *Ibid.*, 473, citing Jeremy Collier, *An Ecclesiastical History of Great Britain* (9 vols., 1852), VI, 612 and Thomas Fuller, *Church History* (1655), Book IX, section 4, p. 119.

early years of the decade, now declined even further into disorganization and drift. The particular catastrophe of Grindal's disgrace came about not through a conscious reaction within the Church against Puritan doctrine and practice but probably as the by-product of local secular politics. Grindal's letter to the Queen echoes the charge that she was listening to lay rather than to clerical advice; her own counter-assertion in the Star Chamber proceedings against the Archbishop has a thoroughly disingenuous ring to it (especially in light of the surviving episcopal responses to Grindal's questionnaire). We do not know who were the informers or how they reached the Queen's ear. It would seem from the record that first rumblings of royal wrath were contained by the intervention of the reformers' Court patrons, but the Southam episode of 1576 proved too much for them.

In any case it was not a religious reaction which destroyed the exercises but the pressure of royal displeasure, stimulated by private parties for factious ends. The consequences, however, were felt throughout the English Church. First of all, the Queen's own conception of ecclesiastical government was thrown completely awry. Her chief ecclesiastical officer refused to obey her explicit commands and, while none of his colleagues displayed equal courage, their general lack of enthusiasm for her policy was evident. The Archbishop's careful argument in favor of prophesyings (which summed up concerned Protestant opinion among the clergy) stripped the Queen's action of any guise but that of mere arbitrary exercise of power. And it was this which the bishops, against their own better judgments, were enforcing against the aroused consciences of the reformist clerics. They were compelled to discipline men of proved moral quality, zealous and effective preachers of the reformed faith, by a bare act of authority, justified by nothing more than the assertion of the royal will. One senses the anguish of men caught between a lively loyalty to the Queen and the demands of their consciences, informed, as they saw it, by Scripture itself.

It was appropriate although ironic that their position was set out most articulately by the Queen's own servant, the chief officer of her ecclesiastical establishment. It pointed up all too vividly the gaping gulf which separated the Queen from the concerned Protestant leaders of her own generation. Grindal addresses her as a fellow-member of his own community of discourse. He assumes she too is a devout Christian, an eager reader of the Bible, anxious to model her conduct on its prescriptions and seeking above all to enrich and deepen the spiritual life of her people. It is in this vein that he dares to address her so boldly, indeed so passionately, warning and reproaching her as one fellow-Christian to another. He was preaching to the tone-deaf; to her his words conveyed the impudence of an impertinent servant, impugning a prerogative which was hers beyond all question or doubt. Grindal's failure to recover royal favor has been usually ascribed to the anti-Leicesterian forces at work at court in the late 1570's. No doubt this was a factor, but much must be ascribed to Grindal's own words, sketched out above. It is a document, unique in the reign, in its principled challenge of a royal decision, made by a leading servant of the Queen. It was surely intolerable to her, for it pierced the very core of her belief in herself and in her office. At the very least she wanted an abject renunciation from the Archbishop (as the abortive Star Chamber proceedings indicate); it is not surprising that she could never bring herself to restore Grindal to his primatial powers. His betrayal of his office—as she saw it—was too gross for forgiveness.

Grindal, having once delivered himself of his forthright criticism of the Queen, seems to have been abashed by his own boldness. Certainly his apology of 1577 hedges in the area of his disagreement with the sovereign to the smallest possible area. In a manner somewhat reminiscent of More, fifty years earlier, Grindal pleads that his was an act of individual conscience only and in no way a public protest or a call to others to share his views. Their rights to hold and, as bishops, to act upon such views, and thereby enforce the Queen's decrees, were unquestionably just. Nor did he question the Queen's right to act or to punish him.[19] He asked only to be exempted

[19] Grindal, *Remains*, 392-94.

from the particular task of acting as her instrument in the prohibition of the prophesyings—an act which his conscience could not justify. Even this most conscientious of Tudor bishops was a servant of the royal supremacy, for the latter doctrine was as strong a pillar of English reformed thought as the authority of Scripture.

The underlying political naïveté of Grindal's letter to his sovereign reflected the ever-widening gap which separated not only the sovereign from the reformers but also the lay court patrons of the precisians. The embarrassments of Leicester, for instance, are made vivid by the reproaches of his long-time protégé, Thomas Wood, after the suppression of the Southam exercises.[20] This servant of the Dudleys, a busy correspondent and much-travelled man of business, in his anger was quite willing to believe that Leicester had betrayed the reformers' cause by acting as the Queen's agent in the order for suppression. Even when the Earl's angry defense had convinced him of the contrary, Wood showed little comprehension of the political limits which circumscribed the Dudley earls' patronage of reform. His apocalyptic prophesies of the wrath to come, which saw the fall of Calais and the sack of Antwerp as signs of greater plagues about to fall upon a sinful Court and country, and his contemptuous rejection of the ruling bishops (some of them Leicester's protégés) mark the distance between him and his patron. In the very letter which Leicester had written him, the earl insisted that he was "so resolved to the defence of that is already established as I mean not to be a maintainer or allower of any that would trouble or disturb the quiet proceeding thereof"; he goes on to deplore "these divisions or dissentions" which if they continue as of late will only harm the Church. "The over busy dealing of some [which] hath done so much hurt in striving to make better perforce that which is by permission good enough already" will end by harming the Gospel everywhere.[21]

These are the words of a pragmatist, anxious to do his human best, in the limits of worldly circumstance, for the Gospel cause. Wood's are those of a singleminded enthusiast with his

---

[20] Wood, *Letters*, 22-24. [21] *Ibid.*, 15.

sights fixed on transcendent goals, who brushes aside impatiently all compromise. If the earls "would do that for the which the Lord God hath placed you in these high rooms, which is above all to seek the advancement of his glory, the promoting of his Gospel, and the wealth of your prince and country and to the uttermost of your powers to suffer nothing to be done (for the will and pleasure of any) against the same," then God might show mercy to England as He did to Nineveh when Jonas had preached its destruction within forty days.[22]

The correspondence between Leicester and Wood throws light on the weakening of the earl's position as chief patron to the Puritan cause. At the beginning of the reign the expulsion of the whole upper stratum of English clergy had given the favorite an unparalleled opportunity to influence a large number of key ecclesiastical appointments. Leicester had used it very much to the advantage of the more evangelically minded of them and had come to enjoy a reputation as their protector and promoter. But the rapid leftward movement of Puritan leadership at the end of the 1560's quickly created problems for the earl. As early as 1572—in the aftermath of the *First Admonition*—he had written of himself as not only a protector of the "sincere consciences of faithful preachers and ministers" but as a reconciler between Protestants of differing views. And in the final analysis the quarrels within the Church were for "matters simply indifferent and nothing concerns doctrine and therefore ought to be concluded in our obedience to the Magistrate."[23] Leicester would not give countenance to those who actively sought to force the pace of change by pressing for a new polity within the Church of England. He would promote to office worthy men and protect them from harassment of their consciences, but he would go no further. Presumably he thought, in vaguely humanist terms, that if the Church were staffed with men of the right kind, the work of reformation would be accomplished more or less automatically, certainly within the existing institutional structures. The inadequacies of this hopeful line of thought were brought home

---

[22] *Ibid.*, 23-24.   [23] *Ibid.*, xxix-xxx.

when the Queen refused to countenance the exercises, just such spontaneous, "home-grown" labors of reform as the earl's vision conceived. Quiet, almost imperceptible internal change which would transform the ancient fabric of the English Church by the labors of its evangelical pastors was not to be permitted.

There were other reasons which made the last years of the 1570's an unhappy time for the evangelical party within the Church and for their protectors and patrons in the Court circle. The Anjou marriage seemed to many Protestants to endanger true religion by bringing in a Popish foreigner, and it was no accident that Stubbs was Cartwright's brother-in-law or that the central impetus of opposition to the match was associated with the left-wing Protestant leaders. Their somber mood in these years is well represented by Spenser's lament for poor Algrind (Grindal) in the *Shepheardes Calender*.

But if the party of reform felt frustrated by the present and pessimistic about the future, the execution of royal ecclesiastical policy also faced awkward difficulties. In the absence of the Archbishop, the chairmanship of the Ecclesiastical Commissioners was confided to Aylmer, promoted from his archdeaconry of Lincoln to the see of London when Sandys replaced Grindal at York in 1577. Aylmer's antecedents were highly respectable; he had begun his career as tutor in the Protestant household of the Greys of Suffolk, with Lady Jane as his pupil. He had joined the exile and had produced a notable Protestant polemic in the *Harborough for Faithful Subjects* (printed at Strasburg in 1559); he served in the disputation with the Marian bishops in the spring of 1559. But Aylmer's rewards were modest, nothing more than the archdeaconry of Lincoln, where he remained for some fifteen years in spite of Parker's efforts to promote him to a bishopric. His early patron was Cecil, but it was Hatton who raised him to episcopal status, the first nominee of this rising court luminary. Aylmer was the first of a new species, one which would become all too familiar over the next decades—the court-bishop. His attitude is summed up in a letter to his patron in 1578: "I study with my eyes on my book and my mind is in the court; I preach without spirit; I trust not of God but of my sovereign which is God's lieutenant." As for his policy in office, Aylmer vowed his intention of disciplining both Catholics and Puritans, "to bring great unity of government to the Church which Her Majesty in her godly wisdom doth so much thirsteth after."[24]

In the city, in his see, and as president of the Ecclesiastical Commission, Aylmer was to win a reputation for harrying the nonconformists. He came to be labelled by the Puritans "oppressor of the children of God." It was not an easy task; he had enemies on the Privy Council, who questioned his authority. He was at least once summoned to appear before the Council to answer for his behavior on the Commission. When he imprisoned Cartwright, the councillors questioned his authority and when he alleged royal command, he was furiously rebuked by the Queen. His fellow-commissioners were lax in attendance; laymen withdrew and fellow-bishops stayed away. Nevertheless Aylmer expanded the reach of the Commission, gradually supplanting the bishops as prime agents for enforcing conformity.[25]

In a letter of 1581 or 1582 to the Queen, Aylmer boasts of achievements in suppressing conventicles, reducing the Church to order, denying the Puritans the use of Paul's Cross, and making the ministry of London a staid and conformable one. But there was another side to the coin. The Queen, who had rebuked him for bailing some possessor of Stubbs's book, was ill informed as to his powers. He could only act with the consent of two other commissioners and most of them shrank from sharing "in these odious matters." And even when they acted, what powers of punishment had they but excommunication? To imprison or to fine meant the risk of *praemunire*. It is hardly surprising that Aylmer pressed for translation to the quieter precincts of Winchester, Worcester, or Ely—but in vain.[26]

Aylmer's efforts in the London see were paralleled by those

---

[24] Hatton, *Memoirs*, 55-56, 58-59.

[25] John Strype, *Life of John Aylmer* (1821), 60, 68-69, 76; Collinson, *Movement*, 205; BL, Lansdowne Ms. 396, f. 3.

[26] Hatton, *Memoirs*, 240, 243-47; Strype, *Aylmer*, 63-65.

of Freake, translated from Rochester to replace Parkhurst in the determinedly Puritan diocese of Norwich. Freake was a striking example of the Elizabethan prelate who failed to come to terms with the local gentry. His efforts to enforce conformity soon came to be tangled with his quarrel with the East Anglian gentry.[27] These men were the local counterparts of the Puritan councillors and could call on them for help. Freake's humiliation was a dramatic illustration of the limits of episcopal power in enforcing ceremonial uniformity. Where the Puritan preachers could summon up gentry support, the bishop was in for a hard tussle and could hope at the best for very limited success.

These were years of guerrilla warfare and as always in such struggles it is hard to calculate victory or defeat. The establishment improved its position to some degree. A new weapon was being forged in the Ecclesiastical Commission. Recommissioned in 1576, it expanded its scope under Aylmer's guidance and began to fulfill the definition Whitgift would later give of it. "The whole ecclesiastical law is a carcase without a soul if it be not in the wants supplied by the commission."[28] The deaths around the beginning of the 1580's of most of the original Elizabethan bishops, particularly those of the exilic tradition, opened the way for the appointment of incumbents more malleable to the royal purposes, more willing to accept the role of royal officers, less conscious of themselves as pastors. But these improvements in weapons and in personnel were not adequate to the task. The Puritans, more determined than ever, were openly contemptuous of episcopal authority, ready to flout it as soon as the bishop's back was turned, and clamorous in seeking lay protection.

Many were deprived by their superiors, but few of them were driven from the battle. They soon reappeared on some other front where a favorable lay patron had found a new post and a new opportunity for them. The prophesyings, in spite of all the salvoes discharged against them, did not disappear from

[27] Collinson, *Movement*, 202-5.
[28] Usher, *High Commission*, 99-100 quoting BL, Add. Ms. 28,571, f. 172.

the scene. There is much evidence to demonstrate that they continued, a little muted perhaps, but a vigorous feature of local religious observance in many parts of the country. These are the years, too, of the Dedham classis, of experiment in presbyterian polity, and beyond that, of the first organized separatism, tokens of disappointment and even of desperation of some within the insurgent ranks.

But the establishment had yet to solve the problem of firmly establishing its own claims to authority. If the bishop were to succeed in his efforts, he needed to assert his presence in the various parts of his diocese, to win the cooperation of the local magnates, and to establish a team of efficient and honest subordinates. These were conditions hard to fulfill—impossible in many of the larger sees or in such small new dioceses as Peterborough.[29] Indeed, what was happening in too many areas was the failure of the Protestant bishop to win acceptance as "natural" successor of his Catholic predecessors. He was unable to obtain that unforced deference, that ready obedience to constituted and unquestioned authority, which lubricated the whole social structure. The bishops would have to become not merely the legal but also the social counterparts of lords and gentry if they were to carry out the functions of social control which the Queen envisaged for them. Whether they could achieve this was still very much in doubt at the close of the 1570's and in the earlier years of the next decade. At the center, Aylmer was making the Commission a more effective instrument than it had been in the past, but he himself lacked the primatial authority; more important, he had not the personal weight which would command royal confidence and royal backing. The death of Grindal in 1583 opened the way for a new appointment to the primatial see. The new incumbent would prove to be not only an effective hammer of the Puritans but also the conscious shaper of a new polity for the reformed Church of England.

[29] See William Sheils, "Some Problems of Government in a New Diocese: the Bishop and the Puritans in the Diocese of Peterborough, 1560-1630," in *Continuity and Change*, 167-87.

CHAPTER 5

WHITGIFT AND

THE VINDICATION OF

THE ESTABLISHMENT

CHARACTERISTICALLY the Queen had refused either to allow Grindal to function as archbishop or to resign. As we have seen, she chose to allow matters to drift until Grindal's death in 1583 forced upon her the nomination of a successor. This time her choice fell upon a man who combined strength of character with certainty of purpose. His appointment to Canterbury marks a term in the history of the Elizabethan settlement and in that of the Church of England.

John Whitgift belonged to the generation which had entered the university when reform was well rooted in the colleges; he took his B.A. in the year of Edward's death.[1] He thought seriously of emigration but was dissuaded by the supple Doctor Pearne, who almost alone among the Cambridge dignitaries kept his footing with equal sureness under Protestant, Catholic, or restored Protestant regimes. Whitgift's ascent through the university *cursus honorum* was steady, flawed only by one slight but soon recovered misstep. Or-

---

[1] For biographical details on Whitgift, see John Strype, *The Life and Acts of John Whitgift* (3 vols., Oxford, 1822), and P. M. Dawley, *John Whitgift and the Reformation* (New York, 1954).

dained in 1560, master of Pembroke and then in 1567 of Trinity, chaplain to Bishop Cox, prebendary of Ely, he was drawn to the attention of Chancellor Cecil by Lord Keeper Bacon, preached before the Queen, and went on to be Lady Margaret Divinity Reader and in due course Vice Chancellor. He worked closely with Cecil, was one of the makers of the new university statutes which reduced the power of the juniors and increased that of the heads of houses, and took an active lead against Cartwright early on. Such a career, under the discerning eye of Cecil, was a sure road to advancement in the established Church.

But Whitgift had not only very considerable administrative gifts but also those of an able polemicist. It was he who responded to the challenge thrown down in the *Admonition*. In the famous series of exchanges, lasting until 1575, between Cartwright and Whitgift, the latter proved himself not merely a skillful debater and a divine of solid Biblical and Patristic learning, but a discerning socio-political thinker. Cartwright had posed an awkward and dangerous question for the Church of England. The statute of 1559 had laid down that the Supreme Governor of the Church was the sovereign. What was the nature and extent of this governorship? From what did it derive its claim to obedience? What was the relation between this temporal and visible governor and the eternal and unseen Governor on High? For Cartwright the answer to all these questions was easily to be discovered within the pages of Holy Writ, and that answer, as he read it, bade Englishmen change the whole structure of their ecclesiastical government.

As Cartwright read Scripture, the bishops were unknown to the Church of the apostles and, as he read history, a later—and Romish—invention, with no claim whatsover to exercise authority in a godly church.[2] Let this Popish remnant be swept away, this creation of an usurping and ungodly regime. Let the Scriptural pattern, plain for all who chose to read it, be

[2] For the arguments of both Cartwright and Whitgift, see Whitgift, *Works* (Parker Soc., 1851-53), *passim*. Since Whitgift builds his argument by quoting his opponent, much of Cartwright's text is reproduced as a preface to the refutation.

the guide of Englishmen. Let the bishops be replaced by presbyters, men whose qualifications were those of preachers and teachers of the Word, experts in the Book, and acknowledged exemplars of the Christian life. What was discreetly left unsaid by the Puritan doctor was how the Supreme Governor fitted into this altered structure of Church government. Nothing was said to impugn her office, but the most innocent reader of Cartwright was bound to raise the question of her relationship to a new and largely autonomous clerical meritocracy, whose dependence on the Supreme Governor would presumably be minimal.

Cartwright's attack of course fell most heavily on the incumbent bishops. They had been appointed at the beginning of the reign, by a kind of reflex action, to fill the places left vacant by the departing Marians. All that was certain about their functions was that they were agents of the Supreme Governor. They themselves were uncertain as to the essential nature of the office they filled, and no satisfactory doctrinal argument had been worked out to explain its inward character. In externals they had simply imitated their predecessors.

The task of answering the whole of this sweeping indictment was a formidable one. Whitgift had somehow to demonstrate that the existing polity of the Church of England was no mere survival of the Roman past, waiting for the cleansing arm of the reformer, but one acceptable to Scripture—at least not contrary to it—and part of a vital and irresistible tradition of authority. To do this he had first of all to break down his opponents' assertion that the liturgy and the government of the Church as they stood were contradictory to explicit Biblical injunctions and thereby offensive to the Deity. Whitgift had by the weight of his learning to counter these propositions as resting on unsound reading of Holy Writ. But it was not sufficient merely to demolish his opponents' argument. First of all there was the obvious practical difficulty that such demonstrations were never sufficiently conclusive to all concerned; indeed, they simply engendered more argument and gave his opponents additional publicity for their illicit views. More difficult still and more important, Whitgift had to prove that the order established in 1559 rested on foundations that were sounder, stronger, more unassailable than either Cartwright's *iure divino* presbytery or Rome's *iure divino* Papacy.

One conventional route—a demonstration that the 1559 order was indeed based on explicit Scriptural injunction—was closed to him. Elizabethan churchmen had never argued that the rites and ceremonies prescribed in the Book of Common Prayer or the authority of bishops—the two issues under immediate scrutiny—were based on sole Scriptural injunction. The apologetic tradition of the Church, so far as it had been worked out since 1559, largely against the Catholics, had rested on a rather loose underpinning which combined Scripture, the Fathers, and the experience of the early Church as touchstones of authenticity. Whitgift, continuing in this tradition, needed to make use of these varying components in composing his defense, giving each its place but none sole validity. Perhaps too he recognized earlier than some of his Protestant contemporaries the ultimate impossibility of securing agreement on any explicit Scriptural argument. It was becoming all too apparent that there was no touchstone whose qualities might be used to still the endless disagreements about the certain meaning of Holy Scripture.

At any rate, what Whitgift did was to utilize a commonplace conception, deeply imbedded in the English Reformation tradition though perhaps insufficiently exploited hitherto. Archbishop Parker in his oft-quoted letter to Burghley at the end of his life had reasserted that it was not the externals of worship which were at stake in the quarrel with the precisians but "the laws established."[3] "The laws established"—how could Whitgift give them the aura of irresistibility with which Cartwright had tried to endow the presbyterian polity? The answer of course for the dean lay in the not very novel doctrine of adiaphora—those things indifferent, not revealed in the Bible as necessary for salvation and therefore humanly determinable. By what human authority? Here Whitgift very shrewdly turned to a very potent English tradition, that of the royal supremacy over ecclesiastical affairs. Cartwright had

[3] Parker, *Correspondence*, 477-79.

made his appeal to the other pillar of English Protestant principle, the authority of Scripture. Whitgift, having to his own satisfaction demolished his opponent's case, used as his touchstone that royal supremacy—or, to put it another way, that lay superiority—which had been invoked by Tyndale in the very dawn of the English Reformation, and by its founding fathers in the decades that followed. Its potency had been illustrated over and over again, not least by the Marian bishops whose consciences had equally forbidden them to acknowledge the royal supremacy or overtly to seek its overthrow, or by Grindal, whose carefully limited protest excluded the least hint of active resistance to the Supreme Governor's will.

Whitgift's position rested firmly on this solid bedrock, but he strengthened the claims of the establishment (and weakened those of its opponents) by a skillful parrying of the Scriptural argument used by them. His was an essentially historical argument which pointed out the force of differing settings—the effect of time itself in altering the institutional framework within which we dwell. A Church struggling under Neronic persecution was a world away from one nursed by such a Christian princess as England's Deborah. Such an assertion meant a long step towards secularizing what had hitherto been sacred. Polity and liturgy were now creatures of time and circumstance, reflections of changing social or political environment. This was a risky, a two-edged, argument which could and ultimately would be turned against Whitgift's polity as he had turned it against Cartwright's. But in the immediate present it immensely strengthened the claims of the Crown and also the bishops to obedience. The former was placed firmly on the rock of a divinely ordained natural order; the latter were hallowed not by apostolic succession but by long and necessary continuance from the earliest days of the Church and by proven social utility.

That Whitgift had been a hard-hitting and tenacious polemicist in defense of the establishment was no doubt an element in his further advancement. But it is more likely his skills as an academic administrator in a university which lay so closely under the observant eye of a chancellor who was also the

Crown's senior councillor were the grounds for promotion. There is no evidence that Whitgift in the 1570's was writing as an official spokesman for the establishment. He had the approval of Burghley in what he was doing, but the Church which the Master of Trinity was defending was not yet a coherent or a self-aware community; indeed, it was very much his work, done as a solitary task, which would provide the rationale for its future consolidation. It was the sober university Vice-Chancellor and the conscientious Dean of Lincoln who was promoted to the see of Worcester and later to the primacy, not the skillful controversialist, least of all the ingenious theorizer.

Nevertheless it was a matter of no small consequence that the new Primate was a man of ideas. He was that rare bird, the theorist who has the chance and the talents to turn theory into practice. The tasks of episcopal government were clear to him; they were to flesh out the skeleton of doctrine which he had so cleverly strung together. Whitgift was no mere facile polemicist, weaving together whatever webs of argument served to win a disputation, but a convinced idealist whose ideas could be given reality in the workaday world of the administrator. He would have not the slightest doubt that the tasks he was to carry out in the Queen's name were sanctioned by every authority to which he or his contemporaries could lawfully appeal.

Hence Whitgift's appointment to Canterbury was a very predictable one. To his academic posts at Cambridge, where he worked in close collaboration with Lord Burghley, he had added the deanery of Lincoln in 1571. Conscientiously, he divided his time between his old responsibilities and his cathedral post. In 1577, on the death of Bullingham, Whitgift was duly consecrated to the western see of Worcester. The Queen's favor was already manifest in her unaccustomed generosity in remitting the first fruits; at the same time she made over to him the right of presentation to the Worcester prebends. Whitgift settled in very comfortably in his new responsibilities, took a prominent place on the justices' bench and other local commissions, entertained the local gentry, and established his place and dignity as a regional magnate. He was shortly appointed to another post, that of Vice-President of the Council in the Marches of Wales; in the absence of the Lord President Sidney in Ireland, Whitgift was for some time the active head of this body. He was the first bishop since Archbishop Young's not very successful tenure as Lord President of the north to hold an important civil appointment.[4]

There can be no doubt that Whitgift's tenure at Worcester won him high marks with Burghley, who admired his great administrative talents, and with the Queen. Catholic recusancy was more of a problem than Puritan nonconformity in Whitgift's remote diocese, but the bishop earned the hostility of the reform party by his conduct in the Parliament of 1581 when he was blamed for the ill success of the petition for religious reforms which was pressed, with some episcopal support, in that year. He had also won a reputation as the defender of clerical property rights.[5]

Whitgift's appointment to the primacy has often been seen as the culmination of a reorientation in Elizabethan policy which had begun as early as the mid-1570's. It was signalled—in this interpretation—by the humiliation of Grindal and characterized by the decline of Leicester's influence in the making of ecclesiastical appointments, as well as by the rise of the new favorite, Hatton, to great influence in such matters. Hatton was in his own time often regarded as an anti-Puritan (a Puritan fanatic had tried to assassinate him in 1573) and sometimes represented as the patron of such crypto-Catholics as Henry Howard or the Earl of Oxford. He is also, on more solid grounds, regarded as the close collaborator of Whitgift. The archbishop's earliest biographer bears witness to this relationship, but there is no direct evidence of their association be-

[4] George Paule, *The Life of . . . J. Whitgift* (1612), 20-25; Strype, *Whitgift*, I, 188. Whitgift was consulted on the appointment of JP's in Worcestershire and Warwickshire. Archbishop Young of York was appointed to be Lord President at York from 1564 to 1568, but his record there was not one of success (see R. R. Reid, *The King's Council in the North* [1921], 194-98).

[5] Strype, *Whitgift*, I, 173, 184-87; Izaak Walton, in *Walton's Lives*, ed. A. H. Bullen (1884), 200-3; Collinson, *Movement*, 205-7.

fore Whitgift's arrival at Canterbury.[6] This interpretation of the late 1570's is discussed elsewhere along with the problem of Hatton's career.

But whatever may be said about these general changes in Elizabethan policy, at the time of Whitgift's actual appointment to the metropolitan see, he must have seemed pretty much the only possible candidate. It was no longer possible to draw upon the exile generation, which had dominated the episcopacy for twenty years after Elizabeth's accession; they were nearly all dead by now. And they had no natural successors. Between them and the younger generation of divines there had developed an increasing alienation. The more ardent spirits among the younger were attracted by contemporaries such as Cartwright or Travers. As in other ages of revolt against the past, the heroes of the young were those who were most outspoken against the existing order. And even the less outspoken, who were not prepared to travel the whole road to presbytery, were likely to be "fellow-travellers" for at least part of that journey. This meant that the pool of younger clergy from which Leicester and his coadjutors at Court could have drawn successors for the aging exile generation was in fact dry. The new generation of zealous divines did not look to their episcopal fathers as models of piety or hope to succeed them in an office which many of them found suspect, if not positively odious.

Moreover, the qualifications for episcopal office had changed. In 1559 a tested Protestant piety and deep learning were the minimal requirements for the pioneer task of establishing a new order in the face of Catholic opposition. Twenty years later the character of the episcopal office in the Church of England had altered in many important ways. The fact that the new establishment was now a generation old would in itself have institutionalized the office, but more important still were the pronounced views of the Supreme Governor as to what she wanted from her ecclesiastical servants. The Queen had never had much enthusiasm for the zealous pastor of the faithful, truly a father in God to the congregations under his

[6] Paule, *Whitgift*, 36.

charge. What she clearly wanted now, after some fifteen years of dispute, dissension, and obstinate obstruction of her orders, was an efficient administrator, a reliable and resourceful servant of the Crown. And he must be a man wholeheartedly committed to upholding the existing religious order as it now stood. Aylmer was the first of the new breed, but Whitgift, with a greater weight of learning and a stronger personality, was obviously a first choice. His writings had made very clear what his convictions were; his career at Cambridge and Worcester displayed to the full his abilities as an administrator. He was surely the man for the job.

Whitgift wasted no time in introducing a new order consonant with his conviction. He would speak often of the "lenity which hath bred this schism in the Church . . . after so long liberty and lack of discipline." There was lost time to be made up for as fast as possible. He had been in office barely a month before he produced a set of articles, drawn up and signed by himself and eight episcopal colleagues, to which, the Primate specifically wrote, "it hath pleased Her Majesty of her princely clemency to yield her most gracious assent and allowance." Comprehensive in character, they forbade such practices as private meetings for worship, or preaching by clerics who refused to celebrate the sacraments. They required the use of the surplice and limited preaching to those ordained within the English Church. But the center and core of the whole code was the requirement that all who exercised any ecclesiastical function should subscribe in writing to three articles. The first, requiring assent to the royal supremacy, was least controversial, but the second and third were plainly designed as tests for all those of reformist persuasion. They demanded that the clergyman subscribe to the proposition that nothing in the Book of Common Prayer or the ordinal was contrary to the Word of God. Further, he had to make the same declaration in regard to all the Thirty-Nine Articles.[7]

In setting up these touchstones of orthodoxy the Archbishop was conforming himself very closely to the norms which the

[7] T. N. Strype, *Whitgift*, I, 228-32, 233-34; Gee and Hardy, *Documents*, 481-84; also BL, Lansdowne Ms. 396, ff. 6-8 for summary.

Queen herself had always insisted on—a strict adherence to the letter of the 1559 settlement (with the addition of the 1562 articles). By the very terms of the subscription—"nothing contrary to the Word of God"—Whitgift forced the clergy to bind their consciences to the Book and the Articles, to accept without reservation every jot and tittle of these documents as at least congruent with the Divine Word.

Whitgift must have known that he was stirring up a hornet's nest by his actions. On every hand, there was refusal to sign, but in addition there were delegations of protesting clergymen, seeking to see the Primate, and organized petitions of protest, not only to Whitgift but, over his head, to the Privy Council. The reforming leadership hit on the shrewd strategy of collecting systematic statistics about the state of the clergy all over the country, which demonstrated all too vividly the low state of clerical learning and the poor quality of spiritual life of many incumbents. This imposing body of evidence was brought to the Council.[8] The lay supporters of the reformist clergy were also in arms, and a delegation of angry Kentish gentry confronted the Archbishop at Lambeth. But Whitgift faced not only this widespread highly organized and skillfully deployed attack from the provinces but also the indignant protests of the Privy Councillors. The opposition of Walsingham, Leicester, or Knollys—Puritans all—was predictable but even the wary and reserved Burghley joined the ranks of his critics. And at times the Archbishop had to suffer the official rebukes of the whole Council acting collectively. At one stage the Primate was forced to defend his actions to the Queen herself. Altogether the years 1584 and 1585 were a tumultuous period for the new Archbishop.

He met the assault of his critics by vigorous counteroffensives. The clergy who appealed to him were in general bullied and scolded—"boyed," as the current phrase went. They were ridiculed as young, unlearned, and unstable, and the Archbishop insisted that the older, wiser heads of the clergy were

[8] This material is included in the general compendium known as *The Seconde Parte of a Register.*

ready enough to subscribe. The gentry who approached the Primate fared little better; the magnates of the Council were treated with more courtesy, but there was little yielding by the obstinate Primate.

The Council, reminding Whitgift that they too had a responsibility to see the realm well governed and to the honor of God, reproachfully urged on him charitable consideration of the poor subjects who were deprived of pastoral care because their ministers although "diligent learned and zealous" were "in some points of ceremonial . . . doubtful only in conscience and not of willfulness." Burghley on another occasion began with some very unflattering reflection on the bishops: "I see such worldliness in many that were otherwise affected before they came to cathedral chairs that I fear the places above the men." He went on to reproach Whitgift for his recent actions "by which certain simple men have been rather sought by inquisition to be found offenders than upon their facts condemned. . . ."[9] He urged that gentleness might prevail over severity.

But Whitgift was not to be moved. To the Council he replied by a counterattack; the protesting clergy of Kent were young and unlearned and leading their people into schism. And in any case the responsibility for ecclesiastical government was his; he asked the Council to forbear his attendance on them. To Burghley he was even more blunt. After a brief defense of episcopal standards, he continued, "I am as yet fully persuaded that my manner of proceeding against these kind of men is both lawful, usual, and charitable, neither can I devise how otherwise to deal to work any good effect." It was lenity which had bred schism and he would rather be blamed for severity. To Walsingham he wrote, "I have taken upon me the defense of the religion and rites of the Church of England to appease the sects and schisms therein, to reduce all the ministers thereof to uniformity, and due obedience; herein I intend to be constant and not to waver with every wind, the which also my place, my person, my duty and the laws, Her Majesty,

[9] BL, Lansdowne Ms. 396, f. 21; BL, Add. Ms. 22,473, f. 12.

and the goodness of the cause doth require." And to the Queen he reiterated that it was the satisfying of his own duty to God and to Her Majesty that moved him.[10]

The vigorous language of the Archbishop reflects the deep conviction of a man who saw himself as much more than a mere servant of the Crown. He was confident that he was acting on the highest cosmic principles and was as certain that he was the agent of ultimate righteousness as his most principled opponents. Yet, if the Archbishop yielded nothing on principle, he proved himself a flexible and shrewd tactician. The sieve which he had devised, in the articles, was a very fine one, which caught not only the radicals who wanted wholesale replacement of the existing liturgy and polity, but also the much larger body of reform-minded fellow-travellers who were prepared to accept the settlement in large but whose consciences and intellects were troubled by the numerous details of imperfection in the Book and in the Articles of Religion as they stood.

The ministers of Kent, for instance, in their appeal to the Privy Council, insisted on their respect for the Book, which they used; it was particular points within the Book, not its whole character, that made them reluctant to sign. The petitions of the East Anglian clergy afford an example of just what these particular points were, which disturbed the workaday ministers of a reformed cast of mind. How could the Collect for Christmas Day be repeated seven days running when it was written specifically for the particular day of the Nativity? How can one say with surety in every burial service—"with sure and certain hope of resurrection"? What is the significance of the sign of the cross in baptism? Is not the sacrament itself a sign? How can there be another—subsidiary—sign of a sign? These were the kinds of imperfections in the Prayer Book, those places where it fell short of or ignored the inspired text, or else violated simple logic. They were details but of great importance to men whose whole mission was predicated

[10] BL, Add. Ms. 22,473, ff. 8, 13, 18-20; Strype, *Whitgift*, I, 249-55, 333-35.

on the careful and accurate understanding of Scripture and the faithful preaching of it to their flocks.[11]

Whitgift's insistence on an unconditional acceptance of every word in the Book and the Articles placed a tremendous strain on just such moderate reformers, and the Archbishop was persuaded by his critics and by circumstances to a tactical retreat. At one point some 300 to 400 clergy were refusing to sign. Some were allowed to subscribe with reservations about such details, provided they accepted the liturgy as a whole; Whitgift may even have backed up far enough to demand subscription only from those who were newly entering an ecclesiastical office. But it seems probable that all but a small minority gave in some form of subscription. This very act, of course, separated out the rigorists, who were not prepared to make any concessions and to whom the whole existing order was anathema.[12]

The Archbishop had already prepared a more formidable and more efficient instrument against the extremists—the famous procedure *ex officio mero* laid out by the Ecclesiastical Commissioner in May 1584. This procedure, drawn from canon-law practice, forced the individual clergyman under oath to answer a rigorous and searching inquisition into every phase of his professional actions for whatever period of the past the judge chose. It was a peculiarly effective system for winkling out damaging information from the unwilling. It also had a great advantage over presentment; that procedure involved the participation of the chief gentleman in the parish, who if he were "so affected" could handily choke off proceedings.[13]

This more rigorous procedure evoked a famous protest from Burghley, who protested its self-accusatory aspect and compared it to the Spanish Inquisition in its severity. But the Primate calmly replied that these were procedures in use at least since King Edward VI's time, that they were no different from those used in Star Chamber or in the Council in the Marches.

---

[11] BL, Add. Ms. 22,473, f. 7, and 48,064, ff. 167-72.

[12] BL, Add. Ms. 22,473, ff. 23-24.

[13] Strype, *Whitgift*, III, 81-87; *ibid.*, I, 318-22.

These were public not private suits, judging the actions of men in a public calling—men who were in fact schismatics, separating themselves from the national Church.[14]

The relentless struggle between the iron-willed Archbishop and his bitterly angry opponents went on for months, a continuous tussle within the court and Council. The results were indecisive; the Primate had to pull back from the extreme position he had taken up initially and to allow exceptions for individual ministers protected by powerful patrons or by the quirks of the administrative system. But many others felt the power of his harrying, and it was becoming quite clear that this campaign for uniformity was not likely to taper off into neglect and forgetfulness, as the earlier episodes had. There was a consistency and driving force which had not been present before.

But the conflict within the inner circle of politics spilled over into another arena when Parliament met, first in November 1584 about a year after the Archbishop's accession to office, and again two years later in 1586. Both Parliaments powerfully affected the course of the struggle. The first one met primarily to deal with the threat to the Queen's life posed by Catholic intrigue and focussed on the Queen of Scots. At the opening of the session the Lord Chancellor specifically commanded the Parliament in the Queen's name to forbear discussion of religion, but the erosion of royal authority over the Houses had proceeded so far by now that this was an empty gesture.

The main religious measure pushed in Parliament—by a broad coalition of leading gentry, minor civil servants, and at least two Privy Councillors, Mildmay and Knollys—was an attack on Whitgift's whole program.[15] Its sixteen articles, couched as a petition to the Lords, would have ended all subscription (except as provided by statute), have prohibited prosecutions for minor variants from the Prayer Book, have ended procedure *ex officio mero*, and have freed preachers from harassment by the bishops. These measures would have rolled back the Primate's advance; but, in addition to repelling the

[14] BL, Add. Ms. 22,473, ff. 18-20, 20-21.
[15] Strype, *Whitgift*, III, 118-24.

enemy, the petitioners proposed to tighten requirements on admission to the ministry, and to expel incompetent incumbents. Then, in an aggressive move of their own, the reformers sought to shift the balance of power within the Church itself. New clergy would be ordained by the bishop in association with six ministers, only for specific vacant livings, and after the parish had had some chance to vet the candidate. There were additional proposals for reform of the ecclesiastical courts. The prophesyings were to be restored. All in all, it was an impressive, reasonably coherent program for restructuring the Church, which summed up the main aspirations of the evangelical party, clerical and lay. Characteristically it would have strengthened all those initiatives coming from below—and virtually ignoring the bishop—which had been so marked a feature of the movement since 1559. It would have established the center of gravity in the Church at the level of the parish clergy, backed by their local patrons.

This petition brought the Archbishop on the scene. It was he who, after long delays in the Upper House, responded to the Commons committee. He followed Burghley, who gave the Queen's views as laid out after a discussion with Whitgift and other bishops. They pushed aside the whole petition; some of the issues were being dealt with by Convocation; some would be handled by the Queen herself; "some were not fit to be reformed as requiring innovation and impugning the Book of Common Prayer."

Whitgift's answer was more specific, dealing with each clause in turn. It was also more abrasive; the deprivations were justly done; the *ex officio* oath was offensive only to those who disliked government and would bring the Church to anarchy. The reform leaders in the Lower House were beside themselves with fury. The committee of the Commons prepared a reasoned reply to the Archbishop, which pushed the argument on to constitutional grounds by asserting the supremacy of statute law and thereby denying the Primate's right to claim subscription.[16]

[16] *A Compleat Journal of the Votes, Speeches and Debates, Both of the House of Lords and House of Commons throughout the Whole*

But the dispute had already moved to a higher quarter. On 27 February, the same day that the Commons committee report was drawn up, there was a dramatic scene at court. The occasion was the reception of a delegation from Convocation offering the clerical subsidy. It included Whitgift, three bishops, and representatives of the Lower House. The Queen received them in the presence of her principal councillors, including Burghley. She made a point in thanking them by distinguishing their voluntary grant from that of the laity who had to be "entreated and moved thereunto." Burghley's interjection that the clerical subsidy was but a mite compared with that of the laity brought a lengthy outburst from the Queen. Turning to the bishops, she condoled with them on the attack made in the House of Commons "tending greatly to your dishonor, which we will not suffer." The Commons "meddle with matters above their capacity, not appertaining unto them for the which we will call some of them to an accompt." Some of her Council had joined them; she threatened those councillors—Mildmay and Knollys—that she would "uncouncil" them.

But the Queen distributed her blame to the bishops as well, not for their severity but for their lenity, their lack of care in making ministers, but, more important, their failure to enforce uniformity. She had heard, she said, of six ministers in one diocese "the which do preach six sundry ways. I wish such men to be brought to conformity and unity; that they minister the sacraments according to the order of this Realm and preach all one truth"; those unable to preach should read the homilies, "for there is more learning in one of those than in twenty of some of their sermons." The bishops were warned not to be moved by "noblemen's letters and gentlemen's letters" to an unwise lenity. Such ministers "will be hanged before they will be reformed." She went on to blacken the reformers even more; reports from abroad, she said, spread the rumor that Protestants disliked her as much as the Papists—that they held

---

Reign of Queen Elizabeth, etc., collected by Simonds D'Ewes (1693), 359-60 (cited henceforth as D'Ewes, *Journal*); Neale II, 65-69; Strype, *Whitgift*, I, 354-60.

she was of no religion; they were indeed but her "pretensed" friends and no better than the Papists.

There followed an exchange between Whitgift and Burghley in which the Queen firmly backed the Archbishop. It all ended on a familiar note, Elizabeth declaring that it was not learned ministers whom she would see appointed, "for they are not be found" in adequate numbers, but "honest, sober, and wise men and such as can read the scriptures and homilies well unto the people." These words echoed sentiments which she had never varied from the beginning of her reign.[17]

This scene was played out before a small and select audience, but the Queen's views on the matter were conveyed to Parliament a few days later, after the committee's reply to the Archbishop had been prepared but before it was presented to the House. The Speaker was chosen to convey her message. It was full of plain speech. The House was rebuked for having pursued the matter of religion against a royal command. It was told that it knew that the whole power to reform religious abuses lay with her, the Supreme Governor. Their proceedings could benefit only the adversary to whom they revealed division and distrust within the Protestant ranks. For herself she resolutely declined any innovation of "the religion or Church of England [as it] standeth established at this day." Abuses she would reform but only when grievances were forwarded in the normal channels from bishop, to metropolitan, to Council and Queen. Elizabeth ended with yet another reiteration of her determination not to change. "For as she found it [the state ecclesiastical] at her first coming in and so hath maintained it these twenty-seven years, she meant in like state, by God's grace, to continue it and leave it behind her."[18]

All this left the reformers within the House very sore indeed, and there were private meetings where they gave vent to their rumbling discontent, turning over such alternatives of action as an attack on the Speaker, a refusal of the royal command as a violation of Parliamentary right, and a bill for ecclesiastical reform. But all these brave words died away, victims of the struggle between religious conviction and the

[17] Neale II, 69-71.   [18] Neale II, 73-75.

deep-rooted habits of deference to royal command. In their cooler moments even the hottest heads must have seen that at this crisis of the reign, when the best safeguards they could devise were all too fragile protection for Elizabeth's life, when foreign enemies loomed on every side, they could hardly afford the luxury of open defiance of the royal will.

For Whitgift and for his policy the reaction must have been immensely reassuring. He could not have stood up to the attacks of the past year, from the weightiest quarters in the court, if he had not expected royal support. But now it was publicly and emphatically asserted; his enemies were discomfited, and the Queen's explicit approval of his course announced by her own lips.

Courtiers, if not Parliament men, must have been aware that a perceptible shift had taken place in those foundation rocks on which their political structure rested. A new and strong presence was now felt in the inner circle. More important still, for the first time since the reign opened, the actual structure of power coincided with the vision of it held by the sovereign. In addition to the Privy Council, that immensely strong and supple instrument for the civil governance of the realm, there was now an ecclesiastical equivalent of equal vitality, enforcing the royal supremacy from above.

But the Puritans in the Commons fought on, regardless, launching bills, one of which would have reduced the bishops to common and statute law control while another would have ousted incompetent, i.e., ungodly, ministers. These and other lesser bills continued to move through the Lower House until the very end of the session, and the Archbishop was worried enough to seek explicit royal support. All this embryonic legislation was aborted before it reached the Crown. No single act for religious matters reached the statute book.[19]

This decisive check and the open manifestations of the Queen's backing for Whitgift did not shake the determination of the more strong-minded reformers; it drove them towards more radical measures. With the summons of another Parliament, in 1586, they made ready for a supreme effort. This time

[19] *Ibid.*, 83; Strype, *Whitgift*, I, 391-92.

all the stops were pulled out. More material was collected to prove the moral insufficiency and professional inadequacy of a large part of the incumbent clergy. Steps were taken to ensure the election of proven supporters and there may have been in November 1586 a national conference of the evangelical leadership. Some more timorous brethren held back fearfully from such determined assault on the establishment's citadel. Field, the great manager of the left-wing drive, put it bluntly to one such hesitating brother: "Hold your peace. Seeing we cannot compass these things by suit or by dispute, it is the multitude and people that must bring the discipline to pass, which we desire." And what he proposed was a campaign to rouse opinion, to lobby MP's, and to prepare a legislative program for Parliament which would press for the most far-reaching changes.[20]

What ensued was one of the more startling episodes in Elizabethan history—a bold-faced attempt to abolish the whole existing ecclesiastical polity, indeed all the ecclesiastical legislation passed from 1559 onwards, and to substitute a Genevan prayer book and a presbyterian system of Church government. The backers of this proposal launched it with care and skill; a series of well-prepared speakers rose to advocate it and they were able to carry the House so far as to order its reading on the next day. The Queen promptly laid hands on the bill and when its sponsors continued the debate and raised the cry of Commons privilege she clapped them into the Tower, where they cooled their heels at least until the end of the session.[21]

The proposal was indeed revolutionary in its boldness, but it was also politically inept and ultimately damaging to the cause it sought to serve. The government brought in its heaviest guns to demolish the radicals; Sir Christopher Hatton in a long and carefully prepared speech stated the establishment case fully while raking the clauses of the radicals' bill. The reformation of King Edward and Queen Elizabeth had, he insisted, established *true* government in the church, *pure* doctrine, purged of Papal error, and a godly order for public worship to replace the barbarous corruption of the Popish mass.

[20] Neale II, 145-48.   [21] *Ibid.*, 148-62.

Drawn up after grave consideration by the doctors and fathers of the Church, it had been perfected by the Queen to such a degree as to become "the chief key and stay of all reformed churches in Christendom." The English Church was not only acceptable to God, but the supreme achievement of the reformed community.[22] Would Parliament throw all this away, "alter the whole form and order of your service? Will you take the book from us that we have been persuaded to think both good and godly?" The substitute would offer no settled form of worship at all since it was riddled with options which left each minister free to improvise. How can a people who cannot read learn the fundamentals of faith from an ever-varying order of service?

Hatton then went on to appeal to economic interest. How was the vastly expanded clerical establishment to be maintained—this staff of pastors, doctors, deacons, elders? The bishops' lands would not suffice; the abbey lands would have to be recovered from their present owners in order to foot such a bill. Impropriators were mere robbers, according to these reformers; in fact they wanted to enrich themselves at the gentry's expense. It was a skillful appeal to all the anti-clerical sentiment in the House.

As to the powers of bishops—whether they were agreeable to the Word Hatton left to divines, but for his part, as a politic man, "I do see the necessity of these dignities and authorities for avoiding of contention and better reputation of their callings. As for the same purpose we have in the civil law nobles and gentlemen." It was precisely the position that the Queen had taken for granted: that the episcopate was the ecclesiastical equivalent of the civil hierarchy with corresponding functions within its own domain.

As for the royal supremacy, it would be quite destroyed by the new proposals by the loss of the very power to make law or to hear appeals in ecclesiastical cases; indeed it savored of those notorious attacks on royal authority mounted in Scotland and France—*De jura regni apud Scotos*, and the *Vindiciae contra Tyrannos*. These men were indeed in the same camp

---

[22] *Ibid.*, 158-60; D'Ewes, *Journal*, 412; Strype, *Whitgift*, III, 186-94.

ultimately as the Papists, as dangerous to all royal authority.

There is another similar document, emanating from the Queen herself and perhaps a response to an appeal from Whitgift.[23] It left little in doubt as to her views, if indeed they needed yet another exposition. "Her Majesty is fully resolved by her own reading and princely judgment upon the truth of the Reformation which we have already and mindeth not now to begin to settle herself in causes of religion. Her Majesty hath been confirmed in her said judgment of the present reformation by the letters and writing of the most famous men in Christendom as well of her own dominions as of other countries." Again there is the confident claim to excellence, to a reformed perfection.

The critics of the present order made nothing but frivolous exceptions; indeed "for the very substance and grounds of true religion no man living can justly control them." And here she moved to a full-blown doctrine of adiaphora: "to make every day new laws in matters of circumstances and of less moment (especially touching religion) were a means to breed great lightness in her subjects, to nourish an unstayed humor in them in seeking still for exchanges."

Effectually the Puritan assault of 1586 was to be their last Parliamentary campaign; a much more modest effort in 1589 produced some discussion in both Houses, but it was the mere swell of the sea after the storm had subsided. The reformers' attempts over a period of more than twenty years to bring about by Parliamentary enactment changes, modest or far-reaching, in the character of the Church of England were over. The established Church was now headed by a heavy-handed but effective administrator, absolutely certain of the righteousness of his cause and of his actions, informed by a coherent view of the Church's polity, and backed by the confidence and trust of the sovereign.

For more than two decades the English government had wrestled with the unprecedented problem of disagreement within the ranks of the reformers—within the Protestant Church es-

[23] Strype, *Whitgift*, I, 494-95; Neale II, 163.

tablished by law. At the root of the problem was the fundamental divergence between an uncompromising sovereign for whom the settlement of 1559 was a finished artifact, permanently serviceable and proof against any further alterations, and that very weighty proportion of her subjects, clerical and lay, for whom at least some measure of additional religious reformation still remained to be accomplished. The result was that the very men who were meant to enforce conformity to the new order—ecclesiastics or magistrates—were at the best half-hearted and at the worst downright obstructionists. The problem was further compounded by the Queen's fundamental indifference to religious issues, her angry impatience with reformers, and her ill-concealed anti-clericalism, which made her more than half contemptuous of her clerical servants. There followed twenty years of muddle in which bouts of royal displeasure punctuated long intervals of relative neglect or indifference. Confused and unhappy prelates struggled ineffectually to enforce a conformity to which they could give no wholehearted allegiance. Opposition in its multiple forms continued, harassed but undeterred. Not until the chances of time and of politics thrust John Whitgift onto the throne of Canterbury was it possible to oppose the many-pronged attacks of the Church's critics with a considered, coherent, and viable polity. At the end of the period we are concerned with, the emergence of the new Archbishop signalled the end of the years of drift and the appearance of royal commitment to an authoritarian ecclesiastical regime which, fleshing out the bare bones of statute with a new conception of right order, demanded the active loyalty of the clergy. The decisive turn towards what we may anachronistically term a distinctively Anglican polity had been made; its architect was also to be its builder. How far he would succeed still lay in the future at the end of the 1580's.

CHAPTER 6

CATHOLIC DISSENT

THE PROBLEM of dissent had, for the Elizabethan regime, an unhappy symmetry. Protestant dissidence, on the left, was matched by the recalcitrance of English Catholics, on the right. In a strictly legal sense both groups stood on the same ground in their refusal to obey the letter of the law, that is to say, of the 1559 settlement. And the government's response was in principle the same in both cases, but there the resemblance ends. Protestant dissenters demurred at the internal arrangements of the settlement, particularly its regulations as to ceremonial and its structure of Church government but until quite late in the reign no Puritan repudiated the established Church *in toto* by denying it to be a true Christian Church. The actively disobedient dissenters were clergymen of the Church of England; the problem of disciplining them was primarily an ecclesiastical one.

The Catholics represented a more threatening issue. Their offense was graver since they repudiated the whole religious settlement of 1559 and at least in theory denied the Church of England to be in any sense a Christian religious community; it was a false Church, a simulacrum of the real thing, infinitely dangerous to men's souls. Their ranks included both clergy and laity, many of the latter men of high rank. The Papal Church provided them with a refuge and rallying point and all the resources of a great international organization now moving very self-consciously from a defensive to an offensive posture. They might reasonably hope for powerful assistance from one of the great continental monarchies, which for reasons spiritual or temporal might be disposed to intervene on their behalf. *Prima facie* the English Catholics presented an ominous threat to the Elizabethan regime; there were all the raw materials for a grand-scale combustion, a confrontation between the old and new faiths of the kind which was already wracking France with civil war. In actual fact the division between English Protestant and English Catholic was to prove a curiously blurred one, and the government's policy of coercion was often to be blunted both in intent and in execution. The hostility of the Elizabethan leaders towards Catholicism never wavered, but in planning and in executing a strategy of attack they showed the same fumbling unsureness of touch which characterized their dealings with Protestant dissent. In both cases, although for different reasons, government policy was shot through with ambiguities which reached deep into the religious consciousness of Englishmen.

These reasons alone would have made the history of government policy towards the Catholics a complex one, but it was complicated even more by the major changes in the nature of English Catholic belief and practice during the decades after 1570. Up to that time it was not unreasonable to assume that the old faith would die out, once a generation of aging adherents passed on; they would have no successors either lay or clerical. The powerful currents of the Counter-Reformation were to reverse this situation within a very few years of the founding of Douay Seminary (1568), and the government would then have to deal with a resurgent faith of great vitality. Along with the wave of young missionary priests who spearheaded this revival came the rise of Catholic political conspiracy, more and more associated with Spain. For the English government the two movements were one; missionary activity was equated with straightforward treason to the Crown. Catholic denials of this identity of purpose won little credence, but the experience of the government in dealing with the whole perplexing problem gradually brought them by the late 1580's to the first glimmering recognition that they might distinguish between a purely religious Catholic community and a political one and that the former might have no other political goal than that of bare survival.

At the opening of the reign the new regime was uncertainly apprehensive of the dimly menacing but still incalculable force of Catholic feeling within the country. Several of the "advices" offered to Elizabeth in 1558 emphasized the strength of the old faith and urged a cautious approach to change,[1] but the resolution of the Marian episcopate and of their clerical and lay brethren remained to be tested. The first such trial of strength came in the Parliament of 1559 when the solidarity of episcopal resistance was demonstrated—as well as the paucity of their lay support. The Marian bishops were eased out of their sees with minimal difficulty and in their refusal to take the supremacy oath were joined by a relatively modest body of clerics, largely from the cathedral clergy.[2] The great inert mass of parish priests sluggishly yielded to this latest change in the official faith of the kingdom, as they had done on three earlier occasions. There were no stirrings of active opposition among the laity, of the kind which the Protestants had so disturbingly displayed in the late reign. The government might reasonably heave a sigh of relief once the new bishops were installed and the machinery of Church government began slowly to turn over.

The regime's policy towards possible Catholic recalcitrance was summed up in the Act of Uniformity.[3] Clause II of the act required that clergy use the statutory services and no other under penalties of imprisonment and eventual deprivation; similar punishment was decreed for anyone who wrote or spoke in derogation of the new establishment. Finally, most important, all persons in the realm were required "to resort to

[1] See MacCaffrey, *The Shaping of the Elizabethan Regime* (Princeton, 1968), 51-55.
[2] Henry Gee, *The Elizabethan Clergy and the Settlement of Religion, 1558-1564* (Oxford, 1898), chaps. 12-14; Henry N. Birt, *The Elizabethan Religious Settlement* (1907), chaps. 4, 5.
[3] *Statutes of the Realm*, 1 Elizabeth, c. 2.

their parish church or chapel accustomed" if at all possible, on every Sunday and Holy Day "then and there to abide orderly and soberly during the time of the common prayer, preachings, or other service of God there to be used and ministered." But the penalties for nonattendance were modest: the censures of the Church and a twelve-penny fine to be levied by the Church wardens of the parish for the use of the poor. The contrast with the Act of Uniformity of 1552 was striking. The requirement for attendance in the earlier act was virtually identical except for the omission of the 12d. fine, but any person who attended any other form of religious service fell under the authority of the common law and, upon conviction at assizes or sessions of the peace, faced serious penalties of imprisonment.

The enforcement procedures of 1559 were clumsy; while the statute rather rhetorically thrust the main burden of execution on the bishops and their officials, it also provided an alternative procedure in the common-law courts. In both cases the initial action would be taken by the church wardens. It is important to note that no sacramental requirement was imposed; nothing more than mere attendance was required. The government's intention was seemingly to lay the barest minimum obligation on the worshipper and to clothe the requirement in a guise which was as much that of a civil as a religious duty. It was unadorned Erastianism in which the absence of any persuasive argument or authoritative dictum was all the more compelling. The power of Parliament to require such a civic duty was simply taken for granted, something quite beyond question.

The assumptions which underlay this policy, although not explicitly spelled out, are not hard to define. The leaders of the new regime believed, especially after the peaceful transitions of 1559-1560, that what faced them was a tractable problem, the nostalgic adherence of aging worshippers to a familiar faith, with no power of resistance other than that of sheer inertia. Once the external ministrations of the old worship were removed, it could only be a matter of time—waiting for natural generational changes—before Catholicism would vanish altogether from England. The government's cue, under these circumstances, was to turn a blind eye towards those whose consciences denied even minimal acceptance of the new order. A corollary of this politique attitude was the government's total lack of interest in any proselytism for the new faith. It was assumed that the younger generation, knowing nothing but the new forms of worship, would easily and imperceptibly slip into new habits of conventional piety. The change in religion was to be effected by a firm but discreet deployment of the Crown's authority rather than by any campaign of persuasion. There was the greatest confidence in the weight of the government's own authority and in Englishmen's habits of obedience to its commands. Nothing which had happened in the later years of Henry or under Edward gave cause to doubt these assumptions.

The second Elizabethan Parliament, of 1562-1563, added something to the armory of repression. Teaching or writing in behalf of the power of Rome subjected one to the penalties of praemunire.[4] Justices (of Assize and of the Peace) were given powers to investigate recusancy and to certify it to Queen's Bench. More important, the oath of supremacy was extended to all courts, sheriffs, feodaries, and escheators; the penalty of a second refusal was that of high treason (but only ecclesiastics were to be preferred the oath twice). The penalties of excommunication were now stretched to include those who refused to have a child baptized or to receive Holy Communion or to come to divine service.

How far the penalties for nonattendance at the parish Church were enforced in the first decade of Elizabeth's reign is impossible to know accurately.[5] The bishops, in their injunctions to their dioceses, inquired with reasonable frequency into the execution of the attendance requirement; and not only mere attendance was to be investigated but also participation in the sacrament of Holy Communion; three communions a

[4] *Ibid.*, 5 Elizabeth, c. 23.
[5] *Ibid.*, 1 Elizabeth, c.2, clauses iv. v, vi; see also W. H. Freer, ed., *Visitation Articles and Injunctions*, vol. 3 (Alcuin Club *Collections* 16, [1910], 22); F. X. Walker, "The Implementation of the Elizabethan Statutes against Recusants, 1581-1603" (University College, London, Ph.D. thesis, 1961), 5-8 (cited henceforth as Walker, "Recusants").

year were set as a minimum. It may well have been the latter requirement (which could be enforced by excommunication) that bore more heavily on recusants than the attendance clauses. But, as with Protestant dissent, much depended on local circumstance, on the Protestant zeal of the parish incumbent and of the resident squire, if there was one.

The government's attitude seems to have been one of watchful but normally passive supervision rather than of active intervention. The bishops were left to keep the machinery turning over without much overt pressure from the Crown or Council. The latter was concerned only with any political (or potentially political) activity. Surviving Marian leaders were kept under surveillance—hence the cat-and-mouse treatment of the deprived bishops. And Cecil was quick to pounce on such important Catholic laymen as the Marian Privy Councillors, Waldegrave and Hastings, in 1561.[6] Concern about the import of "Louvain books," the polemics of the English Catholic exiles in Belgium, began to show up in 1566 and 1567 in episcopal injunctions. The machinery of the Ecclesiastical Commission was brought into play in 1568 in an investigation into the churchgoing habits of the members of the Inns of Court, societies notoriously affected to the old faith.[7] Recalcitrants were threatened with virtual disbarment and required to produce certificates of conformity. Earlier, in 1564, the Council had ordered an inquiry into the religious opinions of the JP's,[8] the returns of which were rather depressing news for the government since they suggested that those unfavorable to the new religion plus the neuters were not much fewer in number than its supporters. But there is no evidence of any extensive purging of the commissions of the peace in the light of this information.

The essence of the Crown's position in the first Elizabethan decade was succinctly expressed in a statement drawn up by

[6] MacCaffrey, *Shaping*, 108-9.

[7] Frere, *Visitation Articles*, III, 182 (Horne's injunction to New College), 226 (Sandys to Worcester diocese); Walker, "Recusants," 17-21.

[8] *A Collection of Original Letters from the Bishop to the Privy Council, 1564*, ed. M. Bateson, Camden Soc. n.s. 53 (1895): *Miscellany* IX.

Secretary Cecil and read by Lord Keeper Bacon in the Star Chamber in June 1570. Its primary aim was to quash rumors that the government was about to initiate inquisition of "men's consciences in matters of religion." This was denied; certain persons who had lately been called before the Council were breakers of the law "in not coming at all to the Church, to common prayer, and divine service" for upwards of a decade. This was "open and willful contempt of breaking of Her Majesty's laws." The Queen went on to say that she would have no one "molested by any inquisition or examination of their consciences in causes of religion," provided they did not flout her laws by open deeds of disobedience.[9]

In that same year these relatively calm waters were ruffled by the issuance of Pope Pius V's bull of excommunication. A royal proclamation of July denounced seditious books, "and bulls as it were from Rome," which spread slanderous untruths about the nobility and the Council and stirred up treasonous attempts against the Queen's government. Nothing is said of religious doctrine and there is only the slightest reference to Rome; the language is deliberately vague, throwing the whole emphasis on the seditious nature of these writings without specifying content.[10]

But if the government's attitude was relatively restrained, that of Parliament, when it met in the spring of 1571, was less so, and the strong Protestant core in the Houses had solid backing within the Privy Council, almost certainly from Burghley himself.[11] A bill which passed both Houses would have required both attendance and communication with a heavy fine (100 marks) for failure to conform to the latter requirement. The Queen vetoed it. What did pass was much less far-reaching. One statute made the use of bulls or the reception of absolution (for attendance at Anglican services) high treason, the concealment of a bull, misprision of treason. The importation of religious objects such as crosses or pictures was forbidden and, significantly, penalties were laid on JP's who con-

[9] Strype, *Annals*, I, pt. 2, 371-72.
[10] *Tudor Proclamations*, II, 341-43.
[11] Neale I, 192-93; Walker, "Recusants," 33-34.

cealed such offenses. The first notice of the exodus of young Catholic recruits to the new-founded seminary at Douay occurred in the statute against fugitives beyond the seas; their property would be forfeited if they did not return. But even here a milder note was heard, for the families of those departing out of "blind zeal and conscience only" were to be provided for out of the forfeited estates.

In 1576 there was renewed evidence of a rising tide of anti-Catholic feeling among the political classes and within the government itself. Another bill for attendance and communication was backed by an imposing committee of lords and bishops, but it did not reach the statute book.[12]

The relative passivity of the government during this decade reflects in large part the events of 1569-1572. The Northern Earls, when they had reluctantly risen against the Queen, sounded the most uncertain of notes, fluctuating between a merely political conservatism and a call for religious restoration. Their own infirmity of purpose was matched by the signal failure of Catholics to respond to any call to action. This almost effortless triumph of the regime was followed by the equally effective crushing of the Ridolfi scheme and the exposure of the Queen of Scots—the presumptive Catholic candidate for the throne—as an intriguer who plotted the invasion of the realm by foreign armies. An organized Catholic movement within England seemed now a thing of the past. On the other hand, events in France and the Low Countries cast a strong and sinister light on what many Englishmen believed to be a grand international Catholic conspiracy against the reformed faith. However, until the end of the decade the link between English Catholics and their continental brethren was not one to cause alarm.

Complacency about the Catholic problem continued through much of the 1570's. Not until about 1577 did English leaders begin to perceive that recusancy was no longer on the decline but was in fact beginning to increase alarmingly. Behind this English phenomenon stood the grander development of the

---

[12] Neale I, 349; Walker, "Recusants," 35.

Counter-Reformation. The revival of a vigorous spiritual life within the Roman Church dated back to the 1540's; it had barely touched the Marian Church in England; but now in the 1560's and 1570's its energizing effects were felt in the recumbent English community. English Catholicism was transformed from an inert body of leaderless and aging devotees of a fading order into a lively community of faith, revitalized by the infusion of young blood. The Douay Seminary, opened in 1568, quickly drew to it a multitude of young singleminded idealists, the counterparts of the Puritan intelligentsia in the English universities. That was the other magnetic pole of religious enthusiasm which engaged the sympathies and devotion of many of the ablest young Englishmen. The importance of these developments cannot be overemphasized. They gave to the English Catholics a framework of leadership and organization as well as the stimulation of a transcendent ideal.

The Elizabethan establishment was slow to recognize what was happening in their midst. The first missionary graduates had arrived in England in 1574; it was another three years before the authorities began to sense the increase in recusancy. Interestingly, the initiative within the establishment seems to have been taken by Aylmer, who was moving at the same time against the Puritans. In 1577[13] he proposed heavy fines as the best means to compel communication. An opinion of the judges and learned counsel of 1578 held that the Supreme Governorship provided subordinate ecclesiastical officers (bishops or commissioners) with power to fine recusants, and such powers were used by the High Commission at York at least by 1580. These may have been isolated cases, but certainly from 1577 the idea of using heavy fines or imprisonment as a weapon against Catholic dissent was gaining headway rapidly. Such a policy was outlined in a conference of bishops, summoned by Walsingham (on behalf of the Council) in 1577. And it was put into execution within the next few months by the joint efforts of Council, High Commission, individual

13 Walker, "Recusants," 37, quoting John Morris, *The Troubles of Our Catholic Forefathers* (1877).

bishops, and local justices. Appearance before the Council, followed by varying terms of imprisonment, was the fate of the leading recusants in a scattering of counties across the country. Enforcement of the 1559 legislation in the ecclesiastical courts continued, although in a rather dilatory fashion. High Commission brought pressure to bear in the dioceses but with only limited success.[14]

In the North, under the vigorous prodding of Lord President Huntingdon, the High Commission for the province of York made a strong and continuing attack on recusancy in the years just before 1580.[15] Fines, imprisonment, bonds were all used; the civic officials at York were nudged into action, and steady pressure was maintained on the rather sizable Catholic population of the northern counties.

What became apparent in the late 1570's was the increasing alarm of Privy Councillors, bishops, and other leading officials as to the extent and tenacity of recusancy. They could no longer look forward complacently to the extinction of Catholic belief by sheer attrition. But the difficulties they faced in dealing with the problem were considerable. There was more unanimity of opinion within the Council than there was in regard to the Puritans, but it is clear that the Queen set her face against new legislation in the Parliaments of the 1570's, and there is no evidence that she lent her authority to the efforts of councillors and High Commission at the end of the decade. Lacking adequate civil machinery for their purposes, the leading ministers made use of High Commission, with its still undefined but promisingly large powers. But these tactics yielded only very partial success. Where there was a powerful and determined Protestant leader, as at York, something could be done in putting pressure on recusants, but elsewhere the bishops found themselves faced by the same kind of opposition that baffled their efforts in dealing with Protestant dissent. Local officials were sluggish at best, often recalcitrant. In most cases their inertia was probably not the result of Catholic sym-

<hr />

[14] Walker, "Recusants," 41-44, 48, 56-58, 60-62.
[15] *Ibid.,* 68-118 *passim.*

pathies but reflected a certain coolness and indifference towards the new faith. The continuance of peaceful relations with their neighbors, especially when the latter were men of substance in the countryside, was more important than the interests of pure and undefiled religion. And once again the ambiguous position of the bishops in relation to the local aristocracies put a damper on episcopal initiatives, even when the bishop in question was zealous in persecution. The parallels with the Puritan problem are interesting—royal neglect, aristocratic opposition, inefficient machinery for repression, episcopal timidity, all are there. And there was the further fact that Catholics, like Puritans, were now revealed as men and women of conscience, who were quite prepared to deny obedience to constituted authority on the highest grounds of faith. The mere assertion of raw authority—the mere command to obey because obedience is owed—was no longer sufficient to deal with the adherents of the ancient faith.

By the time Parliament met again in January 1581 the problem of Catholic dissent was one which engaged the attention of government and of the Commons. Along with increasing awareness of the dimensions and the success of the missionary movement there was the growing activity of the Roman curia. The Popes had contemplated direct intervention of some sort in behalf of the English Catholics since the bull of 1570. At one stage—at the end of the 1570's—they had placed their hopes in Don John. At another, Rome, having failed to interest Philip in direct action against the English regime, gave its patronage to the adventurer, Thomas Stucley,[16] who set off from Civitavecchia (with the honors of a Papal marquissate) for Ireland. He was diverted by the coldness of Philip and the enthusiasms of King Sebastian into the latter's Moroccan fiaasco.

The Papacy tried again, although not more than half-heartedly, when it backed the Irish rebel, James Fitzgerald. He was accompanied by one of the most eminent and influential of

[16] John H. Pollen, *The English Catholics in the Reign of Queen Elizabeth* (1920), 224-25.

the English clerical exiles, Dr. Nicholas Sander. They landed at Dingle Bay in July 1579. Fitzgerald was soon killed in battle; Sander survived to meet the succors sent by the Papal nuncio in Spain when they reached Smerwick in late summer 1580. This expedition was quickly wiped out by the English commanders and Sanders escaped only to die some months later of sheer exhaustion, in the Irish bogs. These two ill-fated and ill-conceived essays of Papal policy had a marked effect on the thinking of the English government. It saw them as incontrovertible evidence of Papal hostility and assumed Spanish backing since the forces sailed from Iberian ports. And indeed Cecil assumed that one of the Catholic powers would naturally seek to stir up civil war in the British Isles by invasion.[17]

These Papal enterprises coincided in time with Spanish designs on the vacant throne of Portugal and with the invasion scare of summer 1580 which led to the issuance of a proclamation.[18] Although English fears were founded on scanty (and inaccurate) information, the proclamation is a measure of English fears of both external and internal Catholic pressures.

Many of these themes were brought together in a major policy speech delivered by Sir Walter Mildmay in the early days of the Parliamentary session of 1581. The main thrust of his speech was simple and direct. The Papists, he argued, "hold this as a firm and settled opinion, that England is the only settled monarchy that most doth countenance and maintain religion." The Pope will not rest in his efforts "to remove this great obstacle which standeth between him and the overflowing of the world again with Popery." There followed a confirmatory catalogue of events: the Northern Rebellion, the maintenance of the rebels after their defeat, the bull of 1570, the two invasions of Ireland. But the Pope, Mildmay said, was

---

[17] *A New History of Ireland*, ed. T. W. Moody, F. X. Martin, and F. J. Byrne, vol. 3: *Early Modern Ireland, 1534-1691* (Oxford, 1976), 103-8; HMC, *Calendar of the Manuscripts of the . . . Marquis of Salisbury . . . at Hatfield House*, etc. (cited henceforth as *Hatfield*), pt. II (1888), 268.

[18] *Tudor Proclamations*, II, 69-71; Pollen, *English Catholics*, 236-37.

too weak to act alone. These acts are done in his name, "yet who seeth not that they be maintained under-hand by some princes his confederates?" And to clinch his point he reminded his hearers from whence the Papal expedition sailed, "and by direction of whose ministers they received their victual and furniture."

Having chilled the blood of his audience with this dire picture of foreign menace, Mildmay went on to retail domestic happenings. The Pope was directly blamed for the obstinate disobedience of the recusants and for the appearance of "a sort of hypocrites, naming themselves Jesuits, a rabble of vagrant friars newly sprung up and running through the world to trouble the Church of God." Under the pretense of religion they seek "to stir up sedition, to the peril of Her Majesty and her good subjects." He called for laws "more strict and severe to constrain them [the recusants] to yield their open obedience, at the least, to Her Majesty in causes of religion and not to live as they list to the perilous example of others and to the encouraging of their own evil affected minds." The rest of the speech called for measures—largely fiscal—necessary to preserve the state against its external Catholic enemies.[19]

We may assume that Mildmay was speaking for his colleagues on the Council, and that he had royal assent. But what followed was a characteristically untidy piece of Tudor legislative history. The Houses, given Mildmay's lead, devised two separate bills, neither of which was to reach the statute book. The effort reflects rather too accurately the strains within the Protestant ranks, which manifested themselves even when they faced the Papist foe.

The Lords, probably mirroring the opinions of the bishops, would have confirmed the existing practice of the High Commission by giving that body power to fine heavily both for nonattendance and for noncommunication. It would have placed the responsibility for enforcement squarely on ecclesiastical shoulders. The Commons' bill, on the other hand, carefully excluded the ecclesiastical authorities and threw the whole burden of executing the act onto the civil officers—the justices of the peace. Its terms were very harsh; capital penalties abounded, as did heavy fines and indefinite terms of imprisonment. It reflected the inflamed passions of the Lower House but also cast doubt on their good judgment, for it would have been very difficult legislation to enforce. Probably it also reflected something else—the Commons' deep distaste for ecclesiastical jurisdictions, even when used against Papists. Once again they were determined to wrest control of religious matters from the Supreme Governor and her ecclesiastical servants and place it firmly in lay hands, their own.[20]

In any case, neither bill passed, probably because of royal intervention. Lacking the intense Protestant conviction of so many of her subjects, the Queen also lacked their bigotry. She could not quite bring herself to believe that her Catholic subjects would place their faith before their allegiance to her. As with the Puritans, Elizabeth failed to understand the dilemma which intense religious conviction thrust upon her most serious-minded subjects. At any rate, the act which now emerged under the auspices of Sir Francis Knollys was widely different in its terms. This statute confined itself to the problem of nonattendance, setting aside altogether refusal of communion. A heavy fine—£20 per month—was now the principal weapon to be used against the recusant, obviously against the wealthier ones since few subjects would have incomes equal to such a monthly drain. Although certification of delinquency was to come from the ordinary, responsibility for detection and information was largely that of the JP's, and legal action would take place at assizes or sessions. Ecclesiastical jurisdiction was mentioned only in a clause at the end of the act declaring that nothing in it abridged existing Church authority.[21]

It is a curious piece of legislation, for the very terms of enforcement which are spelled out in its clauses go far towards blunting the alleged aims of the enactment. It would be hard to administer since responsibility for grass-roots action was too

[20] Walker, "Recusants," 121-28.
[21] Neale I, 387-88; Walker, "Recusants," 130-33.

widely and loosely diffused; and, as Catholic lawyers were prompt to point out,[22] it had many legal loopholes for the more wily recusant. But it was consistent in its obstinate adherence to the original conception of recusancy legislation since it limited its demands to mere attendance at the parish church rather than on participation in the Anglican sacrament. Once again it reflected the Queen's belief, shared by at least some of her councillors, that she was not meddling with laymen's consciences—their inner and spiritual life—but constraining only their outward and formal behavior.

But the new statutes, however inept in formulation, did mark a new stage in the government's treatment of Catholic dissent. Hitherto the Elizabethan government had been pressuring a group of recalcitrant laity into attending the services prescribed by law. Leaderless, disorganized, and politically inconsequential, they could, it was assumed, ultimately be chivvied into the required conformity. But now it was clear that they had found, in the missionary clergy, new and effective leaders, a framework of organization, and the prospect of survival into an indefinite future. Hence a change in strategy was forced on the government. In a continuing effort to coerce them into the fold of the established Church, laity were to be put under the stronger pressures of fine and imprisonment. But the Catholic clergy—new and dangerous enemies—were to be brought under the ban of treason. Against them it was to be all-out war.

For the priests were, in the government's eyes, as much warriors in this contest as the men who landed in Ireland. In addition to the missionary effort and the Irish enterprises, already discussed, there were other pointers which to many Protestants seemed sure and certain proofs of a gathering Catholic conspiracy. Parma's steady advances in the Low Countries were frightening enough, but there was now the prospect of a restored Catholicism in Scotland, where Esmé D'Aubigny had wormed his way into the royal confidence and was about to overthrow the Protestant Regent Morton. In

---

[22] Walker, "Recusants," 140-44.

London the Spanish ambassador Mendoza was fast assuming the role of protector-general to the English Catholics and of arch-plotter against the government to which he was accredited. For the Protestant beholder the pieces were falling into place with an ease which served to confirm his worst suspicions.

All these developments working together widened and complicated the struggle between the government and the Catholics. It now had to be waged on several fronts: at home against the recusant laity and the missionary priests; at home and abroad against the conspiracies hatched jointly by the Spanish ambassador and the militant English exiles; in Scotland against the power of Catholic Spain wherever it was manifest. These battles were to be waged in one form or another for much of the remaining years of the reign. Most immediately they triggered a polemic between the government and the Catholic exile leadership which to some extent parallels that between the established Church and the Puritans and which compelled the regime to examine the principles by which it struck at the Catholics.

Catholic polemic against the Elizabethan regime had been slow to emerge. The slowness of the Papacy to define its position *vis à vis* the regime damped political criticism during the first decade of the reign, and the writers of those years concerned themselves largely with theological issues.[23] But it was not only lack of guidance from Rome which kept English Catholic spokesmen in check; there was also a very basic uncertainty which arose from their own habits of thought and from their principles. The English Protestant regime had not come into being, as in Scotland, by a *coup d'état* or by open rebellion but by an act of state which observed at least the outward forms of legitimacy. Nor were the Catholics willing as yet to challenge Elizabeth's claim to the throne. Hence any criticism of her regime had to be angled in such a way as to avoid a direct assault on its legitimacy. Even the bull of 1570 did not open the way, at least to the English exiles, for a repudiation of Elizabeth's authority as their ruler.

[23] Thomas H. Clancy, *Papist Pamphleteers* (Chicago, 1964), 3.

The first major attempt to mount criticism within the awkward constraints imposed by these conditions was the *Treatise of Treasons* of 1572, perhaps written by the Bishop of Ross.[24] Struck off in the heated aftermath of the Ridolfi episode, the first half of the book is a defense of Mary Stuart and Norfolk; the second half mounts a wide-ranging critique of Elizabethan policy. The author evades any direct criticism of the Queen by the gimmicky device of casting her in the role of a dupe—deluded by two self-serving Machiavellians, Cecil and Bacon, who are seen as the authors of all policy since 1558. Marred by this bit of political fantasy and by polemical overkill, the book nevertheless mounts a fairly coherent attack on Elizabethan policy.

Its idolatrous and quite literal-minded devotion to the old order seems to confirm the government's view of the Catholics as merely nostalgic conservatives who would bring back a vanished past. More than once it echoes very directly the manifestoes of the Pilgrims of Grace a generation earlier. Denouncing the break with an immemorial past and with a universal religious tradition, it calls for a meticulous rebuilding of the fallen temple in complete and loving detail. The present calamity is seen not merely in religious terms but also in broader social dimensions; base-born men have replaced the ancient nobility and the whole social order is in process of dissolution. Manners and morals are hopelessly corrupted and decay proceeds apace. The present regime is pictured as a "Machiavellian state and regiment where religion is put behind in the second and last place, where the civil polity, I mean, is preferred before it, not limited by any rules of religion but the religion framed to serve the time and policy."[25] At a more pragmatic level the present government is assailed for a foreign policy which has broken "with the mightiest and sincerest friend [the Queen] had on earth," King Philip, and for the rupture of the ancient amity with the House of Burgundy, leaving England isolated and vulnerable. The government thought enough

---

[24] *A Treatise of Treasons against Queen Elizabeth and the Crown of England* ([Antwerp], 1572).

[25] *Ibid.*, preface, A5; 101-2.

of the tract to ban it. Cecil scribbled pages of notes in angry rebuttal,[26] but there was no published answer. Perhaps they felt this simplistic longing for a vanished past would defeat itself by its nostalgic fantasy.

It was not until a decade later, in the changed atmosphere of the 1580's, after the execution of the first missionary martyrs (particularly Edmund Campion), that the government felt moved to issue a manifesto of its own which was at once an attack on the militant Catholics and a defense of the regime. The author was almost certainly William Cecil. *The Execution of Justice in England* was aimed, as the title[27] proclaims, "against certain stirrers of sedition and adherents to the traitors and enemies of the realm" and denied that they were being persecuted "for questions of religion, as is falsely reported and published" in their defense. At his trial Campion defended himself against the charge of treason—and the denial was repeated at the trials of other priests—by asserting that the mission of the seminarians was entirely a spiritual one, the rescue of souls, and quite totally divorced from any political aims.

Burghley's response to this claim insisted on lumping the seminarians together with the northern rebels and the English participants in the Irish expedition in one great mass of treason. The link which bound them in a single traitorous enterprise was, according to the Treasurer, the Papal bull of 1570, which did "import that Her Majesty is not the lawful Queen of England"; that her subjects are discharged from obedience and "warranted to disobey her and her laws."[28] Given this premise, any Catholic activity, open rebellion or secret preaching, sought ultimately to overthrow the regime. Reconciliation to the spiritual authority of Rome was in fact a political act, for to acknowledge the authority of the Pope, who had deposed the Queen, was to deny her right to obedience. Renewed allegiance to Rome was automatically treason to the Crown of England.

[26] *Tudor Proclamations*, II, 377 n. 1.
[27] William Cecil, *The Execution of Justice in England* (1583) and William Allen, *A True, Sincere and Modest Defense of English Catholics* (1588), ed. Robert M. Kingdon (Ithaca, 1965), 1.
[28] Cecil, *Execution of Justice*, 13.

Having attacked the Catholics as traitors, Cecil now went on to defend the Crown's right to obedience in matters ecclesiastical. His arguments were almost as old-fashioned as his opponents'; if they harked back to the Pilgrimage of Grace, the Lord Treasurer repeated the arguments of the Henrician apologists. There were the usual Biblical citations such as Romans 13:1 or Luke 22:25-26,[29] and the same appeal to history. Gregory VII was trotted out to play the villain's role as the usurper who was the founder of Papal claims and whose attempts against the Emperor Henry IV were an exact parallel to Pius V's assault on Queen Elizabeth. Other historical instances were drawn from English and French history, and even the quarrels between Mary and Pope Paul IV were pressed into service. The Queen was represented as patiently enduring the Papal persecutions which began with *Regnans in Excelsis*, taking measures only when compelled by the fact of open rebellion. Far from being a deliberate persecutor, aggressively striking at the missionaries, she was merely a sovereign driven by threats to her security and that of her people to take necessarily severe measures of defense.

What is most interesting in Cecil's argument is its bland refusal to deal with the fact of religious revolution. Ostentatiously historical in its reference to the earlier Middle Ages, it was resolutely silent about those statutes of the last thirty years which had revolutionized the religious order in England. It ignored just precisely what the *Treatise of Treasons* had vividly emphasized—the differences in practice and in belief which separated the old and the new religious worlds. Cecil's stubborn insistence on sticking to the Henrician categories—on seeing the issues solely in constitutional and institutional terms, sturdily pushing aside the doctrinal significance of the changes, especially since 1547—is entirely consistent with the government's stance ever since the opening of the reign. It provoked, in the following year, the able exposition of Cardinal Allen, who laid out at considerable length and with creditable intellectual flair a Catholic rejoinder to Cecil's argument.

[29] *Ibid.*, 22-23.

The first part of Allen's *Defense of English Catholics* reiterates Campion's argument at his trial, the solely spiritual goals of the priests' mission, the reconciliation of souls to Holy Church, and the specific prohibition laid on them to deal with anything at all touching matters political. As for the awkward question of the bull of 1570, he attempted to deal with it by softening its implications. First he downgraded its initial significance, not so much a judgment as a warning, and then went on to argue that for the present and the foreseeable future its execution had been suspended by the Pope. For the modern reader it is hard not to feel that Allen, as much as Cecil, skates away from the main issue. The Treasurer insists on ignoring the doctrinal content of the Elizabethan settlement while the Cardinal refuses to admit any link between the pastoral ministrations of the seminarians and the political intentions of the Papacy towards England.

To some extent Allen makes up for this deficiency by the argument in the later chapters of his book.[30] He carefully avoids the particular relationship between the reigning Pope and the reigning monarch of England, leaving that case to the judgment of his ecclesiastical superiors, but he makes quite clear that as a general principle the Pope does have the power to judge and if necessary to depose unrighteous monarchs. The Bible, history, canon law are all pressed into service—the traditional medieval arguments for the *sacerdotium* as opposed to the *imperium*. This manner of argumentation, although a great deal fuller than Cecil's, has much of the same curiously evasive character to it. The rather casuistical argument on behalf of the missionary priests—that their role is purely spiritual —fails to come to grips with the immediate and haunting problem which faced Elizabethan Catholics: what was their lawful relationship to their Protestant sovereign. Allen shifted the burden of his theoretical argument away from the contemporary scene into an historical past. The reader might choose to make his own deductions about right behavior in the present, but the Cardinal evaded the responsibility of stating them himself.

[30] Allen, *True Defense*, chaps. 5-8.

In part this unwillingness on both sides to address the most urgent questions of principle—what was to be rendered unto God and unto Caesar—arose from embarrassing variants of their basic assumptions. The politique Cecil could not bring himself to deal with the problem of the state's doctrinal authority; he was content to live with a faceless Erastianism which asserted, without explaining, the overriding power of the Crown in matters spiritual. Allen, on the other hand, was still unready to deal with the thorny question of deposition, to look fully at the irreconcilable claims of Pope and Queen.

In addition one must take into account another basic assumption of each side: that the opposition did not represent a genuine religion. This cannot be dismissed as mere polemic although that is such an element in the intemperate language used. But for the Protestant, Catholicism was in fact nothing but mere "idolatry," while the Catholic was sincere in dismissing his opponents as "atheists." The gap in sensibilities which had opened up in the generation between 1520 and 1550 had become a wide gulf between those who were deeply committed to either the old or the new faith. For the Protestant the ceremonial, the ritual, the symbolism of the Catholic faith was a kind of toying with holy things, while the Catholic in his turn saw, especially in Elizabethan Protestantism, a kaleidoscopic confusion of sects which was totally at odds with the universality and order which were for him the hallmarks of true faith.

On this inconclusive note the argument was to come to a halt. There would be abundant polemics on both sides in the years to come but no great joining of issues, as occurred in the quarrel with the Puritans. In the latter case there was still some sense of common ground and a conviction that the opposition, except perhaps for a few irrational zealots, could be persuaded by the force of argument. The bishops still hoped for the assimilation of the nonconformists, while even the most ardent Puritans were not quite ready to take the road of separation.

But in the Catholic case there is a sense, perceptible even in the 1580's, of total irreconcilability, of two camps separated by an unbridgeable chasm. And already in the last section of Allen's book there is the first hint of a radical solution.[31] The bloodshed and misery which now afflicted so many Englishmen could, he hinted, be ended if Catholics might "by license or connivance if never so inoffensively" have the exercise of their religion. He pointed to the example of Germany and Switzerland or of the Huguenots of France, or indeed of "the very Turks or very Jews among Christians" as instances of such a tolerated status. Implicit in such a plea was the notion of separation, of a ghetto where a barely tolerated sect might be allowed the minimal privilege of survival. While it seemed totally contradictory to the basic principles which either the English Church or the Roman Church held, the governors of the former body, as we shall see, would move obliquely and reluctantly but visibly to a position approximating that of Cardinal Allen.

But this is to look ahead; the immediate problem in the wake of the 1581 legislation was the enforcement of the new law. The Privy Council threw its whole weight into setting the local machinery in operation, by no means an easy task. It is clear that the Council looked to the bishop and his clergy as the prime movers in winkling out recusancy and bringing the offenders to the attention of the civil courts. Strenuous as the Council's demands were, they were only very partially successful in the primary task of identifying recusants, far less so in their efforts to bring them to judgment. Local parsons and local JP's proved sluggish at best in their responses and in some cases pretty clearly recalcitrant. The sparse success of the government is vividly mirrored in the Exchequer receipt of recusancy fines. For instance, of 1,939 recusants from 22 counties listed by the Council in December 1582, only 55 appear as paying fines in the years over the five years following the passage of the statute. This state of affairs was particularly marked in the North, where the Catholic population was probably largest, but the failures of enforcement repeated themselves in such southern dioceses as Winchester and Chichester. Four years after the passage of the statute, a period in which the Council had been unremitting in its pressure on local authorities, some

[31] *Ibid.*, 261.

55 recusants, from 18 counties and 2 cities had paid in a total of £6,356, a dismayingly poor return on the efforts exerted.[32]

In 1585 the government began to seek other means to harass the Catholic nonconformists. They needed money for the war in the Netherlands, and in November of that year the Privy Council considered extraordinary means for raising money (outside the Parliamentary grants). They apparently considered a levy which would have fallen on the whole population, but in the end settled for a special tax on clergy and recusants to pay for 1,000 horsemen. Lists of well-to-do recusants were drawn up by the bishops, about 200 in number, and it was hoped that as much as £7,000 might be brought in from them. In this case it was the sheriffs who were made responsible for collection; the sum finally gathered in was something over £3,000, far less than had been hoped for but more than statutory fines had brought in any twelve-month period.[33]

In any case it led the Council into an interesting experiment. Recusants were to be given the opportunity to make a yearly payment of a fixed sum in lieu of their fine. For a payment of about a half of the normal annual fine of £240 they would be freed from the vexatious attentions of informers and the exactions of the courts. A kind of bargain was to be struck, with advantages to both sides; there was no alteration in the statutes, nor diminution of the grave offense committed, but there was to be mitigation of the consequences. It was an oblique approach to a kind of legalized toleration. Offers were received from over 300 recusants in 24 counties. They included a substantial number of poorer recusants who had not fallen under the penalty of the fine. But the individual sums they offered and the totals of all their proposals were disappointingly small, a little over £3,000. The local officials had been little more than haphazard in searching out candidates for the scheme, but even allowing for this, it seems likely that the recusants regarded the move as a retreat on the government's part, a confession that the statute was unworkable. The gov-

---

[32] Walker, "Recusants," 149-54, 158-59, 165, 189, 193-95, 200.

[33] *Ibid.*, 201, quoting PRO, SP 12/185/64; Walker, "Recusants," 207-208.

ernment were particularly anxious to avoid any such imputation, especially at a time when there was every indication
that recusants were growing in number. There was nothing
to do but forget the whole proposition.[34]

Indeed by 1586 the Council had good reason to be discouraged. The flow of money from fines was in decline; more important, the record for the past half dozen years was a dismal
one. Only 69 recusants had in fact paid in money, at least half
of them men of enough eminence to be personally known to
the Council. Their geographical distribution was skewed in a
most curious way. The notoriously Catholic North was hardly
represented at all and the three counties of Norfolk, Suffolk,
and Hampshire account for 29 out of the 69 names.[35] Clearly
such enforcement as had been achieved represented either local
pockets of enthusiastic magistrates or, more frequently, simply
the fact that circumstances had made the recusant known to
the Privy Council. Such men were naturally kept under closer
surveillance and felt the full penalties of the law. If the whole
policy of the government towards the Catholics was not to be
nullified, new measures must be adopted.

The meeting of Parliament in 1586 offered the opportunity
for fresh legislation. This time the statute passed swiftly, almost certainly under Burghley's careful direction. It had three
important provisions: (1) a shift in venue from the sessions
of the peace to assizes; (2) one conviction only sufficed hence-
forward to lay one under the repetitive penalty of the monthly
fine; (3) in case of default the Crown was empowered to seize
two-thirds of the offender's lands and to receive the income in
lieu of the fine. No new offense was created nor any new penalty, but the procedure for enforcing existing penalties was
very appreciably tightened up. By shifting responsibility to the
assizes, the Privy Council brought the whole matter much
more closely under its own supervision. Many minor provisions closed loopholes hitherto open to the wilier recusant. It
was a clearcut assertion of the government's determination to

[34] Walker, "Recusants," 209-10, 219, 221-23.
[35] *Ibid.*, 226-28.

make the recusancy code an effective hammer of the Catholics.[36]

How successful was the new act in increasing pressure on the recusant population? On the surface, the gains were impressive. In the nine terms from Michaelmas 1582 through the same feast 1586 the total "take" in fines was almost £9,000; for the eleven terms running from Easter 1587 to Easter 1592 inclusive over £36,000 were credited to the Queen's account. But if we examine these figures a bit more carefully the results dwindle in their significance. It is true that the number of payers of fines had risen by 1593 to 167, of whom only 45 had been paying before 1587; the number of counties had risen from 22 to 32 and included significant numbers from such northern centers of the old faith as Lancashire and Yorkshire.[37] But the most striking fact that can be extracted from the recusant rolls for the years 1587 to 1592 is the high proportion of total income that was being paid in by a very small number of wealthy recusants. Sixteen such gentlemen paid no less than £26,700 out of the total of £36,332 received by the Exchequer. Residents of thirteen different counties, they were obviously men of substance, although for the most part not of the first rank of gentry. Circumstances had made each of them known to the Council; their obstinacy in refusing conformity ensured continuing pressure upon them. But what the results suggest about the government's policy is interesting. These men had in a measure become token recusants; they were probably not the sixteen most wealthy or most prominent Catholic gentry; there were certainly many others of equal wealth and eminence. The sustained pressure upon them (they endured imprisonment, especially during the Armada crisis) was a signal to the whole recusant community of the government's continuing abhorrence of their position and its determination to punish such acts. Yet it was also evident that the government's power to suppress the recusant community was

[36] *Statutes of the Realm*, 29 Elizabeth c. 6; Walker, "Recusants," 238-46.

[37] Walker, "Recusants," 248-49, 252, 277.

limited. In addition to those paying regular fines, there was a second category of men, mostly somewhat poorer, who had to endure the sequestration of two-thirds of their estates by the Crown in order to meet the fines imposed on them. But these two groups taken together were in fact cast in the role of scapegoats for the larger Catholic body. So long as their resources would serve to meet the heavy burden laid on them, they were in a sense vicarious sufferers for the sins of their co-religionists. The Elizabethan regime's persecution of its Catholic lay nonconformists was taking on a certain ritual character in which a representative group were made to act for the whole. Implicitly the government was acknowledging its inability or unwillingness to carry out the specifications of its penal statutes and hence its ultimate abandonment of the original goals which it had set itself early in the reign. Tacitly the government was prepared to allow the continued existence of a nonconforming sect if it were prepared to put up with the suffering which fine, imprisonment, and harassment imposed upon some of its members.

But if the government was disposed to yield a little—very little—to lay recusants, to allow them a bare and harsh survival, it was not so disposed towards the priests of the Catholic mission. Already the legislation of 1571 made the granting of absolution (for attendance at the Anglican service) an act of treason; ten years later this provision was strengthened by declaring any person possessing such powers of absolution to be a traitor. In the session of 1584—in the aftermath of Allen's book—even more rigorous legislation was demanded. In a speech on the first day of the session, Sir Walter Mildmay[38] turned all his heaviest guns on the seminarians. Hammering away once again at the bull of 1570, he portrayed the Pope as would-be universal monarch, the disposer of all earthly kingdoms. Given these ambitions the Pope entertained "against us *odium implacabile* for we can never make our peace with him." Upon him depended "divers other malicious and secret practitioners and of them most pernicious those that are called

[38] Northampton Record Office, Fitzwilliam of Milton Mss., ff. 2-4.

Jesuits and seminary priests, a rabble of vagrant runagates" who seek "to stir sedition and nourish the corrupt affection of evil subjects" under a pretense of saving souls. He then went on to cite those parts of Allen's book which rehearsed the eleventh-century Papal claims against the Emperors. All these assumptions taken together led Mildmay to the inescapable conclusion that the Papacy's aims were the deposition of the Queen, since only thus could they accomplish the restoration of the old faith. In his peroration he demanded that measures be taken by Parliament againt these men who "like raging waters would destroy whole countries"—measures strong enough to terrify them from even setting foot in the Queen's dominions.

The response to this appeal was a statute[39] which in effect outlawed English Catholic priests. Those now in the country were required to leave within forty days; after that their very presence in the realm would be an act of treason; students remaining in the seminaries were also by that act traitors. A move to make the teaching of the Romish religion in itself treason was turned back by the argument that this confounded treason and heresy and allowed Catholics to argue that Protestants dared not answer doctrine with doctrine. Whatever the motive, the defeat of this motion meant that the English government remained resolutely secular in its opposition to Rome, condemning the priests straightforwardly as political enemies of the realm. Other provisions in the statute brought anyone who offered protection to a priest under the penalties of praemunire (softened by the Lords from a Commons provision making it treason).[40] It also prohibited sending children abroad for their education without license.

The government had not, of course, waited for this reinforcing statute to open its campaign against the priests. The first to suffer was Cuthbert Mayne, executed in 1577; in the peak years of persecution, from the passage of the statute of 1581 through the Armada crisis, up to 1590, 103 Catholics died for their faith, of whom 78 were priests (in 1588 there were 21

[39] *Ibid.*, ff. 11v-16v, for debate.   [40] Neale II, 38.

clerical martyrs). In the remaining years of the reign another 88 suffered, of whom 53 were clerics. Hughes gives a total of 67 clerical martyrs for the years 1582 to 1591 and a total of 183 (123 priests) for the years 1577 to 1603.[41] Exact figures are uncertain, but somewhere between 120 and 130 priests were executed after 1577. This figure has to be set against the totals of ordinations in the continental seminaries, Douay-Rheims, Rome (after 1579), and Valladolid (after 1589); they added up to well over 400 (438 according to Hughes). Nearly 100 had reached England before Campion and Persons arrived in 1580; 200 more were ordained, and 216 sent back to the homeland from 1579 to 1585.[42] These are impressive numbers for an organization working under such great disadvantages. (It is worth remembering that Cambridge was awarding about 100 B.A. degrees annually in the decade 1580-1589, some of whom but not all would enter the Anglican priesthood.)[43]

At any rate, these numbers help to make clear the alarm and fear which the English government displayed after 1581 and go far to explain the savagery with which the attack against the Catholic priests was maintained. Every weapon at the command of the regime was employed. A minority of the martyrs (sixteen) were tried under the ancient statute of 1352, the balance under one or other of the acts of Elizabeth's reign.[44] Of these the great majority, 94, suffered under the act of 1584. A set of test questions, six in number, were devised to be put to each prisoner, all of which turned on the validity and the consequences of Pius V's bull of 1570.[45] All were designed to extract from the accused some acknowledgment of the political nature of his activities. To such accusations the missionary priests and their superiors at Rome were vociferous in denial,

[41] Patrick McGrath, *Papists and Puritans under Elizabeth I* (New Haven, 1967), 177. Philip Hughes, *The Reformation in England* (3 vols., New York, 1951-1954), III, 293, 338.

[42] McGrath, *Papists*, 111; Hughes, *Reformation*, III, 293.

[43] See table 3 in Laurence Stone, ed., *The University in Society* (2 vols., Princeton, 1974), I, 94.

[44] Hughes, *Reformation*, III, 342.

[45] *Ibid.*, 360; Allen, *True Defense*, 119-20.

insisting on the purely spiritual nature of their ministrations. The English government with equal vehemence insisted on the necessarily political character of any attempt at reconciliation to Rome. Both claims were honestly made; both, to modern eyes, are flawed. Campion and his fellow-workers were explicitly instructed to avoid all political questions,[46] and we need not doubt that the priests faithfully obeyed instructions. They saw themselves as shepherds of souls, of a wandering and endangered flock, and behaved accordingly.

But the English government viewed the priests from quite another angle. For them the powers which Rome sought to exercise in England were temporal ones; the key document was the bull of 1570, which for them simply implemented the Papacy's ancient claim to ultimate sovereignty over secular rulers. The Jesuits, keenly aware of the problem which this presented for their mission, had asked and received an interpretation of the bull's status from Gregory XIII in 1580.[47] This explicitly stated that the bull did not bind Catholics until its public execution became possible. Hence a missioner priest could with clear conscience give his allegiance to the Queen. But it was a double-edged document which, seen through hostile eyes, could be represented in a very sinister light. Logically, once a sufficient number of Englishmen were reconverted to the Roman obedience, the conditions for fulfilling the bull would come into existence. Seen in this light, the mission was merely a necessary first step towards the destruction of the Elizabethan regime. Unluckily a copy of the interpretation fell into Burghley's hands and the operative clauses were printed by him in the *Execution of Justice*.[48]

But it was not only a logical dilemma which was forced on the missionaries. Their activities were entirely pastoral in character, but the institution which they served, and indeed

[46] J. H. Pollen, "The Politics of English Catholics during the Reign of Queen Elizabeth, III," in *The Month* 99 (1902), 293, and Campion's statement, *ibid.*, 294-95.

[47] Arnold O. Meyer, *England and the Catholic Church under Queen Elizabeth* (1915, reissue 1967), 138-40.

[48] Cecil, *Execution of Justice*, 18.

their immediate superiors, were in fact deeply engaged in straightforwardly political activities aimed at the English government. The oft-cited invasions of Ireland in 1579 and 1580 paled in their significance beside the elaborate conspiracy hatched out after D'Aubigny's arrival in Scotland in 1579. This involved not only Esmé Stuart but also the Duke of Guise, Ambassador Mendoza, and the Papacy. In this, Persons and Allen were directly involved, as were various members of the Society of Jesus.[49] While the English authorities did not have full knowledge of this conspiracy until after the fact, they had plentiful pointers to a large-scale international Catholic conspiracy, in which, of course, most of them implicitly believed even in the absence of confirmatory evidence. Ultimately with the discovery of the Throckmorton plot, they were to see their worst suspicions confirmed. In short, by the early 1580's the English ministers were set in their belief in a grand Catholic plot in which the mission of the seminarians played an important role which justified the most rigorous measures of repression. With far fuller knowledge of the evidence, we realize this was an inaccurate perception of Catholic activities. They were far less well organized and centrally directed than the English supposed, but the latter were not wrong in assuming that the Papacy and its allies would, if it could, use worldly weapons to bring down the heretical regime. Caught between the fears of the regime and the contradictory practices of their own superiors, the heroic priests were hapless victims, protesting their genuine innocence to captors who had strong grounds for refusing to believe their protests.

For the English Catholic laity the prospects were almost equally grim. Those whose faith was reconfirmed or rekindled by the mission and who made a conscious decision to remain faithful to the Roman Church found their position, particularly from the late 1570's onwards, increasingly painful. Their fellow-dissidents, the Puritans, however frustrated and irritated, still thought of themselves as members of the English

[49] Pollen, "Politics," 297-305; Conyers Read, *Mr Secretary Walsingham and the Policy of Queen Elizabeth* (3 vols., Cambridge, Mass., 1925), II, chap. 10 *passim*.

Church, of a body imperfectly reformed, but at least one in which they could remain, striving for better things. But the Catholic faced not the claims of a rival faith but mere chaos. The Church of England was not an imperfect body but no body at all, mere anarchy, pregnant with all imaginable evils. It was a contrast between impenetrable blackness and the purest rays of light.

What strategies were open to the Catholic? In the early years of the reign the simplest and most familiar was resistance by whatever secular means he might grasp: rebellion, conspiracy, and foreign arms. This required leadership and organization and the Catholics possessed neither. The Marian bishops would have faced martyrdom with equanimity but abhorred the very thought of resistance to the anointed sovereign. Some of the laity, a little bolder but utterly confused, did bumblingly attempt all three means—and failed disastrously. It was in the wake of that failure that the missioners appeared on the scene, offering pastoral ministrations and a renewed spiritual life. For the ordinary lay Catholic the revival of his faith gradually opened up a new possibility—bleak, strenuous, barely tolerable. He began to shape a pattern of life which would give him the essentials of his faith, above all, the action of the sacraments, at the cost of social exclusion and heavy financial penalties. Even as early as Allen's book the possibility of some such toleration is hinted at, and in the longer run this ghetto-like existence was to become the goal which the English Catholics sought to attain.

But in the short run the alternatives were not so clear. For the priests and for most of the laity the frightening uncertainties of day-to-day existence were too great to leave much time for envisioning the longer future. For the exiles the temptation to seek foreign aid had a potent attraction since the 1560's when they first flirted with the Spanish ambassador. In 1569 they had of course turned directly to him for assistance. Allen had been aware of the vague plans for using Don John to release the captive Mary.[50] Sander had been directly involved in

[50] Hughes, *Reformation*, III, 315.

the Irish expedition, and after 1579 both Allen and Persons became involved in the elaborate plot built around D'Aubigny and closely linked with the Spanish ambassador, Mendoza. Finally, they looked to the Armada to solve their problem, although their involvement in its inception and preparation was minimal. In short, the exile leaders, both clerical and lay, continued until very late in the reign to pull all the strings they could in the hope of a Catholic restoration brought about by foreign intervention.

The differences in point of view between a resident community suffering under a harsh persecution, largely fragmented, and deeply respectful of and loyal to their sovereign, and an exile leadership, linked to England's great international rivals and increasingly political in orientation, played up the contradictions inherent in the Catholic situation. As an integral part of a supra-national community they were dependent ultimately on the disposition of Rome itself and more immediately on the high-ranking clergy who spoke for them at the Papal court. Their own clergy had to be trained abroad and they were made constantly aware of their subordination to these distant authorities whose knowledge of their affairs was imperfect and whose own goals were shaped by many forces unknown to the English community. The English Catholics could only struggle on from day to day, a community too strong to be exterminated except by weapons which the Elizabethan government did not possess, but too weak to gain any real leverage such as the Huguenots enjoyed in France or, more humbly, Catholics would ultimately possess in the United Provinces.

On the other side of the fence the government's position *vis à vis* the Catholics was not without its ambiguities. Like the Catholics they viewed their opponents with contempt; there was a total lack of respect, for what they saw was not a rival confession but a mindless, a superstitious, tyranny; the very existence of an English Catholic community seemed to them anathema. As we have seen, the first reaction of the regime was the bland assumption that once the deluded survivors of a fading past died out the relics of their worn-out superstition would perish with them. The shock of the Catholic revival after 1574 was all the greater, and the English leaders obstinately refused to believe in its genuineness. Rather than admit the facts of a religious revival of great intensity, they preferred to believe in a political conspiracy, engineered by the exiles and their foreign allies. They persisted in seeing the Roman Church in the terms set out in Henrician times as the alien instrument of a power-hungry priestly caste determined to bend the whole world to obedience, in things temporal as well as spiritual. The priests were the soldiers of this great organization and had to be fought tooth and nail; the laity were deluded men and women, led astray, who needed to be disciplined with enough severity to force their return to the fold of the national Church. From 1580 onwards the fears and the hostility of the government mounted rapidly as it came to perceive the English Catholics as a fifth column within the realm, plotting with its enemies to bring the regime to the ground. Such a view was, of course, consistent with the intensely politique outlook of the English leadership, which more and more thought of Protestantism in political rather than in spiritual terms. Such a vision, blinkered in important ways, could not accommodate the notion of a purely spiritual allegiance. But at least it did mean that Catholics were treated as political enemies whose power must be broken, rather than as heretics whose very existence must be rooted out for fear that the deadly infection they bore would kill the souls of a whole nation. Priests were to be killed, imprisoned, or banished as circumstance dictated; the laity was to be harassed to the last degree of discomfort by fine and imprisonment, but there was never any thought of a campaign of extermination.

There were those among their bitterest enemies, especially those most zealous for the new faith, who would have pursued such a policy had it been within their power. But the politique cast of mind of the English leadership, which displayed no interest in the enforcement of some kind of doctrinal standard as the basis for national unity, assured that the political impotence of the dissenters rather than doctrinal uniformity for all would be the regime's goal. These fundamental differences of opinion as to the very nature of the state and the purposes of social organization were ironically a kind of guarantee to the Catholics that they would never be persecuted to the point of extinction.

It is worth pausing to examine the range of attitudes within the leadership which led to this outcome. Comparison with the Puritan case is instructive. There the strongest impulse for repressive action came from the Queen herself, albeit fitfully. Within the Council and even more among the governing groups in the shires, the Puritans had many friends, some warm adherents, others more vaguely sympathetic, but few enemies disposed to pursue them to the bitter end. It was only when the bench of bishops threw up a leader determined to break them and who won royal backing that suppression of their movement was relatively successful.

The Catholics had no supporters in high places who actively sympathized with their cause. The Queen herself was perhaps their best friend, not because she shared their opinions but because her indifference to religious questions left her without the theological rancor which affected most of her councillors. Coolly viewed as a merely political phenomenon, the Catholics did not stir Elizabeth's fears as they did those of her court. Her insensitivity to religious passions made it difficult, perhaps impossible, for her to grasp the intensity of feeling which moved her most devoutly Catholic subjects and, more important, left her quite unable to imagine an English subject who would place his religious loyalties before his native allegiance. The Queen repeatedly checked proposals to use extremist methods against the recusants, and softened the terms of legislation against them. But, so far as we can tell, she approved of the repressive measures taken against both laity and clergy.

Within the Council there seems to have been little division of opinion about the gravity of the Catholic menace, although Walsingham, the most Puritan of the leaders in that body, may have taken the lead in active persecution. But as we have seen above, all attempts at a really thoroughgoing enforcement of the penal laws were blunted by the uncooperativeness of local officials from JP's down to church wardens. Arguing from the halfhearted efforts of the local authorities even when pressed by the Council to take action, one supposes that most of the local leaders, while cheerfully conformist to the new religion, did not think the persecution of their recusant neighbors worth the candle. It suggests that large segments of the ruling classes were more or less indifferent to the internal Catholic menace. They simply failed to perceive their recusant neighbors as anything more than eccentrics, harmless eccentrics for the most part. Some of them were men of position and highly connected, and to have troubled them for their absence from the parish church would only have involved the accuser in a tangle of dangerous, possibly damaging, rivalries. Consequently it was only those recusants who by the boldness of their posture positively flaunted their views or those whose eminence made them easily visible from Westminster who suffered for their faith. The best the government could accomplish with the laity was to harass and distress a small elite of wealthy recusants. With the clergy they might count themselves more successful, since they quite literally killed about a quarter of the missioners ordained between 1577 and 1603. But high as the percentage was, the ranks of the Catholic clergy continued to be filled by new recruits and the lay community to be served by a devoted and vigorous pastorate.

What the outcome of this confrontation between two adversaries who so fundamentally misunderstood each other, whose goals were at such cross-purposes, and who were so unevenly matched could hardly be predicted in the tumultuous decade of the 1580's. It would take another ten years of experience before the notion that the Roman Catholic dissidents might be a permanent feature of the English scene began feebly to take root. In the later 1580's, given the recent history of conspiracy against the Queen's life and the looming menace of invasion by the ultra-Catholic power of Spain, such a development seemed very unlikely indeed.

PART II

ENGLAND AND
HER NEIGHBORS

CHAPTER 7

THE CHANGING SCENE,

1560-1572

AT THE OPENING of the 1570's the shadows of religious division fell darkly across the international scene. In the generations of the Queen's father and grandfather, relations among the monarchs of western Europe had been regulated after a fashion in an ancient and familiar way. A criss-cross of dynastic and personal ambitions colored to some extent by economic considerations and by the faintest glimmerings of a sense of national interest had served to give some coherence to the international community. England had been particularly fortunate in that she lay more or less on the periphery of the central struggle between the Hapsburgs and the Valois for domination of Italy. Her rulers had been able to opt in and out almost at will. Henry VIII had indulged his fitful impulses towards chivalric fame at vast financial cost and sacrifice of life but without involving the kingdom in life and death struggle. But now, in his daughter's time, England's relations with her continental neighbors were being transformed by the infusion of that virulent new stimulant: religious ideology. The ancient enmities—dynastic, commercial, vaguely nationalistic—persisted, but they were twisted into a different shape by the presence in all the major courts of elements whose view of international politics was determined by impassioned religious zealotry. These men tended to see their political opponents, at home and abroad, as combatants in a cosmic confrontation between absolute right and absolute wrong. Their influence varied from court to court and from one season to another. But their influence went far in darkening the international scene. It meant that the indecisive wars of Henry VIII's time, which ended in some slight territorial adjustment, some ritual exchange of hostages and treasure, and new affirmation of everlasting friendship, were transformed into relentless struggles in which survival itself—not mere trophies—was at stake in the international lists.

In the years after Henry's death there had indeed been an interval of real peril, a frightening decade for Englishmen. Henry and his immediate successor, Somerset, behaved like bulls in the Scottish china shop, threw that nation into France's arms, and opened up the possibility that Scotland would become little more than a French province. England was left dangerously isolated until Mary's precipitate embrace of the House of Austria carried policy to the opposite extreme and threatened her realm with a fate similar to Scotland's, smothered in the bosom of a greater power. Daring diplomacy, bumbling military effort, and sheer good luck combined to rescue England from these dangers at the opening of Elizabeth's reign. There followed a decade of relative tranquillity in England's international relations, ruptured only slightly by the Newhaven adventure, then more dangerously by the seizure of the Spanish treasure ships and the ensuing confrontation with Philip. Here again, skillful diplomatic management coupled with Spanish preoccupations in other parts of their extended empire kept the temperature below the combustion point of outright conflict.

But by 1570 the international community of western Europe had changed its character. First there was the transformation of the Hapsburg realms. In Henry's time they were a dynastic confederation ruled by a peripatetic lord whose dynasty was not specially identified with any part of his scattered dominions. Now Philip, the immobile bureaucrat at Madrid, ruled over a highly centralized and unmistakably Spanish empire.

Both the Italian and the Netherlands provinces sank into a semi-colonial dependence; it was a Spanish grandee who now ruled in Brussels. From the English point of view this meant that her neighbor across the North Sea was no longer a collection of semi-autonomous provinces and cities, loosely bound together under a common but alien lord; instead they were now mere outliers in a consolidated state. A relationship of relative equality was changed into one of inequality between a great power and a small one.

This in itself might not have been dangerous to England so long as Spain had no particular interest in subordinating the island state and so long as France stood as a powerful counterweight to Spanish power. But two transformations had taken place. The decisions of Trent had given to Catholicism a rigidly dogmatic definition (matched by the equally emphatic Protestant formulations of Augsburg and Geneva); the lines between the rival religions were now sharply drawn and each viewed the other with abhorrence and with fear. It was crystal-clear that Philip weighed in on the side of Catholic orthodoxy, not for merely expedient or worldly considerations but as a principled believer. England, from 1559, was less dogmatically but no less certainly Protestant.

The second transformation was also a product of the Reformation; if revived Catholicism provided a focal point of principle for the Spanish monarchy, it was fatally divisive for the French kingdom. Here the Protestants were highly organized, both politically and militarily; the dynasty remained officially Catholic but its power to maintain national unity was eroding rapidly.

For England these changes posed awkward and painful choices. How was she to deal with a Spain in whose official vision the English regime was a focus of virulent infection, a mortal danger to the souls of Christians? And how was she to conduct her policy towards a France which might become— if the Catholics triumphed—as dangerous an ideological foe as Spain? In the French situation the rise of Huguenot power had already forced England to dangerous choices early in the 1560's; as successive bouts of civil strife erupted in the following years these choices became ever more difficult to calculate. Then in April 1572 the potential dangers of an involvement with Spain became actual with the rising at Brill. England henceforth had to deal with grave changes on two fronts.

The breakdown of Spanish control in the Netherlands and the collapse of French royal power, torn apart by the rivalries of the religious factions, did not immediately threaten English interests as the menace of foreign intervention had done two decades earlier; indeed in the short run they were advantageous since they neutralized the two greatest continental powers. But in the longer run the fluid uncertainties which followed upon these two catastrophes were full of potential threats to England's security. The issues at stake and the strategies which might be used to deal with them were far more complex and far more difficult to sort out than any in past experience. Only the religious enthusiasts saw the situation in clearcut terms. For them Protestant righteousness stood starkly arrayed against Papist depravity. While none of the circles close around the Queen took quite this simplistic a view, many were prepared to transmute such views into a straightforward formula of political partisanship which dictated support for all Protestant movements within the Hapsburg or Valois dominions. Such men accepted with little hesitation the existence of a universal Catholic conspiracy dating from the Bayonne meeting of 1565 or even from Cateau Cambresis.

But for most statesmen, even those most firmly committed to the reformed religion, the path to be followed was ill-marked. Protestantism as a European-wide movement was but a shadowy entity. It lacked any institutional apparatus or, worse still, general agreement on central doctrinal issues and the possibility of unified action, doubtful at best, now dimmed perceptibly. Perhaps only half-consciously Englishmen were coming to think of religion as a domestic, a national, matter. Their responsibilities to their fellow-Protestants elsewhere became increasingly uncertain, since they inevitably criss-crossed lines of political force. And, if it was difficult to determine what commitments England had to international Protestantism, it was even more of a problem to divine the extent of the

Catholic rulers' commitment to co-religionists outside their own dominions. How far were they likely to press their ideological commitments beyond the predictable limits of their ordinary secular interests?

The Low Countries afforded a concrete example of this dilemma. Suppose the outcome of current events in the seventeen provinces were to be the restoration of Hapsburg rule; what had England to fear from this return to a *status quo ante*? In the Emperor Charles' time the loose amalgam of states grouped under the Hapsburg scepter had been a comfortable neighbor for England, and at times a sheltering umbrella of great usefulness. The answer, of course, lay in the changed character of Hapsburg policy in a post-Tridentine world. The goals of a restored Spanish government at Brussels had been foreshadowed by Alva's policy of intense religious persecution in the late 1560's. Such a regime would be assertively and exclusively Catholic. Even so, why should England fear these domestic alterations in the Low Countries? What frightened and baffled even the most cool-headed English councillors in assessing the probable course of Spanish policy was the unpredictable ideological component in Philip's views. Would he be content with the restoration of his power and the re-establishment of his faith in his Burgundian provinces, or would the compulsions of religious ideology drive him beyond these traditional aims to the grander tasks of exterminating heresy in general, and, in particular, in the British Isles? In the fevered atmosphere of the 1570's in a Spain where Philip at least listened to the "hard-liners" or a France dominated by the Guises, these questions were difficult to answer. Calculations about dynastic or national interests which would normally have served as sure guideposts in the past were no longer wholly reliable. The familiar sea-marks were being hidden and the English pilots had to take their chances in increasingly uncharted waters.

Ultimate goals—those of England or of her rivals—were hard enough to discern; immediate tactics were even more uncertain. The most familiar ploy was to fish in troubled waters, to patronize neighbors' malcontents. England had used this device in Scotland for several generations; in France there were the examples of intrigue with the Constable Bourbon in the 1520's and more recently the Newhaven venture, in both of which English fingers were badly burned. The intervention of 1562-1563 had pointed up the risks of this kind of tactic under existing conditions. Religion and *realpolitik* had become inextricably muddled—the protection of the brethren or the recovery of Calais? How was one to square the advancement of the faith with the goals of national or dynastic security? This episode had offered little useful guidance, and in its last stages had illustrated yet another flaw in the strategy of meddling. The rebel forces had made their own peace with the French Crown and together both had turned against the foreigner. Collaboration with rebels meant dealing with ephemeral and undependable allies with very uncertain futures. Rebels might be defeated or they might make terms with their own governments, leaving the English alone to face the anger of the French or Spanish Crown. It was very dangerous to risk the limited credit of the English Crown in such enterprises where the probabilities of heavy loss were so high. And these risks were doubled by the fact that the continental powers by making use of a troubled Catholic minority, might play the same kind of cards against England.

One possible out was neutrality; the Queen would certainly have opted for it, did opt for it whenever she could. But the forces which frustrated such a comfortable alternative were overwhelming. The fog of hatred and fear which enveloped western Europe in the 1570's affected the judgment of even the most level-headed. Behind the façade of effusively civil diplomatic intercourse which prevailing protocol required, the diplomats on both sides were signalling urgent and hysterical warnings to their home governments every time a ship or regiment was moved. Every change of tone at Court, every minor shift of political alignments, was interpreted as evidence of impending hostilities. So pathological had the suspicions of the rival courts become that the most routine activities were given bizarre conspiratorial significance. In short, men's judgments were so clouded by their own fears and suspicions that they had lost the power to make those considered and objective judgments on which neutrality must necessarily rest.

But neutrality was also ruled out by another calculation, resting on more familiar ground. In the case of the Netherlands the very survival of the rebellion was for many years a problematic question; for a long time no one supposed the rebels could by themselves throw off the Spanish yoke. Yet once it became clear that the Spanish could not immediately suppress the revolt the question of outside intervention became urgent. When and upon whom would the rebels call for rescue? Almost certainly it was to France they would first turn. For Englishmen the specter of French domination of the Low Countries was a frightening one. It would give that kingdom a throttle-hold on England's main trading partner and secure to her the great financial and industrial resources of these rich provinces. And strategically England would be flanked at every angle from Biscay to the Ems by the single power of France. This last consideration weighed heavily in all English decisions about their neighbors' affairs. There could be no neutrality towards the troubles of the seventeen provinces nor towards those of France so long as the probability of French intervention in the former remained.

CHAPTER 8

ENGLAND AND FRANCE,

1572-1576

BETWEEN 1572 and 1576 Anglo-French relations went through a stormy and deeply disturbing phase. It began hopefully enough with the Treaty of Blois, but even before that document was signed, the revolt at Brill had pushed the two powers into uneasy competition in the new arena of conflict. Before this awkward jostling escalated into open confrontation, they were caught up by the staggering calamity of St. Bartholomew. Yet, however great the shock of this holocaust, Anglo-French relations remained tenuously intact. For the next four years the English government found itself scrambling desperately to keep its footing amidst the quicksands of French politics at a time when virtual anarchy obtained in the Valois dominions. But Elizabeth never quite lost sight of two contradictory and yet complementary goals—the survival of a Protestant interest strong enough to keep the French court off balance and the renewal, in some viable form, of the tentative alliance of 1572. When the Huguenots seemed most in danger, it was the former objective which predominated; when the Queen Mother was able to re-establish some modicum of stability, it was the latter which the English pursued. But neither goal was ever wholly lost sight of. Towards the end of this period the rise of a politique faction in France, in alliance with the Huguenots and under the patronage of Alençon (Anjou after 1573), led Elizabeth into more dangerous paths when the temptation to intervene directly in internal French politics as patron and participant became appealingly strong. Only the skill of the Queen Mother in bringing about a general reconciliation in the so-called Peace of Monsieur (April 1576) checked this surprisingly militant impulse of the English Queen.

AT THE ENGLISH COURT the late spring of 1572 was filled with the festive celebrations connected with the conclusion of the Treaty of Blois. The Admiral of England, newly promoted Earl of Lincoln, set out for Paris to ratify the treaty, accompanied by Sir Thomas Smith, the former ambassador there, and an imposing retinue. A correspondingly dignified French embassy, headed by the great Montmorency, assisted by Secretary de Foix, made its way to London for the same purpose. It was richly feted during a stay of several weeks. But behind the façade of court entertainments and the exchange of compliments the new-born amity was already being put to its first test, thanks to events transpiring across the Narrow Seas.

For some years past, since the great disturbances of 1566, England had been a refuge for the religious malcontents of the Low Countries. Flemish cloth-workers had come in considerable numbers to East Anglia. They flocked also to London, where the French Church, dating from Edwardian days, provided a gathering-point for a refugee community of some size and importance, one which was in touch with important figures in the English Court. In addition to these immigrants, another group of refugees frequented the ports of the east and south coast—the Sea-Beggars, the only remaining active opponents of Alva's government. Sailing under commissions granted by the Prince of Orange as a sovereign ruler, they pursued a precarious existence, as privateers or pirates, according to one's point of view. Collaborating with the Huguenot ships based on La Rochelle, they made life miserable for all traders frequenting the Channel and its approaches. In early 1572 the English government, which had within the past few months revived negotiations with Brussels for the restoration of commercial relations, broken since 1568, issued a proclamation closing its ports to the Sea-Beggars. The damage to English and to neutral shipping was probably as much a factor in this decision as reasons of diplomacy. There is certainly no clear evidence to indicate that the proclamation was issued in collusion with the Flemish privateers. In any case their movements during February and March, once they cleared the English ports, are obscure. In very late March deGuaras, the Spanish merchant who was a kind of chargé d'affaires for Alva in London, warned him of an impending attack on Brill.[1] On 1 April the attack took place. What was intended as a raid unexpectedly turned into an occupation of the port, and this in turn set off a chain of explosions through the provinces of Holland and Zealand. Within a few weeks a substantial part of both provinces was in the hands of rebels, acting in the name of the Prince of Orange, protesting their loyalty to Philip, but repudiating the authority of Alva.

English official reaction to these events was reserved and coolly correct. The Queen expressed herself to Alva's agent as full of indignation against the rebels. But nothing was done to prevent the departure of some hundreds of Flemish refugees with full equipment of war and supplies of food. Even military supplies in the Tower were sold, either by royal connivance or, more likely, through bureaucratic corruption, to the departing Flemings. This first phase of English reaction was aptly summed up by Burghley when he wrote to Walsingham that every covert means was being used "to let them of the Low Countries pass home to the help of the liberty of the country; and I wish it were done rather by themselves than others that percase would not suffer them long to enjoy their liberty when it should be recovered." While proclaiming

---

[1] J. B. Black, "Queen Elizabeth, the Sea Beggars, and the Capture of Brille, 1572," *English Historical Review* 46 (1931), 30-47; J. M. B. C. Kervyn de Lettenhove and L. Gilliodts-Van Severen, *Relations politiques des Pays-Bas et de l'Angleterre, sous le règne de Philippe II* [hereafter cited as KL, *Relations*] (11 vols., Brussels, 1888-1900), VI, *Gouvernement du duc d'Albe*, pt. 2, 350-52.

official neutrality England would help the rebels to help themselves.[2]

Burghley was hinting, of course, at French intervention and these events were watched with equal interest in Paris. There Admiral Coligny was quick to push for action; his whole concept of policy was built on the organization of a grand anti-Spanish coalition and he was eager to seize the opportunity now offered. The King was half-persuaded, but the Queen Mother's cooler counsels prevailed and France, like England, preserved an official but somewhat fictitious neutrality. There was no move to prevent Orange's brother, Count Louis of Nassau, who had spent the last few months at the French Court, from using French soil as a launching pad for an invasion of Hainault. He occupied its capital, Mons, on 24 May, and in June a force of French Protestants under Genlis, a protégé of the Admiral, followed. The latter was promptly defeated; Louis, supported by his brother's entry into the provinces from Germany, hung on through the summer.[3]

The English role in these events had begun to change as early as mid-May when Alva's agent in London reported the departure of English volunteers headed for Flushing; by 20 May the English captain, Morgan, was systematically recruiting a troop. The English government gave no overt permission for these activities, but the companies of English soldiers now in Zealand were reporting to the English government. Morgan wrote at length to Burghley immediately after disembarkation, reporting conditions at Flushing and seeking the Lord Treasurer's instructions. Leicester and Walsingham were also involved in this corrrespondence. Morgan arrived in early June; he was reinforced in early July by another contingent, commanded by Sir Humphrey Gilbert. The English

[2] KL, *Relations*, VI, 370, 393, 414-18; Dudley Digges, *The Compleat Ambassador*, etc. (1655), 189, 203.

[3] J. M. B. C. Kervyn de Lettenhove, *Les Huguenots et les Gueux* . . . (*1560-1585*) [hereafter cited as KL, *Huguenots*] (6 vols., Bruges, 1883-1885), II, chapters 21-26, *passim*.

captains now found themselves faced with a complex situation. Alva's forces were still strong in the neighborhood of Flushing and a constant menace, but Gilbert found rivals almost as dangerous as the Spanish enemy in the French volunteer companies at Flushing. Initially a compromise was worked out with them and with the local governor.

But the problem of the French remained. It had already been canvassed by Burghley in a state paper of 3 June. In his systematic way he wanted, first, a survey of the strategic possibilities at both Flushing and Brill. Next he proposed to find out what Count Louis' intentions were and what were those of the German princes. The core of his deliberations was concerned with French penetration into the Low Countries. If Alva could by himself repel such a penetration, well and good; England should keep carefully neutral, remaining on good terms with both powers. But if the Duke could not keep the French out, the Queen must consider intervention. It was true that English commerce with the Low Countries had latterly been choked off by the Spanish governor, but if France were master there, not only commerce would suffer "but our sovereignty upon the Narrow Seas will be abridged with danger and dishonor." In another document of the same time he wrote, "The French increasing their dominions may be too potent neighbors for us." Alva should be given secret information of Elizabeth's willingness to assist his defense by all honorable means. But she should seek to set conditions—the restoration of the ancient liberties of the provinces and the end of the Inquisition.[4]

These views of the situation were probably shared by Burghley's mistress, and indeed suspicion of French ambitions was general. His proposals for dealing with the internal problems of the seventeen provinces were characteristically nostalgic, harking back to the *status quo ante* of Charles V and would in various forms become a favorite nostrum of Elizabeth for years to come. English observers saw the cur-

[4] KL, *Relations*, VI, 420-21, 425-27; Digges, *Ambassador*, 212; KL, *Huguenots*, III, 47-48; *CSPF*, X, 123.

rent developments in the Low Countries as analogous to those in Scotland fifteen years earlier—i.e., part of an internal upheaval leading to major readjustments within the regime but certainly not to revolution or to the independence of the provinces. This part of Burghley's scheme might recommend itself to all sensible men. But the use of English power to assist Alva was a more uncertain matter. Such a reversal of roles may seem startling, but at least one of the English soldiers in the Low Countries, Roger Williams, was to make just such a switch of employer when fortune dictated it. But for such men as Ambassador Walsingham at Paris such a change of heart was unthinkable. His counsel to Burghley, urging that aid be sent to Nassau for reasons of both religion and state foreshadowed the more radical policy of interventionism which would be the staple of left-wing Protestant aims for years to come.[5]

In the Low Countries themselves the English companies had in June and July joined in an expedition into Flanders, directed at Bruges and Sluys, which, if successful, would have enlarged the scope of English involvement considerably. But this move was a total failure and they soon fell back on Flushing. There is no indication that the English government backed this venture; it was more likely an instance of local initiative which could at the very least embarrass the home authorities. In the meantime the defeat of Genlis and the setbacks suffered by Nassau, coupled with Catherine's determined neutrality, postponed any test of Burghley's proposed policy. And after Genlis' defeat and the firm decision of the French not to intervene further, Walshingham transmitted the desperate pleas of Coligny and his associates that England act more effectively in bolstering the rebel cause.[6]

But on a local scale the problem remained acute. In early August Burghley sent an agent with instructions to Gilbert

[5] Roger Williams, *Works*, ed. J. X. Evans (Oxford, 1972), 149; KL, *Relations*, VI, 451-52, 459.

[6] KL, *Huguenots*, III, 53-55; Williams, *Works*, 112-115; Digges, *Ambassador*, 231, 233.

to assure that the Flushing garrison should contain no foreigners other than Englishmen.[7] It was essential that this important post, controlling as it did the navigation of Antwerp, should not be at the command of French forces. The English role was to remain a resolutely negative one, denying any foothold to the French; but there was no intention of yielding to hints coming from various Sea-Beggar commanders that the Queen become official protector of parts or all of Holland and Zealand.

In this hectic summer while the Queen's subjects outfaced the French in Zealand, their sovereign was about to play another hand in the endless game of cards with the French royalties. They were pushing a proposal which had first come up in the negotiations for the treaty—a marriage between Elizabeth and the youngest of Catherine's brood, Francis, Duke of Alençon. The Montmorency embassy was charged with pressing it; even to the extent of buying the support of Leicester by offering him a royal French match, possibly the daughter of the Duke of Montpensier.[8]

The Queen initially hesitated; after what seemed to be a polite but firm rejection of the suit, she turned around and, while asserting the obstacles of religion and of age (some twenty years between her and the duke), she proposed nothing less than a secret interview, after which she would make up her mind. For Elizabeth's ministers it was the re-enactment of a familiar comedy—another match-making. Burghley, blowing hot and cold, first hoped for the cession of Calais and for Alençon's abandonment of religious privilege. But a few days later he admits wearily that he could "make no choice for no marriage; all evils must be looked for; and by marriage without liking, no good can be hoped, therefore to God I leave it." He saw that at the bottom of the Queen's heart was her fear that Alençon's person (his face was reputedly badly scarred by smallpox) would make him an object

[7] KL, *Relations*, VI, 483-89.

[8] Bertrand de Salignac, seigneur de La Mothe Fénélon, *Correspondance diplomatique* [hereafter cited as Fénélon] (7 vols., Paris and London, 1838-1840), V (22 June and 28 Aug. 1572).

of derision. Nevertheless, she was prepared to use the diplomatic possibilities of a match, and it soon became a staple of Anglo-French diplomatic intercourse.[9]

So the summer passed, England and France nervously watching each other's "volunteer" forces in the Low Countries while slowly warming up for another bout of marriage negotiations. Both sides continued to exchange expressions of amity; indeed, a good deal of ambassadorial time was taken up solely in communicating these messages of good will. The very extravagance of their language betrays at once the brittleness of the connection as well as the continuing search for common ground of interest and even of action. These hopeful beginnings were suddenly blasted by a bolt from the blue —the assassination of Admiral Coligny, followed by the mass murders of Huguenots in Paris and virtually every large city of France. The shock of St. Bartholomew was immense, the immediate consequences quite literally incalculable. The suddenness of the event and the overnight disappearance of much of the Protestant leadership left English observers too stunned and too confused to make sense out of the chaos around them. The tremendous escalation of violence so transformed the scene as to make past experience irrelevant. Protestant fears were raised to a new pitch of hysteria. Most English Protestants readily assumed that the massacre was premeditated, a new chapter in the unfolding conspiracy of the Catholic world—Pope, Guises, Spain—aimed at the extermination of the reformed religion throughout Europe.

Quite naturally the Protestants cast these events in religious terms. Burghley saw them as a visitation of Divine wrath, in which the "devil is suffered by the Almighty God for our sins to be strong in following the persecution of Christ's members"; Leicester used almost the same language. But, while acknowledging the ultimate moral and religious dimensions of the event, they were compelled to deal with the immediate worldly aspects of the situation. The alliance with France had been made possible by the reconciliation of the Huguenots

[9] Digges, *Ambassador*, 218, 226-28, 228-30; Fénélon, V, 15 and 29 July, 7 and 28 August 1572; *CSPF*, X, 171 (Burghley to Coligny).

and the Court. With strong Protestant influences at work about the King, the English could hope for a French line of policy which would emphasize the common interests of the two kingdoms while putting into limbo the official religious differences. Coligny's presence at Court was a personal guarantee of the stability of the arrangement.[10]

Now his murder and the destruction of the Protestant leadership knocked out the props on which the structure of co-operation had been built. The immediate consequence of this overturn was the renewed ascendancy of the Guises, traditionally inflexibly hostile to the English regime. Walsingham at Paris quickly came to the conclusion that France was now transformed into an enemy. "I think [it] less peril to live with them as enemies than as friends," was his pithy advice a month after St. Bartholomew.[11]

Individually the English ministers shared much of Walsingham's fear and dislike for the new regime and his angry disgust of both the King and his mother. But their collective judgment, sent in a dispatch of 9 September summing up both the Queen's and the Council's views, was more reserved. In fact, although the foundation of Anglo-French collaboration had been blasted away by the massacre, the delicate super-structure of diplomatic relations remained intact, perilously swaying over the void beneath. The French, from the very day of Coligny's first wounding, made desperate efforts to preserve and to make use of the fragile outward and formal structures of friendly intercourse. In the first despatch reporting the wounding of the Admiral, the deed was ascribed to the Guises; and as late as 24 August events were described in terms of party conflict between Chatillons and Guises; only after that did the French Court ascribe them to a Protestant plot. From then on, they clung to this story, elaborating and embellishing the details and insisting on the immediate danger to the King and to the royal family which moved Charles IX to act. There was an attempt to separate this from the issue of toleration; it was insisted that the edict would be

[10] Digges, *Ambassador*, 250, 251.   [11] *Ibid.*, 258.

maintained, although this latter promise soon faded from liberty of worship to a shadowy freedom of conscience.[12]

The point of this policy was to stave off direct and angry recriminations or, even worse, an open break in relations. It signalled to the English that the French Court wished at least to maintain civil relations. More important, it offered an opportunity for continuing diplomatic intercourse. The French justifications for their actions provided a topic for the kind of discussion which could be kept within the bounds of ordinary diplomatic exchanges. The tone could be moderated and the temperature lowered to the normal level of routine communication.

The views of the English councillors in early September were varied. Some of them, Burghley for one, would have recalled Walsingham in protest, and the ambassador was given the option of proposing to the King of France that a secretary be left in Paris to represent England. But the main thrust of the councillors' instructions was conciliatory. The Queen had already in her first interview with Fénélon taken this line. He had been received by a sad and silent court and Elizabeth had not spared expressions of hurt surprise and of reproach, but he was allowed to present his case and he secured the royal agreement to withhold judgment until further evidence arrived from Paris. Walsingham in his interviews with the Queen Mother and the King was more contemptuous in his skepticism of the French justification and scathing in his comments on what had been done, but he followed his instructions in continuing discussion with the French. He submitted to the King's refusal to grant him passports, at least for the present.[13]

Thus it was that the Anglo-French entente, so battered by the events of late August, was still in mid-autumn at least formally extant. Nervousness and suspicion were running high on both sides but communication was still just barely

---

[12] *Ibid.*, 242, 246-50; Fénélon, VII, 322-72, for royal French instructions from August to early October.

[13] Digges, *Ambassador*, 253-58, 246-50; Fénélon, V, 14 September 1572.

open. Fénélon reported in late September that no one would speak to him and that only the Queen continued to treat him decently. Things were little better for some months thereafter; it was not until Christmas that the ambassador could report the end of his social quarantine when Leicester invited him to dinner. The intervening months were nevertheless busy ones for both Fénélon and Walsingham. The continued disorders in France were totally destructive to commerce and the cause for constant complaint by English merchants. The gradual revival of Huguenot resistance, in Languedoc and then at Rochelle, excited French fears of English aid. The English, on their side, saw every assemblage of French shipping as a preliminary to intervention in Scotland, where the pro-French party, holding Edinburgh Castle, was given new hopes when the Regent Mar was killed in October.[14]

From the end of August, London was crowded with refugees, including many of the surviving Huguenot leaders. They sought not only refuge but aid in recovering their position at home. The English government's public stance was one of sympathy for their plight and of protection for them as refugees but not as plotters. Privately the English gave cautious consideration to their proposals but waited on events before acting.

In the meantime the most bizarre aspect of this uncertain relationship was to be found in the grim little comedy of the Alençon match. The French, determined to gloss over the events of August and to continue relations as though nothing had happened, brought up the proposed interview again before the end of September and through the ensuing weeks there were desultory discussions as to whether the Queen could go to the Channel Islands to meet her suitor. This she declined, but the French continued to press consideration of the match and the English were willing to take their part in this solemn play-acting. Like the continuing exchanges over the French justifications for the massacre, these hollow negotiations kept intact the fragile diplomatic bridge.[15]

[14] Fénélon, V, 29 September and 25 December 1572.
[15] Ibid., 29 September 1572; Digges, *Ambassador*, 266, 277.

In October Charles IX became the father of an infant daughter, and in December Queen Elizabeth was formally asked to be a godmother. The Queen took the opportunity to deliver herself of a stinging indictment of the King's behavior, but then condescendingly agreed that for the good of Anglo-French relations she would accept the invitation, and shortly afterward an undistinguished but trusted nobleman of Papist inclinations, the Earl of Worcester, was chosen to head an embassy of honor for the baptism.[16]

Parallel to these official exchanges, the English were conducting a very obscure and rather curious underground intrigue. The evidence is both slight and murky, but it is enough to establish the existence of contacts of a private and secret kind between the English Court and that eager suitor, Alençon. The agent who conducted these discussions was Maisonfleur, a minor poet, a courtier, and a member of the Duke's household. Accredited by Alençon, he apparently brought proposals that the Duke should slip away from France (accompanied if possible by his brother-in-law, Navarre, and his cousin, Condé). He would be received by the Queen and (so Alençon hoped) promptly wedded to her. It is difficult to estimate the seriousness of this hare-brained scheme; the English took it seriously enough to delay Walsingham's departure from Paris but the ambassador was scornful of the whole affair. Alençon was a young and very inexperienced hand at this time and this was his first venture on his own into international politics. How seriously he considered actual flight from France, how far the scheme was blown up by Maisonfleur and others of his entourage, one cannot adequately assess. But his willingness to act independently of brother and mother was a clue that the English could use for future reference. The intrigue itself is another pointer to the dangerously unstable relations between England and France.[17]

[16] Digges, *Ambassador*, 297, 298.
[17] For the Maisonfleur intrigue, see KL, *Huguenots*, III, 107-35; *Hatfield*, II, 27, 28, 29-35, 36; *CSPF*, X, 200, 220, 234, 255; Digges, *Ambassador*, 310-14.

The Huguenots were not, as men had feared, exterminated by the late massacres. Rochelle was in arms by November and appealing for English aid. They successfully seized the Ile de Rhé off the harbor mouth; and Walsingham with unwonted hopefulness saw God at work revenging the blood of His saints. "Perhaps we did build too much before upon the courage and wisdom of them that be dead; He can raise up stones to set forth His glory." What this meant was that England had now once again some leverage within France and some hope that the Court of France would be too distracted from within to have the means to dabble in their neighbors' affairs.[18]

By November the Queen had been persuaded to accept Walsingham's request for recall and a successor was being sought. The new envoy was a civil lawyer, Valentine Dale, Archdeacon of Surrey, who had served on a mission to Flanders in 1563. His despatch to France was delayed until March. The revocation of Walsingham marked a period in Anglo-French relations. As an avowed left-wing Protestant, he was an articulate and persistent advocate of English cooperation with continental Protestantism and a natural choice to represent England during the Coligny ascendancy. His withdrawal marked the end of that hopeful collaboration and of English retreat to a more neutral although not unfriendly stance.[19]

There are several clues to the English view of their relations with France at this point. In late November Fénélon reported home that the Privy Council after much deliberation had decided to observe the treaty with France without putting much trust in it while exploring an accord with Spain and sending an embassy to the Protestant princes. They would also keep open connections with the Huguenots in case some kind of intervention seemed desirable. The ambassador was well informed. Negotiations with Alva's envoys continued through these months and contacts with the German princes were maintained. Discreet dealings with the Huguenots continued; in November Rochelle sued for help and even offered

[18] *CSPF*, X, 203, 221-22; Digges, *Ambassador*, 293.
[19] *Ibid.*, 442 (Dean of Wells, 1573).

the sovereignty of the city to Elizabeth; by January the Queen was willing to send clandestine supplies of munitions to the Rochellois. Supplies flowed out and armed refugees followed, and Fénélon in retailing this news expressed his darkest suspicions of powerful assistance to the beleaguered Protestant stronghold.[20]

In the meantime the Queen instructed Worcester, in Paris, to defend her protection of the French refugees in England (on the condition that they did not plot against their sovereign); he was to justify them to their King on the ground that it was religion not sedition that moved them to act. In April 1573 the Queen averted her eyes while the Huguenot refugee Montgomery organized a sizable fleet of French, Flemish, and English components for the relief of Rochelle. He failed in his purpose and retired to Belle Isle. Elizabeth, pressed by French accusations, steadfastly denied any English participation in this enterprise.[21]

The revival of Huguenot strength and the reopening of marriage negotiations with the French Court opened a three-year period of dizzying confusion in Anglo-French relations. Catherine de'Medici's speculation in the "final solution" had proved a failure. She was faced not only by a recrudescent Protestantism but by the ceaseless intrigues of her restive youngest son, Alençon, who found allies in the Huguenot camp and also among the great nobles, notably the house of Montmorency. France was threatened with the kind of alliance between religious dissent and noble discontent which had proved so explosive a mixture in the Low Countries or Scotland. The French malcontents naturally turned to the English Queen for assistance and plied her with one proposition after another, all of which required English money and some of which involved active English intervention in French politics. The tumbling confusion of events which followed must have bewildered contemporaries as much as it does the

---

[20] Fénélon, V, 29 November 1572, 15 and 22 January, 16 and 21 February 1573; Digges, *Ambassador*, 293; *CSPF*, X, 206, 221; Thomas Wright, *Queen Elizabeth and Her Times* (2 vols., 1838), I, 452.

[21] Fénélon, V, 17 April and 8 May 1573.

historian. But behind that confusion there are observable continuities; two themes played a ceaseless counterpoint against one another—one an entente with the French Court built on matrimonial alliance, the other active English support for the French rebels. At moments the latter alternative certainly tempted the ordinarily cautious Elizabeth and led her to the very brink of commitment to dangerous policies. That she did not become involved was in the end as much the result of chance as of policy.

Towards the end of March 1573 the French began again to press the Alençon match and the Queen's response was warm enough to force the English ministers to some serious consideration of the possibility. Burghley worried about the future of the state and of the reformed religion, longed for a marriage, and thought his mistress genuinely interested in matrimony. Alençon was, alas, the only possible candidate; the best the Treasurer could say was "I do force myself to pursue it [the match] with desire." Skeptical of Alençon's religious pretensions, he thought the duke would not "lose a Queen with a kingdom for a priest's blessing of a chalice." Walsingham, queried for information on the suitor, was candid in writing that his person would probably not please, but the ambassador thought the duke had such good parts as one might wish for the Queen's husband and was likely to conform to English religious practice. But he thought the French Court was using the negotiation merely to spin out time until French domestic affairs were less troubled, a view which Leicester shared.[22]

Nothing could more succinctly represent the state of Anglo-French relations in the spring of 1573 than this insubstantial structure of deception built upon deception, of distrust counter-thrusting distrust. Yet the English assessment of their mistress' intentions was that she was more seriously disposed to marriage than at any time since the Austrian match, five years earlier. Certainly the succession problem was no less worrying than in the previous decade. Mary of Scots was a prisoner and her name anathema to many Englishmen, yet

[22] Digges, *Ambassador*, 336.

should Elizabeth die the Scottish claim would probably be the strongest. James VI was still a child, the plaything of warring factions in a violence-ridden kingdom; his chances of survival were poor and he probably was not yet a very serious counter in English calculations about the future. So, whatever fears the royal councillors might have about the unsuitability of the suitor, or the risks of marriage for a forty-year-old woman, state policy and royal desires united to press on with the wooing.

This new dance of state began with a move by the French Court, acceding to Elizabeth's demand for an interview—as soon as the Duke was freed from his current military task by the fall of Rochelle. In the Council Leicester and Burghley vied in supporting the match; Sussex, Smith, and others were well disposed. They agreed to dispatch Sir Edward Horsey, captain of the Isle of Wight and a long-time adherent of Leicester's, to Paris. (Horsey had, in Marian times, been a pensioner of Henry II.) He was to emphasize that Alençon would not be an acceptable suitor while warring on the Huguenots, and he was to offer Elizabeth's services as a mediator between the French King and his Protestant subjects. But the envoy's instructions were rapidly outdated when the older brother, Anjou, was elected King of Poland. In order to pursue this new adventure, he was anxious to liquidate the war with the Huguenots, having in any case failed in several assaults on Rochelle. Peace was patched up in late June, and this bout of civil war sputtered to a close as settlements were made in the various Protestant enclaves. Elizabeth's bid at mediation followed a line of policy which would be tried out again and again, in France and in the Low Countries. It is hard to know how much was intended in 1573; if it had been followed up, it could have created for England a special—and dangerous—*locus standi* in French affairs as umpire and protector of the minority interests.[23]

In any case, the change in French affairs coincided with another circumstance, favorable to the English: the fall of

[23] *CSPF*, X, 319, 322, 376; Fénélon, V, 8 May and 17 June 1573; KL, *Huguenots,* III, 232-35 (the election was known in Paris by 24 May).

Edinburgh Castle, an event which ended the threat of French intervention in behalf of its defenders. The English diplomatic line now veered around to an emphasis on the difficulties which hindered further negotiation, and the French, driven to take the initiative, dispatched the Marshal de Retz, who arrived in the fall of 1573 in great state and was received with reciprocal pomp. His persuasive speeches were listened to with interest; the Duke's stock rose in the English Court; prospects for an interview seemed fairer, and by the spring of 1574 discussions on a possibl meeting place were under way. The ambassador was persuaded that an interview might do all, and he urged that the Duke agree to meet the Queen secretly in Kent.[24]

But all these hopeful approaches were suddenly overtaken by a new rush of events. In March 1574 the Huguenot leader, Montgomery, using Jersey as a base, made a descent on the Norman coast, raised the standard of revolt, and seized several strong points. This immediately strained relations, since the French accused the English of backing Montgomery, while the Queen resolutely denied any knowledge of his doings. In the weeks to come Huguenot unrest spread elsewhere through France.[25]

This renewal of civil war was played out against a background of events in the French Court itself. The King, who had suffered recurring bouts of illness for some months, was now struck down and by early May there was open speculation as to his survival. And in early April a major conspiracy was uncovered in the very heart of the Court. Anjou and Navarre were both seized and held under restraint at Vincennes while a number of the Duke's servants were arrested. For some months past the Huguenots had been preparing some move against Charles IX and Alençon had entered into their intrigues.[26] An initial move had been nipped in the bud a few weeks earlier and both Alençon and Navarre kept under close surveillance. But another move was planned for

---

[24] Fénélon, V, 20 Sept. 1573; *CSPF*, X, 418.
[25] *CSPF*, X, 479; Fénélon, VI, 2 and 6 Apr. 1574.
[26] KL, *Huguenots*, III, chap. 18.

Holy Thursday, at which time the two princes hoped to escape from Vincennes and to join their Huguenot allies at Sedan. They were discovered just before the plot was to be set in motion and placed under guard, while various servants of the Duke were arrested. The fury of the dying King was so great that for some days there was fear for their lives.

The role of the English government in this tangle of conspiracy was considerable, but the remaining evidence is too fragmented to give a clear picture. Fénélon was anxious about the English naval preparations of the spring, which he suspected were being made jointly with the Huguenots and Orange for an attack on the French coast. The Queen insisted that the preparations were precautions against the large Spanish fleet reported about to sail for Flanders and hinted darkly at a new Franco-Spanish alliance.[27] No major naval activity did in fact follow and the general Huguenot scheme did not materialize.

As to the conspiracy at the French Court, it is clear that the English embassy was to some extent involved;[28] they probably had some foreknowledge of what was coming off. One account suggests that the princes might have fled to England rather than to Sedan. Certainly the princes made contact with Ambassador Dale and his secretary, who saw Navarre at Vincennes in late April when the two prisoners earnestly sought to have a secret token from the Queen or Leicester in assurance of friendship. Later still in May, when Charles IX was dangerously ill, the cautious Burghley weighed in with a desperate proposal. Fearing that the "tyrant that shall come from Poland" would take their lives, the Treasurer suggested several secret ways of conveying money to the prisoners to bribe their guards. One of these schemes would have involved Leicester, who would pretend to be buying horses in France to cover the transmittal of funds.

Certainly Dale intervened with the Queen Mother not only for Alençon but also for the Duke's servant, la Mole, who

[27] Fénélon, VI, 19 and 24 Apr. 1574.
[28] For this whole episode, see Wilkes's account in SP 78/1/144-48v; also CSPF, X, 484, 485, 486-87, 491, 506.

had been condemned to death for his role in the plot. But, in addition, a special agent was dispatched to Paris, Thomas Leighton, the Captain of Jersey, with instructions to seek reconciliation between the royal brothers. Leighton arrived almost too late to see the King, with whom he had but one audience before the latter died, but it was he who relayed the fears of the princes for their lives. On 31 May Charles IX breathed his last, and Catherine de' Medici seized power in the name of her third son, whom she anxiously expected to return from Poland. In the meantime, Anglo-French relations, badly bruised by recent events, were wrapped in a cloud of impenetrable uncertainty until the new King declared himself.[29]

The summer of 1574 following the death of Charles IX was a tense one; the English waited anxiously for the coming of a Spanish fleet, which they feared was destined for Ireland, and naval preparations continued fitfully through these months, depending on the latest rumors from the north coast of Spain. Relations with France were no happier; the Queen and her ministers were apprehensive as to Henry III's intentions. Henry III was notoriously Catholic; he had refused the Queen's hand for his religion's sake. Was it not likely that he would ally himself with Spain and the Pope against the heretic kingdom? Negotiations with the Huguenots and particularly with agents of Condé were reopened. All summer long the French ambassador nervously watched what he saw as a struggle within the English Council of pro-French and pro-Spanish elements.[30] It would probably be more accurate to characterize English actions during these months as a nervous jockeying for position at a moment of rapid and unpredictable change. The conclusion of the Convention of Bristol was a step towards better relations with Spain; those with France remained in a state of worrying suspense while Henry III enjoyed the flesh-pots of Italy as he idled home-

[29] SCPF, X, 489, 492, 493, 495, 499, 501, 503, 504-5.
[30] Fénélon, VI, dispatches of 29 May, 3 July, and 13 Aug. 1574; memoir of 27 June 1574.

wards towards his impatient mother, who was waiting for him at Lyons.

In September as Henry III crossed the Alps a new French figure appeared in England, Monsieur de Meru, the youngest of the Montmorency brothers; the eldest, the Marshal, had been imprisoned along with Alençon and Navarre. Meru was joined shortly by an agent of the Calvinist Elector Palatine; there was also a representative from Rochelle in London. The ambassador thought that the German envoys had come charged with the task of a general Protestant consultation on the problems raised by the accession of Henry III. They were thought to be proposing a loan of 200,000 écus for the raising of a German army to be used in France or in Flanders to defend the Protestant cause.[31]

At the beginning of October Queen Elizabeth dispatched Lord North as a special emissary to the Court of France. North went partly to spy out the new political landscape, partly to exhort the King to restore domestic peace by concessions to the Protestants, and finally to convey a formal but not disingenuous offer to renew the alliance of 1572. North, although civilly treated, got little response from the new King and returned in December to England with information on the worsening political condition of France. By the end of the year Danville, the second of the Montmorency brothers, had converted to Protestantism and was in arms in Languedoc, in effective control of much of that province, and in communication with Condé, who lurked on the eastern frontiers of France, and with Rochelle, the great Protestant fortress in the West. The English continued a waiting game, playing off the German princes with fair words while making fulsome offers of friendship to Henry III. By the turn of the New Year, Meru was being received at Hampton Court, presenting the English Court with a detailed manifesto put out by his brother, Danville.[32]

[31] *Ibid.*, 10, 15, and 19 Sept., and 5 Oct. 1574; *CSPF*, X, 548-49, 554.
[32] *CSPF*, X, 560-64, 584; Fénélon, VI, 10, 15, and 29 Oct.; 13 and 17 Nov.; 28 Dec. 1574; KL, *Huguenots*, III, chaps. 6, 7.

This document reflected the changing circumstances of the French political scene. Danville had initially taken arms because of the imprisonment of his brother, the Marshal, which followed on the detention of Alençon and Navarre. The princes had been given a limited and closely supervised freedom by the new King, but Montmorency remained a close prisoner. Danville's recent conversion to Protestantism marked the alliance of the powerful Montmorency interest—essentially politique in character—with the Huguenot party. This brought into being a new coalition headed by the Prince de Condé, explicitly linking the religious minority with a broader, secular opposition. Their immediate goal was the freeing of the captive princes and the Marshal, the reissue of the edicts of toleration and a meeting of the States-General for the airing of grievances, both civil and religious, and their redress by common agreement. Their longer-term purposes were the reform of the body politic, the re-establishment of the *bien publique*. Force was required; the Huguenots already in arms would be assisted by a German army under the Calvinist Elector Palatine. The role of the Queen of England was to provide the necessary money, 100,000 crowns (about £30,000).

What was demanded of England was a greater involvement than hitherto, since the Queen was asked not only to act as banker for the enterprise but also to back a broad-based opposition movement within French politics. This was quite a different role from the protection of Protestant co-religionists. Danville's appeal explicitly made the comparison with England's intervention in Scotland in 1559-1560; he might aptly have pointed to the Sea-Beggars, who similarly blended constitutional and religious elements in their defiance of the established order.

The English government used all due deliberation in dealing with this new situation, negotiating with both parties. In February Thomas Wilkes, lately Dale's secretary, was secretly sent to the Palatine (he was to pretend he was sent to meet Philip Sidney). He was first of all to attempt to persuade the Protestant leaders to come to terms with Henry III—and the

Queen thought circumstances propitious—but, failing that, to seek security and absolute secrecy for a loan to the Palatine to raise troops for use in France. Secrecy was on the whole successfully maintained; the French ambassador picked up only fragmentary reports. Wilkes brought back in May the terms proposed by the Palatine and Condé; the Queen was willing to loan half the sum asked (50,000 crowns equal to £15,000) on the promise of repayment by the Palatine. Her name was to appear nowhere in the legal instruments. The documents were signed on 23 July by the Palatine, the Prince as chief of the Huguenots and Meru for the Montmorency interest.[33]

But the English government did not neglect its relations with the French Court in these months. A constant flow of messages, alternating compliment with complaint, crossed the Channel. In April the alliance of 1572 between Queen Elizabeth and the new French King was solemnly renewed and the latter was elected to the Garter. It was by no means certain that the King and his subjects might not come to an agreement; and it was not until late May that such negotiations failed completely. During these months Dale kept in touch with the captives Alençon and Navarre. But even when the agreement was made with the Protestants, payment of the money was delayed until the fall so that no immediate action was contemplated.[34]

Then in August the hare of an Alençon marriage was once again started. The Duke was still under restraint, and relations between the royal brothers as bad as they might be; Alençon was patently dangerous as long as he stayed in France. It was a gamble whether he would be less so if he were out of the kingdom, but the French Court went ahead in re-opening marriage negotiations in September. These were speedily thrown awry when the Duke escaped from surveillance and made his way to Dreux, where he set himself

[33] *CSPF*, XI, 15-17, 44, 95, 115; Fénélon, VI, 19 and 29 Jan., 4 Feb., 11 Mar., 30 Apr., 12 May 1575.

[34] *CSPF*, XI, 39, 40, 49, 50, 55, 58, 118, 138; Fénélon, VI, 15 and 30 Apr. 1575.

up as "Gouverneur General pour le Roy et protecteur de la liberté et bien publique de France." General confusion ensued as the Duke withdrew south of the Loire. However, the success of the Duke of Guise in destroying the force of German mercenaries in Condé's pay (but not under his command) temporarily improved the position of the Court. The Queen Mother sought frantically to make terms with her younger son and accomplished this when the truce of Champigny was signed on 8 November 1575.[35]

This hardly settled matters, however, since Condé refused to recognize it, and indeed Alençon himself almost immediately dispatched a messenger to Queen Elizabeth, explaining that he still regarded himself as bound to the Elector Palatine. The messenger was to press on the Queen that she actively join the enterprise; finally he was to set up regular intelligence between the Duke and the Queen. The Montmorency brothers (the Marshal was now freed) were included in this negotiation. Condé was also in touch with the Queen, and with Meru was preparing forces on the Rhine for a move on France, accompanied by the Palatine's son, Duke Casimir. By late January Condé was on French soil and Alençon proposed again to resort to arms. He was also seeking aid from the English Queen. At the same time a mission which included the former resident ambassador, Fénélon, was engaged in sober discussions of the forthcoming interview between the Duke and the Queen, to take place possibly after Easter. In early February 1576 the situation disintegrated yet further when Henry of Navarre decamped from the Court and retired to the Protestant west. The Queen Mother as usual worked furiously for a conciliation and at the end of February succeeded in bringing about a forty-day truce. There followed some weeks of fluctuating uncertainties as the all too numerous contending parties struggled over terms of peace; from week to week the probabilities veered from peace to war and back again. During these weeks Alençon's agents intrigued in London and in March received a guarded assur-

[35] Fénélon, VI, 6 Aug., 10 and 20 Sept. 1575; *CSPF*, XI, 123-24, 125, 140-42, 155, 177.

ance of general support from the Queen; to the request that she enter into the league between him and the Elector Palatine, she reserved answer for the moment.[36]

Shortly thereafter, in early April the Queen sent off that hard-worked diplomat, Thomas Randolph, on yet another mission to France. Accredited to the Court, he was to urge the Queen's mediatorial services on the King and Queen Mother, but he was also to deal secretly with Monsieur d'Alençon, to keep him firm in his alliance with Condé and Casimir. But Randolph arrived too late to do any substantial good. Slowly through April the balance inclined towards peace and the so-called Peace of Monsieur was finally signed 27 April 1576.[37]

Much is revealed by the extreme disappointment with which the English Court reacted to the French peace. Randolph wrote a bitter letter roundly condemning the peace as sacrificing the cause of religion and the Queen's interests. The Queen herself wrote to the King of Navarre to express her disgust with the false peace, ruinous to him and his cause and full of dangers for the future.[38]

It was almost four years since St. Bartholomew, and the new pattern of relations with France inaugurated by that event was now discernible. From the morrow of the massacre onwards disorder became endemic in French politics. The inability of either the King or his mother to establish more than momentary equilibrium among the warring factions resulted in veering uncertainties in French policy. It left the English government unable to make any working assumptions about their opposite numbers in Paris. Fulsome expressions of friendship were constantly exchanged but they meant less and less. At those moments when the French monarchy seemed capable of reasserting control over its own destinies, the English seemed seriously interested in the establishment of a

[36] *CSPF*, XI, 190, 191, 192, 193, 202, 206, 234, 239, 240, 241-42, 251, 297; PRO, Baschet transcripts of French dispatches (MSS. without pagination), 23 Mar., 8 Apr. 1576.

[37] *CSPF*, XI, 302-4, 325-29 *passim*.

[38] *Ibid.*, 323; KL, *Huguenots*, III, 638.

working entente with Paris. At such times negotiations for the Alençon match were revived or, as at the accession of Henry III, the alliance of Blois was resurrected. But as time went on and French public order visibly crumbled, the English authorities were more and more drawn to a working agreement with the opposition groups and more disposed to listen even to the most hare-brained schemes proposed by them.

The mere presence of crowds of refugees in England in the months following St. Bartholomew forced the English government to formulate an official position towards them. The Queen declared to the French ambassador that she would shield any Frenchman who came as a fugitive from religious persecution; her realm was to be a refuge for all those fleeing France for conscience' sake. But she made it a condition that the refugees must not engage in political conspiracy while on English soil. This distinction between religious and political dissent was a useful one for diplomatic purposes but it did not provide a policy easy to enforce.

The leaders of the Huguenot exile—Montgomery or the Vidame of Chartres and their associates—saw themselves as the leaders of a political movement and expected England to provide not only asylum but support for the recovery of power in France. And however coolly correct the official policy of the government (the Queen repeatedly denied any knowledge of Huguenot intrigue within her realm), the French Protestants did in fact find powerful and numerous English friends to welcome them. Many of the clergy, and especially those of the more ecumenical left wing, were ardent sympathizers. More important, they had weighty friends at Court. Leicester gave them his forthright and steady patronage. Burghley, in this matter, was pretty much at one with his rival; less enthusiastic and more discreet, he nevertheless took a continuing and benevolent interest in Huguenot affairs. The principal agents engaged in negotiation with the French Court during these years were for the most part protégés of the left-wing Protestant leadership, most notably Walsingham, who after three years as ambassador returned to assume ministerial rank as Secretary in December 1573. Dale, Wilkes, Randolph, Horsey, and Leighton all belonged to this same circle. There could be no doubt that the ideologues of the left, who identified English interests with those of continental Protestantism, were strongly represented at Court. The fruits of their labors were to be seen in the swarm of agents, from Rochelle, Holland, the Palatinate, and from the Prince of Condé, who buzzed about the English Court, where they were received, discreetly, not only by the royal ministers but also by their mistress. English authorities looked through their fingers while supplies (paid for in advance) flowed to Rochelle or even while the refugees prepared for an armed return to their homeland. And apparently some £15,000 of the Queen's money went as a loan to their cause.

All these activities together added up to a modest but clearly conceived English policy: to keep alive the Huguenot cause in France with sufficient strength to harass the French government and to disturb the public peace. The grander strategy, of establishing a strong—perhaps even dominant— Protestant interest at Court had not seemed a viable goal since the death of Coligny. But the lesser strategy was safe, cheap, and, so long as it kept the French Court off balance, reasonably satisfactory to English purposes.

The emergence of Alençon and his noble allies presented both an opportunity and a danger and, if he were to be fully supported, a change of strategy. The Duke was not a Protestant; his aims and ambitions were of an entirely political character; and to plot with him was to venture onto new ground, to enter the inner world of high French politics and to become a player in a new and much more risky kind of game. Dealings with the Huguenots had, over a dozen years, become almost institutionalized; a set of rules, tacitly accepted by all the players, including the French Court, gave a kind of pattern to English patronage of the Protestant party. England in effect limited her efforts to securing the survival of the Huguenots. In such a role she was an irritation to the French government but hardly a threat to its survival. Intervention in behalf of Alençon and his friends would alter this picture in important detail. A new rationale as well as a shift in strategy would have to be found for English participation, for these would-be allies were playing for higher stakes than the Protestants; they sought to dominate the Court and to shape the policy of the state. If they succeeded, with English help, Elizabeth and her government would have a long-term stake in the survival of such a regime (as they already had in Scotland or were to have in the United Provinces) which might ultimately make very heavy demands on English resources and entail graver risks than Elizabeth usually cared to accept.

Yet the evidence suggests that Elizabeth was increasingly tempted by the bolder strategy. She felt more at ease intriguing with grandees who could justify their resistance on more traditional grounds than those of tender conscience. The potentialities were grand indeed; there might emerge at Paris a regime more favorable to collaboration with England than any since Coligny's time; at the very least, the English could hope for a major and prolonged disruption of political order in France and for the consequent paralysis of the royal government. What might have happened we cannot say; at the very last moment the Queen Mother was able to bring to a halt the impending collisions which threatened universal disorder. Elizabeth was unable to disguise her bitter disgust at this turn of events; nevertheless Catherine's success spared Elizabeth from further temptations, which, had she yielded to them, might have dragged her from the spectator's seat she so valued to the arena of struggle she so much dreaded.

CHAPTER 9

ENGLAND AND

THE HAPSBURGS,

1572-1576

RELATIONS WITH FRANCE in the years after St. Bartholomew were difficult enough; those with the Hapsburgs after the seizure of Brill were no less complex but quite different in character. Superficially the problems in each case seemed parallel; in both instances rebellious Protestants turned to England as a natural protector against Catholic oppression. But there the parallel ceased. First of all, the context of previous events was markedly different. England and France had in the spring of 1572 come together in a diffident but viable collaboration and even the events of August did not wholly erode a fund of common interest which served to keep open communications over the difficult years which followed. In the contrary case of Spain there was a history of angry quarreling dating from the seizure of the treasure ships in late 1568; diplomatic relations had been all but severed when de Spes was expelled in January 1572 for his role in the Ridolfi plot. There had been enough relaxation of tension since then to permit the opening of negotiations for renewal of commercial relations. The Flemish commissioners in London in January 1572 remained, and deGuaras, a Spanish merchant, became the recognized although unofficial representative of Alva in London. Hence the rising at Brill took place at a time when England and Spain were barely on speaking terms, with unresolved issues between the two kingdoms and a deep mutual suspicion.

Moreover, events shaped themselves very differently in the two areas after 1572. The very confusion and the kaleidoscopic changes in the French political scene meant that English policy could be opportunistic and flexible, meeting each darting move on the board as seemed best at the moment. In the Low Countries there was from the beginning a certain black-and-white clarity to the picture. The Sea-Beggars, whatever fictional loyalties they might assert, were in arms against the Spanish Crown and proclaimed as rebels by Philip. Any substantial aid to them might lead to a direct confrontation with the affronted power of Spain. Moreover, quite in contrast to the French situation, where the lightning shifts of events seemed to make anything possible, the possibilities in the provinces were, after the first summer of revolt, increasingly limited.

By autumn 1572 it was clear that the impetus of revolt was checked; Count Louis had been defeated; Orange himself, his army dissolved, fled to the refuge of Holland. From then until late 1576 the very survival of the revolt was always in doubt. English hopes for its success were never in question, but English policy had to bend to the realities of the situation. England could not risk open war with Spain on behalf of an ally which might at any moment cease to exist. Hence Elizabeth set her course for an ostentatious neutrality, which meant the mending of fences with Spain—the reopening of commerce and the maintenance of civil dialogue with Philip and Alva. Yet at the same time the rebels were allowed maximum freedom to trade (the sale of their booty) and to recruit English volunteers for their cause. Such a course won the confidence of neither warring party but it kept English options open. This policy of wary tight-rope walking won an unexpected reward when in 1576 the exhaustion of Spain's finances drove her unpaid armies in the Low Countries to mutiny; in the anarchy which ensued, the whole of the seventeen provinces were driven out of sheer agony to revolt and a whole new range of possibilities opened up for English policy.

IN 1572 the initial revolt had sputtered uncertainly across Holland and Zealand like a handful of defective firecrackers. In some towns sharp, clear explosions had blasted the Spanish authority altogether, but elsewhere there were nothing but damp fizzles. Through the summer it looked as though the center of action would be in the southern Netherlands, where the armies raised by William of Orange and his brother Louis of Nassau faced Alva's forces. The speedy defeat of Louis and the ensuing disintegration of William's mercenaries changed the picture radically. In October in desperation William threw himself into Holland and Zealand, where the only remaining foci of rebellion were to be found.

These events, coupled with the withering of the French menace after Coligny's fall, brought an abrupt end to English initiatives in the provinces. English policy was thenceforward to be largely reactive in nature, responding to the ebb and flow of events across the North Sea. First there was the withdrawal of the companies under Gilbert from Flushing in November; they were all home by December.[1] English officers and men still remained in the service of the States of Holland and Zealand, but they were no longer directed from home.[2] Negotiations with Alva's representative for reopening trade were resumed and by the end of winter were complete; orders for opening the ports of both nations were prepared and the resumption of trade proclaimed by the Queen on 30 April 1573.[3]

The rebels had done their best to block this agreement. Agents arriving in London after New Year's offered the Queen possession of certain strong places in Holland in return for her assistance, but all they got for their pains was fine words, empty compliments, and a hint that the Queen

---

[1] Digges, *Ambassador*, 299; KL, *Relations*, VI, 568, 570.
[2] See Williams, *Works*, xvi and 121-48 *passim*.
[3] *Tudor Proclamations*, II, 371.

desired to mediate (indeed an English agent went to Delft to press this suggestion). The most the rebels could achieve was permission to buy military and food supplies.[4]

There followed a season of unaccustomed good will between London and Brussels. Burghley went out of his way to express his friendship to the Spanish agent, deGuaras, taking full credit for pushing the agreement through the Council and boasting of the hostility that his pro-Spanish stance had earned him. He declined a proffered Spanish pension, with the diplomatic excuse that this would ruin his credit and destroy his usefulness to Spain.[5]

Hoping for more substantial advantages from this good will, Alva pressed for a halt to the flow of volunteers. The Queen and Cecil replied that such volunteers were disobeying the royal command by such service, but showed no disposition to staunch the flow, and the supply of English soldiers to Orange's forces continued steady. When the Spaniard sought to buy powder in England, the ministers expressed their desire to oblige but regretted that their supplies were too low to permit sales.[6]

The Spanish also hoped for English mercenary aid and opened a negotiation with Martin Frobisher, who offered to recruit English mariners for Spanish service out of the forces returning from the abortive Huguenot expedition to Rochelle. Frobisher explained that these men had not been paid and refused to follow the French proposal to join the Dutch rebels. In the summer of 1573 an agreement was hammered out providing for some dozen fully equipped ships to join Alva. But when the expedition was about to sail, an order from the Council halted it. This episode highlights the mercenary motives of many of the combatants (even Roger Williams was to serve the Spanish for a time). It is of no small importance that the government winked at support for the rebels but halted help for Alva.[7]

[4] *CSPSp*, II, 455; KL, *Relations*, VI, 661, 720.

[5] KL, *Relations*, VI, 719, 721, 722-23, 737.

[6] *Ibid.*, 736-37, 744, 779.

[7] *Ibid.*, 745, 750, 780, 785, 786, 789, 803, 808; *CSPSp*, II, 469; *CSPF*,

The English also aided Orange indirectly by encouraging the Scottish regency to allow the flow of volunteers after the fall of Edinburgh castle in the spring of 1573, thereby emptying Scotland of unemployed bravoes and contributing several thousand troops to the Dutch without compromising England's official neutrality.[8]

Elizabeth followed up the reopening of the ports with a strong personal initiative to persuade Philip to accept her mediation; she would bring Orange to a truce and to submission. Guaras was repeatedly pressed to win royal consent; eventually, in June, Alva had to write categorically rejecting such intervention. A reproachful Orange addressed a long memoir, rehearsing the familiar argument of a universal Catholic conspiracy aimed at all Protestant regimes; once again offering the pledge of four towns, he proposed a general Protestant league headed by the Queen. But such grandiloquent pleas had little effect at the moment (July 1573) when Harlem was about to fall to the Spanish.[9]

The Prince was not without leverage against the English since his possession of Flushing meant he could prevent the Merchant Adventurers' return to their ancient and preferred haunt of Antwerp. For the moment he allowed trade to pass upstream, but only under conditions which assured a flow of food, supplies, and money into Flushing. The final months of 1573 saw a turn in the tide of military events in favor of the rebels. After the fall of Harlem Alva pressed on to besiege Alkmaar. It was here in October that he met his first reverse when he was obliged to raise the siege; three days later his admiral, Bossu, was captured by the Sea-Beggars. In the same month Alva won release from his task and in December turned over authority to Don Luis Requesens, formerly governor of Milan. In this same season Orange took a definitive step by openly joining the Calvinist Church.

X, 348. See *ibid.*, 462-63, for instance of Englishmen serving Alva. For Frobisher, see G. R. Marsden, "The Early Career of Martin Frobisher," *English Historical Review* 21 (1906), 538-44.

[8] *CSPF*, X, 365, 394-95, 398, 417, 418.

[9] KL, *Relations*, VI, 685, 724, 732, 733, 760, 764-68; *CSPF*, X, 360-63.

So things stood at the departure of Alva from the Netherlands. The rebels were holding on stubbornly; the Spanish were hopeful of success, but clearly had a long road to travel. The English had displeased both sides and were trusted by neither. But the rebels had no option but to accept whatever crumbs Elizabeth was disposed to minister to them since the continuing chaos in France choked off hopes of aid from that direction. The Spaniards resented England's benevolent neutrality but were in no position to hit back; all their resources were absorbed by the rebellion. A dispassionate observer might have judged that on balance the rebels were marginally the beneficiaries of English policy. However coldly their pleas for further aid were rejected, access to the English market plus the flow of English and Scottish volunteers may well have been a determinative advantage.

Developments of 1574 were overshadowed by Spanish enterprises in the rebel provinces. The year began with a setback for them when, in February, the rebels took the major Zealand city of Middleburg after ineffectual Spanish efforts to provision it. But in the same month Requesens chalked up a notable success. Louis of Nassau's attempt to invade from Germany was halted at Bommel, where he and his two brothers were killed and their force annihilated. This episode had sidetracked the attention of the Spaniards from their main effort of the year, the siege of Leiden. In addition to its strategical importance, the defense of the city soon took on psychological dimensions as well; its fall might have given the *coup de grace* to faltering rebel confidence. A summer-long struggle ended with the Spanish retreat in October. For the governor it was a defeat of more than military consequence; his shortage of funds was acute; in May he had summoned the Estates General, hoping to raise money, but was met only by an insistent clamor for the restoration of the ancient liberties and for an end to Spanish domination.[10] The failure to take Leiden shook his prestige and left him less able than ever to withstand the complaints of a hostile populace.

These events were directly reflected in England. The fall of

[10] *CSPF*, X, 514.

Middleburg was publicly celebrated in London while a rich flow of booty reached English markets, and in the next month or so perhaps as many as a thousand new volunteers joined the Prince. At the same time the Queen deftly sidestepped new Spanish demands for the withdrawal of English soldiers.[11]

The Spanish government reacted to these events by assembling a fleet in its northern ports to sail with naval reinforcements for the Low Countries. First reported in England in April, the fleet's existence became certain when the Spanish asked permission for its ships to put into English ports in case of emergencies. The Queen at first responded with complaints about English exiles in Brussels, but in May, in the wake of Nassau's defeat, she conceded permission. This fleet was to haunt English statesmen all summer long. Rumors that Stucley, the Catholic trouble-maker, and the exiled Lord Morley were on board aroused fears that the fleet's true destination was Ireland. Orders were given to mobilize the Queen's ships; Bedford was sent to organize West Country defenses. From early June through late August the government alternately started and stopped the machinery of naval mobilization as conflicting reports filtered through. And in Spain there were rumors of a joint Anglo-Dutch-Huguenot fleet about to assemble. Requesens at one point was so worried that he contemplated a declaration of war; in July Mendoza was sent specially with a letter from Philip to quiet English apprehensions, but it was not until late August that preparations were finally cancelled. The English might have been a little less nervous if they could have seen the perplexed letter Requesens wrote to his royal master in July from which it is apparent that the governor knew neither the size nor the composition nor the destination of the approaching fleet. This whole comedy of errors reflects the deep-lying panic fears of the English, which all too easily surfaced, as well as the totally unsatisfactory state of their intelligence from Spain. The

[11] KL, *Relations*, VII, 65, 69, 75, 79, 85; *CSPF*, X, 473. DeGuaras reported (KL, *Relations*, VII, 70) that Elizabeth was subsidizing Nassau, but there is no English evidence to back this assertion.

cancellation of the fleet by the Spanish government reflects the growing strain on its resources.[12]

Otherwise Anglo-Spanish relations moved along paths already marked out in the past couple of years. There was an exchange of diplomatic small-fire over the issue of exiles. Elizabeth demanded the expulsion of thirty of her subjects, all but five of them among the rebels of 1569. Spain's *quid pro quo* was the recall of all Englishmen fighting in the Low Countries and the denial of English soil to the Dutch rebels. Neither side was going to yield on this question, but the prolonged negotiations over the 1568-1569 seizures were brought to a successful conclusion with the signing of the Convention of Bristol on 21 August 1574. There was talk of resuming diplomatic representation, but the Spanish thought the more favorable tone of English policy arose from fears of the new French king, Henry III.[13]

During this summer the English continued to negotiate with Orange and Requesens for the opening of the Scheldt to their ships. The Orangists, during the desperate days of the siege of Leiden, made another bid for aid in men, money, and arms and received the usual cool rejection, but after the relief of Leiden English policy began to shift slightly but perceptibly. Thomas Wilson, the scholarly master of requests, who had some previous diplomatic experience, was despatched to Brussels to deal with the opening of the Scheldt but also to press once again an English offer of mediation. Proposed as early as the closing months of 1572, the offer had been repeated after the signing of the Convention of Bristol. The Spanish agent at Bristol thought well of the Queen's intentions and, while Requesens did not respond immediately to it, he yielded on the question of the Scheldt by withdrawing the requirement that English trade move via Dunkirk and

[12] *CSPF*, X, 480-81; KL, *Relations*, VII, 93, 104, 168, 174, 196, 201, 205, 208, 209, 215, 216, 222. For an account of the intended Spanish fleet, see Julian Corbett, *Drake and the Tudor Navy* (2 vols., 1898), I, 203-6.

[13] KL, *Relations*, VII, 117, 131, 216, 300-8, 314, 375-77; *CSPF*, X, 543.

Bruges. He also showed some disposition to give way on the question of expelling Westmorland and his fellow-exiles.[14]

The governor had now moved so far as to propose discussions with Orange and at a colloquy at Breda in the spring of 1575 offered a general pardon, the peaceful departure of all Protestants (after an interval for sale of their property) and the departure of all alien (but not Spanish) soldiery. In March 1575 Requesens formally ordered the departure of the English exiles, hoping thereby, but in vain, for permission to export ordnance from England.[15]

At the same time English relations with Orange soured when the Flushingers seized English shipping; England retaliated by seizing all Flushing ships in her ports, and a proclamation of April closed the kingdom to a named list of Dutch leaders while, in less clear language, forbidding traffic with their adherents. In May the Council went so far as to suspend intercourse with Holland and Zealand.[16]

The English pursued detente with Spain by yet another route, the despatch of an ambassador to the Escorial. Sir Henry Cobham, brother of the Lord Warden and an experienced diplomat, travelled by land. He was to seek freedom from the Inquisition for English seamen who gave no offense by their behavior and Protestant worship for any ambassador sent from London. But the core of his instructions was in Elizabeth's renewed offer of mediation. Specific terms were to be laid out: restoration of the ancient liberties, suspension of the Inquisition, and the removal of the Spaniards. On religion Philip should consult the Estates. Cobham had one audience

---

[14] KL, *Relations*, VII, 187, 195, 216, 219, 318, 328, 337, 349-52, 358-62, 375-77.

[15] *Ibid.*, 460, 472, 476, 491; *CSPF*, XI, 28, 84-85, 122; G. P. Gachard, *Correspondance de Philippe II sur les affaires des Pays-Bas*, III (Brussels, 1858), 259.

[16] Samuel Haynes and William Murdin, eds., *Collection of State Papers . . . Left by William Cecil, Lord Burghley, etc.* (2 vols., 1740, 1759), II, 274; *Hatfield*, II, 296; William Camden, *Annals of Queen Elizabeth* (1675) [hereafter cited as Camden, *Annals*], 208; KL, *Relations*, VII, 499, 508, 511.

with the King but was then fobbed off on Alva and got little satisfaction from the Spanish Court. Minimal concessions would be made to English seamen off their ships but none to English merchants resident in the country; the only ambassador who would be welcome would be a Roman Catholic. As for the Low Countries the King replied categorically that no privileges had been taken away, that good terms were offered at Breda, but that he would never yield the exclusive rights of the Roman Catholic faith. At most Philip would permit the provinces to make their submission to him through the Queen. The initiatives taken by both England and the Hapsburgs were pretty well exhausted by now; each side had made its maximum concessions and, until events reshaped the situation in the Low Countries, further negotiations were likely to be sterile.[17]

Relations with the Hollanders were also cool; Orange naturally resented the Queen's proclamation naming him as a rebel and banning his followers from England, and commercial relations were exacerbated by the repeated seizure of English ships by the Zealanders. Daniel Rogers was employed by the Queen and by the Merchant-Adventurers to deal for them at Delft but with limited success.[18]

Both the rebels and the Spaniards were under the severest strain. Respective resources dwindled, but it was the former who seemed about to lose control of vital posts; the latter were rapidly exhausting their financial resources and were in no condition to replenish them. In this contest of endurance it looked as though the rebels would be the first to crack. Orange was already throwing out hints that he would have to call on French intervention and in the autumn of 1575 Elizabeth's own informants were sending in alarming reports of Dutch desperation; they had recently lost two more posts, Oudwater and Schoonhoven and the Spanish were laying siege to Ziericksee. This strategically important town linked South Holland and Zealand; its fall would isolate the prov-

[17] *CSPF*, XI, 75-76, 156; *CSPSp*, II, 510; KL, *Relations*, VIII, 17-31; BL, Add. Ms. 48,084, ff. 32-54.
[18] *CSPF*, XI, 134, 135, 151-52, 158, 163.

inces one from the other. The English agents in Holland confirmed the likelihood of an appeal to France in spite of the Prince's reluctance.[19]

The Queen took these warnings seriously enough to take action. Two envoys were quickly despatched, Sir Robert Corbet to Requesens and John Hastings to the Prince. The latter was a kinsman of Huntingdon, had been an exile under Mary, and had cooperated in Parliament with his kinsman, that outspoken Puritan, Sir Francis Hastings. Corbet was instructed to raise the governor's fears of French intervention; indeed, he was to draw the parallel with their role in Scotland twenty years earlier. He was to intimate that the Queen had secret intelligence of an impending invasion of the Low Countries by Alençon, using the French and German armies then under his leadership. Having frightened Requesens sufficiently, Corbet was then to hold out once again the bait of English mediation and to reassert the arguments in favor of restoring the ancient liberties of the provinces; interestingly enough nothing was said regarding religion. He was to link his mission to that of Cobham.[20]

Hastings' mission was the counter-face of his colleague's. While thanking Orange for his straightforward warning that he must turn to France, Hastings was to warn the Prince that he would only be exchanging one foreign tyranny for another, and one equally Catholic in character. And in any case strife-torn France could hardly act at this point. But Hastings was to be plain in refusing any protectoral role for England, which could only lead to war with Spain. But in his dealings with Orange, Hastings was not to rule out altogether the possibility of war; he was to find out all he could about Dutch resources and to put feelers out to the anti-French States of Holland.[21]

The two English envoys (who were carefully briefed as to

[19] KL, *Huguenots*, III, 579.
[20] KL, *Relations*, VIII, 2-10, 16; *CSPF*, XI, 167-71. On Hastings see Claire Cross, *Puritan Earl: The Life of Henry Hastings . . . 1536-1595* (1966), 47, 88.
[21] KL, *Relations*, VIII, 10-16.

each other's instructions) had varying receptions. Hastings' was cordial and frank. Orange admitted that Condé had approached him asking that he mediate between the King and Alençon so that the latter might divert his forces to the Low Countries. But the Prince declared he would put off the French offer and would instead send a mission to London offering Elizabeth the title of Lady of Holland and Zealand, with an income of 1,000,000 florins per annum. Before the end of November 1575 St. Aldegonde and Paul Buys had been accredited to the Queen.[22]

The Prince used every argument he could deploy. He emphasized the failure of the late meetings at Breda and Philip's determination to maintain absolute Spanish control and undiluted Catholicism. He displayed once again that ancient bogy, the plot hatched at Bayonne for the general extermination of Protestantism. To the English fears of war with Spain he opposed the argument of Spanish financial exhaustion; the Grand Commander had been told that the most recent supply of funds was the last he could expect.

Corbet's reception was initially much chillier; the governor brusquely dismissed the warnings of French intervention with the comment that the French were too busy at home to meddle elsewhere. He went on to blame Queen Elizabeth for Spain's difficulties, declaring that but for her the rebellion would be crushed by now. But after a little time Requesens calmed down enough to agree that if the English brought proposals from Orange they would be forwarded to Madrid. More important still, the governor tacitly recognized the importance of England's role by sending a leading official of his Court to London as special ambassador. The man chosen, Champagny, was a Councillor of State, governor of Antwerp, and brother to the Cardinal Granvelle. Thus by mid-winter there were two rival Low Countries missions in London, each vying for the Queen's favors.[23]

Champagny's instructions were largely negative; he was to build back-fires against the conflagration which St. Aldegonde

<hr />

[22] *Ibid.*, 42-44, 46.   [23] *Ibid.*, 37, 81-83.

sought to fan. He arrived in London to find the Orangists
already there and in consultation with the inner Council—
Burghley, Leicester, Walsingham, and Sussex. His own reception was not cordial; Burghley was sick and the Queen away
from London. Even when he saw them, things went badly.
His meeting with the Treasurer ended in mutual recriminations; the Queen was in an ill humor, constantly interrupted
him, and complained bitterly because he had no letter of credit from Philip. Leicester was hostile; Croft, the avowed friend
of Spain, silent; only Hatton manifested any signs of good
will. Champagny soon came to the conclusion that he could
do no good for his cause in this unfriendly setting; he predicted that the Queen would take possession of the two provinces as soon as Parliament met. But the envoy was pleasantly
surprised when no such event took place and when the English Court suddenly turned a friendlier face to him. Diplomatic civility was restored, but the basic English position was
no more favorable to him and if anything more inflexible.[24]

But the English affability—to both envoys—only served to
point up the inflexibility of the English position. The demands of both parties were turned down. Elizabeth declined
the proffered sovereignty of the two provinces and refused
aid in money or men while at the same time rejecting Champagny's request for a ban on English volunteers and for prohibition of intercourse. The English were in fact in an un-
accustomedly strong position and able to push their initiatives
on both parties with some reasonable hope of success. The
presence of the two embassies in London emphasized the desperation of their respective masters. The rebels feared from
week to week the fall of Ziericksee, while the Grand Commander was haunted by the increasingly mutinous demands
of his unpaid troops. In September 1575 Philip had suspended
payments on his debts; this in turn led the bankers, even the
Fuggers, to refuse any more advances.[25]

Under these circumstances the English spoke forthrightly

[24] *Ibid.*, 98-105, 138-43, 157-62, 188-94.
[25] *Ibid.*, 188-94, 198-200, 201-3, 204-8, 208-13.

to both sides. To Champagny the Queen was frank in admitting her fears of a restored Spanish regime in the provinces, modelled on Alva's. Even the coolly secular Elizabeth was apprehensive of Philip's further intentions once his power was firmly reestablished in his rebellious dominions. What she sought was an end to the Spanish regime in Brussels, the departure of officials and of troops, and a return to the loose, semi-autonomous regime of earlier days.

But if Spain were prepared to make such concessions, then the rebels must make even larger ones. They must give up all thought of the virtual independence which they now enjoyed and return to Hapsburg rule and, as far as religion was concerned, Elizabeth apparently thought they should be content with a mere freedom of conscience—without any legalized Protestant worship—something equivalent to the terms which she tacitly conceded to her own Roman Catholic subjects.

Such a settlement was proposed to Champagny and the Orangist delegation in January 1576, to be carried through by English mediation, preceded by a cease-fire.[26] Neither party found it acceptable. The Dutch felt they had been tricked into a long delay during which they might have sought French aid. The whole history of past relations, they argued, demonstrated the impossibility of compromise with Madrid. Brussels was equally irritated. To accept even an offer of mediation was to betray the Spanish position that their opponents were rebels against royal authority and against an infallible faith. They protested furiously against the very reception of the Dutch delegation, pointing out the Queen's own proclamation against the rebels in the previous year. Elizabeth dodged this attack by insisting that Philip had committed himself to a discussion of terms in his meeting with Cobham and that St. Aldegonde and Buys could be legally entertained until the promised agent arrived from Spain. The frantic denials of such a commitment by the Brussels delegation were turned aside by the Queen's bland insistence. The Dutch sought to gain advantage; they were prepared to believe in

[26] For this whole sequence of negotiations, see *ibid.*, 109-11, 118-20, 121-23, 188-94, 198-215; *CSPF*, XI, 243.

the promised envoy from Spain and improved the waiting weeks by asking for a £30,000 loan to tide them over.[27]

This diplomatic impasse was overtaken by dramatic and determinative events when in the first week of March 1576 Commander Requesens died quite suddenly. The last weeks of his life were rendered miserable by the rising discontent of his unpaid soldiery, and the news of his death was accompanied by reports of mutinies and the choice of *electi* by some of the Spanish garrisons. Power passed nominally to the Council of State but so great was the confusion now prevailing that Champagny received no official confirmation of the governor's death for a fortnight after the event.[28]

The English government saw in the weakening of the regime at Brussels a further opportunity to push their proposals for settlement. The diplomatic offensive was redoubled by the dispatch to the Council of State of William Davison (closely connected with Francis Walsingham and a member of the inner Protestant circle), who began a long career of public service with this mission. He was sent to tell the Council of State of Philip's commitment to Elizabeth (via Cobham) that "upon the submission of his subjects, [he would] receive them to grace and favor."[29] The late commander had denied knowledge of such a commitment; the Queen insisted that there must be an authorization from the King. But even if there were not, Davison was to urge the Council for their own safety and the King's honor to agree to an "abstinence"—a cease-fire. If they would do this, Davison would then repair to the Prince of Orange and ask him to beg an armistice of the King. Thus a move towards a settlement would be initiated by a humble approach from the rebels but with an understanding that there would be negotiations to follow. The English obviously hoped that a weakened and distraught Council would be persuaded to accept such a face-saving scheme. But the authorities at Brussels, divided among themselves, and terrified by ever-growing disorder, were afraid to take any initia-

[27] *CSPF*, XI, 265-67.
[28] KL, *Relations*, VIII, 231-34, 239-47, 244-45, 257-62, 275-80.
[29] *Ibid.*, 303-8; *CSPF*, XI, 291-93.

tive, and excused themselves from such a bold decision by taking refuge in a promise to write to their master in Madrid. By the end of April it was clear that Davison's mission was fruitless.[30]

There followed a summer of muddled events and confused purposes. Until July the Brussels regime was able to maintain just enough control over affairs to continue the siege of Zie-ricksee and two of the best Dutch commanders were killed in efforts to relieve the city. The crowning irony came when the capture of the city by the Spanish troops on 2 July was followed immediately by the mutiny of the victorious army and its dispersal into Brabant. From that point on the power of the Council of State to control either men or events dwindled fast; paralysis of all military efforts followed; and finally in early September the members of the Council were put under arrest by local Walloon forces acting for the States of Brabant and Hainault. Organized armed forces under the command of the States now stood in open opposition to the Spanish army and the new authorities were in communication with the Prince of Orange.[31]

During these months when the Spanish regime was falling apart, the English government was locked in a protracted cold war with the Prince of Orange. Disagreement began with the seizure of the Portuguese ambassador's bride, who was crossing from Calais to Dover. The lady was under English conduct; she and all her bridal treasures were hustled off to Flushing. The Queen was beside herself with fury and promptly ordered the seizure of all Zealand ships in English ports. This occurred in the same week as the death of Reque-sens and virtually coincided with the return of the rebel commissioners, empty-handed, even their plea for a loan denied.[32]

The Dutch retaliated by seizing English shipping in their ports and by harassing English trade in the Channel. By July at least fourteen English merchant ships were held at Middle-

---

[30] KL, *Relations*, VIII, 338-39, 344-47.

[31] *Ibid.*, 409-12, 455-58, and 419, quoting Gachard, *Correspondance de Philippe II*, III, 106.

[32] *CSPF*, XI, 259; KL, *Relations*, VIII, 229-30, 230, 238, 280, 281.

burg while four of the Prince's warships were detained at Falmouth. A tentative settlement negotiated by Robert Beale and William Winter failed to win royal approval, largely because it provided for a kind of forced loan by the Merchant Adventurers to the States of Holland and Zealand.[33]

Pretty clearly the Prince, desperate for money, sought to force the hand of the Queen by these measures, but the result was only to harden her determination not to yield anything to him. His implied threat that if she did not yield some aid, he would seek it at the hands of the French had lost force by late summer. In the autumn he sent a special envoy to cool down the still simmering dispute but the matter was not altogether settled when the general revolt of the provinces made this a dead issue.[34]

Events in the Low Countries between September and November altered the scene almost beyond recognition. Some of the old players remained in the field now in new roles but the emergence of the Belgian magnates made it a whole new game. From the English point of view the changes were all to the good. Spanish officialdom and the Spanish armies had vanished from the seventeen provinces; the traditional local leadership had reasserted itself; and the very conditions which England had pushed in previous negotiations now seemed about to be attained.

The close of the year 1576 was a milestone for English policy. More than four years had passed since the seizure of Brill and the massacre of St. Bartholomew—four tumultuous years, clouded with anxious uncertainties and treacherous turns of events. The English government had moved warily, committing itself as little as possible, although occasionally shaken by gusts of panic, living from day to day and improvising as the situation demanded. Now at last it looked as though there was a pause in the storm, both in France and in the Netherlands.

The death of Requesens and the ensuing breakdown of Spanish authority made for an entirely new and very fluid

---

[33] KL, *Relations*, VIII, 417, 433, 437-39.
[34] *Ibid.*, 423-28; *CSPF*, XI, 400-1, 421.

situation in the Netherlands. The Peace of Monsieur, on the other hand, brought to an end a prolonged bout of anarchy and restored something like general order in the distracted kingdom of France. From the English point of view these two opposite situations brought a breathing-space after four years of almost unbroken tension. It was only a pause; soon enough English statesmen would be brought by external events to painful decisions, but from the historian's vantage-point it is an apt moment to look back and analyze the drift of English policy since the seminal events of 1572, the Treaty of Blois, Bartholomew night, and the rising at Brill.

It is not difficult to catch the tone of English policy of these years, as the preceding account of events shows. Caution and reserve were the predominant note even when the most glittering prospects were temptingly displayed by French agents or those of the Dutch insurgents. The English government's attitudes were cool-headed and singularly sober; the narrow limits of England's resources and the defense of essential English interests were kept determinedly at the forefront of the councillors' thinking and action. They strove with cool concentration to divine the motives at work among the fevered politicians of the continent. One can draw a sharp (and favorable) contrast between the sobriety of the English rulers in these dangerous years and the behavior of their counterparts across the Channel. Irresponsible pursuit of personal ambition seemed to be the keynote of French politics at all levels. The increasingly blindered policy of Spain focussed on the simple goals of restoring her absolute political and religious control in the Low Countries, no matter what the cost and with complete disregard for the deep currents of discontent in those provinces. In one country, there was absence of both goal and direction; in the other a simpleminded inflexibility which slowly destroyed any sense of political reality.

But it is not easy to penetrate to the more particular motives and purposes of the English government. There is a dismaying paucity of direct evidence from the English side. Burghley's position papers for these years are exasperatingly inconclusive, masterpieces of his pro-and-con approach to problems of state but uninformative as to his conclusions. Later on in this book, there is an attempt at assessing the roles of individual ministers; here we are limited to a consideration of collective policy.

Perhaps it is easier to begin negatively by pointing out what clearly was ruled out of the scope of English policy. Elizabeth and her Council were repeatedly approached by Orangist agents offering her the dominion of the two rebel provinces of Holland and Zealand, with their fleets, their trade, and their wealth. Tempting pictures were painted of a new continental empire, strategically placed across the great trade routes of Europe, a source of power and of great wealth. Similarly the agents of the Huguenots suggested a renewal of ancient Lancastrian glories by the acquisition of influence and perhaps lands in western France. Both these propositions were resolutely rejected by the English government; expansion of English power on the continent, the resumption of the role played by Edward III or Henry V, was excluded altogether from the possible goals of English action. England's role, seen in this light, was to remain defensive, and protective in character.

But what about the positive assumptions of English policy? Without doubt what was foremost in the thoughts and words of English statesmen was the defense of the reformed religion —a simple enough conception and yet one which needs definition and interpretation. What the Elizabethan councillors meant when they used these words was essentially the defense of the existing English regime. However reluctantly Elizabeth accepted the role of protectress of the new religion, she found no alternative to the role. The very inertia of events had cast her in the role without effort on her part—and indeed against her will. Mary Stuart's shift towards the Pope and Catholic Spain in the Ridolfi plot; the Catholic cast of the northern rising; the Papal condemnation—all these had made Elizabeth willy-nilly a pillar of the Protestant world, the leading Protestant ruler in Europe. Yet, paradoxically, the very process by which Elizabeth emerged as the champion of the Gospel drained away much of the religious content in English ideology. It was not only the Queen's own indifference to the evangelical religion but the very processes of political life which brought this about. Since 1559 English Protestants no longer found themselves an assault force attacking a tyranny in power but a garrison defending a religion established by law. The existence of the reformed faith was now something to be taken for granted; the strategies of its defense, which were perforce political in character, took precedence over fundamentally religious problems, which could, for the time being, be shunted aside. Such a shift in focus led, unintentionally but very rapidly, to a transformation in thought. The political leaders of the country, irrevocably committed to the new faith, were less moved by its glowing inner vitality. They had, so to speak, externalized it, turning it into an institutional structure which commanded their loyalties and energies but no longer stirred their own inner consciousness.

A second change occurred at the same time. In the years of persecution, Henrician or Marian, there had been a strong sense of the international scope of the new faith, of the brethren in Germany, Switzerland, or more recently Scotland and the Low Countries, who were members of one great evangelical community. Now the reformed faith had become much more narrowly the religion established by law in England. That there was a common interest with French, Dutch, or Scottish Protestantism was by no means lost sight of, but that common interest was now found in a political rather than a religious identity. It rested on an alliance of divergent communities rather than on common membership in one great brotherhood. The exhortation to seek first the kingdom of God, that all else might be added, lost its force as religion was toppled from a transcendent position to mere equality with other political goals. One could now balance the interests of the faith against considerations of worldly power. The claims of the Gospel had to compete with those of *Machtpolitik*, the commands of God with those of Caesar.

What in fact were these other elements in English interest? One can begin with the question of national security; what threats imperilled it in the decade of the 1570's? Here the ghosts of the past played as much of a role as the living actors then on stage. It is difficult to understand but no less dangerous to underestimate the ancient English fear of the French. It was not, of course, merely a matter of inherited memories. The Queen's father had fought three great bouts of war with the French, two before the divorce and a third in the 1540's. Cecil's generation had entered politics when the French threat in Scotland was taking fearsome shape and the first great crisis of the current reign had been the struggle to oust France from Scotland. There had then followed the undeclared war of 1562-1563 when England had momentarily hoped to recoup the loss of Calais. The cast of mind acquired in these struggles was not easily reshaped. What Englishmen specifically feared from France in the 1570's was not so much an invasion of their kingdom as another French intervention in Scotland. Until the spring of 1573 there was still an active Marian force there, in close contact with the French, and even after the fall of Edinburgh Castle the treacherous uncertainties of Scottish politics offered all too many opportunities for outside interference. Hence every movement of French vessels on the Breton or Norman coasts produced a tremor of nervousness at the English court.

But even more worrying was the possibility of French expansion into the Low Countries, the focal point for English export trade. French ambitions had been directed towards Italy for more than two generations, but her ancient claims in Flanders and Artois were only dormant and the burial of French ambitions south of the Alps at Cateau Cambresis diverted French energies into old channels. From the time when the disturbances in the Low Countries first became serious in the 1560's, English statesmen narrowly watched to see what move France might make. French interest in the Netherlands was all too evident at the very outbreak of the revolt and, as we have seen, only the explosion of St. Bartholomew checked French movement in those provinces.

The other potential menace to England's security, Spain, was both more and less fearsome. The immense prestige of Spanish arms, the awesome wealth of her crown, and the unchallenged authority of Philip in his many kingdoms spoke for themselves. But Spain was a distant power, preoccupied for many years by Mediterranean affairs. The long reign of Charles V had accustomed Englishmen to thinking of Spain as one of the many dominions of a peripatetic sovereign rather than as the focus of a great empire. They were slow to grasp the changes signalled by Philip's decision to settle in his Iberian inheritance. But Philip's association with England in his second wife's reign had identified him with the Catholic cause and cast him as an ogre in English Protestant eyes. Since then, his unbending Catholicism had intensified this image and his politique civility towards England, indeed his support of English interests at Rome, had done nothing to dissuade Englishmen of their growing fear of him. Cecil's bold stroke in 1568, when he persuaded his mistress to seize the treasure ships, had led to an angry clash between the two powers and reflected England's somewhat insouciant attitude towards this remote giant. Hence English fear of Spain, though real and growing, was not nearly so urgent as their suspicions of France.

How had these general attitudes towards their great neighbors altered in the course of the four years of intense activity between 1572 and 1576? Take first the case of France. At the beginning of the 1570's the problem was a familiar one, and a model for dealing with it had been established. After the unlucky intervention of 1562-1563 Elizabeth had set her face against another such experience but in the civil war of 1568-1569 she had somewhat reluctantly acceded to a cold war technique by which the French Protestants—the Rochellois especially—were permitted easy access to English supplies, provided they paid for them, and the English government turned a blind eye on the collaboration between English privateers (or pirates) and the Huguenot seamen. Once it became apparent that French Protestantism would survive the blow of August 1572, the English returned to this strategy. It was a useful one in the highly fluid state of French affairs, but there was a new element in French politics which it did not so handily fit. After the departure of Henry for Poland, his younger brother of Alençon (now Anjou) rapidly asserted his independent role. He had been put forward as a candidate for Elizabeth's hand by his mother and brother and that negotiation remained in their hands, but Anjou himself established secret communications with the English court. There had been an earlier episode in the Maisonfleur affair in the fall of 1572; much more serious was the involvement with the Duke in the last months of Charles IX's reign, when there was talk of his flight to England (accompanied by his cousin of Navarre). Later still, when Damville took up arms in the new reign and allied the Montmorencies with the Huguenots, the English government was drawn into cooperation with the coalition which included beside Damville, Alençon, Navarre, and Condé. To their enterprise Elizabeth contributed a loan of £15,000 to finance the Palatine's mercenaries sent to Condé's aid.

These latter intrigues signalled a slight but significant shift in English policy. To play the role of protector of the persecuted Protestants was a relatively safe tactic, proved by experience and tacitly accepted by the French Court. The intrigues with Alençon and his allies was of course a reaction to a change in French politics; they were no longer characterized by a more or less straightforward religious conflict; the rogue male Duke was on the loose, prepared to join whatever forces of discontent might serve his insatiable but unfocussed ambitions. But the English move was a risky one since England seemed about to abandon a backstage role for one of public appearance on the stage of French civil conflict. When the Queen Mother patched up a peace which sent home all the protagonists—except the English—with something to show for their efforts, Elizabeth was profoundly disgusted, but in fact the peaceful termination of the threatening French conflict spared England the further involvements which developing civil war would have entailed. As it was, she had committed and lost nothing more than £15,000.

It is not easy to explain this shift in policy; the English documents are few and mostly merely formal. Circumstances, of course, encouraged it. Elizabeth was already involved with the Duke and when he showed his independence of his mother and brother, she could hardly afford to let him slip altogether out of her orbit. At this early stage of his career he was still something of an unknown quantity; if his abilities matched his ambition, he might become a centrally important figure in French politics. As it was, Elizabeth had to take out insurance against all possible contingencies at the French Court.

All the same, Elizabeth's willingness to press this kind of intervention to the danger point is somewhat startling; at one stage she contemplated receiving Alençon and Navarre as refugees in England; at another was egging them on to war against their sovereign, even providing a modest subsidy to encourage them. And when the latter scheme fell apart, Elizabeth could not conceal her chagrin. The Queen's inclination to dabble in shady conspiracy of this risky kind is not altogether uncharacteristic. It reflects her fondness for the devious, for underhanded conspiracy rather than for open intervention —as well as a certain royal snobbishness which found plotting with Anjou or Navarre far more acceptable behavior than dealing with the bourgeois magistrates or provincial nobles of the Low Countries. What the consequences of this line of action might have been we cannot know since the Queen Mother's skill finally stilled the troubled waters of French politics. But the drift of English policy towards an involvement from which it would have been difficult to withdraw is perceptible. It may be argued that England came close in these months to a Tudor Vietnam, to a long-term entanglement in the morass of French civil war which might have proved ruinous to all the goals which Elizabeth valued.

The bewildering uncertainties of the Valois Court forced on England a line of action which would enable them to deal with whatever combination emerged from the kaleidoscope of French politics. In the case of Spain the situation was much more clearly blocked out in black and white. Philip II was beyond all doubts in full control of Spanish policy and Spanish power; his aims, as an outraged monarch faced by rebels who were also heretics, were straightforward: the suppression of insurrection and heresy. The uncertainties here lay in the potentialities of rebel success. Hapsburg power, the mightiest in

Europe, could, if concentrated, surely crush the puny forces of the Sea-Beggars, unable to win full control of even two remote provinces. But the Hapsburg empire was a very clumsy giant and one with many enemies. It was possible either that Philip, distracted by many problems in the Mediterranean world, might accept some compromise in the Low Countries or, alternatively, that some foreign prince might intervene on the rebel side. It was the first outcome which the English government ardently hoped for and the second which the rebels assiduously sought.

For over two years events gave no clear signal in either direction; Spanish successes on land were countered by rebel control of the sea and of the waterways. Through these years England's stance remained one of carefully balanced neutrality. If the rebels had unlimited access to English ports and to English supplies, Spain on the other hand was gratified by the reopening of trade relations. Indeed, trade was a central concern of the English since Antwerp was still the focal mart of western Europe and the staple for English cloth. A great deal of diplomatic energy was put to work at the awkward task of maintaining access to the blockaded Flemish port, which involved the consent of both Orange and the Spanish governor. English success in this difficult feat is a proof of the value of her friendship to both protagonists. But the events of 1575 eased the English government out of the paths of caution it had hitherto trodden into a bolder course. The failure of Escobedo's relief fleet even to sail from the northern Spanish ports, the continued stalemate at Ziericksee, and the declared bankruptcy of the Spanish treasury persuaded the Queen to take the initiative. England's hopes now focussed on such a softening of Philip's policy as would lead to political and religious compromise with his rebellious Low Country subjects. The moment seemed to have come when England could move actively to press the mediation which she had so frequently suggested over the past three years. The English program envisaged submission by the rebels to Philip's authority in return for the removal of Spanish troops and officials, a restoration of provincial autonomy, and a vaguely defined freedom of conscience for his Protestant subjects. In pressing this scheme on the Brussels government, England went beyond the role of honest broker; it was made clear that England's interests required this relaxation of Spanish power in the Low Countries. Elizabeth could not afford to live with neighbors who were merely provinces in a centralized Spanish empire. It was a significant shift in English policy, for it meant that England now forthrightly asserted that a change in Spanish policy within its empire was a desideratum for English security. It was in fact an abandonment of neutrality, at a moment when it seemed very likely that Spain would find it wiser to loosen her control over the Burgundian provinces rather than to continue an exhausting war. Significantly the Queen was not prepared to press any conditions about religion in the compromise she pushed forward. Her hope was that Philip would turn the same blind eye to private religious conviction (and even worship) which she displayed towards her own Catholic subjects.

In France Catherine de' Medici's diplomacy resolved the crisis from which England had hoped to profit and thus left English schemes for intervention untested. In Spain the final breakdown of Spanish authority after the death of Requesens similarly made English proposals no longer relevant. It looked —by the fall of 1576—as though Lowlanders by their own exertions would throw off effective Spanish authority in their territories and achieve by themselves the aims which England had hoped to realize by her mediation.

But the shift of events both in France and in the Netherlands does not disguise the fact that England in both cases had moved from a cautious reserve which gave only minimal aid to the Protestant rebels on the continent to a much bolder and increasingly dangerous participation in continental politics. It was more forthright in the French case with the subsidy to Condé, but more far-reaching in the Dutch case, where a major alteration in the distribution of power was made a condition for England's own security.

CHAPTER 10

ENGLAND AND

THE LOW COUNTRIES,

1576-1578

In the wake of the Spanish collapse in the Low Countries, the English leadership stirred to a new and more venturesome policy, but the conclusive initiative remained in Madrid. Would Philip acknowledge the force of events and bend his policies accordingly, or would he stubbornly press onward to the same unchanging goals, yielding nothing to time or circumstance? The next two years would provide answers to this query.

The breakdown of Spain's power in the Low Countries inaugurated a whole new phase in her relations with England, which was to last until Don John's successor, the iron Prince of Parma, made felt his strong grasp on the provinces at the beginning of the 1580's. On the face of it, the situation was most favorable to England; the mainspring of Spanish authority in the Netherlands was broken, seemingly past repair, while the new provisional government of the States was pushing a program which coincided with a solution pushed by the English Queen since 1572—a return to the *status quo ante*. Elizabeth would be led to an unwonted support for direct intervention with men and money to back the States government, to the delight of Leicester and Walsingham. But events were to disappoint expectation. The internal disagreements of the Low Countries were to prove stronger than their common fear of Spain. The Queen's response to the growing dissension in the States's ranks was to back away from active intervention, first to indirect support by paying for the mercenaries of the Palatine prince, Casimir, and then, when that ploy failed, to reluctant sponsorship of the Duke of Anjou as a stalking-horse against the now resurgent power of Spain. This too proved a vain project; with the coming of Parma to power as Philip's governor, Spanish power gained a momentum which would not be arrested until all of the southern provinces were again in Philip's hands. Possibilities of compromise or of reconciliation would fade fast. The Queen kept free of wholehearted commitment to the rebel cause, but she drifted a long way from the posture of discreetly colored neutrality which she had maintained hitherto. The measure of involvement, although undefined and ineffectual, was yet too great for easy or safe withdrawal. It was in fact to deepen into a more dangerous enterprise than any the Queen had ventured on hitherto, more far-reaching than any commitment to continental affairs made by her predecessors since Lancastrian times. But in the early months of 1576 all this was in the future.

THROUGH THE SUMMER and early autumn of that year the Low Countries drifted rudderless while Philip in his deliberate way cogitated over a successor to the late Grand Commander Requesens. His ultimate choice had about it an air of uncertainty and indecision. In early April a first offer of the governorship had been made to the King's half-brother, the hero of Lepanto, Don John of Austria, but it was not a settled matter until September. This brilliant, insecure young man had been kept on a very short tether by his royal brother since 1571. Restless, full of unfocussed ambition, Don John dreamed of a throne of his own, with the kind of security and status which had hitherto eluded him. As early as 1572 English Catholic exiles had thought of him as a suitable match for Mary Stuart. In 1573 the Pope recommended Mary to the care of Philip and although the latter excused himself on the grounds of his pre-occupations in Flanders, the Papal nuncio at Madrid kept up a steady drum-fire of pressure in favor of the Scots Queen. Now, in the approaches to Don John, Philip's secretary, Perez, was allowed to hold out the bait of an English expedition—once the Low Countries were pacified—to rescue the captive Catholic princess. The King in his wily, distrustful way made no direct promises and in the end negotiations between the brothers were cut short by urgent news of increasing disorder and of the emergence of Orangist power at Brussels. In great haste Don John left Spain in late September and travelling incognito crossed France safely, arriving in Luxembourg on 31 October. Since Don John's experience was almost entirely military, the appointment might have suggested that Philip's policy in the Low Countries was to be one of reconquest. In fact the royal instructions were conciliatory in tenor and authorized the new governor to dismiss the Spanish troops in the provinces, once Holland and Zealand submitted, and to yield on most issues other than that of religion. There was a sense of hesitation and drift in Philip's actions at this point. He had entrusted his Netherlandish provinces to a young, impatient, and ambitious warrior, who, however, was to bear an olive branch rather than a sword. This incongruous combination of a man of war with a policy of peace was unlikely to lead to successful conciliation. Yet the new governor also lacked the necessary resources for the alternative policy of force.[1]

The secret instructions which followed the prince in early November dealt with quite another topic: the putative invasion of England.[2] Very cautiously couched, they emphasized certain preconditions—a solid peace in the Low Countries, assured French neutrality, and a precise understanding with the English Roman Catholics. The rationale of the expedition would be provided by a Papal bull in behalf of Mary, the le-

---

[1] For this paragraph, see P. O. de Törne, *Don Juan d'Autriche et les projets de conquête de l'Angleterre . . . 1568-1578* (2 vols., Helsingfors, 1915, 1928), *passim*, esp. I, 143-44, 169; and II, 47-48; KL, *Relations*, VI, 223.

[2] KL, *Relations*, IX, 15-21.

gitimate Catholic sovereign. But all this was contingent on Don John's precedent completion of a Herculean task, the pacification of the provinces.

On almost the same day that these instructions were drawn up, the States-General at Brussels, acting for all the provinces, was issuing another set of instructions for the first of the many envoys they would accredit to the Queen of England.[3] This decision followed closely on two events. The first was the agreement of the provinces known as the Pacification of Ghent, which united them against the Spanish troops and Spanish officials still on their soil. The second was that fearful outburst, the Spanish fury—the sack of Antwerp—perpetrated by the mutinous, unpaid royal garrison. The States-General in their representations to Elizabeth rehearsed not only present conditions but also the brutalities which they had suffered at Spanish hands for a decade past and thus justified their decision to take up arms in their own defense. They took great pains to emphasize their loyalty to their royal master and to the Roman Catholic faith; they spoke longingly of the golden days of Charles V and called for a return to that happy age.

Most immediately men's eyes turned to three central figures —Don John, the Prince of Orange, and the Duke of Anjou. Of these the Prince was most forthright in his intentions. Deeply suspicious of the new governor, he urged that no recognition be given him by the States until the Spanish troops were gone and until Don John had conceded new constitutional arrangements which would leave all real power in the hands of the States-General. Anjou's interest was immediately apparent although his intentions were anything but clear. Don John quickly yielded to the demand for the removal of the Spaniards but his further policy remained a matter for suspicious speculation. Both the States and the governor turned their attention towards England; as we have seen, an envoy from the former was accredited in November and one from the latter followed in December. The States's emissary was to ask that the Queen send an intercessory agent to Philip to back up their demands and to this request she responded

[3] *Ibid.*, 23-24.

quickly; Sir John Smith was dispatched to Madrid with instructions to offer his mistress' service once again as mediator, urging Philip to recall the Spanish soldiery and to be reconciled with his Low Countries' subjects.[4]

At the same time Elizabeth sent Edward Horsey, Leicester's dependent and a recent emissary to France, to attend upon Don John. Like his counterpart at Madrid he was to urge on the governor all possible pacificatory measures, warning him sharply of the probability of French intervention. Don John was to be offered a carrot in the form of an English offer to join with him in expelling any French forces sent into the provinces. Horsey had orders also to confer secretly with some of the States's leaders and with Dr. Wilson, the English envoy already in Brussels.[5]

In the meantime the States on their side had dispatched yet another agent across the Channel, again a familiar figure in London, Councillor Sweveghem. His task was to raise a substantial loan from the English government. He arrived in London in mid-December; the Queen's response to his request was made with unaccustomed promptness; by Christmas Eve he could write home of the royal promise that if Don John did not accept the States's terms, she would loan them £100,-000 for eight months. Sweveghem was pressing the Privy Councillors for an immediate installment of £20,000 which he could take back with him. In this he was only partially successful since instructions were issued to Dr. Wilson not to turn over the £20,000 until all hope of accord with Don John had failed. Wilson confirmed this tentative commitment to the Council in Brussels, even extending it to include possible armed aid, always on the conditions of continuing loyalty to the King. The States returned their thanks in early January 1577, taking occasion to reassert their determination to change neither prince nor religion.[6]

[4] *CSPF*, XI, 427-28, 428-30, 437, 438; KL, *Relations*, IX, 23-24.

[5] *CSPF*, XI, 442-44; BL, Add. Ms. 48,084, ff. 32-35, for Burghley's views, and f. 36 for mission to Spain.

[6] KL, *Relations*, IX, 82-83, 96-97, 98-100, 102-3, 139; *CSPF*, XI, 456, 480-81.

The months that followed through the spring of 1577 were filled with the buzz and hum of diplomatic activity. The English agents in the Low Countries were dealing with the States, with the governor, and with the Prince of Orange, who still controlled independently his northern enclave in Holland and Zealand. Don John politely but firmly rejected Elizabeth's offer of mediation;[7] he could now use the excuse that the Emperor had already stepped into that role and sent his representatives to referee between the governor and the States. English relations with Orange steadily warmed as his influence throughout all the provinces grew. And in turn, States, Prince, and governor all maintained their agents at the English Court during these months. Elizabeth's special messenger to Philip, Smith, had in the meantime arrived at Madrid in early February.

The central negotiation was that between the governor and the States and this resolved itself into a fragile agreement in the Peace of Marche-en-Famine (12 February 1577). This pact was far from settling the great issues troubling the provinces, but it had the immediate effect of clearing out the remaining Spanish forces and—more important from the English point of view—ensuring their departure by land and not by sea. It had been a great hope of Don John's that the Spanish forces leaving the Low Countries could somehow be used against England, and his agent, Gastel, sent over in the winter, was charged to request landing privileges in case of emergencies. The glittering mirage of the Scottish match and an English throne which had helped to draw Don John to his Low Countries charge was fading rapidly.[8]

The uncertain peace which was inaugurated in February lasted until mid-summer. It never truly comprehended Holland and Zealand, where the Prince of Orange remained in control while negotiating with Don John and the States. The Peace of Marche-en-Famine was really nothing more than a truce which dealt with the immediate problem of the Spanish

[7] KL, *Relations*, IX, 161.
[8] *CSPF*, XI, 517-18; KL, *Relations*, IX, 80.

forces but did not touch the central issues at stake: who was to be the real ruler of the Low Countries; which religion was to prevail?

In April Orange had again proposed to the Queen (by means of Daniel Rogers) an alliance between his two provinces and England; believing that no lasting peace was possible because of religion, he looked for a renewal of war. English assistance, in such a case, was as much in Elizabeth's interest as the Prince's. He invoked yet again the ghost of Bayonne and insisted that Philip would not rest until Protestantism was everywhere overthrown. The Queen's answer to these bold proposals delivered through Rogers was surprisingly mild. Her rejection of the offer was not an absolute one and she countered with a scheme for a general Protestant league comprehending England and the German Protestant princes, and part of Rogers' mission was to broach this to the Palatine. Even while these discussions were going forward, open rupture between Don John and the States took place with his retirement to the citadel of Namur late in July. Accusations of bad faith flew back and forth and both sides moved slowly towards a resumption of open warfare.[9]

At this juncture the English government, which had more or less marked time since the late winter, moved actively into the affairs of the Low Countries once again. William Davison was sent in early August 1577 to Brussels, officially accredited to the governor but with instructions to work with the States and with Orange. Officially and openly he was to urge conciliation; confidentially to those who were "discreet and good patriots" he was to make it clear that the Queen put no trust whatsoever in Don John and would not fail to assist them so far as stood within the Queen's honor. In addition he was also to urge acceptance of Orange as their only possible leader. On his arrival in Brussels, Davison found the Estates successful in quashing the plots laid by Don John to gain control of the citadel of Antwerp and other points of strength. But he noticed their disposition to take a purely defensive stance and

[9] *CSPF*, XI, 583, 600, and XII, 22-25; KL, *Relations*, IX, 356-62.

their unwillingness to give much authority to Orange. The latter arose partly from the rivalries between the house of Croye and the house of Orange but even more from Catholic fears of the Prince's religion.[10]

Davison almost crossed paths with a new envoy being sent by the States. The Marquis d'Havré, brother to the Duke of Aerschot and a leading member of the house of Croye, was instructed to seek another loan on the order of £100,000, and to propose that Leicester be sent to the Low Countries to take command of the English and Scottish volunteer forces already in being. As a persuader he was to offer copies of letters from Spain, intercepted by the States and already shown to Rogers, which revealed Spanish designs on England. Havré was to pay special suit to Leicester, who was already regarded as the friend and English patron of Orange and of the States of Holland.[11]

Through the late summer and early fall of 1577 the Low Countries magnates, the Prince of Orange and Don John, jockeyed uneasily for position, each distrusting the other party. Official negotiations between the States and the governor to patch up a peace dragged on with no great expectation of success on either side. That peace endured through these months was the effect of a shortage of money on all sides rather than of good will or trust on either part. But the States were also at odds among themselves. The preeminence of the Prince of Orange as the only man who could give them leadership awakened jealousies among the other magnates as well as fears for the Catholic religion. Already there was talk of summoning the Hapsburg Archduke Matthias from Vienna to act as governor of the provinces. His royal blood would provide a modicum of legitimacy while his innocence of any Spanish association would make him acceptable in the provinces; above all, he could be used as a counterweight against Orange. By October the Archduke had left Vienna on his way to the Low Countries. The English agents could only watch with dismay the growing disunity within the ranks of the

[10] *CSPF*, XII, 54-55, 74-77.
[11] *Ibid.*, 120, 123; KL, *Relations*, IX, 487-91.

States and convey their fears to London. In France another Huguenot-Catholic confrontation had been cooled down by the Queen Mother before actual fighting began. The Peace of Bergerac in September 1577 opened anew the worrying possibility of French intervention led by Anjou.[12]

It was fear of the last which had precipitated the States's plea for English aid; by the time the Marquis d'Havré presented himself before the Queen in late September 1577, he had sharpened his requests to include not only an immediate loan of £100,000 but also the prompt despatch of 6,000 English soldiers (of which 1,000 would be cavalry) under the command of some great English seigneur, *if and when* French forces entered the provinces. With a quite extraordinary alacrity the Queen granted the loan and offered the soldiers should need arise. Leicester rejoiced to see his mistress in such "very good minding in those matters as ever I saw her." He was anxious that the Prince bring pressure for the immediate despatch of English forces; to wait until the French moved would be fatal (given the fact that the English had the disadvantage of a sea crossing).[13]

But the Low Countries leadership was in fact deeply divided over English aid. They wanted English money but they were very doubtful about English soldiers. The Catholic nobles, led by the powerful and numerous house of Croye, jealous of the Prince of Orange and fearful of the religious change which he favored, feared an English contingent, especially one led by Leicester, who was so closely linked with Orange and with the reformed religion. And indeed the Prince was zealously urging Leicester's immediate arrival. The Croyes' counter-move had already been made as early as August, when they secretly invited Archduke Matthias to come as elected governor; the secret had to be revealed to Orange in September and in October the Austrian was already at Cologne. His coming stirred debate in the Council of State and an open clash between the head of the Croye family (Aerschot) and the Prince. In the States the Catholic nobles were powerful enough

---

[12] *CSPF*, XII, 171-72, 226-27.
[13] *Ibid.*, 201-4; KL, *Relations*, IX, 540, 550-51, and X, 103-5.

to persuade the States to decline the English offer of armed aid, alleging the approach of winter and the need to establish order within the provinces. They were still clamorous for their £100,000 and reserved the right to ask for armed aid in the future, but they were clearly backing away from too close an entanglement with England.[14]

The fragility of the Croye power became apparent when the Duke of Aerschot and others of his family and adherents unwisely ventured into Ghent at the end of October. The citizenry, populist and Protestant, rose under the leadership of the urban magistrates and imprisoned the Duke and his entourage, openly accusing Aerschot of intrigue with Don John and with Anjou and with using Matthias as a stalking-horse for their own ends. The Duke was released at the request of the States and the Prince, but the Councillors of State arrested with him remained in custody.[15]

These developments were watched with considerable resentment by the English Court. As late as 14 October Leicester had been eagerly planning the composition of his expeditionary force, which he had earlier referred to as "being such a picked company as has not passed the seas these forty years for their number." But by the 18th he was writing in dismay about the uncertainties which surrounded Matthias' arrival and warning that the Privy Council might reverse its recent recommendation to aid the States. Walsingham expressed the Queen's resentment at not having been informed about the Archduke's coming; and the States's ambassadors in London warned their masters of the growing coolness felt by the English government.[16]

Leicester's resentment turned even against the Prince, whom he accused of indifference towards the English offer. Davison, more aware of the realities of Low Countries politics, pointed out the Prince's limited power within the States General and his need to compromise with the other elements in the Brus-

[14] *CSPF*, XII, 170-72, 222-24, 226-27, 240, 249, 287-92, 320-23; KL, *Relations*, IX, 461.

[15] *CSPF*, XII, 292-93, 303-5, 318, 320-23.

[16] *Ibid.*, 204, 260, 266, 267, 268, 271-72.

sels regime. At this point in November Davison had a very frank discussion with the Prince, who quite coolly advised the English government to temporize for a while, without any show of sympathy; if the ambassadors insisted upon the first installment of the loan (£20,000 to £30,000) the Queen should assign the money to Davison with instructions to dawdle over the details of payment as long as possible.[17]

The States, in fact, chastened by recent experience, now began to warm towards English intervention even as the English Court's sympathies cooled. On 19 November they reversed their earlier vote and agreed to accept English armed aid, and on 2 December their ambassadors in England presented this proposal to the English. Within a fortnight they had the Queen's agreement to a general treaty of alliance, including an expeditionary force to be paid by the States. The alliance was to be reciprocal, with the States committed to aid England in case of need; and to all future negotiations with any other prince Elizabeth was to be party. If a reconciliation with Philip were achieved, these articles were to be confirmed by the King as part of such a settlement. At the same time a treaty was drawn up between Matthias and the States, which gave him the title of governor, but virtually no power, all important decisions being reserved to the States or the Council nominated by them. It was not until the end of January that the Archduke formally took his oath and was proclaimed Governor-General at Brussels. Although Matthias had come as the Catholics' nominee, Orange was strong enough to secure to himself the important post of Lieutenant-General to the Archduke.[18]

In the meantime the Queen, following up her promises to the States, prepared to send Thomas Wilkes, another of her all-purpose diplomats, to Spain to expostulate with Philip. His instructions ordered him to make the strongest possible plea for the acceptance of the pacification; he was also to urge the recall of Don John and to make much of the intercepted correspondence, with its talk of a prospective invasion of Eng-

[17] Ibid., 307-9, 320-23, 327-28.
[18] KL, Relations, X, 137, 219-21; CSPF, XII, 364-69.

land. Wilkes was to tell the King that Elizabeth had promised money and men to the States on their promise to observe the pacification and maintain the old religion. She hoped for Philip's approval of her measures; if under a new governor the Estates refused obedience on the terms outlined above, she would join the King of Spain in coercing them. It was the strongest stand the Queen had yet taken *vis à vis* Spain. At the same time Thomas Leighton was sent off, accredited to the States and to Don John, with the thankless task of urging a truce on these two parties.[19]

These busy negotiations were rudely interrupted at the end of January 1578 when Don John fell on the States's army at Gembloux and decisively beat them. Even before this news reached London, the Queen was hesitating on following through on her commitment of men. Orders had been sent to the shires for the levy, but now Elizabeth, strongly pressured within the Council by Leicester's opponents, balked at further action. After the news of Gembloux, the Queen instantly despatched Leighton once more across the Channel, excusing her delay on grounds of reports of serious dissensions among the States. He was, however, to reassure them that her troops were still available.[20]

The months following saw a steady shift in English policy; the steps by which it was brought about are quite unclear, but in early March Daniel Rogers was sent off to the Netherlands with a startling new proposal. The Queen declared that she could not send forces to the Low Countries because such a move would certainly provoke the French into matching the English with a force of their own. Hence she proposed that Duke Casimir, the Palatine prince, be hired to bring 6,000 Swiss and 5,000 reiters to the provinces. That veteran entrepreneur, always ready to sell his services to the Protestant cause, was now in negotiation with the States. Elizabeth was willing to provide £20,000 immediately and the same sum in addition on days of musters, to be charged against the loan of £100,000. A crestfallen letter from Leicester to Davison of

---

[19] *CSPF*, XII, 370-73, 388-92.   [20] *Ibid.*, 490-91.

the same date reveals something of the struggle in the Council which preceded it. Bitterly disappointed, he feared that God had "found us unworthy of a longer continuance of his former blessing." The States rather reluctantly consented to the proposed alterations before the end of March.[21]

Just at this point Don Bernardino de Mendoza arrived in England, Spain's first resident ambassador in some seven years. He came in part as a response to the Smith embassy.[22] His very appointment was a score for the Queen since it meant that Philip had at last been persuaded to turn his attention directly to England; it was a somewhat irritated regard which he now bestowed on his one-time kingdom, but the choice of Mendoza was gratifying to English pride since the new ambassador was a Spaniard of high rank and distinction. The line which he followed (based on royal instructions) was at once stiff and flexible—stiff in its defence of the King's actions and those of Don John, flexible in that the ambassador insisted that peace could be achieved if only the Catholic religion were maintained and the States returned to their obedience as in the time of the King's father. This latter declaration was taken by the Queen as a hopeful sign that she might yet arrange a mediated peace. Her secretaries both took the far less optimistic view that Spain was merely playing for time. The ambassador eluded any acceptance of an English mediation, alleging the lack of instructions.[23]

Through April and May 1578 the English government pursued two goals—on the one hand, seeking, through Mendoza and through another agent sent to Don John, to bring about a cease-fire. On the other hand, they went ahead with arrangements for the loan to the States and by early May Casimir had received his first £20,000. But the States and the Prince were far from happy about a succor which would be two to three months in arriving, and worrying reports began to come in of their renewed interest in Anjou's tempting offers of assistance. Some within the English Council felt the situation was

[21] *Ibid.*, 529-30, 531, 556; KL, *Relations*, X, 281-82.
[22] *CSPF*, XII, 541-44; *CSPSp*, II, 553-60.
[23] *CSPF*, XII, 552-53.

so desperate that the least evil for English policy now would be to support Anjou as an ally of the States (and thus keep him out of Don John's clutches).[24]

The question of Anjou's intervention became more than an academic one as the spring wore on. By the latter half of April commissioners of the States were negotiating with deputies of the Duke. The States desperately tried to divert Anjou's energies by proposing that he should occupy the County of Burgundy and other territories beyond the Meuse, i.e., Hapsburg provinces not affected by the revolt and lying outside the Belgian heartland. These negotiations came to no conclusion but the probability of Anjou's intervention steadily grew. In the meantime the Queen had sent yet another envoy, Wilkes this time, to persuade Don John to a cease-fire. The governor rather tartly replied that the Queen seemed not to have understood his reply to her previous messenger, Leighton. He categorically refused a cease-fire and brusquely suggested that the Queen mind her own business.[25]

These events disturbed the English government deeply, and in early May the Queen began to consider the despatch of a high-level mission to the Netherlands, possibly headed by Leicester, who eagerly sought the post. To stall off an immediate agreement between the States and the Duke of Anjou, she ordered Davison to demand that as condition for payment of the second £20,000 due to Casimir, the States should proceed no further with the French prince. By late May the States and Anjou were on the verge of a treaty; the Duke offered to serve for two months with 10,000 foot soldiers and 2,000 horsemen at his own charge; if after three months they decided to change masters, he was to be their choice. In the meantime he asked that three or four towns be handed over to him. The Queen was now in a fury and wrote off peremptorily to Davison that he was to cut off all supply of money and to stay Duke Casimir unless the States suspended their French negotiations until the arrival of her new ambassadors, Secretary Walsing-

[24] KL, *Relations*, X, 384-85, 475, 525, 531-32, 558, 562; *CSPF*, XII, 630-32.
[25] *CSPF*, XII, 624-25, 636-37, 644-51.

ham and Lord Cobham. Orange's behavior in this affair was very harshly judged in London; it was assumed that he was now resolved on independence from Spain, hence opposed to the Queen's efforts to obtain reconciliation with Philip, and thus pro-French. This ultimatum proved unnecessary since negotiations with Anjou failed in the end, largely because he sought sole and supreme command of all the States's forces without regard to the Archduke.[26]

Cobham and Walsingham set off from Court on 15 June. Tokens of the importance attached to their mission were the rank of the ambassadors and the state in which they travelled (with a suite of 120), quite unlike their modest predecessors. But the contents of the instructions given the ambassadors were all too familiar. The Queen still hankered after a cease-fire to be followed by mediation and a return to the old order. She was realistic enough, however, to envisage other alternatives. If peace with Don John were not possible, then an alliance with Anjou, regarded as intolerable only a few weeks ago, might be unavoidable. If the States's forces backed by the armies of Anjou and Casimir were insufficient to withstand Don John, she was willing to send armed aid from England. They were to make minute inquiries into the resources of the States and to insist that if aid were given, cautionary towns, preferably Sluys and Flushing, would have to be delivered to the English.[27]

The dispatch of the Walsingham-Cobham mission marked the last phase of an era which began with the collapse of Spanish power in the Netherlands in early 1576. By now some of the fog of confusion which had so densely shrouded the political landscape had cleared. Initially the alliance against the Spaniards had united all groups, nobles, townsmen, Protestants and Catholics, and the rival magnate houses. But Don John had had a modest success in drawing a party of nobles to his side, especially from the southern provinces, and he had clearly established himself as the standard-bearer of Catholicism. Orange, whose control over Holland and Zealand had

[26] *Ibid.*, 665, 671, 689, 690-92, 702-3, 704-7, 722-26.
[27] *CSPF*, XIII, 10-13, 17-18.

been far from complete in 1576, had made wide gains. Amsterdam was now in his hands; he was governor of Brabant by the States's appointment and lieutenant to the Archduke; he had re-entered Netherlandish politics by his return to Brussels, and his influence in the States was very great although by no means unchallenged. The house of Croye did its best to maintain a foothold against him. The invitation of Matthias had been their boldest move but hardly a successful one since that puppet prince was effectively at the beck and call of the Prince.

These dynastic rivalries sputtered and flared, but until the spring of 1578 the far more dangerous question of religion was carefully muted, largely by the Prince's own efforts. In the course of that season the tinder of Protestant discontent took fire and in one Flemish and Brabantine town after another the Protestants emerged from their semi-clandestine underground to a fully public assertion of their religion.[28] They seized churches for their use, expelled the religious orders, smashed altars and images, and demanded the right to public observance and propagation of their faith. The dangers which threatened the fragile unity of the States as a result of these religious divisions and the opportunities they offered the Spanish government were increasingly apparent.

These changing circumstances also opened the door to the Duke of Anjou. He had been hovering hopefully in the wings for the last two years. Now the fears of the Catholic nobility of Hainault gave him leverage within the provinces. More and more of the States leaned to this French and Catholic prince as their best guarantee against Don John and his Spaniards, on the one hand, or Orange and his wild-eyed reformers, on the other. The Queen had always averted her eyes from the facts of religious division in the Low Countries, to the distress of the Prince of Orange, and now, ignoring Anjou's religious preferences, she bent her policy to take account of his improved position. Contact with the Duke was made through clandestine agents while the ambassadors to the

[28] KL, *Relations*, X, 435-57, 569-72; *CSPF*, XII, 613-16, 704-6, 726, 727.

States were grudgingly allowed to discuss the terms of a possible arrangement with the French prince. This was an important shift in English policy. Unwilling to enter the scene directly, Elizabeth had first tried to use Casimir. Now she was turning instead to the French duke; these were the first steps towards a major alteration of English policy—one which would shape that policy for some five years.[29]

The ambassadors, once arrived in the Netherlands, found themselves painfully squeezed on all sides. High expectations had been aroused by their coming, a situation which distressed Walsingham even before he left England. The very "slender matter" contained in their instructions made for a chilly reception once it was known. The States were blunt in their rejection of any accommodation with Don John and blunter still in pointing out that any talk of going back to the old footing of the Emperor Charles' time—the favorite shibboleth of earlier negotiations—was now beside the point. The question of religion demanded radical change and must be left to the States's decision. Moreover, the whole network of relations had been fatally damaged by Don John's bad faith and could not now be restored. But there was also a loss of confidence in English good faith, compounded by the fact that the Queen would do no more than act as guarantor for a second £100,000 loan, a futile gesture under the circumstances, given the difficulties of actually raising funds. The Netherlanders were driven willy-nilly to look towards the Duke of Anjou as their best—or rather, their only—hope. The Duke was pressing in his offers of aid and full of effusive assurances as to his altruistic motives. In fact the Belgian magnates and the English ambassadors remained baffled by the Duke's behavior, unable (1) to decide whether he was acting with his brother's consent or not and (2) whether he came to aid Don John or the States. The harried States, torn between suspicion of Anjou and distrust of Elizabeth, continued to hesitate until the Duke took things in his own hands by entering Hainault, occupying

[29] KL, *Relations*, X, 575-76; *CSPF*, XII, 435-37, 531; *ibid.*, XIII, 18, 39-43.

Mons, and laying siege to Maubeuge (recently taken by Don John).[30]

Elizabeth chose this moment to throw one of her customary tantrums, angrily denouncing her ambassadors because they had not demanded the first due repayment on the earlier loan of £100,000 while turning on the States, full of indignation at their request for more money. Her ambassadors suffered even more, for they had pledged their personal credit for an immediate loan of £5,000, hoping to be reimbursed by their royal mistress.[31]

There followed a month of uncertainty as agents from Anjou came and went, within the Low Countries, and across the Channel to the English Court. The Queen remained unyielding in her refusal to provide money for the States or even to cover the money guaranteed by the ambassadors. Walsingham waxed grimly humorous in a letter to Randolph; rumor had it that he and Cobham would be hanged for their performance in the Low Countries; he hoped only for a Middlesex jury trial. Burghley and Wilson lamented the Queen's obstinacy; the latter declared "that *fatum regit mundum* or rather that will bears sway instead of reason." One ray of light brightened this dark landscape when an engagement was fought between the States's forces and Don John's at a place called Rymenam near Mechlin, in which the latter suffered a severe check and the English forces led by Colonel John Norris covered themselves with glory. Duke Casimir's English-paid forces lingered on in the meantime, begging for more money.[32]

English diplomacy was now fumblingly shifting course. Since the Queen was plainly determined to do nothing more for the States out of her own resources, it was necessary to accept some form of French intervention as a necessary counterweight to the Spaniards. Anjou himself professed the desire to act only under the direction and favor of the Queen and even hinted that he had moved on Hainault with her approv-

[30] *CSPF*, XIII, 18, 32-35, 54-57, 64, 65, 83-85, 88-89; KL, *Relations*, X, 588-90.
[31] *CSPF*, XIII, 74, 81, 82-83; KL, *Relations*, X, 635-39.
[32] *CSPF*, XIII, 100, 101, 102, 114, 115-16, 118-19.

al. In addition, he furbished up anew his old and well-worn suit for the Queen's hand. The Queen's response to this was to offer a very reserved approval to his participation in Netherlands affairs if the States felt they could not fend off Don John by themselves. Burghley, Sussex, and Leicester were very dubious of her action, pointing out that Walsingham had no leverage other than words by which either to persuade the Duke to withdraw or to limit his participation.[33]

Leicester in an uncommonly frank letter to Walsingham summed up the Queen's mind at this point. She suspected that Anjou had in fact very slender resources for his Low Countries venture and thus could be held on the silken lead strings of hopes and promises. In this delicate situation it was important that Walsingham play up to the Duke, concealing any hint of distrust and yet probing as deeply as possible into the Prince's motives. This required the Secretary to play the role of favorer to an Anjou marriage. This bit of plain speaking between two intimates throws suggestive light on the distrust they both felt for the French duke and their very equivocal attitude towards a renewal of the wooing.[34]

For a moment, after the English success and with the weight of her ministers' anxious fears of French success in the Low Countries weighing on her, the Queen gave way and swung around to a full acceptance of the States's demands from the English—a force of 10,000 to 12,000 men or else the £100,000. But the States had already made terms with Anjou. The agreement was cautious in its clauses—the Duke was to serve until the end of October at his own charge and thereafter, with a reduced force, he was to garrison the places assigned him. He was to be called Defender of Belgic Liberties but without power in the conduct of government. A league including the Duke, the States, England, Navarre, and other Protestant princes was envisaged; the Duke was given a kind of reversionary claim on the governorship. The Queen, although demurring to some details, gave her tentative blessing to this agreement and finally allowed the States to keep the

[33] *Ibid.*, 121, 122-24, 125-26.   [34] *Ibid.*, 121-23.

first £28,000 raised instead of requiring they be handed over for repayment of the English loan.[35]

The ambassadors were now able to obtain a hearing from Don John, suffering from his recent defeat, a visitation of the plague on his camp, the final arrival of Casimir and his army, and the new agreement with Anjou. They met him in an open field near Louvain; both sides rehearsed their well-worn arguments without yielding and after a few days of desultory discussion prospects of agreement faded altogether. These final weeks of the embassy were deeply discouraging to the ambassadors. The Queen in her most miserly frame of mind allowed the £28,000 to the States only after they provided collateral in the form of jewels and plate. The various armies—those of the States, of Anjou, and of Don John—maneuvered sluggishly as the plague took its terrible toll. The Hainault towns pledged to Anjou by the treaty balked at being turned over to him. Duke Casimir, unable to pay his troops, sulked off to Brussels. Amid these miseries the ambassadors made their way homeward. The news which followed hard on their heels was that of Don John's death at the very beginning of October and his replacement by Alexander Farnese, Prince of Parma. At almost the same time news filtered through from the Mediterranean world of the crushing defeat of the Portuguese king in Morocco. Men worried uneasily over the looming consequences of this distant battle for all Western Europe. But more immediately the long-simmering discontents of the southern Belgian nobility flared up in a clash between them and the radical Protestant oligarchy of Ghent. The threat of a fission in the ranks of the States just at the moment when their great opponent died clouded whatever hope they entertained from that event. Low Countries affairs were about to enter a new phase.[36]

THE COLLAPSE of Spanish power just before and after the death of the Grand Commander had radically altered relations between the English government and the Low Countries.

[35] *Ibid.*, 128-29, 131-34, 138, 153-57, 158.
[36] *Ibid.*, 150-52, 201-2.

First of all there was now something like a legitimate regime with which England could deal. The Council of State at Brussels was the lawful successor to Requesens and it was they who in September 1576 summoned the States General, into whose hands power soon fell. The States could speak with all the authority of law and tradition and for the whole of the provinces. This was a very different voice from that of William of Orange, self-proclaimed leader of an irregular force asserting but not achieving control in two of the seventeen provinces. There was a distinct psychological advantage since the new circumstances went a long way to overcoming the Queen's deep distaste for dealing with rebels. But there was great practical advantage also since the States were potentially an authentic governmental body, able to command obedience, to tax, and to carry on the normal functions of a state. Moreover, their initial program was almost identical with the one Queen Elizabeth had urged steadily upon Philip—a return to the regime of his father. This meant effectually the end of rule by Spanish officials and the restoration of the traditional loose, semi-autonomous Burgundian regime. The ancient religion would be left untouched.

But in fact these fair-seeming prospects were soon to be flawed. The meeting of the States General opened up new opportunities for the Prince of Orange; the magnates at Brussels could hardly ignore him although by entering into relations with him, they implicitly legitimized his status and, worse still, that of the Protestants. The rapidly increasing influence of Orange was particularly gratifying to the left-wing faction in the English Court, gravitating around Leicester and Walsingham. These men now saw their long-time hopes of a Protestant and nationalist regime in the Low Countries given new life. Hence both the Queen and the politique wing of the English establishment, on the one hand, and the Protestant ideologues, on the other, were encouraged to try a more "forward" English policy in the Netherlands than had yet been hazarded, of which the first fruit was the loan proffered with such surprising readiness as soon as Havré asked for it.

Yet the very circumstances which encouraged English action darkened the prospects for Netherlandish unity. At the best the States-General was a mere Continental Congress rather than a Parliament—a body of delegates representing a cluster of autonomous provinces, bound together only by common lordship. Its dominant figures, moreover, were great provincial magnates, linked by family ties, divided by dynastic rivalries, agreeing only in obstinate assertion of equality. All this was discouraging enough, but much worse was the grievous fissure which religion drove through their ranks. The majority of the nobles were Roman Catholic, frightened of what they saw as the egalitarian aspects of the new faith, and the whole question of religion had to be held in abeyance by a kind of gentleman's agreement to ignore it for as long as possible.

The proposed English intervention speedily put a cat among the pigeons. The Queen's ready consent to Havré's request for money was gratifying indeed, but the proposal that the money should be followed by an English expeditionary force was disconcerting, for it immediately stirred up fears that the unsteady balance within the States would be overturned if Orange and his co-religionists had behind them the backing of English armed force. Hence the house of Croye was able to push aside the English offer of men.

From this point on, relations between the would-be allies slipped badly out of phase. Don John's shift from conciliation to belligerence depressed the prospects of the States regime; his victory at Gembloux threw them on the defensive and heightened their need for some sort of foreign assistance. Yet at this very time English policy was drifting in the opposite direction—away from any form of open intervention. Divergence appeared within the English Council, where Leicester and Walsingham fought unceasingly for intervention, becoming themselves increasingly identified as partisans of Orange, while the Queen backed away step by step to her old favorite stance of the would-be mediator, urging a return to the *status quo ante* in government and in religion. Leicester's hopes of leading an expeditionary force faded; the best he could do was to facilitate the flow of volunteers from England and Scotland.

In July 1578 the English contingent in the States's camp at Bois le Duc numbered as many as 3,000 to 3,400 out of the 11,600 infantry, while at Enghien there were 4,000 Scots among the total of 15,400 foot.[37]

Under these circumstances the question of relations with Don John and his royal master took on new importance. It became all too apparent from the summer of 1577 onwards that the former was a formidable factor in the situation. He was hardly *persona grata* in the English Court since his ambitions to play St. George on behalf of Mary Stuart—and to marry her—were widely known. But the English sensed that the ultimate decision would come, not from his camp, but from the Escorial—hence the successive missions to Philip's court.

What took shape as the English government maneuvered among these magnetic fields of differing and rapidly changing force was a gradual weakening of the policy of direct intervention. Stage by stage it was diluted into indirect off-stage efforts to influence events. The first move was to substitute for the proposed English expeditionary force the subsidized mercenaries of Duke Casimir. This looked better on paper than in military fact. As the Prince skeptically prognosticated, the slowness and uncertainty of this German aid rendered it of little value. The English loan, originally a generous £100,000, dwindled away to a subsidy of £40,000, while the balance became a useless guarantee for funds which could not be raised. Most of the cash found its way into the pockets of Casimir. And in the summer of 1578 the Queen was ill-temperedly insisting that any money raised be used to repay the cash already laid out by her treasury.

As all English efforts at aid faded, the Queen turned more and more to her old policy of mediation. Reconciliation of Philip and his subjects was to take place on the platform of Charles V's system. But such a scheme, which had a color of plausibility in 1576-1577, was soon outdated by Don John's successes as well as by the rise of militant Protestantism within the revolting provinces. The probability of either party's yield-

---

[37] *Ibid.*, 48, 178.

ing rapidly diminished under these circumstances. The dispatch of the Walsingham-Cobham mission seemed momentarily to revive the possibility of English intervention, but it was in these very weeks that the Queen turned her face definitively against open English support while abandoning for the nonce the hopes of mediation. She was swinging around now to a policy which only a short time before had seemed abhorrent—to backing Anjou's entrance into the provinces, as a counter-force to Spain, drawing him to accept English direction by the lure of matrimony and, if all else failed, of money.

What is to be made of English policy towards the Low Countries during these crucial years? At the beginning it lurched in an unexpected way from the carefully shaded neutrality of the previous half-decade to the very brink of actual involvement of English soldiers and ships. The explanation for this shift probably lies, as has been suggested, in the extraordinarily propitious circumstances of 1576, along with the concentrated drive of the Leicester-Walsingham coalition to carry their policy. Presumably the Queen went as far as she did because she thought there was a real chance that Philip and his recalcitrant subjects could be brought together to the great advantage of England. Very probably the offer of troops was seen in her mind as a diplomatic ploy rather than as a real commitment of resources. It could serve as a useful lever in bringing Spain to agree to a compromise which circumstances were in any case forcing upon her. The initial coolness of the States towards the offer and their subsequent failure to jell as a government made it apparent that the offer would have to be turned into a real expedition if it was to bear weight, and at that point the Queen began hastily to back away, taking refuge in the cut-rate substitute of the Casimir subsidy. Her emissaries exhausted themselves in reading homilies to the States, to Don John, and to Philip on the advantages of peace, the dangers of French intervention, and the necessity for a commonsense compromise—all very edifying, but quite ineffectual.

The results of these maneuvers were a decrease in Dutch confidence in English reliability and an increase in Spanish suspicions as to English intentions. English actions had roused the strongest expectations among the rebel leaders, particularly the Prince of Orange. He would continue to look to England not only for immediate material aid but for a patronage which could be transmuted into overlordship. His goal was not absolute sovereignty for the provinces but rather a change in dynasty. The Netherlanders were used through generations of experience to the rule of one alien house or another. What Orange sought now was another such lord, who would accord them a maximum of local autonomy while providing protection against their late masters. The Queen of England was an obvious choice among the limited number of possibilities, and their hopes ran high in the autumn of 1577. But Elizabeth's delays, her endless obstructions, her fits of temper or of coldness, her seeming fickleness, exhausted their patience and eroded their confidence. English credibility sank to a dangerous low.

Nor were there offsetting advantages in English relations with Spain. Neither Don John nor his half-brother trusted the Queen; her move towards open intervention, even though not carried out, hardened their suspicions and deepened their conviction that England was the greatest obstacle to a reconquest of their revolted dominions. Philip's advisors were not slow to point out the obvious remedy: a preventive attack on England herself. Philip was willing to listen, although as yet not to act.

What was revealed was the poverty of England's arsenal of diplomatic weapons. She could threaten armed intervention, but to carry it into effect was to risk full-scale war with the mighty power of Spain. In such a struggle England would play the role of auxiliary to the States, who would have to bear the main brunt of the military effort. The success of English arms would really be dependent on the capacity of the States to create a viable government and to wage war. In other words, England would have to take the terrible risk of entrusting her destiny to the fathomless uncertainties of a Netherlands society convulsed by unmanageable civil disorder. And yet, if the threat of intervention were withdrawn, England had no other lever to bring into action. When she drew back, the Queen rapidly lost face with the States and her withdrawal hastened the widening fission between those who looked towards France (in the shape of Anjou) and those who tended to drift back into the Spanish embrace.

This impotence was all the more worrying in that English policy had not stood still in the years 1576-1578. The carefully defined neutrality of 1572-1576, ever so slightly colored in the rebels' favor, had been abandoned by the actions of 1576-1578 and there was no possibility of return to the earlier situation. Dutch expectations, in spite of their disappointments, had been aroused and were to grow in strength; Spanish suspicions were permanently deepened; and at home the possibility of war in support of the rebels was becoming a familiar, a thinkable, alternative.

But for the moment, with the tide of events running against them, the English were left in the humiliating position of being forced to pin their hopes on the manipulation of that wayward French prince, sometime suitor for Elizabeth's hand, always an erratic meteor among the fixed stars of the European system.

CHAPTER 11

ANJOU, 1576-1579

In 1576 Sir Thomas Wilson rather grandiloquently wrote that the whole fate of Christendom depended on three men—Don John of Austria, the Prince of Orange, and the Duke of Anjou.[1] The first of these was to die two years later, young, disappointed, and frustrated; the second was to win a prominent niche in the pantheon of European national heroes. The third was to die unlamented, having failed at everything he set his hand to, and having won an unenviable reputation for faithless double-dealing and for almost unrivalled political fecklessness. Nevertheless, Anjou for a few years played a leading role in English political calculations and for a fleeting moment seemed likely to fill the role of consort to Elizabeth. He is in himself a negligible figure, but the English phase of his career, examined with care, serves to throw a good deal of light on more important topics. The flirtation with Anjou—marital and diplomatic—was part of a major episode in English foreign policy, a critical turning-point in England's unsettled relations with the Hapsburg power. The decisions made in these years (between 1578 and 1582) were of long-term importance, but the way in which they were shaped is hardly less important than what was decided. It was at this time that the

---

[1] Much of the material in this chapter appeared in a different form in "The Anjou Match and the Making of Elizabethan Foreign Policy," in *Essays Presented to Professor Joel Hurstfield* (Leicester, 1979).

Queen herself emerged from relative passivity to vigorous activity, abandoning her traditional policy of cautious neutrality —even of isolationism—in order to launch a new policy of active intervention.

In doing this, she pushed aside the urgings of the left-wing Protestants, led by Leicester and Walsingham, who had tried hard to press her into overt support of the resistance of the Low Countries. She instead preferred alliance with France, with the goal of common action in the Netherlands. The first phase of this policy was highly personal since it turned on a match between the Queen and Anjou, the heir to the French throne, and would have linked the two countries very closely indeed. When it failed, because of resistance within England, Elizabeth turned to the more straightforward goal of an offensive and defensive alliance with France. This too proved impossible of realization, and what was substituted was a scheme by which England subsidized Anjou as governor of the Low Countries and leader of the rebels in their struggle against Spain. This in its turn failed and led to the final bankruptcy of the Queen's policy. After the deaths of Orange and of Anjou, when the rebels' cause seemed to be almost lost, England was forced to enter war with Spain under the precise conditions which Elizabeth had striven to avoid—quite without an ally except for the disorganized forces of the provinces of Holland and Zealand.

To UNDERSTAND Anjou's career in this period, we need to step back to 1576. Ever since the summer of that year he had been prowling hopefully around the fringes of Low Countries affairs. The Peace of Monsieur, concluded in May, had freed him for new adventures just when the need of the Orangists was at its greatest. Coldly rejected by Queen Elizabeth and threatened by Spanish military successes, they turned desperately to Anjou, offering him nothing less than the countships of Holland and Zealand. Condé, the Duke's rival, reproached Orange for what seemed to be treachery to the Protestant cause, and made his own bid. But neither of these initiatives came to anything; the first was squelched by the Queen Moth-

er; Orange refused to respond to the latter. The Prince's fortunes were about to take a turn for the better as the Requesens
regime fell apart.[2]

The Duke, constant only in his inconstancy, now veered off
on the opposite tack and made advances to Madrid, hinting at
a marriage with the Infanta Isabel. He was politely but firmly
rebuffed. Rapidly reversing direction, he once again wooed
the Prince of Orange. This time it suited the latter to encourage Anjou, who might be useful as a rival to the newly arrived Don John. During the muddled negotiations which followed, the Duke asserted that he had actually been invited to
become governor by the States and he reproached the latter
for their failure to follow up the invitation. Whatever the facts
of the situation, the Duke was denied his ambition. The majority of the States certainly wished nothing more than to keep
on civil terms with him while conceding nothing; the Queen
Mother and her son were determined to maintain French
neutrality towards Spain; and, finally, the Queen of England's
offer of a loan, brought by Sweveghem in January 1577, was
conditioned on the States's refusal to accept French aid.[3]

Moreover, from the end of 1576 on, the Duke saw new opportunities at home. His unsteady compass had now swivelled
around to the Catholic pole. The Catholic leaders had responded to the Peace of Monsieur and its concessions to the
Huguenots by organizing the Holy League. This in turn
brought the Protestants into the field in arms in January
1577, and it was Anjou who commanded the forces raised
against them. No fighting ensued; after months of maneuver
in which the Protestants with assurances of Elizabeth's financial backing again sought Casimir's aid, another peace was
patched up at Bergerac in September 1577. Anjou resumed his
intrigues in the Low Countries, but the inauguration of the
Archduke Matthias as governor made this an unpropitious
moment.

In February 1578 the royal brothers had another falling out;

[2] For these episodes, see KL, *Huguenots*, IV, 48-60; see also *CSPF*,
XII, 405-6, 320-23, 324-27.
[3] KL, *Huguenots*, IV, 75-88, 125-33, 227-29, 230-31.

Anjou was arrested, escaped, fled to Angers, and from there wrote to Ambassador Paulet expressing his devotion to Elizabeth.[4] By March the negotiations with the States discussed in the previous chapter were underway. As we have seen, the Queen's angry intervention was sufficient to hold up an immediate treaty. But by the summer of 1578 she was moving towards her new policy of patronizing Anjou's ventures in the Low Countries, while keeping him on English leading strings. As part of this new line of action, she encouraged the renewal of the Duke's courtship, lapsed now for some two years.

The two aspects of the new policy took shape at about the same time. As early as April 1578 an agent of Anjou had visited the Queen, and by early June the Queen Mother could congratulate Elizabeth on the renewal of marriage negotiations. Almost at the same moment, Walsingham and Cobham, departing for the Low Countries, were cautiously instructed to explore the possibilities of Anjou's assistance to the States on terms which would be satisfactory to the English. Paulet, ambassador at Paris, was informed of the Queen's intentions at the same time—that "in some sort Her Majesty would be content that he [Anjou] should deal in the Low Countries." And the Queen herself, speaking to an agent of the Duke's, circuitously allowed that if his master wished to help the States win their liberties from the Spanish tyranny without any effort to impose his own rule, she would gladly join with him.[5]

These grudging concessions were sufficient to permit the States to move to a preliminary treaty with the Duke in August. To this the Queen gave her approval in principle but with a strong reservation against any future transfer of sovereignty to Anjou and with strict reservations as to his power. Duke Francis was in fact formally proclaimed Defender of the Belgic Liberties against the Spanish tyranny at the end of August, but the alliance with the States remained a paper

[4] *CSPF*, XII, 548-49.
[5] *Ibid.*, 597, 650-51; *CSPF*, XIII, 4, 11-13, 14, 18, 42; PRO, Baschet 31/3/27 (4 July 1578).

one. The towns which were to be handed over to the Duke balked at such a measure. His forces were then shifted to the siege of Binche, which they took from the Spanish in early October.[6] The outbreak of hostilities between the Protestant oligarchy at Ghent and the Catholic nobles of Hainault gave the Duke a chance to weigh in on the side of the former. But this inveterate double-dealer was at the same time intriguing with the Catholic Malcontents of the southern provinces, hoping to use this as a weapon in his negotiations with the States. They were indeed driven to consider offering him the governorship. However, his army, like those of Casimir and the States, was steadily disintegrating. By the end of December 1578 the disillusioned Duke was ready to throw in his hand. He returned to France early in the new year.

In the unhappy provinces which he left behind him, the opponents of Spanish rule had little to rejoice over. After the hopeful victory at Rymenen and the uncovenanted blessing of Don John's death, the affairs of the States had ceased to prosper. Their army, unpaid, disintegrated; Casimir, allied with the Gantois in their quarrel with the Catholic Walloon nobles, allowed himself to be frightened off the field by the threat of the Prince of Parma. Casimir went, in the new year, seeking to mend his fortunes at the English Court. Parma, by a shrewd stroke, bought off the Palatine's leaderless reiters, by paying their arrears and sending them home to Germany.[7] Parma resolutely opposed the imperial suggestions for a cease-fire and made his preparations to besiege Maestricht.

To add to their misfortunes, the States lost their capable commander, Bossu, by death at the close of the old year. Lastly, worst of all, was the fission within the provinces. In the autumn the aggression of the militant Calvinists of Ghent led to open warfare between them and the forces of the Catholic Walloons, known as the Malcontents. Parma, quick to exploit the fissure opening in his enemies' ranks, got into communication with the Malcontents. It would take some six months

[6] *CSPF*, XIII, 123-25, 131, 139-41, 153-57, 169, 191, 196, 237-42.
[7] Léon van der Essen, *Alexandre Farnèse* (5 vols., Brussels, 1933-37), II, 88.

of careful maneuvering before he drew them back into the Spanish fold, but the unity of the provinces was already visibly ruptured as the new year 1579 opened.[8]

It was this melancholy state of affairs which led to Walsingham's despondent reflections at the close of the winter. Ambassador Davison might as well return since there was little for him to do in Flanders. There was no disposition at Court to deal further in Low Countries causes "in respect of the low ebb we see them fallen into, of which we have as little regard as if we were not [at] all interested in their fortune." The new marriage negotiations took "greater foot" than first looked for and received "no small furtherance upon occasion of the decayed state of things in the Low Countries." The Queen, seeing that Philip would have his will there and that he would prove no good neighbor, must seek her safety in the match "though otherwise not greatly to her liking."[9]

Walsingham always saw the bleakest side of any situation, but he was accurately noting the Queen's turn of policy. Even before the appointment of Parma—and the discovery that he was unyielding in his determination to restore royal authority and Catholic orthodoxy—Elizabeth had turned against both interventionism and mediation. Now she moved definitively towards the policy of using the opportune ambitions of Anjou to counter Spanish recovery in the Low Countries. It was a logical alternative and one which suited her temperamentally. If Anjou actively entered the provinces' affairs, there would be the assumption—justified or not—that Henry III backed him and of a consequent falling out between the Catholic and the Christian kings. In fact, the Queen's calculation was that the King of France, pressured by the Catholics and distracted by civil disorder, would be unable to give any substantial assistance. Hence the younger brother would be compelled to turn to England for aid and these circumstances would bind the French Hercules in a web strong enough to keep him amenable to English control.

Elizabeth's ministers were not so optimistic. Sussex wrote

[8] *Ibid.*, chap. 4.   [9] *CSPF*, XIII, 437-38.

that nothing less than actual marriage would give the Queen sufficient leverage to control the Duke. It was futile to "dally with him in talk of marriage thereby to stay his other actions; he will give fair words and proceed in deed to his best advantage." Leicester agreed with Sussex, but he saw that his mistress, whatever her deeper feelings, was eager to display unfeigned affection and trust in her suitor, and he warned Walsingham—still in Flanders—not to show any signs of distrust towards the Duke, regardless of his private opinions.[10]

In the meantime, Anjou's wooing of the Queen had followed an uncertain course. It was renewed officially with the arrival of his agent, Bacqueville, in late July. This gentleman was overwhelmed by the attentions of the Queen and courtiers, and Elizabeth renewed her favorite proposal: that the Duke should come himself to England so that they might meet face to face. If they suited, the match could go forward; if not, the Queen promised her unabated amity. All this was very well, but the French, experienced in the royal manner of matchmaking, treated this display with due skepticism. The negotiations in fact continued to mark time; the Duke intrigued with the Malcontents and was rumored to be flirting with Spain once again. It was not until the Duke's failure in the Low Countries and his return to France in January 1579 that his master of the wardrobe, Jehan Simier, finally appeared in England.[11]

On his arrival, Simier was no more than another in the series of French envoys despatched on special mission to London, but within a few weeks he found himself cast in a glittering role in the English Court, feted and honored by the greatest in the land, admitted to the Queen's circle of intimates and re-christened her "ape." For what had seemed to be yet another conventional diplomatic exercise in matrimonial bargaining, a handy device for arriving at some kind of entente was metamorphized into an intense, almost breathless, courtship of Francis of Anjou by Elizabeth Tudor. One cannot demonstrate with absolute certainty that the Queen did

[10] *Ibid.*, 121-22.
[11] PRO, Baschet 31/3/27 (14 August 1578, 16 September 1578); *CSPF*, XIII, 183-84.

really intend marriage to the Duke, but the arguments in favor of such an interpretation are laid out below.

The game of match-making opened as soon as Simier arrived at Court. Every stop was pulled out in an effort to persuade him of Elizabeth's desire for marriage to his master. Entertainments of the most extravagant kind—feasting, dancing, jousting, masques—were lavished on the Frenchman. While the lords of the Court vied in their attentions, the Queen herself was constantly passing over little gifts—handkerchieves, gloves, or miniatures of herself—to be sent to Monseigneur. She talked incessantly about marriage and about the Duke to anyone who would listen and the ambassador wrote, perhaps somewhat hyperbolically, that she seemed fifteen years younger in the excitements of the wooing.[12]

About a month after Simier arrived, Leicester sought out the resident ambassador, Mauvissière, almost certainly at the Queen's direction, and in a long interview did everything he could to persuade the Frenchman of the Queen's sincere desire for marriage. He emphasized his own commitment to the match, declaring that he had already bought clothing, horses, and equipment for the nuptial celebrations. He retailed his successful efforts to win over the strongly Protestant Earls of Huntingdon and Bedford as well as other magnates such as Shrewsbury, Pembroke, Rutland, and Arundel. Leicester insisted that the Duke would have nothing to do once he presented himself at the English court but to make love. The Earl's flow of encouraging speech was slightly marred only by his nervous inquiries as to the real sentiments of the French Court.[13]

The Queen herself followed up her favorite with similarly auspicious references and even suggested the possibility of a marriage immediately after Easter. Every inducement was laid on to persuade the skittish Duke to press his suit before the lady herself. The comedy had a very long run, and one of many acts.

In March there were rumors which rumbled on intermit-

[12] PRO, Baschet, 15 January 1579, 8 March 1579, 29 April 1579.
[13] *Ibid.*, 22 February 1579.

tently that Anjou was a suitor for a Spanish infanta, but at the very end of that month actual negotiations on the terms of a marriage treaty were begun between Simier and the English councillors. There was the usual bargaining over the Duke's position: was he to be crowned, would he share the exercise of royal power, what income should he have? The English constantly cited the unfavorable terms granted to Philip of Spain in the previous reign.[14]

But what differentiated this act from its predecessors was the unwonted eagerness displayed by the Queen. She redoubled her attentions to Simier, who was made to seem almost one of her own servants; she talked incessantly of marriage and urged that Monseigneur come as soon as possible. She made light of Anglo-French rivalries in Scotland and the question of religion—always used as a reserve weapon in previous rounds—was brushed aside with promises of easy accommodation. The Council had expected the Queen to use her usual tactics of seizing on every possible means of delay, but to their surprise she told them in late June that she wished arrangements for the interview to proceed with speed so that Anjou might arrive by 15 August.[15]

Even at this point there were moments of hesitation; in an interview with Sir Amyas Paulet, Henry III was told by the ambassador that, even if the match fell through, the Queen was anxious for alliance. But this proved only a momentary halt and was quickly explained away by Elizabeth. And at last all difficulties were overcome; on 17 August the Duke of Anjou arrived at Greenwich for a visit which lasted some ten days. He travelled under an incognito which, however, was of the most transparent kind. The Duke's arrival in England was speedily known to the Spanish ambassador, who was able to pass on a good deal of detail about the visit to his master; Anjou's presence was certainly no secret in other circles.[16]

This first phase of the Anjou courtship signalled a great shift in the direction of English foreign policy; it also marked

[14] *Ibid.,* 25 March 1579; *Hatfield,* II, 291ff.
[15] PRO, Baschet, 14 June 1579, 18 June 1579.
[16] *Ibid.,* 6 July 1579; *Hatfield,* II, 293; CSPSp, III, 688-95.

a striking change in the Queen's role in the making of that policy. The wooing of the Duke was, so far as we can see, very much Elizabeth's own doing. The earlier French courtship, that of the first Anjou (later Henry III), was promoted from France and sustained by powerful interests in the French Court. The proposed match with the Archduke Charles had been almost entirely the doing of a group of English courtiers. But the courting of Francis of Anjou was an act of the royal will. As we have seen, not many months earlier the Queen had believed she could make use of the French prince for her own purpose in the Low Countries without necessarily marrying him. But sometime during the intervening period, her mind had changed. Through the spring and summer of 1579 it was she who sustained the courtship in the face of French skepticism, bordering on indifference, and the oblique obstructiveness of most of the English Court. This whole action stands in sharp contrast to the Queen's usual stance, which was one of watchful passivity in which she listened to the proposals showered on her by her councillors, accepting or rejecting them but almost never taking the lead. She frequently exercised her veto power but hardly ever took the initiative herself. Now it was clearly the sovereign who pushed boldly forward, dragging her reluctant courtiers in her wake.

What was the policy she now embraced? It was one of close collaboration with a France linked to England by the marital bond. It assumed that France would be attracted by a scheme which would aggrandize the younger royal brother while withdrawing him from the domestic French political arena. The match accomplished, joint action between England and France would follow easily. Elizabeth and Francis would be the protectors of the French Protestants, ensuring them against further Catholic oppression, but also guaranteeing to Henry III the loyalty of his Reformed subjects. The reverse of this coin would be the end of French (i.e., Guisan) intrigue in England and Scotland. But Anglo-Spanish relations would also be powerfully affected by a match. Such an Anglo-French combination would be too powerful for Philip II to ignore and he would be constrained to come to some reasonable compromise with his Low Countries subjects, thus restoring stability in those lands. One stone was to kill a whole flock of blackbirds.

The assumption underlying this proposed line of action—repeatedly brought forward in the various deliberations on the marriage[17]—was the underlying hostility of both France and Spain towards England, which, sooner or later, would eventuate in an intervention in the Queen's affairs. At this very juncture the arrival of the Fitzmaurice expedition in Ireland, patronized by Spain, was taken as striking confirmatory evidence. D'Aubigny's arrival in Scotland later in the year would be yet another confirmation. In short, one of the great continental powers had to be not only neutralized but drawn to alliance. It could only be France, first, because of the unique matrimonial opportunity, secondly, because of the somewhat less rigid attitude towards the Reformed religion which circumstances forced on the French Crown. Roughly speaking, this was the rationale put forward to justify the Anjou marriage to English opinion. A variant, hinted at from time to time, was alliance without marriage, but this would give the Queen much less leverage over the wayward French Prince than would the bonds of matrimony.

What moved the Queen to shift to so activist a policy, one which would require English initiatives, which might well lead to confrontation with Spain and one so riddled with dangerous contingencies? The earlier alternative, which the Queen had favorably entertained for a time—that of backing the States-General—had soured as the internal fissures among the Low Countries magnates became visible. At the same time Anjou, by his eagerness to intrude himself into Netherlands affairs, had become a serious menace. It seemed all too probable that, following on his flirtations with the French Catholics, he might enter the provinces as the ally of Don John (or his successor), and in English eyes this would mean he was merely a stalking-horse for French ambitions to dominate the Netherlands. A third, remoter, element which gradually bore on English political calculations was the probability after the

---

[17] *Hatfield*, II, 250.

disaster of Alcazar in the late summer of 1578 that Philip would add Portugal to his dominions and thus dangerously overweigh the balance of power in western Europe. Under these circumstances it would become imperative to hold Spain in check wherever possible. As early as September 1579, the Queen was expressing to the French and Spanish ambassadors her concern over the Portuguese problem.[18]

But the sum total of these policy considerations does not yield an entirely convincing explanation of this far-reaching shift in Elizabethan policy. We have, I think, to turn to the Queen herself, who suddenly transformed a conventional round of diplomatic sparring into an intensely personal drama. The diplomatic pretense suddenly acquired a startling and vivid reality. There is no direct evidence of Elizabeth's emotional life, now or at any other time, but the circumstantial proof is strong. From January onwards it was the Queen who led and her advisors who followed. It was she who pushed aside the traditional obstacles—income, status, power, and, above all, the religious observances of the proposed consort. It was she who pressed for the interview, abandoning all the convenient pretenses for delay which had served so well in the past.

As to Elizabeth's underlying motives we can only guess. She had reached the very last term of years in which marriage would be possible for her. Once she passed the child-bearing age the diplomatic value of a match vanished, and, equally important, those emotional gratifications which so delighted the Queen. It was this knowledge of time's panting urgency which presumably overpowered her normal repugnance to marriage and drove her in headlong pursuit of Anjou. She was not, I think, in love with him as she had been once with Robert Dudley. But there was immense pleasure for her in his rank and dignity; her royal snobbery was gratified by a prospective match with the first prince of the blood of the oldest of the great dynasties. It was possible to paint a plausible picture of the match as a necessary—and wise—act of state policy, but in 1579 the driving force behind the negotiations

[18] *CSPF*, XIV, 225-26; *CSPSp*, II, 696.

was the overpowering attraction which matrimony now exerted on Elizabeth.

But, as in 1561, the Queen would not take the final plunge unless she had the strong and urgent backing of her councillors. For them it was a bewildering dilemma; for years they had urged on her the necessity of marrying and begetting an heir. The dreadful uncertainties of the succession were no less frightening now than at any time in the past. Yet an elementary knowledge of physiology told them what the risks of any marriage would be for a forty-six-year old woman. They whistled in the dark by dredging up stories of successful late pregnancies, but few of them can have doubted that any marriage was a frightful risk for the Queen and the kingdom. Secondly, there was the question of the particular candidate now proposed; the heir to the French throne and a prince whose antecedents were, to many, dubious and, to some, unsavory. Dared they risk the very existence of the political and religious establishment on the chances of this incongruous mating?

These were the questions the Council was drawn to debate in October 1579, but their official and private deliberations were overtaken by a public and popular outburst of a novel kind. Sermons had been preached against the marriage since March, and an angry Queen had threatened to have the preachers whipped. Public criticism was being noised abroad during the summer and during the Duke's supposedly secret visit.[19] A few weeks later, lampoons against the marriage were posted on the Lord Mayor's door. But the matter exploded into the open in September with the publication of John Stubbs's *The discovery of a gaping gulf wherein England is like to be swallowed by an other French marriage, if the Lord forbid not the banns by letting Her Majesty see the sin and punishment thereof.*[20] The Queen's fury at Stubbs's book was almost beyond bound. A proclamation ordering its public destruction

[19] For references to the anti-Anjou sermons see *CSPSp*, II, 658-59, 692, 701; and Edmund Lodge, *Illustrations of British History*, 2nd ed. (3 vols., 1838), II, 148-50; for other criticisms see PRO, Baschet, 30 July 1579.

[20] *John Stubbs's "Gaping Gulf" with Letters and Other Relevant Documents*, ed. Lloyd E. Berry (Charlottesville, 1968).

denounced it as the work of a seditious libeler, whose object was to "alienate the love and estimation which her people have of her. . . ."[21] The proclamation defended Anjou's reputation and scornfully repudiated the suggestion that the marriage treaty endangered either the Church or the Commonwealth and made the point that any conditions agreed to with Anjou would have to have Parliamentary confirmation. The Privy Council sought the assistance of both the London corporation and the episcopal bench in calling in all copies of the book. Bishop Aylmer reported his success in checking sermons hostile to the match but had little doubt that the weight of opinion was against it.[22]

The Queen's anger is understandable since Stubbs's production had to be taken seriously. It was much more than a zealot's shrill polemic; a literarily respectable piece of work, it was addressed to an educated audience. Its central arguments were shrewdly considered, comprehensive, and very knowledgeable. Indeed they were so well informed—and so close in content to the actual Council debates—that the Queen had some ground for her suspicion that someone in the Council was behind Stubbs.[23]

Stubbs himself was a lawyer and country gentleman, a Cambridge graduate and a member of Lincoln's Inn, with left-wing Protestant associations aplenty. His sister married Thomas Cartwright and he was a friend of both Walter Travers and William Davison and kin by marriage to the great Protestant house of Willoughby de Eresby. He had a connection with Burghley also, through his lifelong friendship with Michael Hickes, secretary to William and friend to Robert Cecil.[24]

Stubbs, his bookseller, Page, and his printer, Singleton,

---

[21] *Tudor Proclamations*, II, 445-49.

[22] Hatton, *Memoirs*, 132-34; Folger Library MS. Vb 142, f. 54, quoted in introduction to *Stubbs's "Gaping Gulf*," xxviii; Strype, Grindal, 584-86; *APC*, XI (1578-80), 276.

[23] PRO, Baschet, 29 Oct. 1579.

[24] Alan G. R. Smith, *Servant of the Cecils: The Life of Sir Michael Hickes, 1543-1612* (Totowa, N.J., 1977), 92-96.

were apprehended shortly after the book was suppressed and swiftly brought to trial. Sentence was pronounced on 30 October and the punishment carried out on 3 November. Its nature is a measure of the royal wrath. Stubbs and Page were tried under a statute of Philip and Mary against publishers of seditious writings. Some lawyers thought the statute had expired with the late Queen, and although the Chief Justice, Wray, defended its validity, one lawyer who protested against it was sent to the Tower and one of the Justices of Common Pleas was "so sharply reprehended that he resigned his place." The penalty was an unusual and brutal one. Stubbs and Page both lost their right hands, chopped off with a cleaver. Camden gives us an eyewitness account and soberly records the silence of the multitude "either out of an horror at this new and unwonted kind of punishment, or else out of commiseration towards the man, as being of an honest and unblamable repute; or else out of hatred of the marriage, which most men presaged would be the overthrow of religion."[25] The unlucky lawyer was then taken back to prison, where he was to remain until his release in early 1581. But in the course of the 1580's Stubbs would be employed by Burghley to answer Cardinal Allen's *Defense*; later he sat in Commons for Great Yarmouth and had the Lord Treasurer's (unsuccessful) backing for an Exchequer post. He was to die serving Lord Willoughby in France.[26]

The book which Stubbs had written displays a wide command of the arguments of all kinds adduced for and against the marriage. He set out to show and to prove "that this is a counsel against the Church of Christ, an endeavor of no well-advised Englishman, as well in regard of the common state, as of Her Majesty's good estate, to every of which it is pernicious and capital."[27] The argument that the marriage would endanger the reformed faith was the first to be taken up. Drawing heavily upon Old Testament precedent, Stubbs cast the English in the role of the Chosen People and likened a

[25] Camden, *Annals*, 270.   [26] *DNB*, s.v. "Stubbs."
[27] *Stubbs's "Gaping Gulf*," 5.

match with a Popish prince to a Hebrew marriage with a Canaanite. "Or shall it not be much more ugly before God and his angels when an Hebrew shall marry a Canaanite?"[28] It would be a sin "to give one of Israel's daughters to any of Hamor's sons, to match a daughter of God with one of the sons of men, to couple a Christian lady, a member of Christ, to a prince and good son of Rome, that anti-Christian mother city."[29]

He went on to demonstrate that the family of France collectively and this prince singly had been and were enemies of the Gospel, "a principal prop of the tottering house of Antichrist." Catherine de' Medici was identified with Athaliah and the massacre of St. Bartholomew evoked in bloody detail.[30] The argument that Anjou would be converted to his wife's faith was mocked by copious references to the Duke's religious tergiversations. The conclusion was plain: marriage with the French Duke would be ruinous to true religion in England and would call down the wrath of an angry God upon a faithless generation.

Stubbs turned from the religious argument to the nationalist one. "It is natural to all men to abhor foreign rule as a burden of Egypt, and to us of England if to any other nation under the sun." It was against nature that an alien could have those "natural and brotherlike bowels of tender love towards this people which is required in a governor."[31] Not so much as a petty constableship should be entrusted to one foreign-born. Stubbs pinpointed his argument by a telling reference to the recent past. The first and chief benefit done by the Queen to her people was to redeem them, with the Lord's help, from a foreign king.[32] A marriage with a foreign prince —above all, one of the ancient enemy house of France—would be to undo this good work, to re-enact the miseries of Philip's years as Mary's husband, with the added horror of destroying true religion. History was invoked—from the marriage of Matilda to Geoffrey of Anjou onward—to prove the disasters

[28] *Ibid.*, 9.   [29] *Ibid.*, 6.   [30] *Ibid.*, 22-23.
[31] *Ibid.*, 34.   [32] *Ibid.*, 36.

of French marital alliance. To those who boasted of the wealth which Anjou would add to English coffers, Stubbs scornfully cited the parallel of Philip, far richer than this French prince, who stripped Mary's exchequer bare by his demands on English resources.

More gravely dangerous were the risks which arose from Duke Francis' position as his childless brother's heir. If he were to succeed to the French Crown, Elizabeth must either follow him across the Channel to be a mere "borrowed majesty as the moon to the sun" or stay at home, "without comfort of her husband, seeing herself despised or not wifelike esteemed and as an eclipsed sun diminished in sovereignty."[33]

Countering yet another argument—the hope that the royal marriage would bring the long-awaited heir—Stubbs quite baldly pointed out the high probability, for one of Elizabeth's years, of the death of both mother and child; he went on to accuse the French of expecting just this event and of rejoicing in the anarchy which would follow.[34] But even if there were a living son, his very succession would reduce England to a mere Naples or Sicily ruled by a French proconsul. No ingenuity of the lawyers could devise legal bonds strong enough to constrain the French Prince once he became the husband of the English Queen.

The strongest argument for the marriage, Stubbs admitted, was the alliance with France and the support of the Protestant party within that kingdom which Monsieur would bring in his train. Stubbs quite sensibly pointed out that Anjou had in fact no base in French politics, no body of steady or respectable supporters either Protestant or Papist—nothing resembling the power which stood behind either Condé or Guise.[35] And as for the argument of a French alliance, he summoned up history—the long saga of Anglo-French enmity—as a witness against its utility. In addition, such an alignment would break the old Burgundian link, still economically vital, cut off the new entente with Scotland, "a brother in Christ," and forfeit the respect of the Protestant princes of Germany. And all this

[33] *Ibid.*, 49.   [34] *Ibid.*, 51-52.   [35] *Ibid.*, 59-61, 64.

for the deceptive mirage of alliance with an ancient enemy, the protagonist of a false and hostile faith.

Stubbs then moved on to more personal considerations. How would Anjou, the man, suit Elizabeth, the woman? Although he eschewed direct accusation, his prose was laden with innuendoes, all of them more than hinting at the depraved tastes and habits of the Duke. Nor were Anjou's motives in seeking the marriage above suspicion; he was, Stubbs argued, likely to be no more than a pawn for the Catholic interest in France and at Rome, a confidant of Guise, and a favorer of the Queen of Scots. In short, the marriage might be no more than a barely disguised scheme to bring in the old religion.

Stubbs then returned to one of the central arguments supporting the marriage: that Anglo-French power would suffice to bring Philip to terms in the Low Countries. If this were so, why had the Duke not already joined England instead of intriguing against Orange and flirting with the Malcontents? And indeed if French forces provided by the King were made available, it would be a French, not an Anglo-French, settlement. There was no more point in England's fighting France's wars against Spain than there had been in fighting for Spain against France in Queen Mary's time.[36] The assumption of those who supported the French alliance was that Henry's jealousy of Monsieur would lead him to support any move which took the Duke out of French politics. But was this realistic? First of all, would the King advance his brother to another kingdom—to two, England and the Low Countries? And at bottom did such jealousy really exist; would not brothers and mother rally together to support the joint interests of their house? Certainly the least of their cares would be the welfare of England.

Appealing again to national pride, Stubbs argued that no alliance was really necessary to protect England; had she not won her freedom from Popery by her own exertions? "The best bridle, therefore, that we can have to keep in proud France are [sic] the naturally bridling bands of the sea wherewith God hath compassed us about and the surest girths which

[36] *Ibid.*, 82.

hold us in our saddle are the peace and good order of our land."[37] Anjou would bring in his train a whole flock of cove-tous French or French-Italian cormorants, to batten off the people of England.

In his peroration Stubbs reiterated that neither would religion be preserved, nor the strength and gain of the land maintained, nor English honor served by bringing in "this odd fellow, by birth a Frenchman, by profession a Papist, an atheist by conversation, an instrument in France of uncleanness, a fly worker in England for Rome and France in this present affair, a sorcerer by common voice and fame."[38]

The Gaping Gulf was all in all a powerful and persuasive attack on the whole program of the Anjou marriage. It assailed the basic policy assumptions of the pro-French party, denying the advantages which would accrue to England by such an alliance. It brought out into the open the worrying contingencies involved in a match with the heir of France. It painted an unflattering but altogether plausible picture of the Duke himself. And as a propaganda piece it appealed powerfully to all the ancient English prejudices against the French and to the Protestant convictions of so many of the Queen's most weighty subjects.

The timing of Stubbs's book was important, for it was published at the very height of a long-drawn-out duel in the Council. Discussion of the match had begun in the late spring and continued up to the Duke's arrival.[39] Opinion within the Council was divided, and quite certainly opposition to the marriage was now openly led by Leicester, who, for a long time, had posed as a friend of France and of Anjou. He was treading on dangerous ground, for in the previous year he had secretly married Lettice Knollys, the widowed Countess of Essex, daughter of that staunch Puritan, Sir Francis Knollys. The favorite suffered a shrewd blow when Simier was able to reveal this event to the Queen—thanks to the assistance of two crypto-Catholics, Henry Howard and Charles Arundel, both

[37] *Ibid.*, 88.   [38] *Ibid.*, 92.
[39] PRO, Baschet, 29 May, 26 and 30 July 1579; KL, *Relations*, XI, 407-11; BL, Add. Ms. 4,149, f. 104.

of them protégés of the Earl of Oxford.[40] The latter was now enjoying a considerable ascendancy at Court and had awakened the jealous hostility of the Leicester-Sidney faction. It was some time in this summer that the young Philip Sidney had his famous tennis-court quarrel with Oxford, an incident which heightened the rivalry between the two men. In late August it was reported that Leicester was holding meetings at Pembroke's house with that lord and with Henry Sidney.[41] Pembroke had been a nephew by marriage of Dudley since his marriage with Mary Sidney in 1577. The deep dismay of the Leicester faction is reflected in Spenser's *Shepheardes Calender*, published in December of 1579.

Discussion in the Council had begun as early as March,[42] but up until the Duke's visit the councillors had evaded the main issue by concentrating on such ancillary topics as the consort's authority (he was to have none), his income or his coronation (decisions shuffled onto the shoulders of a future Parliament). But in October they had to bite the bullet. For the first time the objections voiced hitherto in pulpit and pamphlet were heard at the Council board. Their content was hardly novel; indeed it was so like Stubbs's arguments that it is hardly surprising the Queen should suspect a collaboration between the pamphleteer and some member of the anti-Anjou faction in her Council. Those favoring the match emphasized the alliance against Spain, joint action in the Low Countries, and the protection of the Huguenots. They made much of the grim consequences of rejecting Anjou; he would marry an infanta; Spain and France would ally against England. Conspiracy at home, focussed on that center of all discontents, Mary Stuart, would blend with schemes for foreign intervention. And as Burghley warned the Queen, this would entail English reactions—to keep alight the fires of dissidence in France and the Netherlands would mean "conjunction with heads of factions," soldiers and money, probably a guaranteed annual subsidy.

[40] Camden, *Annals*, 232; *Hatfield*, II, 277.
[41] *CSPSp*, II, 693.
[42] For Council debates, see *Hatfield*, II, 238, 239, 249, 253.

The opponents of the marriage averred that the marriage "could not be but dangerous to religion, unsure to Her Majesty and unprofitable to the realm."[43] And if the Spanish ambássador's informant was correct, virtually the whole Council, led by Leicester and Hatton, recommended against the marriage; only Burghley and Sussex favored it. They warned the Queen that if she persisted, there would have to be a campaign of persuasion before Parliament met and that that body would certainly demand the nomination of a successor.

Mendoza may have got the drift of discussion in the Council right, but he was wrong as to the actual recommendation made to Elizabeth by that body.[44] What they reported to her was not an outright rejection but a stalling motion, i.e., that they could only report the *pro* and *con* arguments without coming down on either side. The Queen was indignant, fell to tears, and declared she should never have put the question to discussion. In a second interview she reproved those who opposed the match, made light of their fears of Anjou's Catholicism, and expressed astonishment that there should be any doubt of the advantages of the match; indeed she had thought there would have been a universal request that she proceed. The Council under this pressure sullenly gave way and agreed "to offer their services in furtherance of the marriage if it should so like her"; they still evaded any forthright statement of approval. So the matter stuck through October. In early November Mendoza reported that Elizabeth had told the Council she would marry; we know certainly that she did order a newly appointed committee of ranking councillors to draw up a treaty of marriage. The articles were signed by Simier on 24 November and taken to Paris by him and Edward Stafford in December. Significantly they had a proviso tacked on, suspending the treaty for two months, to give the Queen time to persuade her people to the match; Parliament was prorogued until January. And sometime before the end of the year the Queen was writing to Anjou, bemoaning the ill will of those who objected to his faith but admitting that

[43] *Ibid.*, 267, 271.   [44] *Ibid.*, 272.

public opinion was too strong to allow her to yield to her inclinations.[45]

Elizabeth had been frustrated in her desire to marry Francis of Anjou. The definitive check had come in the Council itself. After months of polite evasion during which they no doubt hoped that the Queen would prove no more serious in this wooing than in previous ones, they had to face the fact that she plainly demanded their enthusiastic support for the marriage. What answer were they to give? With two exceptions—Sussex and more doubtfully Burghley—they obstinately opposed the match. The gross defects of the Duke, private and public, the risks of a match with the heir of France, the dangers to the Queen's own life, and last but not least the peril in which such a marriage would place the Protestant faith, made a conclusive negative case. And so the councillors politely offered "their services in furtherance of the match" if the Queen on her own chose to make it. Resolutely withholding their explicit approval, they refused all responsibility for the marriage and threw the weight of decision back on the unwilling shoulders of their mistress.

The obstinacy of the Lords of Council was sufficient to hold back the Queen from marriage, but their opposition was backed up by the great strength of an effectively mobilized popular resentment. Stubbs's book was only the tip of the iceberg. In addition to the sermons preached against the marriage (now lost), there was Philip Sidney's letter, Bishop Cox's treatise, and a body of popular ballads, some still extant. All contemporary witnesses agree as to the extent and the intensity of feeling.[46]

The most sophisticated response is to be found in Edmund Spenser's *Shepheardes Calender* (printed in December 1570

[45] *CSPSp*, II, 704-6; *CSPF*, XIV, 95, 97, 108-9; *Hatfield*, II, 273, 275, 293, 298.

[46] For Sidney's letter, see *Complete Works of Sir Philip Sidney*, ed. A. Feuillerat (3 vols., Cambridge, 1923), III, 51-60; for Cox, see BL, Lansdowne Ms. 28, 70; for a contemporary Puritan view, see Hatton, *Memoirs*, 162-66. The ballads are printed in F. J. Furnivall and W. R. Morfit, eds., *Ballads from Manuscripts* (1873), II, 114.

but circulating in manuscript before that date). It was printed by Stubbs's printer, Singleton. The November and February eclogues are the two most relevant sections.[47] The first of these dramatizes the ruin of religion, and of the Protestants' patron, Leicester, which the Anjou match presaged; the second echoes the Court quarrel between Leicester and Oxford, a supporter of the match. The role of the Leicester connection suggests that the outburst of public indignation was by no means an entirely spontaneous phenomenon. We need not doubt, although we cannot prove, that the Leicester-Walsingham faction in the Council made the most of their case. What is important is the existence of this latent body of opinion which needed only a little stimulation to spring to life.

The public opposition to the marriage reveals something else about the nature of the Elizabethan regime. Since the very beginning of the reign, the myth-makers had been busily at work in the service of what the twentieth century would call the cult of personality. Poets, preachers, and painters all lavished their art on the task. Some of their efforts were devoted to celebrating those royal characteristics on which Elizabeth particularly prided herself—her virginity, with the related implication of her sole devotion to her people's welfare, her prudence, wisdom, and justice.[48]

But, in addition to these celebrants of the Queen's "official" virtues, there was another school composed of those who set up an image of her as the protectress of true religion. This "unofficial" enterprise was first shaped by the conceptions of that prophet-historian, John Foxe, who in his great book built up a framework of historical and Biblical interpretation which provided a stage into which Elizabeth's career could be fitted.[49] She was the English Deborah, the princess set by God's special providence upon the English throne to revive and to fulfill the

---

[47] Paul E. McLane, *Spenser's Shepheardes Calender* (Notre Dame, Indiana, 1961), chaps. 4, 5.

[48] See, for example, Frances Yates, *Astraea: The Imperial Theme in the Sixteenth Century* (1975), *passim*.

[49] See William Haller, *The Elect Nation*, etc. (New York, 1963), *passim*.

work of reformation and of renewal. Lesser writers in prose and verse had in the 1560's and 1570's[50] continued this tradition, linking religious and nationalist aspirations in a common pattern. (Spenser's climactic work, of course, still lay in the future.) But this unofficial cult was being built up without the approval of the goddess herself. Indeed, the role of Protestant champion which it assigned her was one deeply repugnant to the secular-minded Queen. Nevertheless, she could not avoid the fact that the loyalties massed around this religio-nationalist conception had become a substantial proportion of the monarchy's moral capital. The immense popular enthusiasm for the Queen rested in no small part on the widely held vision of her as the defender of a faith at once evangelical and distinctively English. To have married Anjou would have sadly marred that image. In one sense Elizabeth was right in seeing Stubbs's book as an attempt to alienate her people from her. He sought to constrain the Queen to act within the stereotype and implicitly threatened her with the loss of popular affection if she did not conform.

While one cannot assess the exact proportions of each of the forces which turned Elizabeth away from marrying Anjou, it is possible to understand this episode as revealing new energies at work within the English political order which were to have a permanent place within its structure. A deep anti-Catholic prejudice, as much a xenophobic phenomenon as a theological one, had taken deep root within important strata of the English political nation. It was a latent force but easily aroused and immensely powerful.

[50] Elkin C. Wilson, *England's Eliza* (1939; reprint ed., New York, 1960), *passim*.

CHAPTER 12

ENGLAND AND

THE LOW COUNTRIES,

1579-1583

THE FIRM though gentle pressure of the councillors had brought the royal train to a halt in its headlong progress towards matrimony. It was to remain stalled for nearly a year and when it began to move again it had been switched to a track which led not to marriage but to alliance. After a year of drift and hesitation a great effort was made in 1581 to achieve a working league with France against Spain. By now the Spanish annexation of Portugal had added a new dimension to Philip's power and the Elizabethan government sought collaboration with the French on two fronts—in the Low Countries and in the Portuguese empire. (Portugal and most of the overseas dominions had passed under Philip's sway in 1581, but some fragments remained in the hands of the Pretender, Don Antonio.) The culmination of their efforts was the mission of Secretary Walsingham to Paris in 1581 when he presented the English case with all possible force. Spain, he insisted, was now so powerful that she threatened to overbalance the combined strength of the other European states. It was essential to both English and French security that Philip be checked; the two states shared a fundamental common interest which neither could possibly ignore. But all of Walsingham's eloquence was wasted on a court which could not be convinced of Elizabeth's sincerity in seeking alliance. The French royalties would accept nothing less than the marital tie as an earnest of the English Queen's intentions. Hence Walsingham labored in vain; in the wake of this disappointment the English government had to turn to a *pis aller*. The only weapon they could muster against Spain in the Low Countries was Anjou, whose sponsor (and banker) Elizabeth became late in 1581. The Duke was formally installed as Duke of Brabant. What followed was a display of incompetence and faithlessness almost staggering in its dimensions. The Duke signally failed to check the inexorable advance of Parma through the Belgic provinces and capped his career by a failed coup—an attempt to seize Antwerp and other cities. Routed, he had no alternative but an undignified scramble back to the safety of French soil. His formal abdication in June 1583 wrote finis to this dismally unsuccessful strategy. The Queen's support of her feckless protégé had left her poorer in pocket and bankrupt in policy; worse still, Spanish suspicions of England's intentions had deepened appreciably, and Philip was so much the more likely to listen to those advocates of direct action who urged him to launch a full-scale attack on England as a necessary prior step to the final reconquest of the Low Countries.

THE EXCITEMENTS of 1579 faded away with the old year; at home and abroad discussion of the marriage subsided as other issues claimed more immediate attention. The year 1580 saw the end of the short reign of the Cardinal-King of Portugal, the last of his dynasty, and the moment of decision arrived for that country. The various native claimants put out feelers to the powers, including England, and in Paris Ambassador Cobham found that the French court shared his government's alarm over the prospective increase in Spanish power. But the English reaction to the Portuguese approaches was coolly unresponsive and nothing came of the discussions in France. Nearer to home, there were disturbing occurrences. In 1579 and again in 1580 small Catholic expeditionary forces landed on the south coast of Ireland. Nominally under Papal sponsorship, their personnel was largely Spanish and Italian and they had clearly come with Spain's barely veiled approval. Intended to spearhead native rebellion, they seemed to Englishmen an oblique riposte by Spain to English intervention in the Low Countries.[1]

In the southern provinces Anjou had renewed his flirtations with the Walloon faction and at Cambray was accepted as lord. Simultaneously another bout of France's chronic disease set in as religious tensions mounted again. In June the English government was embarrassed by Condé's appearance at Sandwich; he sent immediately to Leicester and Walsingham. The Queen took hasty measures to reassure the King of France of her neutrality, offering her mediation, urging the dangers of renewed civil war, but emphasizing that she had no foreknowledge of Condé's coming. The prince himself was treated civilly but coolly and departed at the beginning of July with no satisfactions other than those of a courteous reception. In France great efforts were made to maintain the shaky religious peace and by late autumn a precarious balance was being reestablished.[2]

But the prospects of renewed civil war in France as well as Anjou's seizure of Cambray and Bouchain were causes for much anxious consultation in the English government. In July the Council, meeting at Nonsuch, addressed themselves to the glum prospect that the Netherlands would accept Anjou as their governor with the further probability of future annexation to France. The leading councillors, including Burghley, Sussex, Leicester, Hatton, and Walsingham, were prepared to urge the Queen to send men and money to Orange on condition that he stave off acceptance of Anjou by the States. At the same time they would send a mission to Spain, pointing out the imminence of a French take-over and urging a compromise in the Low Countries; other emissaries should be sent to the Flemish Malcontents and Anjou himself should once

[1] *CSPF*, XIV, 206-10, 238-40, 267-69.
[2] *Ibid.*, 311, 317, 323.

again be offered the bait of marriage. But another memorial of about the same date, endorsed by Burghley, suggests an alternate policy. Rejecting any opposition to the French in the Low Countries, this scheme would concentrate on stirring up trouble in France by subsidizing Duke Casimir to support the Huguenots.[3]

The former of these schemes undoubtedly represents the urgings of Leicester and Walsingham, the consistent backers of a policy of direct intervention in the Low Countries; they seem to have won the assent of their colleagues, at least for the moment, but presumably the Queen remained unwilling, as in the past, to risk backing the unsteady States regime and the possibility of war with Spain. The second alternative faded away as the French patched up a religious truce. Anjou continued to negotiate with the States and in September the latter seemed ready to conclude with the Duke. Daniel Rogers, a member of the radical Protestant diplomats' clique patronized by Leicester, was dispatched to try if possible to block this development. His mission was quickly aborted when he fell into the hands of a petty Rhineland baron who, with Spanish approval, held him for ransom.[4]

All this was discouraging, but, as 1580 closed, new possibilities were opening up, of a more hopeful nature. The French government was even more uncertain of its direction than Elizabeth's but one option which the French had hinted at as early as April was collaboration with England against Spain. Little could be done to realize this so long as the domestic religious situation remained unsettled, but, once that had been steadied, the French could renew their gestures of friendliness towards England. In September 1580 there were hints at a rapprochement, regarded with suspicion by Cobham, but two months later he was taking these moves much more seriously. The treaty of 1572 was unearthed for use as a working model and by Christmas there was agreement to explore the terms of a general alliance to common action which might include Portugal, Ireland, and the Low Countries in its scope.[5]

[3] *Ibid.*, 343-52.   [4] *Ibid.*, 416-17, 433-36, 464-70.
[5] *Ibid.*, 231-32, 424-28, 510, 535-36; *CSPF*, XV, 106, 131.

These negotiations automatically revived the marriage question; the commissioners sent by France were formally charged with a marriage treaty but it was understood that this would be the prelude to a formal alliance, offensive and defensive. These new approaches meant that after a year of uncertain drifting English policy was coming into focus again, clearly directed towards an entente with France. The possibilities were far-reaching.

The Queen made much of the marriage proposals in conversations with the French ambassador, but she took the opportunity to float a trial balloon by pressing the need to check Spanish aggrandizement wherever it was manifest. She even hinted at joint Anglo-French action in the Netherlands as the most effective strategy. At the same time Cobham in Paris was urging on Henry III the need for "further association for withstanding of the Spanish King's growing greatness." The Prince of Orange weighed in with his contribution—a solemn warning that since Portugal was crushed, Catholic power would now be turned on the British Isles; he argued that Spain now believed she could not recover the Belgic provinces until she was sure of the island kingdoms. The two successive expeditions into Ireland added plausibility to the Prince's reasoning.[6]

It was given further emphasis by events in Scotland; in January the Regent Morton fell from power. His position had been weakening for some time, but his ruin was the work of a party led by James's cousin, the Sieur d'Aubigny. This young man, newly arrived from France, was quite rightly thought to be a protégé of the Guises and his appearance on the Scottish scene aroused deep concern in London. At the very least, recent events in the North signalled the end of a pro-English regime which had lasted almost a decade; at the worst, they heralded a new effort at Catholic intrigue, backed by France or Spain. The immediate reaction of the English government was to dispatch Randolph once again to Edinburgh and to concentrate troops on the Borders.[7]

[6] *CSPF*, XV, 27-31, 58-59; PRO, Baschet, 6 Jan. 1581.
[7] PRO, Baschet, 10 Feb. 1581.

Yet another twist was given to Anglo-French relations by the renewed activity of Anjou in the Low Countries; it was reported in early March that he would respond to the States's offer and take his oath as Count of Flanders; he was expected to arrive shortly, accompanied by Navarre as his lieutenant and with many Huguenot companies at his back. This threat of an overt move with its direct challenge to Philip's authority angered the Queen, for it seemed to foreshadow major French intervention. The States's expectations of early assistance were in fact disappointed by the slowness of Anjou's movements, but by 10 May he was writing optimistically of his immediate plans to relieve Cambray.[8]

By the time the French commissioners for the marriage treaty arrived in England in April, the English were quite openly shifting their strategy, pushing the marriage into the background and pressing instead for an alliance. Formulae for postponement of the marriage were being devised; Parliament had just met and sounding of opinion among the MP's, so the French were told, revealed deep fears of the Duke's Catholicism as well as nervousness about English involvement in the Low Countries.[9]

But it now became apparent that the two courts were fast slipping out of phase with each other. Even as the English warmed to the advantages of alliance, the French rapidly cooled. Elizabeth, alarmed, thought it well to speak bluntly to Mauvissière. She did not hide her skepticism as to French intentions, all the greater because of their long delays in the Portuguese matter. She could not move, she insisted, unless assured that if Monseigneur went to war in the Low Countries it would be with his brother's full backing. She could not risk being left alone in so great a quarrel. This plain speaking was repeated when the commissioners arrived at court on 24 April. They were handsomely entertained, but early in the discussions the Queen came straight to the point. Did they have powers to make an alliance? For her alliance was a precondition for marriage; without a commitment to the former from

---

[8] *CSPF*, XV, 82, 156, 163, 165; *Hatfield*, II, 395-96.
[9] PRO, Baschet, 10 Mar. 1581; *CSPF*, XV, 142-43.

the French government she could not suppose them serious about the latter. The commissioners could only respond helplessly that their powers extended only to the match.[10]

This effectually brought negotiations to a dead halt. Walsingham expounded the government's position with great emphasis on English fears that Anjou would involve them in war without their consent; indeed he went so far as to predict a rising of the Queen's subjects in such a situation. In the end the commissioners had to settle for a meaningless document which spelled out all the details of a marriage which, it was almost certain, would never take place.[11]

This impasse led to a new phase in the negotiations in which the English, taking the initiative, shifted the scene of action from London to Paris. In new instructions, Cobham was ordered to ignore the marriage altogether and to propose an alliance against Spain, to include the Low Countries and Portugal in its scope. The offer was not a generous one since it proposed that all the costs of a Low Countries expedition should be borne by France while England grudgingly offered to carry a quarter of the expenses of a Portuguese enterprise. Nevertheless, the offer broadened the scope of the English position into an explicitly anti-Spanish stance. The French held back on any response, marking time, so Elizabeth now followed up her first ploy by sending Somers, a Clerk of the Signet and an experienced second-string diplomat, to press much the same terms as Cobham. This brought a French counter-offer of alliance, offensive and defensive, once the Queen set a firm date for her marriage and entered a secret agreement to back Anjou in Flanders. The English agreed to bargain on this; pushing aside the marriage, they proposed a league to aid Don Antonio, the Portuguese pretender, and *sub rosa* contributions for the support of Anjou. Apparently the Queen went so far as to offer to pay one-quarter of the sum paid to Anjou by the States-General. But the French clung to their set terms, unwilling to yield a jot.[12]

[10] PRO, Baschet, 2, 9, and 28 Apr. 1581; *CSPF*, XV, 172.
[11] PRO, Baschet, 30 April, 12 and 26 May, 14 June 1581.
[12] *CSPF*, XV, 206-18, 234-35, 255-63.

The English now saw that they must mount an all-out effort if they were to persuade the French to alliance without marriage. To make plain their seriousness, no less a personage than Secretary Walsingham was sent off to Paris. He was instructed to break his journey by a visit to Anjou at Chateau-Thierry before proceeding to the French court. The object of this visit was to persuade the Duke to accept indefinite postponement of the marriage but to assure him of English aid for his Low Countries schemes. This achieved, Walsingham was to lay before Henry III the terms of alliance, offensive and defensive, much more far-reaching than the treaty of 1572.[13]

Two central points were to be made to the French King. First, that it would be gravely dangerous to both crowns if Anjou were to give over his present enterprise in the Low Countries, for it was imperative that Spanish aggrandizement be checked, and this was the obvious area in which to move. Secondly, Anglo-French collaboration to this end could best be achieved without a matrimonial link. If Elizabeth married Anjou, her kingdom would necessarily be dragged openly into war in Flanders. Such a war would be "ingrateful" to her people and would only increase dislike for a marriage that was already deeply unpopular. Englishmen would not accept such a war, and the Queen would not embark on it. But she was willing—as Somers had already declared—to provide a secret subsidy to Anjou and a similar *sub rosa* contribution for Don Antonio. The Queen was willing to make a public alliance with France. Walsingham was to lay the strongest emphasis on the mutual interest of the two powers, "for no bond is of more force than that which is grounded upon necessity and where both parties profit by the confederacy."[14] This was a stronger cement than any matrimonial tie.

These were the first set of terms which Walsingham was to lay on the table. But he was given reserve instructions.[15] If France absolutely insisted on the match, he was to be allowed

[13] See Digges, *Ambassador*, 352-54, for the original instructions, and *CSPF*, XV, 271, for the additional instructions.

[14] *CSPF*, XV, 209-13.

[15] *Ibid.*, 279-81; Digges, *Ambassador*, 355-56.

to reopen the marriage negotiations, lest "we shall be left alone without any aid from the King, subject to the malice of Spain, and not free from the evil neighborhood of Scotland and lastly uncertain of the good will of the French king or his brother or of both." The Queen would bring herself to marriage if she must, but on one point Walsingham must not yield; any aid which the English provided must be given in the most secret manner—hidden even from her own subjects.

With Anjou at least, Walsingham was successful; after initial resistance, he gave in on the marriage. The French court listened, interested but skeptical. The King and his mother were forthright as to their doubts. Elizabeth, they said, would only wait until France was fairly entangled in the Netherlands and then slip the collar; once Spain and France were at one another's throats, England would retire comfortably to a spectator's seat. To such argument Walsingham urged the brutal facts which dominated English thinking: Spain had refused to renew the old Burgundian alliances, had backed the Norfolk match and the rising in the North, sheltered English rebels, and most recently sponsored intervention in Ireland. Sheer necessity, he insisted, would keep the English Queen faithful in her commitments to France.[16]

There followed a complicated diplomatic play. The French first countered with the offer of a full alliance, France bearing the whole cost of Low Countries operations—upon the celebration of the marriage. But then, upping the ante, they went so far as to discuss the possibility of alliance, shared costs—and no marriage.[17]

Elizabeth, reacting to the first French offer, seemed to waver and to intimate informally that she reopen the possibility of marriage, going so far as to say that if she must face open war, she would prefer to meet it as a wedded queen. The French promptly backed away from their second offer and returned to the old demand for precedent royal nuptials. The discomfited envoys in Paris, bewildered by their mistress' acro-

---

[16] *CSPF*, XV, 294, 299; *Hatfield*, II, 414, 415; Digges, *Ambassador*, 360-63.
[17] *CSPF*, XV, 294, 299; Digges, *Ambassador*, 397-99.

batics, found their flank dangerously exposed. The Secretary raged to Burghley in an angry letter that the Queen was destroying her credibility in the courts of Europe. It was said "that when Her Majesty is pressed to marry then she seemeth to affect a league and when a league is yielded unto then she liketh better of marriage. And when thereupon she is moved to assent to marriage, then she hath recourse to the league, when the motion for the league or any request is made for money then she returneth to marriage."[18]

There was substance in what Walsingham wrote; when France had seemed to yield on the marriage and when discussions about sharing costs in Flanders began, the Queen instructed her ministers to commit no specific sum of money to France. The latter would certainly receive the lion's share of the benefits and must bear the main burden of costs—at least treble England's contribution. And when there were some preliminary talks about specific terms of alliance—men, money, arms, and ships—the English agents were ordered to plead absence of instructions. All this of course only strengthened French suspicions that the English ruler was not serious in her dealings.

The French themselves, according to Walsingham, were making overtures to Parma for a truce and angling at Madrid for a Spanish princess for Anjou.[19] In any case, with neither side prepared to accept the good faith of the other—with French skepticism and English coyness—it is not surprising that the negotiations petered out by mutual consent. In September Walsingham returned to England empty-handed.

Thwarted at Paris, the English found themselves driven by circumstances into compromising their position and making concessions to Anjou. The latter had during the summer succeeded in relieving Cambray and driving off its besiegers, but the effort had exhausted his slender resources, and his unpaid troops began rapidly to dwindle away. In desperation Anjou sent Viscount Turenne to Walsingham, begging for 100,000 ducats from the Queen. The Secretary urged the Queen to

[18] Digges, *Ambassador*, 377-78, 387-88, 389-90, 390-99, 406-7, 407-8.
[19] *Ibid.*, 380-83.

grant the request; she as always procrastinated, agreeing in principle but declining to name a specific sum. But her hesitations were less protracted than usual and sometime about the beginning of September Lord Henry Seymour set off for Flanders with the first installment of a £30,000 loan while the French King also contributed a sizable amount. Anjou had become the pensioner of the English Crown; that clause of the abortive treaty which would have provided secret English aid proved to be the only one to achieve reality.[20]

The Queen's willingness to go so far no doubt encouraged Anjou to another, and bolder, move; he resolved to present himself in person before Elizabeth. On 20 October his agent in England wrote of the forthcoming visit and of Leicester's determination to make good cheer for him. (He had in fact planned a visit in June and only adverse winds had turned him back at Dieppe.) The Duke arrived 2 November. He came not without hopes of marriage; much more realistically he was anxious for guarantees of continued English support in the Netherlands. His footing there was at the best uncertain and his principal asset popular belief in continued English support. This visit, unlike the previous one, was quite unabashedly public. He was shown great honor by the Queen and her courtiers on all possible occasions. He stayed on for the celebrations of accession day and it was just after that the most melodramatic event of the visit took place. In Camden's discreet prose, "the force of modest love in the midst of amorous discourse carried [the Queen] so far that she drew off a ring from her finger and put it upon the Duke of Anjou's upon certain conditions betwixt them two." According to Mendoza, she actually said, "he shall be my husband," to the assembled courtiers.[21]

The Orangist agent, St. Aldegonde, who was present, sent off a dispatch immediately and in Antwerp the bells were rung in celebration. "At home the courtiers' minds were di-

[20] CSPF, XV, 206, 299, 304, 305, 310, 313, 320-21; Hatfield, II, 424; Digges, Ambassador, 367-68, 397-98.

[21] CSPF, XV, 190, 194, 341-42; Hatfield, II, 449-51; Camden, Annals, 267-68; CSPSp, III, 226.

versely affected; some leaped for joy; some were seized with admiration; and others were dejected with sorrow." The Spanish ambassador was confident (from the time of Anjou's arrival) that there would be no marriage; he noted that it was Leicester, the opponent of the match, who was most to the fore, not Sussex, its advocate. Hatton and Huntingdon, he averred, were both cooling in their enthusiasm. Camden wrote that Leicester, Hatton, and Walsingham stormed at the news of the match, declaring the realm and religion both undone. The Queen's very gentlewomen "lamented and bewailed and did so terrify and vex [the Queen's] mind that she spent the night in doubts and cares without sleep." The historian continued that next day the Queen saw Anjou by himself and that after that interview the Duke went to his chamber and threw the ring from him, taxing the lightness of women and the inconstancy of islanders.[22]

Mendoza's account was somewhat different in detail;[23] in his version a gout-ridden Burghley exclaimed, "Blessed be the Lord that this business has at last reached a point where the Queen on her part has done all she can; it is for the country now alone to carry it out." The cynical Spaniard took the latter phrase to mean that the Queen had no intention of marrying but was cleverly shifting the blame for her refusal to public opinion. He, like Camden, emphasized the opposition of Leicester and Hatton, whom he pictured lecturing the Queen on the risks to her security which the marriage offered. Finally, in his account it was Walsingham who was given the (for him) congenial task of breaking the news to Anjou.

The Duke remained in England for another two months, feted by all, and constantly in the company of the Queen. A draft proposal of these weeks, in Burghley's hand, suggests general support for the Duke and specific financial aid if the King of France gave his share. In November the Queen had authorized Cobham in Paris to proceed with a marriage treaty if Henry III would bear the whole charge of war in the Low Countries and give an iron-clad guarantee to declare war on

[22] *CSPSp*, III, 221; Camden, *Annals*, 268.
[23] *CSPSp*, III, 226-28.

Spain if that country attempted anything against England. This may coincide with the ring episode. In December the French Court responded by again insisting on the marriage and promising no more than one half of the war costs.[24]

Whatever we are to make of the scene in the gallery at Greenwich between the Queen and her "frog," it is certain that no marriage eventuated. But if the Duke was not to be a husband, he was at any rate not to be cast out altogether from royal favor. A bit shop-worn perhaps but still serviceable to the English, he was the instrument by which they might yet hope indirectly to work their will in the Netherlands. So in December Anjou was granted another "loan," this time totalling £60,000 in two installments, the first due fifteen days after he crossed the seas, the second fifty days later. With cash in hand, the Duke was ready for another venture into Flanders. In early January, even before his arrival, his troops marched into Bruges. A sorry sight they were said to be, too weak to attack the enemy but just strong enough to ruin their friends. Skepticism about the Duke remained high in the Low Countries, but when he finally landed at Flushing on 10 February one irreverent Italian observer wrote that he was awaited "not otherwise than as the Hebrews awaited the coming of their Messiah but with much greater certainty of his being already on the road, perhaps arrived in the country." The Duke came attended by the Earl of Leicester, the Lord Admiral of England, and the Queen's cousin, Lord Hunsdon. At the same time the Queen wrote to the Prince of Orange recommending her protégé in the warmest terms and promising her continuing support for him. The English lords stayed to witness the solemn inauguration of Anjou as Duke of Brabant. This was an event of no small significance. The provinces had now formally cast off their allegiance to Philip, and Anjou was therefore nothing less than a new sovereign. Implicitly England was giving diplomatic recognition to a shift of sovereignty in the Netherlands.[25]

The subsequent course of events in the provinces is dealt

[24] *CSPF*, XV, 368, 388-89, 420, 526.
[25] *Ibid.*, 409, 449-51, 484, 489, 500.

with in a subsequent chapter. Anglo-French diplomatic relations, after months of intense activity, slowed almost to a halt. Spasmodically through 1582, the English government renewed talk of the marriage or of the alliance. But nothing new was added to the terms of discussion: the English continued to demand alliance without the marriage; the French were agreeable to an alliance—and even to carrying the financial burden of Netherlands operations—but only after Elizabeth married their King's brother. But the fiction that the marriage was still under consideration was maintained for many months.[26]

During one of these flurries of renewed discussion, in July, when the French again offered to discharge Elizabeth of all charges of war if she married Anjou, Burghley jotted down some very blunt reflections on the problem. Paper promises were all very well, but it was lamentably easy to evade them; marriage on the other hand, once entered into, was irreversible. Before the Queen took such a step she must have concrete evidence of French commitment to an active policy in the Low Countries. The promises made must be seen to be profitable for Henry III and his brother and feasible of performance. The unspoken implication in Burghley's reasoning was that no such promises could be made.[27]

Walsingham, reflecting on the same problem later in the year was equally hard-headed in his views. For him the French insistence on the marriage was the surest sign of their insincerity. France needed an heir as desperately as England; Henry III would not produce one; Anjou was their only hope. Given the English Queen's age, she could not possibly give her husband a child; ergo the French clamor for marriage only masked their opposition to this particular match.

In fact Anglo-French relations had entered a phase of hopeless stalemate at a time when Low Countries affairs daily gave increasing cause for anxiety. Parma, slow but deliberate and single-minded, continued to press his advantage; in July 1582 the key fortress of Oudenarde fell to his arms after a long siege. Anjou had been unable to do a thing to relieve it. Day

[26] *Ibid.*, 564-65; *CSPF*, XVI, 22-23, 47; PRO, Baschet, 17 July 1582.
[27] *CSPF*, XVI, 199-200.

by day he displayed his supreme incompetence; month by month the States regime withered on the vine.[28]

THERE WAS another front on which Anglo-French collaboration might have been possible. Even before the death of the Cardinal-King of Portugal, both governments were expressing their apprehensions about Spanish expansion in the Iberian peninsula. In 1581 the Spanish king entered his new kingdom after only minimal opposition. In the very month that Walsingham went to Paris to push the alliance, Philip was received in Lisbon. Don Antonio had fled from Portugal earlier in that same year and eventually turned up in France. The Queen Mother had a shadowy claim to the Portuguese throne, which she did not intend to press for herself but which gave her some vague legal basis for French intervention. As early as March 1581, Anjou was being tempted with the bait of a Portuguese venture; in May Antonio's agents were proposing to England the sending of 4,000 Englishmen, provisioned for three months, to join with the French in an expedition in the Azores. They were offered as security the Portuguese post at St. George d'Amina in West Africa and the concession of free trade to the East Indies. About the same time an English agent was negotiating with a Portuguese representative in France. But the Queen made it clear to the Portuguese that she would take no risks for them; unless the French were involved also, she would run too great a danger of war with Spain.[29]

The Pretender himself, disappointed by French dilatoriness, came to England in the summer of 1581 under Leicester's auspices. Negotiations involved the Pretender, the French, and the English. The Queen was apparently willing to put up a small sum of money, initially £5,000 and then reluctantly £10,000, but when she was asked for yet another £2,000 she exploded in anger. Drake and Hawkins had been involved but they now drew back; in the end, little was done although a few Englishmen did reach the islands still held for Don Antonio. The Queen's basic objection to a significant English

[28] *Ibid.*, 439-40.
[29] *CSPF*, XV, 98, 108, 132-33, 135, 143, 165, 166, 187.

participation was her insistence that here, as in the Low Countries, England could not afford to go alone without France.[30]

In 1582 the French fitted out a large expedition to the Azores under the command of the Italian admiral, Strozzi. There were discussions with the French and with Portuguese agents about English participation in this expedition, which apparently included some English ships manned by foreign sailors. Strozzi himself asked for 2,000 soldiers with their equipment. However, England did not participate and in late summer the unwelcome news of his overwhelming defeat trickled through. Don Antonio's forces maintained a toe-hold in the Atlantic islands for a while longer and small contingents of Englishmen afforded them some aid. But a major opportunity for Anglo-French cooperation against Spain had been missed.[31]

One last act in the tangled history of the Anglo-French dealings which had begun with the wooing of 1579 remained to be played out. Anjou was now installed—in the spring of 1582 —as the chosen sovereign of the seventeen provinces, or at least of as many of them as chose to accept him. This meant primarily Brabant and Flanders. Anjou had a small French force of his own to add to the States army now under his nominal control. Expectations had run very high at this first coming to Antwerp. He gave out that much larger forces would soon be coming from France; the Queen of England was his public backer; the Prince of Orange made every effort to welcome the newcomer, to cooperate with him, and to win support for Anjou among the Low Countries population.

But from the beginning there was friction between the French and the Flemings. Roger Williams compared their relations to those between Englishmen and Irish. An awkward problem arose in connection with Anjou's religion; the re-establishment of Catholic worship for him and his followers stirred hopes among the oppressed Netherlands Catholics and angry denunciations from the dominant Protestant clergy.

[30] *Hatfield*, II, 408-10, 420, 421; Digges, *Ambassador*, 388-89, 393, 394, 419-22.

[31] *CSPF*, XVI, 78, 91-92, 131, 133, 261-63; *CSPSp*, III, 409, 417, 459-60. 478, 501.

The misfortunes of the Low Countries were augmented when in late March an assassin shot the Prince of Orange in the face; for some weeks the Prince hovered between life and death and virtual paralysis gripped political life. By the time he recovered, murmurs against Anjou were rising. Months had passed without any sign of the promised succors from France; the key fortress of Oudenarde was now invested by Parma; the French forces in the country were so disorderly that the peasantry were fleeing their villages and farms in despair. Anjou remained secluded at Antwerp, his French followers dwindling away. The commander of the promised reiters arrived by sea, leaving his force in France. Despairing of relief, Oudenarde surrendered in early July. The dismal story continued through the late summer and fall; there were some minor successes by States forces, but any attempt at a campaign in the field was given over, although Parma remained in the field well into the winter.[32]

At last in December the promised French forces crossed the frontier at Gravelines, and a brilliant array of French aristocrats came to wait upon the Duke at Antwerp. But the arrival of the French only exacerbated relations with the local people; at Dunkirk, the French garrison and the burghers fought one another. In some places rumors floated about that Anjou would like an arrangement with Parma; in others it was believed that Anjou was allowing things to slide just in order to reduce the Netherlands to such a state of helplessness that they would have to accept French rule.[33]

These vague fears became all too vividly real early in the new year 1583 when Anjou, having concentrated his forces around Antwerp, attempted a coup.[34] He failed to seize the city and some hundreds of his men were felled in bitter street fighting. French attempts elsewhere in Flanders were hardly more successful, and Anjou had to make an ignominious retreat, leaving his household and many of his followers prisoners. The French still held a few towns in the province, but

[32] *CSPF*, XV, 524, 530, 569, 642-43; *ibid.*, XVI, 98.
[33] *CSPF*, XVI, 459, 462, 463-64, 482, 514-15, 518-19; *ibid.*, XVII, 5.
[34] *CSPF*, XVII, 19-22.

their situation and that of their commander was precarious in the extreme.

During the following months the Prince of Orange exerted all his diplomacy in an effort to repair the damage, but in fact the disaster was quite beyond anyone's skill to retrieve. The Netherlanders were confirmed in their worst suspicions of this foreign and Papist prince. The most that could be accomplished was to negotiate a face-saving retreat. Characteristically Queen Elizabeth saw the Duke as the innocent victim and discharged the vials of her wrath on the heads of Orange and his fellow-countrymen, while Walsingham, equally in character, suspected a put-up job between Anjou and Parma. The unlucky Colonel John Norris, commander of the English forces in the country, found himself caught between two fires. He was ordered by the States to hold a key position which denied the French access to provisions. Anjou denounced Norris, and the Queen angrily ordered Norris to obey the Duke. The colonel sturdily held out, appealing from the Queen misinformed to the Queen better-advised. In the end he saved his reputation both with the Low Countries rebels and with his sovereign.[35]

The final episode in this sorry history came in June 1583 when Anjou, now at Dunkirk, announced his withdrawal to France; he spoke of his continued concern for the provinces and blamed the States for failing to meet his demands. He gave his sponsor, the English Queen, no advance notice of his intentions. His departure was immediately followed by a series of disasters in maritime Flanders. Dunkirk, Nieuport, Dixmude, Menin followed one another into Parma's pocket in a matter of days. It was a fitting end to the muddled intervention of the English Queen and the French Duke in the affairs of the Low Countries.

In September a plea for money from the Duke brought down on his head the Queen's wrath; abandoning her usual flowery prose style, she rounded on him bluntly, declaring he was surrounded by such contrarient and confused advice that

[35] *Ibid.*, 47-49, 66-68, 95-98, 100, 102, 144-45.

he did not know how to act. Stafford, the new English ambassador at Paris, reported in November that Anjou's capital was now spent, that the sole remnant of reputation which clung to him was the reputed trust of the Huguenots (who in fact deeply distrusted him) and the continuing confidence of the Queen of England.[36]

WHAT ARE WE to make of this protracted bout of Anglo-French diplomacy lasting from 1581 to 1583? It followed on the attempted marriage scheme of 1579, which had drifted into abeyance after the great outburst of domestic opposition. After a year of uncertainty, about the end of 1580, the Queen, with whatever regrets, had put aside her hopes of marriage and deliberately set out to transform the Anjou wooing into a straightforwardly business-like offer of full alliance. Viewed in the perspective of English foreign policy over the decades since Elizabeth's accession, this was the boldest and by far the most ambitious initiative taken by her government since the Scottish enterprise of 1559-1560. The intervention in France in 1562-1563 had been a hasty and ill-considered undertaking, almost certainly the product of Robert Dudley's novice statesmanship and an essay in confessional diplomacy. There had been an inglorious but not a perilous retreat. The Queen had burned her fingers, not seriously, but quite enough to induce a permanent distaste for this kind of intervention.

The brief, sharp clash with Spain in 1568-1569, engineered by Cecil, was another matter; it was more dangerous, much was risked. But extremely skillful management contained the action within safe limits, and it marked no longer-term shift of direction. The use of such powerful, but non-lethal, weapons as the embargo prevented an escalation into hot war. Once tempers had simmered down on both sides, it was possible to move cautiously but decisively towards a detente—the Treaty of Bristol of 1573. This truce left England and Spain much where they were in 1568, on civil but distinctly chilly terms, certainly not friends but not yet foes. The old alignment of

[36] *Ibid.*, 405-6; *Hatfield*, III, 10; *CSPF*, XVIII, 197.

England and Burgundy was little more than a ghostly presence in English diplomatic thinking. It had seemed in 1572 as though England was about to shift definitively from the Burgundian link to a new-found entente with France, a hundred-and-eighty-degree reversal from the stance of previous Tudor governments. But the initiative had lain with the French clique then dominant, and the disaster of St. Bartholomew totally numbed without quite killing the new-born entente. It retained just enough vitality to be utilized from time to time in the small change of Anglo-French diplomatic intercourse.

When the possibility of entente revived in 1579, and again in 1581, the initiative clearly came from the English side. But the contrast between English policy in these two years could not have been more sharply etched. In the earlier year the needs of the state were muddled confusingly with the emotional drives of a middle-aged spinster princess. Two years later it was the interests of the state and the goals which could satisfy them, which were spelled out with hard-headed clarity. What was offered to Henry III not only put aside the personal preferences of the English Queen but was also free of any ideological component. There was to be a straightforward collaboration between two state powers based on a common threat to the security of each. That one was Catholic, the other Protestant, and that their common foe was the most Catholic of sovereigns was quite beside the point. It was the growing greatness of the Spanish King which menaced both his neighbors, irrespective of their religious preferences. This willingness to put aside religious difference had already been made manifest by the English in the ease with which Anjou's Catholicism had been dealt with in the marriage negotiations. It was envisaged that the marriage should be celebrated in a most ecumenical mode by an Anglican and a Roman Catholic bishop.[37] This self-consciously *Realpolitik* stance was one to which the English steadily adhered through the whole sequence of negotiation.

The deliberate seeking of an alliance was a sharp turn away

[37] *CSPF*, XV, 176-80.

from the carefully guarded neutralism, not to say isolationism, which had been the keynote of Elizabethan foreign policy, particularly in the decade of the 1570's. After the marriage was laid aside, Queen and councillors collaborated in a determined effort to mobilize an Anglo-French joint effort which by its active opposition would call a halt to Spanish expansionism. What led to this change of direction? Two widely separated trains of causes may be discerned. One was the course of events in the Low Countries, the other the loss of Portuguese independence after the disaster of Alcazar.

As we have seen, England's policy towards the Burgundian provinces had shifted after the collapse of Spanish authority in 1576. Under the urging of her left-wing Protestant councillors, Elizabeth had moved cautiously towards overt support of the rebel cause. Now that there seemed a good chance that the seventeen provinces could by their united exertions restore the old, loosely autonomous "Burgundian" regime with which England had lived comfortably in the past, Elizabeth was disposed to give them just enough assistance to tip the balance decisively in their favor. How far she would have gone in backing such a regime must remain problematical. Her instinctive distaste for rebels was a powerful deterrent, and Elizabeth became noticeably skittish when it became evident that the States government would require substantial provision of financial, and even military, aid to survive. In any case, the palpable weakness of the Brussels regime and its all-too-visible inability to assume the responsibilities of a real government gave the Queen an excellent excuse for drawing away from direct support of the States.

But her withdrawal of direct support for them did not signal a return to the guarded neutralism of the past. The Queen was no less committed to a continuing English role in the shaping of Netherlandish destinies; what she sought was an alternative and—to her—better strategy. What she strove for was a transformation of the three-sided relationship among France, England, and the Low Countries. The two former shared a common fear of restored Spanish power in those provinces, but each eyed the other askance, fearing that its rival would supplant Spain as overlord. For the English this would have been as alarming as a Spanish recovery; the French would have been hardly less comfortable in seeing the English reestablished on the continent in an area so strategically central. Elizabeth's hope was that common fear of Spain would enable each of the rivals to put aside, at least for the time, his mutual suspicions in pursuit of a basis for common action. Indeed, Elizabeth and her ministers could see no other viable path for them; single-handed intervention was more than England's strength could bear; only the united might of the two monarchies would be sufficient to check Philip's aggressions.

English concern over Portuguese affairs had a very different origin from their involvement in the Low Countries; the latter area had stood for generations in the foreground of English diplomatic calculations. Portugal, on the other hand, no near neighbor, had been only peripherally in the traditional orbit of English diplomacy. But from the time when the first news of the disaster at Alcazar filtered through to England, the government had become increasingly preoccupied with its consequences. They were a subject of discussion between the English and French courts before the death of the Cardinal-King in 1580 left the Portuguese throne vacant. These discussions assumed increasing urgency once Philip moved to secure his claims. What might be done to assist Portuguese resistance to the Spaniard was a topic of frequent though fruitless debate between the two courts in 1581 and 1582. But English interest in the Iberian kingdom was not directed towards the specific problems of Portugal as such; England had as yet little direct stake there. It was the European-wide consequences of the Spanish acquisition of her neighbor which focussed English attention. Indeed it is not too much to speak of a quantum jump in the dimensions of England's diplomatic horizons. They were extended now from the narrower bounds of those lands bordering the North Sea and the Channel to the wider limits of the whole European comity.

The clues to this change of outlook are embedded in many of the diplomatic instructions and dispatches of these years, particularly those connected with Walsingham's mission to Paris in 1581. They are also to be found in Burghley's cogitations at a slightly earlier time, in 1577 and 1578, when the shift in English policy was being meditated. It is not too much to say that in these years the English leaders came to recognize and respond to the classic dilemma which their successors were to encounter in their various futures, and which is loosely denominated the "balance of power." The concept is most explicitly spelled out in a document probably of 1577 or 1578.[38] It declares that the "old policy observed by the Kings of England, France, and Spain . . . is whensoever two of these princes seeth that one of them groweth to be a conqueror, the third will give aid to the weaker to restrain the mightier from growing overgreat." The notion is certainly implicit in the English diplomatic documents of these years.

In the instructions given Walsingham when he was sent to France in July 1581, the deep fears of the English government are unambiguously expressed.[39] He is to urge at Paris "how necessary it is for the Crown of France as well as for ours, yea, for all Christendom, that the King of Spain's greatness should be impeached." In the same document the Queen states what an error it would be both in the French King and in herself "to leave the King of Spain to increase to such greatness as hereafter neither the force of France nor England nor any that may be confederate with them shall be able to withstand any thing that the King of Spain shall attempt." And finally at the very end she returns to the larger theme "so great a good to Christendom as the conjunction of the King and us might bring." And it is fear of the "greatness of the King of Spain" which is reiterated again and again in the arguments used to persuade the French King to alliance.

The more specific theme of an intervention in Portuguese affairs was not spelled out so clearly, although in Elizabeth's instructions to Ambassador Cobham on first launching her diplomatic offensive she stressed what treasures Philip would

[38] BL, Add. Ms. 48,094, ff. 2-56 *passim*, esp. f. 19.
[39] Digges, *Ambassador*, 352-56. See also *ibid.*, 377-78, 429-33, for other instances in which fear of Spanish domination is expressed.

draw now from the East and the West Indies if allowed quietly to possess them; and then moved on to the ecumenical theme—the dangers not only to the two crowns of France and England but also to all of Europe.[40] Unspoken but perhaps not unconsidered was the fact that the addition of Portuguese resources might well give Philip just that added margin of power necessary to beat the Dutch rebels—a margin which recently had seemed to be missing.

In a more speculative vein one must raise the question as to why Hapsburg power seemed now so much more threatening than it had in Charles V's time, when it had been at least as great as it presently was. What had altered the views of the English ministers?

Two major considerations blended in reshaping their outlook. One was the familiar theme of international Catholic conspiracy; this had been a matter of faith among the more left-wing councillors, such as Walsingham, for some years. And now in this post-Tridentine world, religion did indeed seem to be the ruling passion of politics. "Princes contend not so much for rule as they do for religion, not who shall enjoy this country or that but what God we shall profess."[41]

The more secular-minded among them might subscribe to this proposition less certainly, but they did very much fear Spain because they believed Philip's malice towards the English, intensified by their aid to the rebels, would lead to active intervention when he was free to act. Fear of actual invasion began to grow.[42] It would be fatally easy to accomplish once the provinces were overwhelmed. With the Flemish ports and the maritime resources of the Low Countries at his disposal, it would be easy to choke off English trade.[43] And Philip could bring to bear the whole resources of his many dominions. The centralizing policy he had pursued since the late 1550's had gone far in fusing she loose dynastic cluster of

[40] *CSPF*, XV, 209-13.   [41] BL, Add. Ms. 48,084, ff. 6-8.
[42] *Ibid.*, ff. 26-28.
[43] This argument appears in 1586 in the parliamentary discussions (BL, Harl. Ms. 6845, ff. 30-42).

Hapsburg lands into a much more focussed and national Spanish state power.

Beyond that there was the simple geopolitical fact of Philip's acquisition of Portugal, the first shift in the international power structure since the retirement of Charles V; the transfer of the Portuguese throne to its new occupant—however unpremeditated the action, however plausible his claim—was a shock to the nervous system of a delicately balanced international organism. More particularly, Philip's new dominion substantially increased his power in the one area where it had been relatively weak, the Atlantic. Spain's inability to maintain regular sea communications with Flanders or the effective protection of her own Indies might now be redressed with the Portuguese ocean-going navy at Philip's disposal. Taken altogether these facts forced upon the English leadership a radical, and painful, reorientation of their basic ideas about foreign relations.

Who was responsible for the shift in foreign policy? The theoretician, as always, was Burghley. There is a substantial cache of papers written or annotated by him, organized in his characteristic *sic et non* fashion and filled with cogitations on the Dutch problem. They do not, however, come to any conclusive recommendations, although the arguments in them may well have influenced the Queen's decisions. The active lead was certainly hers, not the Treasurer's. As long as the marriage formed part of her whole policy, she had to drag a recalcitrant Council behind her, but once that issue was set aside, she had the wholehearted backing of most of her councillors. Many of them had had more enthusiasm for the policy of direct support for the Prince of Orange and the States General. Walsingham, Leicester, and Hatton had certainly opposed the match; Burghley had favored it *qua* marriage but without much enthusiasm for the chosen bridegroom. Sussex alone was a wholehearted supporter. But an alliance was an option which attracted backing in every quarter. There can be no doubt that Walsingham, sent to press it on the French Court, used all his skills in an effort to succeed. He was convinced that, whatever the risks of such an entanglement, England must enlist the support of France if Spain were to be checked. There is no reason to suppose that his colleagues did not share this conviction.

It is hard to overestimate the consequences of this great swing of the tiller; it brought the English ship of state hard around and set her on a new, unknown, and danger-laden course. Not the least surprising aspect of that shift was the Queen's own change of heart. Since the far-off days of the Scottish crisis at the opening of the reign, a cautiousness verging on timidity had been the most obvious feature of her personality. At the most she could be moved to an underground intrigue, provided her participation was securely masked; the conspiracy with Alençon/Anjou in 1575-1576 is a good example. Towards the Low Countries her attitude had always been one of coldly correct neutrality. The urgent pleas of Orange and his adherents had been brusquely, even brutally, rejected. Even when events favored them after 1576, the Queen, after a brief softening of her attitude, soon retired to a chilly distance.

Now Elizabeth of her "own mere will and motion" sought a public alliance with France, offensive and defensive, aimed, for all the world to see, at checking the growth of Spanish greatness by joint action in the Low Countries and elsewhere. Such a move shifted the gears of English foreign policy from a neutral to a forward position and implied a willingness to set the engines of state in motion. The Queen seemed ready to spend money, to mobilize troops and ships—in short, to engage in that kind of political and military activism which hitherto she had abhorred with her every fibre.

What internal processes jarred Elizabeth's political consciousness into such unwonted activity are hidden from us as is so much else of her opaque personality. It has been suggested above that a middle-aged spinster's last desperate bid for marriage had been one of the impulses which launched the wooing of Anjou in 1579, but if that was the case, since then, as in 1561, the Queen's vigorous political instincts, her cool-headed grasp of political reality, had reasserted themselves. Personal motives had been put aside and replaced by the claims of policy; the private persona once again vanished into the public. Elizabeth's masterful grasp of the whole machinery of diplomacy was never firmer than in these years. The shape of her thinking at this time is best revealed in the assumptions which underlay the new policy of alliance.

Probably the most crucial was the realization that England at some point in the past half dozen years had crossed over an invisible but nevertheless real Rubicon in her support of the Low Countries regime. From 1572 on, English leaders had hoped that the revolt would lead to a permanent weakening of Spanish authority in the provinces; up to 1576, circumstances enforced a prudential circumspection which allowed only the most modest forms of assistance. After that date, the existence of an indigenous regime in the Low Countries forced England to gamble on its survival. The Queen had—in modern terms—given diplomatic recognition to the States and followed that up with a modicum of financial aid. The gamble had paid off in the short run; they had survived. But from 1580 on, Parma's alarming successes in the resuscitation of Spanish power gave reason for increasing discouragement. But there was no withdrawing; an irreversible step had been taken, the first of its kind since the invasion of Scotland in 1560— and this was a far riskier move. The new regime at Brussels, however ramshackle in nature, was too valuable an asset to be sacrificed. Moreover, in quite another part of the world, Englishmen, acting with the Queen's knowledge if not at her direct behest, had struck at Spain's vulnerable under-belly, the coast of Peru, where Drake had suddenly appeared in 1579. This was only the dramatic culmination of a series of buccaneering raids which disturbed the security of the Indies.

The immediate response of Madrid to Drake's enterprise was apparent in the angry complaints which Mendoza was ordered to lodge with the English government. But well before Drake's return, Spain had given the English a fright by the two successive Papal expeditions to Ireland—in 1579 and 1580—which had been launched with scarcely veiled Spanish assistance. They awakened more alarm in England than their magnitude or the probable intentions of the Spanish government warranted, but they did serve notice that Spanish ire at English meddling in the Low Countries was rising. In the past Elizabeth had spurned the views of those councillors who saw Philip as an inflexible Catholic ideologue, waiting for the first opportunity to crush heretic England. But now she came to the recognition that her actions in the Low Countries were regarded with growing irritation in Madrid, where there were voices telling the King that England was the greatest hindrance to any successful repression of the revolt. The mounting resentment of the Spanish monarch coincided with a marked renascence in Catholic activity within England, and for many the two phenomena were links within a great chain of international conspiracy.

Elizabeth's own fears were revealingly displayed by the *cri de coeur* recorded in the reserve instructions to Walsingham when he went to Paris in 1581. She allowed him, if the French remained obdurate, to discuss marriage lest "we shall be left alone without any aid from the King [of France] subject to the malice of Spain, and not free from the evil neighborhood of Scotland, and lastly uncertain of the good will of the French king or his brother or of both."[44] This dread of isolation in the face of an irate and determined Spain was a nightmare which haunted the Queen from this time forward and was the mainspring of her efforts to achieve alliance with Henry III.

And, as we have seen, events in far-off Morocco forced English statesmen to broaden their horizon to include the whole west European state complex. In this much grander dimension the limited goal of hindering Spanish reconquest of the Low Countries was subsumed in the larger task of bringing to a halt general Spanish expansion and restoring a balance of power within the system. The aid of France was now even more imperative; if without it not even the lesser goal could be accomplished, how much more was it necessary for the larger aim.

The vision which informed the new policy was clear and wide-ranging, but the strategies for achieving alliance and then for common action by the allies were cloudier and more

[44] *CSPF*, XV, 279-81.

uncertain and probably not viable. The basic schema was simple; its purpose was to block the expansion of Spain on all fronts—in the Low Countries, in Portugal and in its empire—by means of an alliance between the English and French crowns. That alliance would be implemented by their joint support of Anjou's governorship of the seventeen provinces. Such a strategy was itself the result of a choice; the rejected alternative was direct support for the States-General, that is to say, for the Prince of Orange, the preference of Leicester and Walsingham. This would presumably lead either to the establishment of an independent Burgundian state or—what was really their preference—an English protectorate over the provinces.

One important consequence of this choice was the virtual abandonment of serious diplomatic representation in the Low Countries. Since 1576 a series of envoys, capped by the mission of Walsingham, had maintained close relations between the English government and the two embryonic regimes in the Netherlands—that of the States and that of Orange. In addition, special representatives were sent from time to time to Don John and to his successor, Parma. But now these contacts were neglected; most of the information the government received from the Low Countries came from resident English merchants or through private contacts. More important, the whole thrust of English policy in the Low Countries was directed to the support of Anjou.

Elizabeth had rejected the alternative of direct intervention for strategic reasons. It would involve her in war with Philip with no support other than that which the provinces themselves could muster. The very shaky character of the States regime made this a dubious gamble; as allies they seemed likely to be non-starters. In addition there were psychological aspects to the problem which were highly important to the Queen. She shrank from cooperation with a regime based on revolt against lawful authority, most particularly when the leaders were for the most part men of inferior social rank, mere townsmen, lawyers or officials—at the best, provincial nobles. Such a leadership only evoked Elizabeth's sneering contempt and she could not seriously entertain them as diplomatic or political equals.

Hence the brute facts of *Realpolitik* as well as the less tangible realities of a complex royal psyche combined to favor the French strategy. A traditional alliance with a fellow-monarch and the employment of a prince of the blood royal as commander and governor satisfied the Queen's sense of the fitness of things in a way which cooperation with a regime of estates, mere inferior councils, would never do. So much for the fixed assets of this enterprise, but what about operations? How were they to be carried out? Here the picture was necessarily a good deal hazier, but undoubtedly what the Queen hoped was that the very mobilization of such a coalition would persuade the stubborn King of Spain to cut his losses—to compromise with his Low Countries subjects along the lines which she had so frequently suggested. She clearly did not want, and probably did not visualize, a sustained military campaign. The threat alone, once it was made real, would suffice.

This brings us to the first, and very serious, flaw in the Queen's grand strategy and reveals those idiosyncracies of temperament which dangerously weakened the royal statecraft. Elizabeth was quite capable of seeing all too clearly the realities of her international position. She saw that Spain must be restrained by alliance with France, but the terms she wanted to set were less than realistic. She wanted the alliance—quite desperately—but she wanted it at the cheapest possible cost and on conditions which would leave her the largest possible freedom of action. Concretely this meant that she would not sacrifice her own independence by marriage and that she would not commit her government in advance to any specified sum of money or number of men or of ships. Moreover, whatever was disbursed to Anjou or Don Antonio was to be so veiled as to be invisible; what she really hoped was that no disbursements at all would be necessary. The confrontation with Spain was somehow to be kept at a diplomatic level where the two protagonists might continue civil conversation across the table even while kicking one another sharply underneath it.

To provide maximum freedom of action for England while making minimum commitments of national resources was a prudential pursuit of national interest, especially when dealing with a would-be partner of greater wealth and population. But in her pursuit the Queen parted company with political reality. Her own egotism, as in her dealings with Mary Stuart in the 1560's, blinded her to any perception of the necessary calculation of interests which her intended ally would also be making.

From the beginning a central question was how far the French, on their side, really desired an alliance. France—so the King and his mother declared—could not look on unmoved at Spain's access of power, but their view of the whole situation was not necessarily the same as England's. Except for the first few months of the revolt France—or Frenchmen—had played a minor role until the Duke of Anjou entered the scene. His interests were by no means identical with those of the French Crown; his was a highly personal venture and his band of adventurers stood in sharp contrast to the stream of English volunteers who came with powerful sponsorship and at least the tacit permission of their monarch. Nor was there the religious sympathy which motivated many of these volunteers. In short, France had accumulated a much smaller burden of Spanish resentment than that felt towards England.

France undoubtedly had long-term ambitions for eastward expansion, manifest in Henry II's time and again when the Colignys were in the ascendant. But the proved incapacity of the Valois kings to deal with the terrible internal rifts within their realm had put the quietus on any expansionist ambitions that the French Court might entertain. The gradual recognition by the English Court that their ancient enemy, whose aspirations in the Low Countries haunted English policy in the 1570's, was now neutralized by her own weakness was an element in encouraging an alliance in the 1580's. In any case, the stimuli which might have quickened French rivalries with Spain in the Low Countries now lay dormant.

And, for France, intervention in the Low Countries was bound up with the strains within the royal family between the two brothers and with the enmity, engulfing Court and country, between the two great religious parties. To give money, men, and arms to Anjou was a risky business, since no one could be certain how this dangerously irresponsible man would use them for his own feckless ends. And since intervention in the Netherlands more and more meant support for Protestantism it was bound to rouse the ire of the Guises and their followers—which might precipitate another bout of civil war and even invite Spanish intervention in French affairs. In short, a calculated weighing of the advantages to be found in an English alliance hardly brought the balance down in its favor. The English were likely to have a hard time in persuading their neighbor to accept their bid.

Under these circumstances it was important for England to use every available diplomatic weapon to convince the French not only of the intrinsic value of such an alliance but of England's real desire to enter into it. The French Court had every reason, based on past performance, to doubt the Queen's honesty of intention. Her very considerable skills in evasion, delay, in the endless spinning out of negotiations, had served her in good stead in the game she had played with her French opposite number over the past decade, but they had also undermined her credibility. Her querulous complaint that she was not trusted by the French Court hardly arouses our sympathy. Obviously the one really clinching action which alone would carry conviction was marriage with Duke Francis. It is hardly surprising that the French Court kept coming back to this point in the negotiations; it was for them the one-way bridge which would block off all possibility of her retreat. The only other possibility open to her, if she would not make the supreme sacrifice of her independence, was—as Walsingham in his hectoring way told her—to make specific commitments of men and money to the Netherlands enterprise and to the support of Don Antonio. The Queen must bind herself to the spending of money and to the running of risks if she expected to move the French. But when they insisted that she put her cards upon the table, her refusal was to them clear proof of her ultimate unreliability.

The historical observer may feel that French distrust was not unjustified, but Elizabeth's refusal to give them satisfaction resulted from a complex of quite varying causes. One was highly idiosyncratic, a kind of failure of nerve. She could not really bring herself to bear the risks entailed by open struggle on the battlefield or the high seas. She could not brook the loss of control over events which necessarily followed, once they moved outside the orbit of her own personal presence, away from the Council-chamber to the muddy fields of Flanders or to the troubled waters of the Bay of Biscay. This deep-seated reluctance would reveal itself again and again in the years of action which lay ahead.

But there were also very tangible political reasons which held the Queen in check. The Anjou marriage would have been intensely unpopular with important segments of the English political world and would have risked dangerous instability within the realm. And Elizabeth's argument, so often repeated to the French, that her subjects would not stomach an expensive war fought for the benefit of the unpopular Duke, was more than diplomatic rhetoric. Events would prove them willing to give more than asked for in the Low Countries—if their Queen would herself assume the protection of Holland and Zealand—but they were unlikely to show much parliamentary enthusiasm for pouring out English money to make a French Papist governor of the Netherlands. Hence the Queen's insistence that her aid be, so far as possible, clandestine—at least unofficial—had some reason to it. Money could be paid over to the Duke without any of the full-dress publicity that more overt intervention would necessarily entail. The Spanish government might not be deceived, but English public opinion would not be so openly outraged.

Indeed, this factor of public opinion, as made manifest in the House of Commons, was an element with which Elizabeth had always to reckon. The capacity of the Tudor government to tap the nation's wealth for its purposes was more limited than the taxing potential of its greater neighbors. Any substantial increase in royal expenditure could be financed only through new parliamentary grants. The Commons were not prepared absolutely to close the nation's purse to a royal demand, but the extent of their generosity would be related to the popularity of the cause for which it was asked. These circumstances may serve to explain the Queen's diffidence in fleshing out the alliance, but they also substantially diminished any real hopes that the alliance would come into being. Elizabeth's own unwillingness to take the risks which were necessary to convince the French of her sincerity, compounded by the very real obstacles which were thrown up by Protestant opinion within the country, cast a shadow of unreality over the grand strategy which Walsingham so ardently pressed upon the French. In the end the tactics of implementation were not equal to the grandness of conception.

The failure of the strategy was not total; the corpse of the matrimonial negotiations was given a little artificial respiration; the Duke donned his suitor's costume once again. The little comedy which followed provided the necessary fiction for setting up the Duke as an English protégé in Antwerp. And the French King was induced to bear a modest share of the expenses of keeping his brother afloat in the Low Countries. About a quarter of Anjou's expenditures from 1581 through 1583 came from English sources; another quarter came from the King and his mother; a third was raised in loans; the balance was provided by the States-General.[45] So the Duke's enterprise was a rather shabby simulacrum of what the Queen had intended.

We have detailed elsewhere the dismal history of Anjou's exploits in 1582 and 1583. His failure arose not from the lack of funds but from his own sheer ineptitude. The episode casts a cold, ironic light on the whole strategy of Anglo-French cooperation pursued by the Queen of England through these years. The ultimate error in the program lay neither in the goals nor in the design for action; the fatal flaw was to be found in the key figure chosen to execute the whole scheme, a man whose total unsuitability for such a role had been visible from the start.

For this the Queen has to bear the responsibility; it was she

[45] PRO, SP 78/10/339, ff. 308-35.

who backed him through thick and thin, even after the clinching evidence provided by the "French fury" in Antwerp. She insisted on continuing to bet on a horse whose inability ever to get away from the starting-post was clear to the rest of the spectators well before the race began. It has to be admitted that she had little choice; her only real alternative was Orange and that would have meant abandoning the whole strategy of the past several years. Her blind loyalty to the Duke until the bitter end throws light on Elizabeth's unwillingness to face unpleasant facts, and on the limitations of her judgment. She was in some measure blinded by her own royal snobbery. Anjou's royalty dazzled the usually clear-seeing eyes of the Queen and endowed him with a panoply of imperial virtues which he never possessed. The fantasm she beheld was a man of bravery, decision, and integrity, and it was an illusion which she was very slow to yield. The cost to England was very high, quite apart from the treasure squandered on the Duke's antics in Flanders. For the Queen had been forced to abandon one of her prime objectives: her determination to keep her support for Anjou at the lowest possible profile. In lavishing her royal approbation on the Duke, in sending her nobles to stand witness at his inauguration at Antwerp, and in the pressure she put upon the States and the Prince of Orange to accept him as governor, she had taken up that public posture of opposition to Spain which she had so ardently sought to avoid, and thereby assured herself of an accumulating weight of Spanish anger.

No wonder Elizabeth's ministers were in a grim mood as they looked on the wreckage of their policy in the summer of 1583. Far from being checked, Spanish power had grown steadily as Parma relentlessly pressed on, adding town to town and fortress to fortress in his program of reconquest. Anjou's intervention had served only to disrupt even further the disordered ranks of the States leadership so that their chances of continuing resistance seemed dimmer than ever. In Portugal and its empire Philip had now made good his claim to rule. And Spanish resentment towards England, strong enough at the beginning of the decade, was now more bitter than ever.

CHAPTER 13

THE COMING OF WAR,

1583-1585

From 1576 on through the next half dozen years the English leadership had taken a series of initiatives by which they sought to bend events to their own ends. Their struggle was marked by successive disappointments; the total bankruptcy of their efforts became apparent in the summer of 1583. For the next two years the English watched helplessly the frightening course of events in the Low Countries. The prospect was all the more terrifying because they themselves, far from being mere observers, were caught by this relentlessly flowing tide and carried towards threatening catastrophe.

Many divergent streams of events were beginning to flow together in these hectic years. One took its rise at Brill in 1572 and its course has been followed in detail; another, which is discussed below, can be traced back even earlier, to the pioneer voyages of that enterprising Devonian, John Hawkins, in the 1560's. They had been followed by the buccaneering exploits of Francis Drake and his fellow privateers. Drake's famous voyage of 1577-1580 escalated what had been an irritating but minor harassment of the Spanish Indies into something more serious, although still falling short of open warfare. These activities came to fill almost as much space in the dispatches of the Spanish ambassador at London as did Low Country matters.

Another, almost contemporaneous, event, outside the borders of the Netherlands, was as important in its consequences. This was the death from natural causes in June 1584 of Francis of Anjou. Although spasmodic negotiations between this prince and the States continued up to the last weeks of his life, he had really ceased to be an important factor in their affairs. But in the larger equation of West-European affairs, his death shifted the balances very dangerously. The next heir to the French throne was the Protestant Henry of Navarre. The French succession, like the English succession or the lordship of the Low Countries, was now a locus of intense rivalry between the two great international religious parties. Developments in Britain, the Low Countries, and France were ever more intricately and sensitively intertwined.

IN THE AFTERMATH of Anjou's departure, the defenses of Flanders crumbled away with appalling rapidity.[1] Parma's clocklike tactical precision secured one town after another with little actual fighting. His technique of blockade and starvation seemed to have a basilisk effect on the defenders, whose resolution steadily cooled, until in numb helplessness they surrendered on the Duke's terms. By the end of 1584 only Brussels, Mechlin, and Antwerp survived in the southern provinces: the first two effectively blockaded and the last just beginning to feel the iron grip of Farnese's encircling armies.

While the Duke inexorably advanced, a more sudden, although hardly unforeseen, catastrophe overtook the rebel cause. In the spring of 1582 an assassin had made an attempt on the life of the Prince of Orange which left him hovering between life and death for weeks, although he ultimately recovered. In July 1584 a second attempt succeeded. The rebels' cause was bereft of its one great leader just as its affairs became desperate.

In the year preceding these events the English government did little but mark time. In the autumn of 1583 a new ambassador was sent to Paris; Edward Stafford replaced Henry

---

[1] See Van der Essen, *Farnèse*, III, chaps. 8-13.

Cobham. Significantly the new ambassador's instructions[2] were exclusively concerned with the problems of Scotland, of piracy in the Narrow Seas, and of the Huguenots. Stafford was to make discreet contact with Navarre and Condé and assure these princes of the Queen's interest in their well-being. Nothing at all was said about the old familiar topics of diplomatic intercourse—Anjou, marriage, alliance, or the Low Countries. And for many months Stafford found his time taken up with the items listed in his instructions.

In the late winter the French Court let slip vague hints about the revival of the proposed Anglo-French alliance. At the same time Walsingham, worried by Spanish naval preparations, was fretting over the need for some such arrangement and was trying to push his mistress into some friendly gesture towards Paris. The Queen did instruct her ambassador to follow up these hints. When he did so, he at first got no clear answer; in a later interview the King was frank in admitting that his internal problems were too great to allow him to risk war with Spain. So matters stood when after weeks of contradictory reports about his health, alternately gloomy or hopeful, Anjou finally died in early June.[3]

The Queen used the opportunity of a mission of condolence, undertaken by Sir Philip Sidney, to press once again for joint action in the Low Countries. She floated an initial balloon with the French ambassador and followed it up with instructions for Sir Philip and for the resident ambassador. They met with a barely civil repulse; Sidney's visit was put off on the flimsiest excuses and it was clear that France would not respond to the English overtures.[4]

Relations with the Low Countries were equally uncertain. The Queen's main interest in the States continued to be the repayment of the £98,000 which they owed her. In the autumn of 1583 she went so far as to authorize the seizure of ships, nominally for piracy, but actually to offset the debt. Orange, while fending off Elizabeth's obstinate demands for

[2] *CSPF*, XVIII, 115-17.
[3] *Ibid.*, 345, 377, 388, 435-36, 476-81, 506, 508, 548-49.
[4] *Hatfield*, III, 41; *CSPF*, XVIII, 594, 601-2, 603-5, 611-13, 622, 633.

her money, was still hoping for a continuance of the aid which had previously been funneled through Anjou. Letters were exchanged, through Norris, between Elizabeth and the Prince and in the fall there seems to have been serious discussion in the English Council about what road to take. Some were clearly urging the Queen to take the initiative in pressing for a mediated peace. Orange's recent assertion that no peace with Spain was possible was to be ignored; so were French interests. The Queen's response to all these proposals was a brusque letter carried to Holland by Walsingham's servant, Burnham, in late November. In it the Queen expressed her displeasure that the Prince did not communicate with her, urged him to make peace with Spain while he was still strong enough to bargain, and once again pressed him to depend on Anjou. She concluded by asserting that she regretted ever having aided a set of ungrateful men who by their own confusions wasted their chances. Walsingham's agent may have held back from the Prince this peculiarly ill-tempered composition.[5]

But in the new year 1584 English intentions seemed to swerve in another direction. Leicester's friend and protégé, Edward Dyer, made a brief visit to the Low Countries. Apparently he was authorized to express English concern about Spanish naval preparations and to discuss the terms of a possible maritime alliance, with each side contributing quotas of ships for common defense. No immediate conclusion was reached, but negotiations continued and in April the States-General accredited two envoys to ask for men and money. But they had more than one arrow in their quiver, for they sent a mission to Paris in June, shortly after Anjou's death, to offer Henry III his late brother's title along with the right to garrison the principal Flemish and Brabantine towns still in rebel hands. This apparently was at the urging of Orange.[6]

A fortnight later the Prince was dead and the future of the rebel cause more clouded than ever. In England there were anxious consultations and an agent, John Somers, the experi-

---

[5] *CSPF*, XVIII, 45-46, 73-74, 101-2, 120-22, 187-90, 233-34, 245-46, 508-11, 563-65.
[6] *Ibid.*, 338, 461, 513, 553-55, 584, 628-29, 653-55.

enced Clerk of the Privy Seal, was ordered to repair to the States-General.[7] He was to assure them of her care for their future and to make careful inquiry as to their resources and what they proposed now as a form of government. If he went, he must have crossed the path of messengers from the other side of the Narrow Seas, bearing the urgent pleas of the rebel leaders for the Queen's protection. The States of Brabant specifically asked Leicester to back their request for men and munitions, and more specifically they sought permission to recruit 1,500 English soldiers for immediate service, to be paid by them and commanded by Colonel Morgan or some other English leader. Their agents arrived in London in August with the additional proposal that the Queen send succor of 6,000 foot, 3,000 horse, and 300,000 lbs. of powder while embargoing shipments to the Spanish-held provinces, choking off supplies of grain from the Eastland. They also intimated that negotiations with France were far advanced and that several provinces had already committed themselves to accept French sovereignty. However, Holland, Zealand, and Utrecht would prefer (they suggested) to place themselves under her protection. The Queen brushed aside all these requests, declaring them unreasonable on the grounds that there was no adequate security for the money she would have to spend. The most she would do was to offer to urge the French to joint consultations with the States and the English at Boulogne on the plight of the provinces.[8]

In this Elizabeth was as good as her word. She had already been pressing her views on the French Court; even though Sidney's mission was choked off by the King's excuses, the resident ambassador made the strongest possible representations to the Queen Mother. This was followed up by specific proposals for the Boulogne conference. While there was no acceptance of these offers by Paris, the Queen Mother did commit her son to an embargo on shipments to the Spanish provinces. When the States envoys arrived in Paris, they were

[7] *Ibid.*, 598-99, 607. It is not clear he went. See *ibid.*, 640, 642-43.
[8] *Ibid.*, 598-99, 600-1, 622-23, 625, 635; *CSPF*, XIX, Add. p. 699, and 40-42.

held in play by the French Court while des Pruneaux, one of
Anjou's agents, was despatched on a fact-finding mission to
the Low Countries.[9]

There followed some confusing weeks in which rumors of
an impending treaty betwen Henry III and the Estates-Gen
eral circulated widely. By mid-October an unofficial proposal
was made by the Estates-General, offering Henry III the place
which Charles V had once occupied in their provinces. The
French secretary, Pinart, communicated these proposals to
Stafford quite frankly and asked for the English Queen's
views on them. Walsingham's instructions are revealing. The
English ambassador was to withdraw the reservations he had
been ordered to express earlier about French possession of the
Low Countries. The Queen, Walsingham declared, was now
so convinced of Spanish bad will that she preferred the risks
of French domination to Spanish restoration. The Secretary
himself thought England was not running much risk since
the French would move into the provinces only if they were
given absolute sovereignty (which the States would never
concede).[10]

The Dutch themselves were far from united on their approach to Paris. The religious views of the French Court, its
past treatment of the Huguenots, and their own experience
with Anjou gave pause to the Dutch leaders. The English
Court made the most of these uncertainties by despatching its
first official envoy to the Estates-General since Walsingham's
return in 1578. Once again the emissary was William Davison.
Davison went with instructions under the royal sign manual,
countersigned by the Secretary. He was to sound out the state
of the French negotiations and if, as the Queen suspected, they
had not really gone far, he was authorized to offer English
protection in return for the handing over of cautionary towns.
However, his initial reports back to London suggest he must
have been ordered to proceed very cautiously, holding these
far-reaching offers in reserve. He did no more than make a

[9] *CSPF*, XVIII, 644-45, 646-47; *ibid.*, XIX, 14-15, 20-21, 26-27, 49-
50, 54-55.
[10] *CSPF*, XIX, 37-38, 55, 61-62, 101, 103-6, 119-20.

general offer of English aid, declining to discuss any specific terms until more was known of the state of negotiations with France. Indeed, he asked whether he should remain in the Low Countries or return to await a ripening of the situation. The French party was, he observed, very strong at present and the pro-Spanish elements were willing to go along with them, counting on a failure which would throw the provinces back into Philip's arms. Walsingham responded by ordering Davison to stay on to see what happened at Paris.[11]

Davison was also allowed to carry on a subsidiary scheme by exploring the affairs of Cologne, where the Elector-Archbishop had turned Protestant and attempted—unsuccessfully—to hang on to his dominions. Davison was given a credit of £6,000 which might, if it seemed a good risk, be handed over to the Elector.[12]

In the meantime, dealings between the States and the French Court dragged on slowly; in November 1584 Stafford thought the ultimate decision would be for French intervention. But it was not until January 1585 that the States mission finally set foot in France, and then the French found means to delay their arrival at court. Stafford was instructed to act very circumspectly. He was to hint at English willingness to collaborate but to avoid any commitment of English resources until it was quite clear what Henry III intended to do. Nevertheless, Burghley feared that ultimately France would be a more dangerous neighbor in the Low Countries than Spain. Therefore his immediate policy was to win time "wherein many accidents may ensue."[13]

The French King continued to listen to the States deputies without giving them any answer. However, the French Court could not continue its "timorous silence" indefinitely, and at last in early March Henry told the States deputies that his own estate was "so tickle and unsound" that he could do nothing for them. The poor substitute, the most he would offer, was

[11] *Ibid.*, 82-83, 123-24, 129-32, 149-51, 176-81, 204-5.
[12] *Ibid.*, 208-9.
[13] *Ibid.*, 148-49, 235-36, 237-39, 239-41; PRO, SP 12/176/15, 11 Jan. 1585.

a joint Anglo-French approach to Philip, urging him to reconciliation with his subjects. Bellièvre, the French Secretary, confided to Stafford that it was fear of the Guises which motivated
the King's refusal to act, and indeed within a fortnight the
Guises' seizure of Chalons signalled the outbreak of new civil
disorder in France.[14]

The news that the Guises were in arms was as worrying as
the news from Antwerp. Stafford was immediately instructed
to sound out Henry III's intentions. Was he in underhanded
alliance with Guise? If he were prepared to stand by the edicts
of toleration, Elizabeth would assist him against foreign foes or
domestic rebels. Within a few days the Guises made public
their demands, for the maintenance of the Catholic religion
and the appointment of a Catholic successor. The Queen now
sent off two special missions. Sir Thomas Leighton went once
again to Paris to strengthen the King's resolve to back the
Huguenots, while Arthur Champernoun sailed from Dart-
mouth en route to the Court of Henry of Navarre. Yet another
mission was set on foot by orders sent to Thomas Bodley, then
in Germany; he was to stir up the German Protestant princes
and the King of Denmark to assist Navarre.[15]

Stafford did his best at the French Court; the King acknowledged his gratitude to Elizabeth but kept her offers carefully
at arm's length. Navarre was now pressing the Queen, through
the agent he was sending (Segur-Pardeilhan) for immediate
help. And she on her side was already writing to her old protégé, Duke Casimir, to inquire what forces he could bring to
the aid of the Huguenots; she suggested, without promising,
that English money might be forthcoming. Casimir promptly
replied, asking for £100,000; nothing less than an army of
20,000 men would serve the purpose. Henry III in the meantime was steadily yielding to Guisan demands; he agreed to
recall the edicts, giving the Huguenots six months to change
their faith. This was in spite of—or because of—a stinging letter from Elizabeth to the French King, scornfully reproachful

[14] *CSPF*, XIX, 273-76, 295-98, 315-21, 318, 354-55.
[15] *Ibid.*, 369-70, 380-81, 393-94, 415-16, 433-34.

of his apathy, hectoring in tone, and on the whole treating him as a delinquent adolescent, lectured by his schoolmaster or by his father.[16]

By late June the Queen had decided to give at least some money for Navarre's use but under humiliating limitations since it was to be provided in Germany and used—at English discretion—only if the German princes and Denmark agreed to collaborate. These terms were all the more depressing since Bodley's reception from the princes and at Copenhagen had been polite, even cordial, but altogether evasive. Each prince sought to thrust the decision on one of his fellow-rulers: the negative reaction of the Saxon Court served as an excuse for all the rest to back away. None of the English initiatives, at the French Court or northern Germany, had achieved anything, and so, for the time being, French affairs hung in suspense as the two great parties maneuvered nervously towards confrontation.[17]

The Dutch, now that their last hope of French aid was gone, had no alternative but to turn to the English. The English on their side had reluctantly to pick up the burden they had sought to cast on French shoulders; now it could not even be shared with France. Nevertheless, both sides moved warily and slowly towards agreement. The English Queen wrote to give general assurances of support as soon as the French denial was known. Leicester wrote Davison deploring the French decision but asserting that if the Dutch "heartily and earnestly seek it, the Lord hath appointed them a far better defence. But you must so use the matter as they must earnestly seek their own good though we shall be partakers thereof also. If they deal effectually and liberally, they will bring themselves to a better end than ever France would have brought them." What these phrases masked was the Queen's determination to have air-tight guarantees for reimbursement for all future outlays in the Dutch behalf and of obedience to her will during the time of her protection. Davison's role now was to

[16] *Ibid.*, 434-35, 447-48, 499, 513-15, 541, 552-55.
[17] *Ibid.*, 494, 508-12, 563-67, 577-78, 584-85, 588-89, 618, 636-39.

tutor the Dutch leaders in their conduct of negotiations; he was to return with their mission when it came to London. But the Low Countries authorities were far from certain even yet of the seriousness of English intentions; there had been too many unfulfilled half-promises in the past.[18]

Both in England and in Holland there was seemingly endless discussion of the details of alliance. So the months wore away; Brussels had surrendered in March 1585, and now in Flanders and Brabant only Antwerp and Mechlin in the interior and Ostend on the coast held out. Antwerp's position was becoming more desperate each week as successive attempts to break Parma's blockade failed in their purpose. By May the States-General was driven to beg for immediate aid for Antwerp, to precede the signing of a formal treaty. Davison drafted a letter from the Queen to the magistrates of Antwerp, promising relief forces. By 23 June Walsingham could write that John Norris would take 3,000 foot and 200 horse to the Low Countries. At the same time the long-delayed mission from the States-General—twice driven back by contrary winds —reached Margate. It was very late for any of these actions since newsletters from the continent were already, before the end of June, carrying accounts of the approaches St. Aldegonde, the governor of Antwerp, was making to Parma. A second letter to the magistrates of that city from the Queen was smuggled in and reached its destination by late in the month, but Mechlin had fallen by then. Moreover, Elizabeth had been seized by one of her constitutional fits of indecision and although the letters for levying the expeditionary forces had been signed, the Queen could not bring herself to determinative action.[19]

Events elsewhere were working in favor of the interventionist party. In May Philip suddenly seized all English ships lying in Spanish ports; his excuse was that he needed shipping for a fleet assembling at Lisbon. Englishmen feared this was an invasion fleet aimed at England, which it was not; but Philip

---

[18] *Hatfield*, III, 96; *CSPF*, XIX, 333-34, 336-37, 365-67, 423-24, 427, 431, 450-51, 465.

[19] *CSPF*, XIX, 490-91, 515-16, 557, 558, 578-79, 618-19, 630-31.

may have been acting on Mendoza's oft-repeated advice, to strike at England by embargoing her trade with Spain. In any case, it left the English merchants trading to Spain angry and desperate. At the same time their colleagues in the Antwerp trade were petitioning the Queen to save that city. Whatever economic considerations had held in check English policy towards Spain were now crumbling away; war could hardly worsen an already desperate situation.[20]

Finally, at the beginning of August, the Queen moved closer to action by signing the warrant which appointed William Huddleston Treasurer for the Wars in the Low Countries and authorizing transport and pay monies of about £18,000. At the same time Norris received his patent as colonel-general of the Queen's forces in the Netherlands. On 10 August 1585 the preliminary treaty between the Queen and the States-General was signed at Nonsuch and in the last week of August Norris was writing from Middleburg of his arrival there with 2,000 foot. Early in August Walsingham's Zealand correspondent had warned that Antwerp could not hold out until the end of the month and Norris' arrival coincided almost to the day with the city's fall.[21]

OF THE TWO ROADS which led England to overt intervention in the Low Countries and to open confrontation with Spain, one was that just traced; it ran through the Netherlands and began with the English "volunteer" forces at Flushing in 1572; its milestones included the loans to the States after 1576, the Anjou enterprise, and the vain attempts to bring France into a collaboration against Spain in the Netherlands. There was another road less clearly marked and consequently harder to map out. This ran directly from London to Madrid with no by-passes. The record of direct diplomatic relations between England and Spain is a baffling one and not easy to interpret. This delicate and vital relationship—one which would ulti-

[20] *CSPD*, II, 244; *CSPSp*, III, 536, 543; Richard Hakluyt, *The Principal Navigations*, ed. Walter Raleigh, Hakluyt Soc., extra series (12 vols., Glasgow, 1903-5), VI, 413-18.

[21] *CSPF*, XIX, 646, 648-49, 655, 666, 668-69, 709.

mately deteriorate into war—had been, during the decades
since Elizabeth's accession and the coming of open conflict, a
peculiarly ambiguous one. It was compounded of at least two
layers, one uneasily superimposed on the other. Overtly the
English and Spanish crowns were on warily civil terms.
Through the first decade of the Queen's reign the Spanish embassy in London functioned with reasonable smoothness in
spite of the polar differences between their established religions. English aggressiveness and Spanish ineptitude brought
about a dangerous clash when Philip's treasure ships were
seized by the English; embargoes imposed on both sides halted
trade and war seemed a real possibility. But Cecil and Alva,
enemies in so much else, found common ground in devising
the formulae of compromise. Even the scandal of Gerau de
Spes's involvement in the Ridolfi plot and his consequent
ejection from England was not allowed to interfere with the
plodding negotiations which eventually, after three years, resulted in the ironing out of difficulties; ports were reopened
and the merchants' claims for seized goods sorted out. Formal
diplomatic relations were not resumed for another five years,
but the merchant deGuaras, as the recognized Spanish spokesman in London, kept open communication. In March 1578 a
major Spanish diplomat, Bernardino de Mendoza, reopened
the Spanish embassy and continued at his post until his expulsion in January 1584. Yet underneath the deliberate civil-
ities of overt intercourse there was an underlay of deeply felt
fear and hatred.

The gulf which separated London and Madrid in the latter
half of the sixteenth century was of the same quality as that
which divides the Communist and the Western capitals in
the twentieth. There was on both sides disagreement about
fundamentals and a profound moral abhorrence. How absolute this division was is illuminated by a casual comment of
Philip's in 1578. Thomas Wilkes, the Clerk of the Privy
Council, was then in Madrid with letters from the Queen.
Philip was coldly indifferent to the Queen's advances, but the
significant comment lies in his order that Wilkes be sent
home as quickly as possible "before he commits some indis-

cretion which will force us to burn him."[22] In a capital of such inviolate orthodoxy as Madrid, the mere presence of a Protestant emissary presented a dangerous center of infection which must be quickly eliminated. The logic of such a regime could tolerate no exceptions to its rule of absolute conformity.

It was this attitude which made impossible the maintenance of an English embassy in Madrid and limited the occasional visits of English envoys on special mission to men whose dignity would not be compromised by the humiliating treatment they were accorded. The successive agents Elizabeth dispatched from time to time found their reception progressively chillier, and every proposal which they carried to Philip was coldly, often contemptuously, rejected. In the far more open society of Elizabethan England it was possible to allow celebration of the mass within the embassy walls, but the sense of moral outrage was hardly less profound. Everything that happened since 1560 had served to harden hostility and deepen fears. The Papal decree of deposition in 1570, the revelations of the Ridolfi plot, and the massacre of St. Bartholomew had led many English Protestants to believe that there existed a Catholic internationale dedicated to the extermination of their faith and that its fulcrum was Madrid; events in Rome or Paris were to be referred back to the true center of Catholic power, His Most Catholic Majesty.

And yet, as we have seen, these deep-seated animosities were contained for well over two decades within a framework of "peaceful coexistence," or perhaps one should better say of "cold war," in which both sides strove consciously to avoid open confrontation. In the 1560's ideological differences were not coupled with direct conflicts of interest. Spain had urgent preoccupations in the Mediterranean, at least until the victory of Lepanto in 1571, while Elizabeth's cautiously defensive policy was usually founded on the avoidance of unnecessary frictions. This situation changed when the Dutch revolt did in fact create a conflict of interest for both ideological and strategic reasons. Yet even then, as we have seen, both sides veered away from overt confrontation, and the patching up of the 1569

[22] *CSPSp*, II, 552-53.

quarrel and the resumption of normal trade was carried through successfully during the years after 1572.

Hence the spirit of Philip's instructions to his new ambassador at London, Bernardino de Mendoza, dispatched there in March 1578, was conciliatory in tone.[23] It seemed important to the Spanish King to reinstate representation at London at a time when his governor in the Low Countries was about to make a decisive bid to reestablish Spanish power there and when the English government seemed to be giving the most serious consideration to supplying financial and even military aid to the rebels. Mendoza was to do everything possible to dissuade the Queen from such a move, but it was the gentle weapons of argument which he was to use, not the implied threat of force. As the representative of the Catholic King, he was to receive English Roman Catholics, who would approach him, in a friendly and kindly way, but the Ambassador was explicitly prohibited from entering into conspiracies against the Queen.

The role of an ambassador in these circumstances was a peculiarly difficult one. It was necessarily a relatively passive one in which he could do little but watchfully observe and patiently persuade. He had no lures to offer and no effective threats to hold over English heads. Philip hoped that England could be persuaded by simple reasons of self-interest to remain neutral. Just as Elizabeth assumed that cool-headed calculation would lead Philip to see that compromise was preferable to continued war in the Low Countries, so the Spaniard trusted that his former sister-in-law would see that England's best interests required avoidance of war with Spain. Mendoza was a nobleman of high birth and extensive diplomatic experience and his appointment was a compliment to Elizabeth and a token of the importance Philip attached to the London mission. Yet he was hardly the ideal man for such a delicate task, which required the lowest of profiles. High-tempered, self-confident, imbued with a deep sense of Spain's greatness, and devoutly pious, his normal impulses were to treat the English rather as a Victorian colonial governor might have dealt with

[23] *Ibid.*, 553-60.

a backward native state. For a time he reined in these tendencies, but in the long run they were to get the better of him.

The new ambassador was received with all due ceremony and continued for some time to be treated with common civility. Yet from the beginning of his mission he felt his sense of isolation; even in the 1560's so level-headed a diplomat as Gusman de Silva was acutely uncomfortable in the English capital and since then the gap between the two countries—between two rapidly diverging societies—had widened perceptibly. Mendoza soon came to sense the distrust and suspicion which surrounded him. As early as May 1578 he was writing anxiously home that Leicester and Walsingham were pressing for his dismissal on the grounds that he had no business to transact, and Mendoza urged that some matter be devised to justify his continued stay.[24]

One real difficulty he faced was that of obtaining information, since so many channels were closed to him. He rather naively assumed that a sufficient amount of Spanish gold would solve these difficulties and was constantly begging such funds from Philip. The King, more doubtful or more economical, resisted any large grant of funds until 1582, when it was already too late. Among the councillors the Ambassador found Sussex and Burghley more cordial than the others, and it was a loss to Mendoza when the Lord Chamberlain's illness and death in 1583 cut off one of these links. Walsingham and Leicester were always open enemies to the Ambassador, although from time to time the earl made advances towards Mendoza, usually when the favorite had reason to be on an anti-French tack. But the best sources the Ambassador had were paid ones: the Comptroller, Sir James Crofts, who became a regular pensioner of Spain, and a clerk in Walsingham's employ who had access to the Privy Chamber. Unluckily for Mendoza, this second informant died in February 1579. Not until December 1581 was he able to open up another channel. This came about seemingly by accident when Lord Henry Howard, the late Duke of Norfolk's younger brother, knocked at Mendoza's door one midnight, asking for sanc-

[24] *Ibid.*, 584-85.

tuary. His alarm turned out to be groundless, but the incident opened up a fruitful source of information to the Ambassador since Howard had access to the Privy Chamber and was on friendly terms with Sussex; he was well paid for his efforts.[25]

Through most of his first two years Mendoza had little to do but watch, report, and gently to nudge the English government away from support of the Low Countries rebels. Philip's instructions hardly vary from one to another in this period, reiterating their message of friendly persuasion. And by the first fall of Mendoza's stay the English were pulling away from contacts with the rebels, following the fruitless mission of Walsingham and Cobham. Mendoza and the Queen were on friendly terms at this time and she even honored him with confidences about her intended matrimony with Anjou. The Ambassador was full and informative in his reports on the wooing of the French Duke in 1579; both he and his master were entirely skeptical of the Queen's matrimonial intentions, and the Ambassador had little to do but report. The proposed French alliance broke down without the Spaniard's needing to raise a finger. But before the end of the year the Ambassador's mission became a more active one; the days of watchful waiting were giving place to a season of growing tension as new clashes of interest between England and Spain emerged in several different areas. Separate in origin, they quickly became entangled. And as entanglements grew, tempers rose and relations between the two courts degenerated from coolly civil intercourse to irritated and ever-more-heated recriminations.[26]

First Portugal, then Ireland, and finally the triumphant return of Francis Drake in his booty-laden ship, provided points of friction. And over against the strident notes of these new quarrels there was the steady obbligato of complaint from the English merchants trading with Spain, whose treatment became part of the diplomatic struggle between the two powers.

Even before the death of the old King of Portugal, Mendoza detected English uneasiness which he diagnosed—not incor-

[25] *Ibid.*, 586-87, 605-6, 652-54, 663-64, 673-74; *CSPSp*, III, 126-28, 167-68, 389-91.

[26] *CSPSp*, II, 594-95, 615-16, 618-20, 621-23, 624-26.

rectly—as a force behind the renewed negotiations with France. In the summer of 1579 an English agent was sent to Portugal, although with what results the remaining evidence does not reveal. When the Spanish actually moved into Portugal, English reactions were impeccably correct, the Queen going so far as to express her satisfaction with Philip's success in the lesser kingdom. The agents of the pretender, Don Antonio, were admitted to the kingdom but denied access to the court. But in 1581 the pretender himself was received in England. His presence plus English interest in the Terceira expedition were important contributing factors to the general diplomatic tensions which agitated Anglo-Spanish relations in the summer and fall of that year.[27]

A second cause of friction developed nearer England's own shores with the arrival of the first of two Catholic, Papally sponsored expeditions in Ireland in 1579; it was followed by another in the next year. (There had been an earlier abortive scheme, that of Thomas Stucley, which was diverted to Morocco when Portugal's crusading King persuaded the English adventurer to accompany him on his fatal venture.) The force which landed in 1579 was composed largely of Italians and Spaniards, and these invaders, and their successors in 1580, became the subject of diplomatic exchanges between the Queen and the Ambassador. The Spanish took a leaf from the Queen's manual of diplomatic practice, proclaiming their innocence and insisting that these expeditions were entirely Papal in sponsorship. This was in large part true, although of course the 1580 expedition sailed from a Spanish port and the Spanish government was keenly interested in its progress. In November 1580 Cardinal Granvelle was urging the reinforcement of the Irish forces by January. The English, in any case, saw these expeditions, particularly the second, as a Spanish attempt to divert the English from the Low Countries.[28]

Ireland—a subject for English complaint against the Spaniard—was soon diplomatically linked with a Spanish grievance against the English: Sir Francis Drake's exploits in South

[27] *Ibid.*, 636, 669, 683-84; *CSPSp*, III, 45, 49, 126, 142.
[28] *CSPSp*, III, 20, 41, 66-68; Camden, *Annals*, 242.

America. As early as August 1579 the King was passing news of Drake's depredations received from his viceroys to the Ambassador. And upon the sailor's return in September 1580, Mendoza kept close watch on proceedings. His information was that the Council divided as to what to do with the booty; Sussex and Burghley were for depositing it in the Tower and, if Philip would give satisfaction on Ireland, returning it to him. Leicester and Hatton opposed using the booty as a bargaining counter; rather, it should simply be appropriated. The Queen listened to both sides and told the Ambassador that Drake had done no harm in his master's dominions and that she would not give an official audience to Mendoza until the Irish matter was elucidated. Elizabeth had thus taken the opening move in this game by pushing forward her Irish pawn before Spain could bring up its complaints about Drake. It was a month later before Mendoza was ordered to demand reparations and punishment of the guilty. In fact, Philip's whole treatment of the Drake case was a very restrained one; he was prepared to regard the matter as a private rather than a public one and to seek reparation through a special commissioner. The matter was pursued in such a desultory way as to make it clear that the Spanish government was prepared to use it as a diplomatic counter in much the same way as the English were using the Irish expeditions. The Queen, on her side, was willing to concede something, and at least partial restitution was made.[29]

But in the summer and fall of 1581 there was an intensification of Anglo-Spanish rivalries. The two central areas of conflict—Portugal and the Low Countries—both came to the fore. The Portuguese pretender, Don Antonio, was actually in England, sponsored by Leicester, and extensive plans were being made for English participation in an Azores expedition. At the same time the Walsingham mission to Paris showed how serious was England's desire for an alliance aimed at Spain, both in the Low Countries and in the Portuguese dominions.[30]

[29] CSPSp, III, 59, 60, 65, 78, 83; Corbett, Drake, I, 344; Hatfield, II, 515.

[30] CSPSp, III, 126, 142; Corbett, Drake, I, 348-49.

Mendoza, faced with these urgent demands on his skill and nerve, did not show himself at his best. Already in 1580 one detects a new hectoring note in his accounts of his audiences with the Queen, in which he emphasizes Spanish power and utters barely veiled threats. Deteriorating relations were not improved when the Queen, catching Mendoza off balance, used her Irish grievance to limit his access to Court. He had lost the ball to his opponents and was now forced into an awkwardly defensive stance which compelled him to beg for each audience at court. Humiliated and frustrated, he sought recall from his master in the fall of 1580. But Philip was at this juncture particularly anxious to keep open his communications with the English court. He was urgent with his envoy to do his best "not to snap the thread of negotiation, as you will do if you leave and will plunge me into obligations which at present are best avoided." The Ambassador had nothing to do but make the best of it, although he grumbled that it demanded "more prudence than I possess to deal with people so evil-minded, cautious, and fickle."[31]

The truth was that Mendoza had blotted his diplomat's copy-book by letting the English maneuver him into a tactically vulnerable corner. The Queen had taken the line that she would not see the ambassador in his official capacity until she had an explanation of Spain's role in the Irish ventures of 1579 and 1580.[32] This was initially intended to fend off questions about Drake, but it was now fashioned into an instrument to make difficult any approach by the Ambassador to the Queen or indeed to her government. It was this that prompted his request for recall. Now that he was urgently needed to do his master's business, he found himself hindered at every turn.

Finally in June 1581, after a lapse of nearly nine months since he had had audience with the Queen, the Ambassador found a workable ploy in an alleged violation of the embassy's privileges. Even now he was put off and in a fit of pique Men-

[31] *CSPSp*, III, 10, 20, 86-87, 111-13.
[32] *Ibid.*, 60.

doza demanded his passports. The Queen defused this bomb by an appeal to his chivalry—that as a favor to her as a woman, he withdraw the request. There followed in quick succession an interview, seemingly amicable; then a rude letter; and another ambassadorial demand for passports. The Queen dealt with this second ultimatum by declaring that she would let him go only for personal reasons, simply refusing to regard his departure as having an official character. The Ambassador gained the desired audiences with the Queen, but they did his master's cause little good since they merely led to displays of bad temper on both sides.[33]

Actually during these weeks things were moving in favor of the Spaniards as the English backed away from support of Don Antonio, while in Paris the negotiations with the French foundered on their insistence that alliance be built on marriage. The time lag involved in sending dispatches between Madrid and London left Philip ignorant of these developments. His most urgent and far-reaching orders to Mendoza were both irrelevant at the time when he penned them. The first, written in mid-August 1581, demanded the surrender of Don Antonio by the English under the threat of an immediate embargo but also offering all possible concessions on English exiles in Spanish territory. If this were not sufficient, the Ambassador was solemnly to warn the Queen that the departure of Don Antonio from England for any destination in Philip's dominions would be understood as an act of war. In October the King, equally worried by the prospect of an Anglo-French alliance against him, took a quite different tack and authorized his minister to offer a renewal of the old Burgundian alliance, re-written to suit Elizabeth's desires.[34]

Both of these instructions were out of date by the time they were received, and Mendoza felt free to act accordingly. He used the opportunity of an audience on 11 October to rehearse the whole litany of Spanish grievances about Portugal, Drake, and the Low Countries. This led the Queen to the angry retort that for three and a half years he had uttered nothing but

[33] *Ibid.*, 128-29, 132-36, 140-42.   [34] *Ibid.*, 159-60, 161, 181-82.

complaints. Mendoza, losing his temper altogether, snorted that perhaps cannon would make her hear better. This stormy interview ended with the Queen's declaration that in the future he would see only Privy Councillors.[35]

The envoy's first angry reaction was to propose to his master a trade embargo on English merchants and goods in the Spanish dominions; later he admitted that this could not be done during the vintage. In a cooler mood he admitted that he was no longer of any use to his master in London and urged the appointment of a successor who could overlap him long enough to be clued in to current business. The King promised in December to recall Mendoza; in actual fact he lingered for nearly two more years, but he had an audience with the Queen only once more—in March 1582—on the formal occasion of the Portuguese Ambassador's departure.[36]

The King continued to press much the same policy of persistent persuasion; English suspicion of French intentions was to be aroused while the Queen was to be warned of the risks of Spanish displeasure if she gave further aid to Don Antonio or to the Dutch. For a moment in the spring of 1582, when Philip believed the Prince of Orange to be dead, a more active policy was proposed. Armed with a new letter of credence, the Ambassador was to press on the Queen the grave danger of French control, which now threatened, and to sound out her willingness to act as a mediator in the Low Countries. Although the Prince did not die, Philip was still toying with the idea of mediation in a later dispatch.[37]

But Mendoza was in no position to carry out any line of policy now. His isolation from the court grew as he was frozen out by one councillor after another. Burghley would see him only in the presence of another councillor, for fear of being branded as pro-Spanish; Croft would no longer deal with him at all since Leicester had awakened the Queen's suspicions of the comptroller's loyalty. Sussex, who had at least

[35] *Ibid.*, 185-90.
[36] *Ibid.*, 190-92, 208-9, 211-15, 242, 303-5, 405.
[37] *Ibid.*, 294-95, 359-60, 373-75.

been civil, was an ill man who would die in 1583. By the end of 1582 Mendoza was complaining that he had no contact with the court at all since no Privy Councillor would deal with him and Henry Howard remained his sole contact. The Queen herself had already rather contemptuously wondered why the King of Spain bothered to keep an Ambassador at her court any longer.[38]

In truth Mendoza was ceasing to function as the King of Spain's Ambassador to the Court of England. He was to remain at his post for more than a year longer, virtually cut off from relations with the government to which he was accredited. More and more his correspondence reflects another kind of activity—that of conspiracy. His busy intrigues with Mary Stuart, with the Duke of Guise, and with a small army of English and Scottish Roman Catholics mirror his transformation from an envoy whose business it was to maintain peaceful relations between his master and the English Queen to a conspirator, working hard to overthrow the English regime. These activities would lead to his ignominious expulsion from the realm.

ANY DIPLOMAT sent by Spain to reside at the Elizabethan court found himself cast willy-nilly in another role besides his ambassadorial one; he was inevitably regarded by the English Roman Catholic community as their advocate and protector. Such a role was singularly delicate and full of dangers which were enhanced by the haunting presence of Mary Stuart. Her tenacious adherence to the old faith made it difficult for the Catholic King to ignore her, yet to support her claims either in England or in Scotland was to run head-on against the Elizabethan regime. Mendoza's instructions, when he first arrived, prescribed the greatest circumspection. He was to treat those Roman Catholics who approached him with kindness but he was carefully to abstain from dabbling in any designs against the English Queen. The whole point of his mission was to quiet English fears and to keep them as neu-

[38] *Ibid.*, 324-26, 362-64, 406-8.

tral as possible. So far as the record goes, the Ambassador seems to have followed these directions faithfully during the first year or so of his mission.

It was events in Scotland rather than in England which first lured Mendoza (and ultimately his master) from the straight and narrow path of virtue to the hidden, winding trails of intrigue. James VI was now entering his adolescence, and in early 1579 Mendoza and Elizabeth were already chatting about matrimonial possibilities—and agreeing on the risks of a French bride. But beyond James's approaching maturity there was the immediate fact that the stability which the Protestant Regent Morton had maintained with an iron hand for a decade was now crumbling. Spain was drawn into this ambit when the anti-Morton nobles sought money from Philip through Mary Stuart's agent in Paris in January 1579. Mendoza, consulted on this matter, took a dim view.[39] The Marian party in Scotland was neither Roman Catholic nor pro-Spanish; indeed it was patently pro-French; there was no profit here for the Spanish. Mary Stuart's best hope, he argued, lay in a union of English and Scottish Roman Catholics aiming at her release and at the seizure of both crowns. So for the present the matter lapsed.

But what is interesting is the Ambassador's unselfconsciously stated desideratum—the overthrow of the Elizabethan regime. Philip, at least for the immediate future, accepted that regime as an unpalatable but intractable political reality, and he had sent his ambassador to England to cultivate good relations as a rationally perceived necessity of Spanish policy. Yet when the possibility of overthrowing—or even of seriously embarrassing—the English government emerged, it was all too tempting to be drawn into intrigue at whatever risk to the overt pursuit of amity. The continued ambivalence of the Spaniards on this issue was in the long run to prove fatal both to good relations with England and to the conspiracies halfheartedly patronized by Philip.

For the time being there were no further temptations since Morton fended off the armed attempt on his power. But

[39] *CSPSp*, II, 626-27, 645-48.

through the year 1579 his star steadily waned, while that of James's first favorite, his French cousin, Esmé D'Aubigny, as steadily waxed. By the end of the year D'Aubigny (now Duke of Lennox) was the head of a strong anti-Morton (and anti-English) faction, and Scottish politics had become fluid in a way which alarmed the English but excited the hopes of the Marians and of the French and Spanish governments.

The next move came from Mary Stuart herself when in early 1580 she offered, through her agent in Paris, to place herself, her son, and her realm under Philip's protection. It was a direct bid for Spain's active intervention in her behalf. Philip's gain would be the establishment of a Catholic and pro-Spanish regime in both British kingdoms. His response was reserved but friendly. In these preliminary dealings Mendoza was little more than a messenger between Mary and the outside world; the main arena of discussion was in Paris.[40]

But early in 1581 Mendoza began to take a more independent line of his own and launched into a series of intrigues which lasted until his expulsion in 1584. He became the confidant and counsellor of the Queen of Scots and her advocate with his master. He entered into close relations with English Roman Catholics and with their co-religionists in Scotland, making use of Jesuit missionaries as his agents. Through the indiscretions of one of them the Duke of Guise was drawn into the action, which in turn led to complex negotiations among Mary Stuart, Mendoza, the Spanish ambassador in Paris, and, of course, Madrid. Mendoza struggled manfully to keep in his hands all the skeins of this tangled intrigue but with no measure of success. Mary, even in her prison, was a willful woman, who insisted on having her way. The Jesuit agents were enthusiastic amateurs, whose zeal carried them beyond their instructions. Guise had his own fish to fry and Mendoza was intensely jealous of a rival Catholic influence. He insisted that a Roman Catholic Britain must be entirely dependent on Spain.[41]

But the fundamental difficulties lay in the political fantasies

[40] *CSPSp*, III, 4-6, 22, 26-27, 30, 33-34.
[41] *Ibid.*, 362-64, 492-95.

on which the whole scheme was built. The fall of Morton, who was executed in June 1581, and the rise of the French favorite, Lennox, offered hopes of greater changes in Scotland, and ultimately, in England. The Queen of Scots was convinced that her son and his favorite were at her command. She would legitimize his position by associating him in her sovereignty; James would then change his faith.[42] This would lay the pre-conditions for an alliance (and perhaps a marriage) with Spain. James indeed might be sent to Spain to be reared under the fatherly care of Philip. Spain, on her side, with Papal cooperation would have to provide an armed force to land in Scotland to ensure the victory of the new Catholic regime. There might well follow an English rising in Mary's favor.

These Alice-in-Wonderland politics were largely the product of Mary's prison-house fantasies, although for a brief time the mirage seemed about to transform itself into reality. In March 1582 Lennox, approached by the Jesuit Creighton, agreed to support a Catholic restoration but only if Spain sent 15,000 (later raised to 20,000) troops to Scotland to back him up! Guise, drawn in by Jesuit intervention, might command this force, under Papal auspices, or land a diversionary expedition in Sussex. But before any of these highly ambitious (and expensive) schemes got past the purely speculative stage, the rug was pulled out by events in Scotland. Lennox lost control over the young king when James was kidnapped by an opposing noble faction in the Raid of Ruthven (August 1582). By the end of the year Lennox had left Scotland, and died in France a few months later.[43]

In all the excitements of this extravaganza Mendoza did his best to keep a grasp on political reality. He had no confidence that either the English or the Scottish Roman Catholics could by themselves free Mary or overthrow the Protestant regimes in either country. And the dispatch of large foreign armies to their assistance would only evoke national resistance (and, if they were Spanish, French intervention). Mendoza tended to

[42] *Ibid.*, 98-100.
[43] *Ibid.*, 313-16, 362-64, 370-75, 377-79.

favor a much more gradualist approach, based on bribery, pensions, and a missionary campaign, aimed above all at James. Yet, although Mendoza never quite lost sight of reality and fairly consistently came down for moderation and caution, the fact remained that he had allowed himself and his master to be pulled into a network of intrigue which, however self-deceiving in its assumptions and moonstruck in its expectations, was nevertheless aimed at destroying the Protestant Elizabethan government of England. They were patronizing the Queen's enemies.[44]

Philip's role in these schemes in many ways mirrored that of his ambassador. The King sent reassuring messages to the Queen of Scots, declaring his willingness to receive James in Spain, and asked for more information on the proposals for action. But the decline and fall of Lennox came just when Philip had finally nerved himself up to commit forces to Guise's aid. A new scheme was now concocted in Paris. The French Duke proposed to invade England with forces provided by Spain and the Pope; Mendoza protested a scheme which would not be firmly in Spanish control, but Philip agreed to the proposals—with the proviso that Rome paid all costs.[45]

Mendoza's unwilling involvement in this conspiracy was to prove his undoing. The Queen of Scots's agent in Paris, Morgan, put him in touch with an English Catholic conspirator, who had served as a link between Paris and Mary's prison for a couple of years.[46] Francis Throckmorton came of the recusant branch of that well-known family and had dabbled in

---

[44] *Ibid.*, 121-25, 169-71, 285-94.

[45] *Ibid.*, 22, 26, 202-3, 400-1, 412-13, 463-64, 475-76.

[46] For full details of the Throckmorton plot and Mendoza's role in it, see R. Holinshed, *Chronicles* (6 vols., 1807-8), IV, 536-48, and *A Discoverie of the Treasons Practiced and Attempted against the Queene's Majestie and the Realme, by Francis Throckmorton* (1584; reprinted in *Harleian Miscellany*, with annotations and notes by Oldys and Thomas, III [1809], 190-200; Latin and Dutch editions in 1584 and 1588), which repeats much of the same material. See also *A Complete Collection of State Trials*, comp. W. Cobbett, T. B. Howell, *et al.* (42 vols., 1816-98), I, 1111-27 (the Northumberland case).

conspiracy with the exile Englefield several years earlier. His role now was to provide the conspirators with vital information—the names of likely Catholic gentry, suitable landing places, and strong-points to be secured. Even now Mendoza was doubtful about the enterprise and Throckmorton's pessimistic responses did not reassure him, but in any case the former provided lists which he had drawn up previously for Englefield. At this juncture another exile, Charles Paget, was sent over by Guise and Morgan to reconnoiter in Sussex, where he met his brother, Lord Paget, and the Earl of Northumberland.

What Mendoza did not know was that the English government had tracked Throckmorton's dealings with Mary Stuart some months earlier and were only waiting for the opportune moment to pounce on him. His arrest came not long after Paget's visit. Throckmorton's confession spelled out in painful clarity the details of the Ambassador's involvement. The English government, with this evidence in hand, moved swiftly to the public condemnation and the ignominious expulsion of Bernardino de Mendoza in January 1584. This dramatic episode terminated Spanish representation in London in such a way as to damage what vestigial goodwill still existed between the two courts.

Elizabeth, it is true, made a halfhearted gesture of explanation by dispatching a Privy Council clerk, William Waad, to Madrid with letters to the King detailing the English version of events. But Waad had a very cold reception in Spain, was denied access to the King, and forced to leave the country after a brief and ineffectual stay.[47]

These feckless and muddled conspiracies, resting on little more than wishful thinking, went far to blacken Spain's image in Englishmen's eyes, quite beyond hope of redemption. The government took pains to publish an account of Mendoza's expulsion, making as much play as possible out of his connection with the Guise plot.[48] A faint measure of decorum was pre-

[47] *CSPF*, XVIII, 391-99, 422, 444.
[48] *A Discoverie of the Treasons, passim.* See also the public meeting in Star Chamber after Northumberland's death, *State Trials*, I, 1111-27.

served by the careful omission from the pamphlet of any direct reference to Philip, but this discretion was probably lost on most of its readers. The Throckmorton plot was to provide a formidable element in the articles of indictment drawn up for public consumption when the English government intervened openly in the Low Countries.

THE HISTORY of Mendoza's mission is a melancholy one. When he arrived in London, the two courts were on civil terms. The Ambassador brought with him very conciliatory instructions, and initially he hit it off reasonably well with the Queen, while in Sussex and Burghley he found sympathetic listeners who were not unwilling to hear his arguments against a French alliance. But unluckily for Mendoza he could rely on nothing but persuasion to keep England neutral; he had in his instructions no positive or concrete inducements to sway England in that direction. The most Philip could bring himself to, and that only for a moment, was acceptance of English mediation in the Low Countries. And even if this offer were serious it came too late, for from about the end of 1580 relations between the Ambassador and the English Court chilled almost to the freezing level.

Much, of course, happened in these years. Spanish power began to recover in the Low Countries; Philip laid hands on Portugal; and English negotiations for a French alliance, marital or otherwise, sank of their own weight. In all these events Mendoza could play but a passive role. He could do little to hinder the negotiations with France; he could not allay English fears about the consequences of Portugal's absorption into the Spanish empire. We know that the English were moving during these years into a much more emphatic anti-Spanish stance although they still looked for a peaceful accomplishment of their aims through diplomacy rather than through arms.

But the change in atmosphere coincided with the return of Drake from his voyage of circumnavigation and more particularly with the public honors bestowed on him in the spring of 1581. The very fact of the voyage necessarily stirred the Spanish government and thereby their ambassador to action. We have seen how he was outwitted by the Queen and how he lost his temper; from that point onwards his relations with the English Court rapidly deteriorated. At this distance it is hard to sort out the sequence of causes—whether it was the Spaniard's arrogance which wrecked his own chances or whether his English opponents successfully goaded him into intransigence. But it is quite clear that the English government changed its own public attitudes towards him; the evidence lies in their treatment of Drake. And this in turn brings to the fore the whole question of English actions in the Indies, a sequence of events dating back more than a decade. Although parallel in time to events in the Low Countries and often involving the same personnel, they remain, at least in the records, curiously separate from English policy in Western Europe. The left hand and the right hand obviously knew what each was doing, but the directing intelligence was making very different use of each. English actions in Europe were the result of carefully controlled policy, devised step by step under the Queen's close direction. It was, so far as events permitted, planned and calculated in every detail. But English actions in the Indies, although hardly less consequential in affecting relations with Spain, were given, so far as we can see, only the loosest oversight by the Queen. Others took the initiative; the Queen's role was largely permissive. Many of her ministers were deeply involved, but in their private capacities as sponsors of private enterprise. It was only at the very brink of war that actions in the two theaters of English dealings with Spain were coordinated under close royal supervision.

As long ago as the 1560's Sir John Hawkins had aimed, by a combination of force and persuasion, at establishing a trade in slaves between West Africa and the Spanish colonies. In his 1564 voyage and again in that launched in 1567 the Queen was at least a sleeping partner, contributing the use of one ship on the former and two ships on the latter expedition.[49] She also allowed him—or so he said—to make use of her name in his dealings with Spanish colonial authorities. These voyages,

[49] James A. Williamson, *Hawkins of Plymouth* (1949), 64, 102.

semi-piratical at the best although advertised as trading efforts, culminated in the bloody episode at San Juan de Ulua in 1568, in open collision with the Viceroy of New Spain. After that, English ventures into the Indies had rapidly turned into straightforward plundering raids, entirely private in character, aimed at the accumulation of as much loot as possible. Drake's voyages in the early 1570's inaugurated this phase; he had numerous successors in the year following.[50] Although the ships sailed without any royal commission, there were patrons in high places. In the early 1570's Sir Edward Horsey, Captain of the Isle of Wight, Leicester's adjutant in more than one enterprise, had moved on from partnerships in Channel privateering to the patronage of West Indian enterprise. In 1576 a Bristol merchant named Barker sailed with two ships significantly named the *Bear* and the *Ragged Staff*; he was almost certainly a protégé of Leicester. It is hardly surprising that the left-wing leaders, who had already been cooperating with the Huguenots and the Sea-Beggars against the Spanish in European waters, should turn their attention to the Caribbean, where the possibilities of damaging the enemy were coupled with opportunities for great personal gain. While these activities naturally kindled anger and fear among the Spanish authorities, they do not appear to have been the source of much diplomatic interchange between the two courts prior to Mendoza's arrival. Both parties entered into a kind of tacit agreement to keep American and European affairs separated into two seemingly unconnected compartments. The terms of competition, clear enough in the ancient European arena, were yet to be established in the vast and little known realms beyond the seas. Both were content for the present to live with these ambiguities.

Drake's expedition of 1577, which ended in the circumnavigation, marked a shift in the Crown's attitude towards English activities in the Spanish empire. In 1574 a group of Devonians, led by Richard Grenville and William Hawkins, sought a pat-

---

[50] *Documents concerning English Voyages to the Spanish Main, 1569-1580*, ed. I. A. Wright, Hakluyt Soc., 2nd ser. 71 (1932), xlvii-lxiv.

ent from the Queen authorizing them to explore and to exploit lands "southwards beyond the equinoctial." Additional evidence suggests that the lands in question were those southern regions of South America still unoccupied by Spanish settlements.[51] The application was refused by the Queen, possibly under Burghley's prodding, because the adventurers' activities might involve them with the Spanish. In the immediate wake of the Convention of Bristol, Elizabeth had no desire to stir up new occasions of quarrel with Philip. Yet three years later the Queen quite clearly gave her consent to Drake's enterprise, which almost certainly was intended to make money by plundering the Spanish colonials. It was initially sponsored by the inner circle of Elizabeth's councillors—Walsingham, Hatton, Leicester, Lincoln (but not by Burghley).[52] The Queen was drawn into the enterprise at a later stage although there is no evidence of a royal commission and it is highly unlikely that one ever existed. Preparations for the voyage were made in the deepest secrecy and with elaborate arrangements for concealment. (The crews were hired on the understanding that the destination was Alexandria; the Spanish agent thought it was in fact Scotland.)[53] All this makes it clear that this enterprise was sponsored by the interventionist party in the Council and that for once they had won the Queen's approval. Almost certainly Burghley disapproved of the scheme, although there is no evidence that he actively sought to halt it.

What brought about this volte-face by the Queen? It is true, of course, that Drake sailed just at the time when the Queen had been won over to a promise of armed aid to the Dutch rebels, and in the very weeks when he was preparing to depart Leicester was girding himself to lead an expedition to the Low Countries. Corbett argued that both expeditions were part of a general plan. But Elizabeth in fact was more than halfhearted

[51] K. R. Andrews, "The Aims of Drake's Expedition of 1577-1580," *American Historical Review* 73, no. 3 (Feb. 1968), 733.

[52] E.G.R. Taylor, "More Light on Drake," *Mariner's Mirror* 16 (1930), 135-47 and "The Missing Draft Project of Drake's Voyage of 1577-80," *Geographical Journal* 75 (1930), 46-47.

[53] Corbett, *Drake*, I, 224; *CSPSp*, II, 545.

in her backing of the forward party and almost immediately reversed her offer of aid to the rebels. Moreover, the Drake enterprise would necessarily be a delayed time bomb; the proposal put forward by his backers assumed a voyage of thirteen months and they must have known from experience that it might be much longer than that. His exploits could hardly be expected to influence Spanish policy in the crucial months just ahead. How then are we to explain the Queen's change of heart?

The answer may in part be simple greed; the returns on such expeditions had already proved to be excitingly large; the risks were slight since there were no Queen's ships involved and as far as we know no royal funds. The strict secrecy observed kept the Queen's name out of the picture. If Drake never returned, nothing was lost; if he came back laden with treasure, a large share of it would go into the royal coffers. And the Queen's participation perhaps reflects that underside of her character which was the obverse of her usual extreme caution. She was not unwilling to gamble when the risks were as near zero as possible—when neither her money, her name, nor her policy was at stake.

It was three years before Drake reappeared and by that time much had changed. The rift with Spain had perceptibly widened; the English government was about to attempt the construction of an anti-Spanish alliance and was prepared to back Anjou against Parma. The two recent expeditions to Ireland rankled in English minds and were seen as Spanish fifth columns. However, Elizabeth certainly did not contemplate an open break with Spain; indeed her whole policy was founded on the assumption that threat rather than force would bring Philip to terms. Yet she chose to flaunt her patronage of Drake and to celebrate his achievements in a way most calculated to ruffle Spanish sensibilities and to increase Spanish suspicion as to her ultimate intentions. In April 1581 there took place the famous scene at Deptford when the Queen instructed Anjou's emissary to give Drake the accolade of knighthood.[54] She took

---

[54] Corbett, *Drake*, I, 336; Camden, *Annals*, 255.

the occasion to mock the King of Spain openly, saying that since he had demanded Drake's head, she had now brought a gilded sword with which to strike it off. Thus Sir Francis, who had set off in 1577 under a cloak of the strictest secrecy, was now publicly glorified by the Queen and by her subjects. What were the Queen's motives in flaunting her patronage of the great sailor? We cannot be certain, but it is arguable that by 1581 Elizabeth had lost hope of any direct diplomatic approach to Madrid; she had been disappointed too many times. She may have felt that only more brutal tactics would serve; the public approbation of Drake would thus form a secondary motif in her general policy of pressuring Philip, the major theme of which lay in the proposed French alliance.

Certainly over the next year or so Elizabeth's contemptuous treatment of Mendoza effectually blocked any possibility of fruitful exchange between the English and Spanish governments. Mendoza's abrasive personality certainly played a large role in this breakdown, but which came first, English belligerence or Spanish arrogance, we cannot tell. Clearly anti-Spanish feeling in the court mounted steadily in the early 1580's; even Cecil feared the consequences of association with the Ambassador to the point where he fairly refused to see Mendoza. The least one can say is that Elizabeth was content to let ordinary diplomatic relationships with Spain lapse and to face quite boldly whatever consequences this might bring.

Yet at the same time the Queen did not abandon caution in her handling of American affairs. She allowed Drake and his colleagues to treat with Don Antonio for proposed action in the Azores, but only on the condition that France shared the risks. When that did not transpire—in part because of her coolness—she withdrew her sanction from active English support of the Portuguese pretender.

Frustrated in this move, the interventionists at court found other openings for their energies. In 1582-1583 an elaborate enterprise was set on foot—a proposed voyage to the Moluccas by way of Good Hope, to be financed in major part by Leicester (but also by the city interests involved in the Muscovy Company and even by Burghley). This ambitious project foundered on the incapacity of its leadership; the fatal attraction of piracy drew the navigators on to the coasts of Brazil, where their own quarrels and Spanish sea power brought an end to the expedition. The Hawkinses were luckier in 1582-1583.[55] Setting out under the authority of Don Antonio on what was intended to be a pioneer trading voyage to Brazil, they ended up by plundering Spanish shipping and returning home with very satisfactory profits.

In addition to these large-scale private ventures, backed by courtiers and Londoners, which mingled in a very confused way merchants' hopes for the opening of new markets with privateers' greed for immediate returns by plunder, a good many smaller men were engaged in straightforward piracy, using the cover of the Portuguese pretender's flag and preying largely on Portuguese shipping. At the same time, among the leaders of the anti-Spanish party, larger strategic schemes were being mulled over. As early as 1579 John Hawkins had proposed that a fleet be sent to search out and capture the Spanish plate fleet; the proposed Terceira expediton of 1582 would have established a kind of pirate base in the mid-Atlantic athwart the Spanish communications with their empire. Hawkins in 1584 had another scheme for organizing privateering under Antonio's flag, which with the cooperation of the Dutch, the Huguenots, and Portuguese rebels would have the same effect of paralyzing the trade of the Spanish empire.[56] All these enterprises had the patronage and in some cases the participation of Leicester and Walsingham; the same men who sought to bring England into action against Spain in her Low Countries possessions were taking steps to assail her in her overseas dominions. But even more important is the fact that from 1580 onwards the Crown more and more averted its eyes and ceased to place any hindrances in the path of the adventurers. They were allowed to harass Spain at will; the Crown, of course, still disclaimed all official knowledge of them. The consequences of their activities were manifold: the accumulation of loot, the gradual development of larger strategies for attacking Spain

[55] Williamson, *Hawkins*, 218-24.
[56] *Ibid.*, 396-97, 409-10; Corbett, *Drake*, I, 347.

through her colonies, and, necessarily, the augmentation of Spanish resentment and of Spanish fear.

One cannot but be impressed by the wide gap between the Queen's views of Western European affairs and those beyond the seas. At home her ministers were kept on the tightest of leashes, under the most careful royal control, every individual move in the game made only with her specific consent. Their initiative was limited to the giving of advice; all decisions, even the most minor, were hers. The most modest gestures of independent action—such as Walsingham and Cobham's guarantee of a loan for £5,000 in 1577—were met by severe rebuke. The contrast with the position of the great adventurers in American seas needs hardly to be drawn. Obviously the very facts of geography and of communications placed them quite beyond the royal reach once the coasts of England faded from view. Nevertheless, at least from 1577 onwards, the restraints placed upon them before departure were steadily loosened. It was their decisions and their actions which were carving out a whole new realm of enterprise for Englishmen; more immediately, it was they who were shaping the fast-growing rivalry between England and Spain beyond the line.

In the late summer of 1585 England stood trembling on the brink of open conflict with Spain. As Burghley soberly wrote, the nation was about "to sustain a greater war than ever in any memory of man it hath done."[57] The immediate occasion of war was the succor of the Dutch rebels, and the decision to intervene openly was the final move in a sequence of events reaching back to the spring of 1572. But the decision to confront Spain was determined not only by English concern over the fate of the Netherlands but also by a larger anxiety over the ever-increasing "greatness of the King of Spain." As we have seen above, the Spanish seizure of Portugal triggered English fears of a power so great as to over-awe all Christendom. The Elizabethan government faced a problem which would be a classic one for their successors in later centuries—

[57] *CSPF*, XIX, addenda p. 705.

how to deal with the emergence of a single continental power so great as to overbalance all rivals.

English response was an attempt to draw the other great European state, France, into an alliance against Spain, operative not only in the Low Countries but also in the Portuguese empire. We have seen the failure of this policy: France would not be drawn into alliance; lesser schemes for cooperation in the Azores or in the Netherlands did not come off; and England was forced back on the *pis aller* of subsidizing Anjou. That too had failed and now, as the rebels' resistance crumbled, England found herself with a moral obligation and a diplomatic commitment to support the States which could be fulfilled only by the dispatch of English soldiers to the Low Countries. England had at last stumbled into the situation which for thirteen years she had struggled to avoid—war with Spain, unsupported by any allies other than the battered remnants of the Netherlands confederation, in effect the provinces of Holland and Zealand.

The decision was one dictated by desperate circumstances and made reluctantly and with hesitation. It was made with much debate within the ranks of the English leadership. Only fragments of that debate survive, but they are enough to give us some sense of the arguments used. Proposals for English intervention dated back almost to the beginning of the Dutch revolt and there had been what was in effect a draft treaty drawn up in 1577.[58] But the final and definitive debate had begun after the assassination of the Prince of Orange in July 1584.

Extended discussions—probably a Council meeting—were held in October, and the surviving notes from this meeting are our best source for the thinking which went into the final decision in the next summer.[59] In October there was still hope that the King of France would assume the burden of protecting the Low Countries, but the English councillors had to consider what to do if he refused. All considerations had to begin with

[58] *Ibid.*, 443-47.
[59] For these discussions, see *ibid.*, 95-98; *Hatfield*, III, 67-70.

the awkward fact that the King of Spain was at peace with England, and in the fall of 1584 there seems to have been no concrete knowledge of any immediately threatening moves by him. Hence, if England intervened in Holland, she would deliberately be choosing war with Spain. Therefore, those who wanted intervention had to demonstrate that war was the only option open to England, that it was an imperious necessity for her national security. It is clear that this central issue was debated and that the case for neutrality was made. The evidence for the latter lies in Camden.[60] His full report of the opposition argument stands in the italic print which usually indicates that he is quoting a direct source. The argument tacitly accepts their opponents' main contention: that Spain had hostile intentions towards England. Allowing this as a possibility, the opponents of war argued for an armed neutrality. The best course would be for the Queen not to intermeddle in the Low Countries but to fortify her own kingdom, strengthening her navy and the border fortresses against Scotland. "So would England become impregnable and she on every side be secure at home and a terror to her enemies." This was the way to avoid war. No one would provoke a country so well prepared to revenge any injury.

As for the Low Countries, it was argued, they were rebels in arms against their lawful prince, and by their disloyalty had forfeited whatever liberties they held by their sovereign's grace. Indeed those men who called themselves the "Estates General" were but a band of pretenders, "most of them of the vulgar sort, masked under the shew of Estates." And if the Queen aided them she would be met in the end with the same ingratitude and betrayal the French Protestants had shown in 1563. It was, succinctly, an isolationist argument: no foreign entanglements abroad; at home a "Fortress England" strong enough to deter any would-be aggressor.

The central thrust of the interventionists' argument took its force from their belief in Spain's hostile future intentions. Once the Low Countries were overcome, there could be no trust in Philip's "quiet neighborhood." He would pick quar-

[60] Camden, *Annals*, 319-20.

rels with the Queen, block trade, and make war. Possessed of the harbors of Holland and Zealand and of their fleet, and aided by the English malcontents, without an enemy in Europe, the Spanish would have all the advantages on their side; far better to export an inevitable war from English shores to the Low Countries. And far better to fight with at least one ally, for once Spain succeeded in the Netherlands, she would be "so formidable to all the rest of Christendom as that Her Majesty shall no wise be able with her own power nor with the aid of any other neither by sea nor land to withstand his attempts." She will be forced to give place "to his insatiable malice, which is most terrible to be thought of, but most miserable to suffer."

But how could they be sure that Philip's intentions were so malign? Since there was as yet no overt act of hostility, they could only point to recent history. In Burghley's systematic, albeit pedantic, note-taking there are the two Latin headings, *Voluntas* and *Potestas*.[61] Under the first is a long list of Spanish actions going back to the Norfolk marriage, the Earls' Rebellion, the Ridolfi plot, and continuing with the harborage of the northern rebels, the Irish enterprises, and Mendoza's plottings revealed in the Throckmorton confession. Under *Potestas*, Cecil included the new lordship of Portugal and the East Indies, Spanish freedom from the Turkish menace and from French intervention. He had an army at his disposal in the Low Countries and once on shore could hope for help from the discontented in England who backed the Scottish claim and the old religion. To the interventionists Philip's past actions and present opportunities were infallible clues to what might be expected from him.

They were not unaware of the risks of alliance with the States—that is, with Holland and Zealand. To the argument that the Dutch were merely factious rebels, they riposted with the rather interesting assertion that the Spanish aimed at destroying "the natural people of the Low Countries" and at replacing them by new-planted aliens. They sought to dissolve an ancient confederation and to destroy the intercourse be-

---

[61] *CSPF*, XIX, 95-98.

tween the "natural nations" of England and Scotland, on the one hand, and Holland, on the other. Admitting the weakness of the provinces, the interventionists insisted that the Queen must take cautionary towns to assure the eventual repayment of her expenses and that she must appoint an English peer to head the army and Englishmen to supervise finances. Interestingly, the advocates of war were also nervously aware that war might not be popular among the English population. When the Anjou marriage was rejected, the Duke was told that English unwillingness to fight in the Low Countries was one principal reason. It was a convenient excuse—difficult to justify or deny—but it may have had real force. Certainly in 1585 Mildmay, an ardent Protestant and an advocate of war, was doubtful how much subjects would contribute to what most would regard as an unnecessary war. In June 1585 Burghley was cogitating how to communicate the news to Parliament.[62] Hatton was to speak for the government, emphasizing the rebuffs which the Queen's repeated efforts at amity had received, rehearsing hostile Spanish behavior, and painting vividly the dangers which would result from Spanish victory in the Netherlands.

In October the Queen ordered the publication of "A Declaration of the causes moving the queene of England to give aid to the defence of . . . the Lowe Countries." The pamphlet was intended for both domestic and foreign consumption; editions appeared in all the principal European languages. Two main arguments were pushed in this carefully written defense of English policy. The first put great emphasis on the special relationship between England and the Low Countries; there had been "perpetual unions of the peoples hearts together." Indeed "the same mutual love had been inviolably kept and exercised as it had been by the work of nature." There had been alliances for generations and a continual intercourse of trade and of people. By implication the Crown of England had special responsibilities towards such neighbors. Continuing the argument, the pamphlet related that Philip, badly counselled by his Spanish advisors, had imposed "stran-

[62] *Ibid.*, 521.

gers of strange blood" upon the provinces, who had violated their ancient liberties and established an absolute government. The provinces had appealed to the Queen for protection and she had repeatedly made representations to Philip, urging clemency on him, but to no avail. She had even lent them money to defend themselves, on the condition of their continuing obedience to the King of Spain. But her embassies were turned away at Madrid and no hearing given to her urgings.

The pamphlet then swung into its second main argument—that Spain was now a menace to England. There had already been the attempt on Ireland and, more recently still, the plots of Mendoza with English malcontents and exiles to mount a foreign invasion. "We did, we say again, manifestly see in what danger ourself, our countries and people might shortly be. . . ." But, backed by her subjects, the Queen would meet this common danger "seen and feared by the subverting and rooting up of the ancient nation of these Low Countries and by planting the Spanish nation and men of war, enemies to our countries, there so near unto us."[63]

Rather interestingly, the declaration compared the present crisis to that provoked by Guisan aggression in Scotland in 1559-1560. There too the Queen had intervened to protect her neighbors' liberties and her own security and God had blessed that action. The peaceful reign of James VI as well as the amity between England and France bore witness to His favor.

One other particular passage deserves singling out. This was the attempt to dissociate the Duke of Parma from his master, paying tribute to the former's clemency and implying that he was under constraint from his Spanish advisors, who prevented him from pursuing a more moderate policy. The attempt was in line with hopes voiced elsewhere that Parma might be detached from Spain, bringing over the Catholic Malcontents with him.

All in all, the proclamation mirrors pretty faithfully the discussions in the English Council of which we have some record. The King of Spain is held up as a tyrant who has violated the

---

[63] Reprinted in *A Collection of Scarce and Valuable Tracts . . . of the Late Lord Somers*, 2nd ed., ed. Walter Scott (1809), I, 410-19.

ancient liberties of his Low Countries subjects. He is also represented as a menace to English safety. Here the supporting arguments are vaguer; most of the onus is laid on Mendoza and the Throckmorton plot. Unlike the papers presented in the Council, the proclamation leaves out reference to earlier events—such as the Ridolfi plot—and makes no effort to picture a crescendo of rising tension beginning early in the reign. More significantly, nothing at all is said about religion; this in part reflects a sensitivity about French Catholic sympathies, but this first edition was intended for an English audience. It is consistent with what we know about the Queen's own reluctance to pose as a Protestant champion and with her past policy in the Low Countries. Although she had urged Philip to let his subjects "go to the devil in their own way," she had never denied that religion was an internal matter to be decided by each sovereign. Moreover, the whole tenor of the declaration was defensive, arguing that only the most urgent concern for English safety had moved the Queen to action; championship of the reformed faith would not be consonant with such a stand.

The decision to act had been taken. How was it to be implemented? The expeditionary force for the Low Countries was only one of two major actions which, after much hesitation, were decided on in the summer of 1585. Since the news of the Spanish seizure of the English ships in May, Drake had been permitted to assemble a considerable fleet, to which the Queen contributed two of her ships, while the balance was made up of privately owned vessels. Officially the fleet was authorized to make a demonstration to secure release of the seized shipping; unofficially Sir Francis had unlimited scope. His intention, of course, was to attempt the capture of the treasure fleet and to do as much damage, and secure as much plunder, as possible in the West Indies.[64]

In addition to these two direct assaults on Spanish power, Burghley and his colleagues had sketched out an intensive diplomatic campaign. England was not only to secure a Scot-

[64] *Papers relating to the Navy during the Spanish War, 1585-1587,* ed. J. S. Corbett, Navy Rec. Soc. 11 (1898), viii-xvii.

tish alliance (with the bait of a pension), but also was to stir up the King of Navarre to action in the Pyrenees and—by privateers—in the Indies. Duke Casimir was to be called in for the defense of Friesland and Guelderland (at Dutch expense). And the Flemish Catholic Malcontents were to be wooed and persuaded of the bad faith of the Spaniards. On the success of these multiple initiatives rested English hopes of success in the unequal struggle they now faced.

As WE LOOK BACK over the more than a dozen years which had elapsed since the Sea-Beggars' seizure of Brill and since St. Bartholomew's night, what can we make of the pattern of English foreign policy as it had evolved in that troubled time? Two elements stand out: first, that these were years when England was quite helplessly at the mercy of events outside her borders and quite beyond her control. The eruption of volcanoes in the Netherlands and in France presented dangers which could not be evaded. Various strategies of defense were possible, but none of them could be exploited without the utmost risk to English security. Willy-nilly, England had to play a dangerous game in which the stakes, high at the beginning, mounted as time passed until, for the leadership, they became all or nothing.

A second feature of equal significance is the Queen's tenacious grasp on the making of every decision which these external pressures forced upon the English leadership; every move in the complex interplay of events was hers. Her style of play varied, responding to circumstance, and more obscurely to her own inward impulses. Low-keyed and cautious in the uncertain years after 1572 when fortune frowned on England, she responded quickly to the more hopeful auguries of 1576-1577 when Spanish power in the Low Countries crashed of its own weight. From that point down to the departure of Anjou from the provinces in the summer of 1583 the Queen took a vigorous lead in conducting a bold and clearly conceived foreign policy. There were several phases: loans to the States coupled with diplomatic pressure on Spain to accept a compromise peace; marriage with Anjou linked to an Anglo-French entente; alliance without marriage, aimed at checking the over-all growth of Spain's power; and, finally, the sponsorship of Anjou as leader of resistance to Parma. After 1583 one senses a certain loss of control. The Queen's strategies had failed; and while she was still at the helm, it was the gathering current of events, not her steering, which carried the ship onwards.

Between 1572 and 1576 there was very little room for ma-neuver, little scope for any English initiative. But when the Spanish fury and the Union of Utrecht cleared the stage for English movement the Queen's initial response was a bold one. Her earlier attempts at mediation were now renewed, but with a formidable stiffening, with the threat of English intervention and more immediately the provision of English loans. The Queen presumably hoped these measures would suffice for a diplomatic victory. Some of her advisors hardly bothered to conceal their hopes for a more definitive English intervention —with arms—which would make England the permanent pro-tector of a Protestant regime. At the least, all could join in hoping for a solution which would bring into being a regime strong enough to stand on its own feet, still a part of the Haps-burg empire yet not merely another Spanish viceroyalty. Such a government would of necessity look to England for counte-nance; it would be at once a stable and friendly neighbor, a secure market, and a buffer against possible expansion of Span-ish (and Catholic) power on the coasts of the North Sea.

But Elizabeth did not long abide by this strategy; within a very short time she reversed gears and swerved off on a very different course. It proved to be a decision crucial to all that followed. She would not return to the tactic of direct inter-vention until compelled by harsh realities in 1585. What led to this change of direction? Overtly it was the growing signs of weakness in the Brussels regime, its indecisiveness, its lack of staying power, above all, its inward contradictions. For all that there is enough evidence to hand, enough indeed to depress the most eager English friends of the rebels. Under these circum-stances to commit English resources and to assume the role of patron to such a dubious protégé would be the sixteenth-century equivalent of America's twentieth-century involvement in Vietnam. It is a plausible argument and perhaps a sufficient explanation for the decision. Yet we cannot ignore another factor, the imponderables of the royal personality, even if we cannot document them. This kind of large-scale overseas enterprise, beyond the royal control of men and of events, was calculated to bring to the surface all of Elizabeth's temperamental hesitations. How far the shift in strategy reflects the influence of the royal temperament rather than a cool calculation of the alternatives available, we cannot guess. Undoubtedly the Queen felt far more comfortable with the indirect strategy of French alliance to which she now turned. It meant dealing with a recognized and established power, and it opened large possibilities of shifting the burden to other shoulders—or even the glittering hope of evading them altogether.

Certainly the next phase of policy—the Anjou courtship—was shaped by the direct impulses of the royal personality. Elizabeth, in her mid-forties, clutched at the last possibility of marriage and came closer to actual matrimony than at any time since 1561. It would be easy to share Mendoza's cynicism about her intentions and to assume that this episode was merely meant to repeat the politic maneuvering of the first Anjou match or the barren flirtation with the Archduke Charles. But contemporaries bear strong witness that it was something more than that. It is not only the forced pace of developments during the summer of 1579 but also the obvious distress of Leicester and the left-wing camp at that time. They thought it necessary to explode the bomb of Stubbs's book in order to halt the Queen. Their stricken condition is vividly reflected in the laments of the *Shepheardes Calender*. There can be no doubt as to their genuine fear that she intended to marry the Duke. As in 1561 the refusal of her councillors to give any sign of encouragement ultimately chilled the Queen's ardors and renewed the nervous self-doubts from which she never had been free. That encouragement which she both hoped for and feared had not come.

When the Queen, after an interval of inaction, returned to

the fray it was in a more sober frame of mind. Aware that her backing of the States, however ineffectual, and her bid for a French alliance had measurably increased Spanish suspicions and fears, Elizabeth had at the same time to face the daunting consequences of Spain's recently augmented power. This led to the almost desperate campaign to secure a working alliance with Paris against Madrid. Yet, sustained and deliberate as the effort was, it was flawed at every turn by the Queen's own unwillingness to give *bona fides* in the form of men, money, and ships in order to convince the French of her honesty of purpose. This failure left her with little alternative except the *pis aller* of supporting Anjou's feckless efforts in Flanders.

At each stage the architect of policy was unmistakably the Queen. The special style of policy reflected all too perfectly her curious blend of political intelligence and wayward temperament. A down-to-earth pragmatist, singularly free of the illusions that arise either from ambition or from idealism, she approached politics with a cool clarity of understanding. Yet there was an ultimate failure of nerve, for she was quite incapable of acting upon her knowledge. She lacked altogether the gambler's courage: to cast the dice by putting an army in the field or a fleet at sea, to leave all to the arbitrament of battle or the vagaries of the winds was more than she could face unless forced to act by sheer brute fact—as in 1585. And even then, as we shall see, having set foot in the current, she struggled fiercely to get back to the firm safety of the shore. These qualities of the royal temperament played a large and in the end a decisive role in the veering course of English policy from the 1570's onwards. Based on clear perception of fact and upon intelligently conceived strategy, policy nevertheless failed in its purposes. The grand alliance against Spain, which seemed so urgent and which by its very existence would check Spanish expansion, failed to materialize. In the end England had to face the might of Spain alone, except for the aid afforded by the two distracted provinces still in arms against Philip. In a long run which was quite invisible in 1585, circumstance would prove more favorable to English purposes than anyone might then have guessed. But this was a closed book to the men who were about to risk the national safety in single-handed war against the greatest European power. All that they could see was their worst fears realized—the long-dreaded struggle coming upon them under the most unfavorable conditions they could conceive.

CHAPTER 14

THE LEICESTER EXPEDITION

IN SEPTEMBER 1585 Drake sailed away and, after he left the coast of Spain lost contact with his government; he was on his own, and Queen and ministers could only wait for news of his further fortunes. Those left at home had to turn to the novel problems posed by the Low Countries expedition. This enterprise was by far the most ambitious yet undertaken by the Elizabethan government; it made unprecedented demands on the physical resources of the country and strained the administrative machinery to the utmost. It required all kinds of decisions about new and complex situations. They had to be made in the knowledge that the survival of the regime and the security of the kingdom were at risk. Within this national crisis individual ministers—and many lesser men—found their own personal destinies put to a hard test. Fortunately for the historian the remaining evidence is extensive in quantity and rich in quality. It is an incomparable opportunity to study the working of Elizabethan government when it was stretched to its utmost.

Specifically, the agreements of the summer and early fall had committed the Queen to sending some 6,400 infantry and 1,000 horsemen to the aid of the States.[1] The Queen was to pay an annual sum of about £126,000 for their maintenance; any ad-

[1] See BL, Harl. Ms. 285, f. 196: "Memorials of treaties with Low Countries, 6 July 1585—5 Feb. 1586."

ditional costs were to be met by the States. They were on the conclusion of peace to repay all English outlays and as a security for repayment were to hand over immediately the two key ports of Flushing and Brill to English keeping. The Queen agreed to dispatch a nobleman who would command her forces in the Low Countries and also assist and advise the States in their military efforts.

This much was reasonably clear; little else was. The whole enterprise was hastily patched together—using a model sketched out in 1577—under the white-hot pressures of events. Originally conceived as a relief operation to rescue Antwerp, the scheme had to be recast overnight when that city fell. But the enterprise remained primarily a relief expedition designed to halt the inexorable advance of Parma's forces across the provinces. All the thinking that went into it seems to have been short term in character. Reinforcements were being rushed from England to the Low Countries to back up the faltering soldiery of the States. But what strategy were they to follow? What was to be their role in relation to the States own forces? How long was the enterprise to endure? And— the most urgent question of all—how was the whole cooperative effort of English and Dutch to be led? None of these questions seems to have been given much consideration in the hurried negotiations of the summer.

But the first question to be dealt with—who was to be the nobleman promised by the Queen—seemed easy to answer. Everyone in England and in Holland assumed that Leicester would be chosen. Ever since the first rising of the Sea-Beggars he had been their patron at the English Court. He had never ceased to press his mistress to enter into overt alliance with them. The English agents in the Low Countries had been almost without exception his protégés; in 1577 he had made ready to lead the expedition then planned and its cancellation by the Queen had been a bitter pill for him. In Holland and Zealand his name was a household word; he had numerous contacts among the leading political figures in the provinces. And indeed once the treaty was signed every correspondent from the Netherlands wrote of his appointment as a thing al-

ready done; one enthusiast declared that the Queen was bringing back to life "the late Prince of Orange in the person of the
Earl of Leicester."[2]

A more detached observer might have been less certain of
the wisdom of appointing the Earl. He was well over fifty years
of age; his last and sole military service was in the St. Quentin
campaign in 1556, where he was a volunteer in the English
auxiliary forces fighting with the Spaniards. He had served in
none of the military enterprises of Elizabeth's reign; his civil
experience was of course much richer but it was that of a
counsellor and courtier, not of an administrator or diplomat.
Yet he was expected to give leadership in the Low Countries
at the very nadir of Dutch fortunes, to reorganize a demoral-
ized army, to halt the victorious advance of one of the great
captains of the age, and to bring order to the chaotically disorganized political world of the provinces. It was a task which
would have tried genius, let alone this untested middle-aged
courtier. Yet circumstances hardly left the Queen or her favorite any choices. Clearly the English commander must be a man
of high rank and great prestige, enjoying the full and unquestioned confidence of the sovereign. He must also be someone
well known in the Netherlands, whose very name would revive the lagging spirits of the beleaguered provinces. No one
but Leicester could possibly fill this role.

Leicester himself shared the expectation of appointment. It
was the fulfillment of a long-delayed ambition, but whatever
pleasure the Earl may have felt in this was sharply alloyed by
his own painful apprehensions. These were not so much of
his own abilities to handle the job as they were of his royal
mistress' commitment to the new policy.

At the end of August Walsingham wrote to the Earl of the
Queen's decision to persevere even though Antwerp had fallen;
she now wished to know if Leicester were still minded to lead
her forces there. His answer was one of wholehearted acceptance;[3] the service of God alone was sufficient reason for pro-

[2] *CSPF*, XX, 67.
[3] *Hatfield*, III, 108; PRO, SP 12/181/68.

ceeding, had not the Queen's safety and that of her realm also required it. However, having affirmed his own convictions, Leicester went on to give vent to his own somber doubts. He feared the Queen's commitment was but a shaky and uncertain one, likely to be altered "as turns and changes fall out." Unless she was prepared to employ all the ways and means that God had given her, it were better to do nothing. "Yea, Mr. Secretary, I must deal plainly with you. . . . I do find all sorts of men . . . so daunted with this conceit as those who would have run to this service at the beginning will slowly go now if they be entreated for they will not believe that Her Majesty will so deal in it as they may hope either of good assurance or such counsel as is fit for men that must go hazard their lives." Leicester no doubt had in mind the nervous hesitations of the summer, when the Queen had stalled, week after week, until driven by the sheer force of events. Her hesitations had included not only the Low Countries expedition but also Drake's naval enterprise. That commander had counted himself lucky to escape from Plymouth before he was countermanded.[4] But once gone, he was out of the Queen's reach. Leicester was not so fortunately situated.

The Earl's doubts were speedily borne out by the royal behavior over his appointment. In the same week in which he wrote the Earl, Walsingham was telling another correspondent that now there would be no forwardness in sending a nobleman to Holland and that it would in any case not be Leicester; possibly Lord Gray, the former Irish Deputy, would be sent. And Leicester had already written of a nobleman who was to be preferred over him. The reason given was Elizabeth's belief that he would "carry with (him) too great a troop." This theme—the royal fear that Leicester would assume too great a state for a mere subject—was to be an abiding one in the months ahead. But another, more intimate reason, emerges in a later letter in which the Earl confides in Walsingham his mistress' very personal fears about his absence. "Often disease taking her of late," she dreads that she will not live to see his

[4] *Papers relating to the Navy*, xxii-xxiv.

return. Leicester was hopeful that these feminine fears would be overcome and indeed by 24 September the Queen had given her consent to his going. But the royal stop-go sequence was not yet over, for on 27 September the Queen suddenly ordered the Earl to suspend the preparations he had already entered on, for reasons not revealed. But then with the same inconsequence she reversed herself once again and allowed preparations to resume. It was not until 22 October that the formal commission appointing Leicester to command the expedition was issued. In November he wrote wearily but hopefully, "No man hath had more discouragements but the worse is past here."[5]

Nevertheless, Leicester threw himself into the preparations for his departure, straining all his resources to provide a suitable entourage and adequate equipage for his great venture. The archaic nature of English military institutions was never more apparent than in the Earl's preparations. He assembled around him an entourage which was more like the great household of a medieval baron than the headquarters staff of a Renaissance captain. For his immediate attendance he had a staff of about 75 persons, including a steward, secretary, treasurer, gentleman of the horse, comptroller, two gentlemen ushers, four gentlemen of the chamber, two divines, a physician, apothecary, and chirurgeon. Two noblemen, the Earl of Essex (his stepson) and Lord North, along with some 20 knights and gentlemen, accompanied him as volunteers, with their 40 servants. All in all the ordinary household of the Earl may well have numbered 200 persons.[6]

But in addition to his immediate attendants the Earl had license to raise as many as 500 of his own tenants to serve at his own expense. He did in fact levy 400 foot from his tenants and paid out of his own pocket for some 350 horse. He had

---

[5] *CSPF*, XX, 8, 172; PRO, SP 12/181/1; 182/24; 182/32; T. Rymer, *Foedera* (20 vols., 1704-32), XV, 799; John Bruce, ed., *Correspondence of Robert Dudley, Earl of Leycester . . . 1585 and 1586*, Camden Soc. 27 (1844), 4, 5, 8.

[6] Dudley Papers, Longleat House (Marquess of Bath), box III, f. 63; *CSPF*, XXI(ii), 110; BL, Cotton Mss., Galba D III 211-15, Nov. 1587.

an allowance of £6 per diem from the Crown, but he claimed to be spending £1,000 a month of his own money.[7]

To pay for these immense outlays Leicester had raised a loan of £25,000 from the city, guaranteed by the Queen, who was in turn protected by a mortgage on Leicester's estates, which she had granted with ill grace. By March 1586 the Earl claimed to have spent £11,000 of his own funds. When he died in 1588, he owed the Crown £20,000 over and above the value of his goods and chattels.[8]

In addition to this personal following, the Earl was attended by two English members of the Dutch Council of State, provided for in the treaty. One of these, Henry Killigrew, was a long-time political dependent of Leicester's; the other was a civil lawyer, Dr. Bartholomew Clarke of the Court of Arches. Two other important appointments were created by the treaty —the garrison commanders in the cautionary towns, Brill and Flushing. The latter fell, after some difficulty, to the Earl's nephew, Sir Philip Sidney. Leicester had been insistent on this appointment; he had to provide a political *quid pro quo* by giving Brill to Sir Thomas Cecil.[9]

It would be another two months after his appointment before Leicester set sail for his command; it was mid-December when he left Harwich for an uneventful voyage to Flushing and a triumphant entry into the Hague (27 December).[10] He was to remain in the Low Countries for eleven months, and to return a battered and—in a fundamental sense—a broken man. He had met the great test of his career and failed. Much of the blame must fall on Leicester's own inadequacies, but it is hard to believe that a far abler man would have succeeded under such disabilities as he faced.

From the beginning Leicester was dogged at each step by his

[7] *CSPF*, XX, 129; Rymer, *Foedera*, XV, 599; Bruce, *Correspondence of Dudley*, 5, 166; BL, Add. Ms. 48,084, f. 134v.

[8] PRO, SP 12/182/49; Dudley Papers, box XX, ff. 3, 94; *CSPF*, XX, 196; Bruce, *Correspondence of Dudley*, 31.

[9] *CSPF*, XX, 53; Bruce, *Correspondence of Dudley*, 10, 23.

[10] See R. C. Strong and J. A. Van Dorsten, *Leicester's Triumph* (1964), 34-49.

mistress' deep-seated irresolution. The fears he had expressed to Walsingham in August were too well founded. The Queen's reluctance to enter the war was reflected in every aspect of her policy—in her contemptuous mistrust of her general and the obstacles she strewed in his path; in her obstructiveness towards every forward move he proposed to make; in her semi-public diplomatic flirtations with Parma; and in the barely veiled disdain with which she treated her new allies.[11]

In addition, the leaders of the expedition had to struggle with the gross imperfections of a military and administrative machine at once primitive and clumsy. Save for the endemic guerrilla warfare in Ireland, England's last overseas effort had been the ill-fated expedition to Le Havre in 1562-1563, and some of the precedents used in 1585 dated back to Pembroke's expedition to the Low Countries as a Spanish auxiliary in 1556. The country's military institutions had been designed largely for defense and although there had been some improvement in the training of the militia in recent years, most of the arrangements for an expeditionary force had to be improvised on short notice.[12] Men were levied from the shires, hustled to the ports, fed, clothed, and paid by local officials pressed into service for the occasion; on their arrival overseas they were in the care of a hastily assembled and very sketchy military administration. The inadequacies of these arrangements, at home and abroad, might well have defeated a commander who could give them single-minded attention. But Leicester was called on to fill yet another role—and that singularly ill-defined. He was not only the commander of the Queen's forces in the Low Countries but her representative, something more than an ambassador, something less than a viceroy.[13]

The role of the Queen's commander in the government of the provinces was left unresolved in the initial treaty; in fact

[11] For the Queen's reservations as early as October 1585, see BL, Add. Ms. 48,127, ff. 83-85.

[12] See C. G. Cruickshank, *Elizabeth's Army*, 2nd ed. (Oxford, 1966), *passim*.

[13] See Leicester's instructions, November 1585, in BL, Add. Ms. 48,084, ff. 42-53.

Elizabeth and the Dutch leaders had widely differing ideas as to what it should be. The Queen, determined to limit her involvement and anxious to avoid any imputation of annexationist designs, wished her general to confine himself largely to military matters, leaving his position in Low Countries domestic matters deliberately undefined. But, since the English were to have two seats on the Council of State, the executive organ, they were to play some role. The Queen insisted that it be advisory and unofficial.

This hardly squared with the expectations of the Netherlands leadership. Their affairs were in a state of almost unbearable confusion and there was a general clamor for strong leadership. Traditionally, executive government in the provinces had been vested in a governor-general, representing the absentee sovereign. When the revolt had broken out, there had been several efforts to fill that post, first with Archduke Matthias, later with Anjou. But then the declaration of independence of 1581 had vacated the sovereign office itself and Anjou had been sworn in in 1582 as the new Count of Flanders. In Holland and Zealand the Prince of Orange, as *stadhouder* (regent) stood in for the sovereign authority and after the departure of Anjou there had been some talk of making him Count of Holland and Zealand in his own right.[14] His death had vacated the *stadhouder*'s office, although in the other two provinces, Friesland and Utrecht, there were still functioning regents. After the assassination of Orange, the rebel leaders sought to persuade the King of France or the Queen of England to accept the vacant sovereignty. When the latter agreed to become their protectress, the Dutch leaders minimized the distinction and tended to regard her representative as yet another governor-general.

This was the situation in which Leicester found himself upon his arrival in Holland. Within a very few days after his arrival at The Hague on New Year's the Earl was solemnly approached by the States-General, who offered him nothing less than the government of all the provinces as it had been

[14] See *CSPF*, XVIII, 10, 34.

held in Charles V's time. Their argument was straightforward: they had offered—and the Queen had declined—the sovereignty of the provinces, but she had sent as her representative one of her most trusted servants as the commander of her expeditionary force and it was entirely fitting that the States should express their confidence in the Queen by choosing him as their governor. They laid great stress on the prevailing disorder—"the confusion of officers hath undone their government"—and only the Earl's assumption of supreme power could remedy this. If he refused, "all will be yet lost."[15]

Leicester's attempt later to claim that the States proposal came as a surprise was less than ingenuous. The issue had been raised more than once before his departure from England. Dutch correspondents had raised it, urging that the Queen insist that Leicester be treated as though he were her own person and that he be vested with the same powers as former governors—or, more ambiguously, as those held by the late Orange. And the Earl had evidently discussed the matter with the Queen and had expressed his own views. In a minute in his own hand he claimed as much authority as "any other governor or captain general hath had heretofore." In another note he declared in disgust that he would "as lief be dead" as take the office under the restrictions which the Queen would impose. What those were is made clear in the treaty, in which Elizabeth promised to send a nobleman of quality to take charge of her forces and to assist by advice and counsel in their government. She repeated this phraseology in her official nomination of Leicester to the States in November.[16]

Leicester took the bit in his own teeth and accepted the offer of the States-General without consulting his mistress. On 22 January the States acted on his appointment and 27 January he was proclaimed Governor-General. The Earl knew he had stretched his commission but clearly hoped to get away with a *fait accompli*. As he wrote later, he trusted in his mistress to allow him such discretion, given his long and faithful serv-

[15] Bruce, *Correspondence of Dudley*, 57-63.

[16] *CSPF*, XX, 6, 140-41, 175, 192; Bruce, *Correspondence of Dudley*, 20.

ice to her. He wrote Burghley a rather shuffling justification of his action and dispatched Davison to defend him at Court.[17]

The Queen's response to this effort to secure some freedom of action was an almost volcanic explosion of royal wrath. A letter from the Privy Council conveyed the royal command that he lay down the newly accepted office, but the Queen followed this up by sending Sir Thomas Heneage, Treasurer of the Chamber, as special emissary to the General and to the States-General. His instructions had been ever so slightly modified by the efforts of Burghley and Hatton, but they still conveyed a stinging and humiliating rebuke to Leicester and a haughty reprimand to the States. The Queen commanded the Earl publicly and solemnly to renounce his office, making clear the extent of the royal displeasure. He was to recite that he, a subject of the Queen—"a creature of our own"—had acted in contempt of her authority and dishonored her in the eyes of the princes of Europe. This was to make clear that she had no ambitions to territorial aggrandizement in the Low Countries. Elizabeth's anger was no doubt the fiercer because Leicester's action would compromise the efforts she was already making to open a negotiation with Parma.[18]

These official considerations were as always intertwined with the Queen's personal resentments. She constantly suspected the Earl of a dangerous vainglory which would rival her own state, and his assumption of the style of "Excellency" infuriated her. Her worst suspicions and her deepest jealousies were aroused by the (untrue) rumor that the Countess of Leicester was about to pass over to Holland with a great train to hold a rival court.[19]

Davison was unluckily held up in his winter passage and did not arrive at Court until mid-February, when he had to bear the brunt of the royal anger. He did his best in prolonged audiences with the Queen and brought her to admit at one point that it was not the substance of Leicester's powers to

---

[17] *CSPF*, XX, 277, 287, 303, 311, 326, 450; *Somers Tracts*, I, 420-21; Bruce, *Correspondence of Dudley*, 57-63, 95-98.

[18] *CSPF*, XX, 322-24; Bruce, *Correspondence of Dudley*, 105-6.

[19] Bruce, *Correspondence of Dudley*, 112.

which she objected but only to his taking the title. Others tried their hand at soothing the royal anger but to little avail. For two months the matter simmered on. The Earl, driven into an agony of self-pity, talked of resignation—indeed he asked for his recall—and gloomily spoke of retirement. It was unclear whether or not he would remain at his post. All this had to be aired in the States-General, who were also treated to a royal scolding. But at last the sustained efforts of Burghley, Hatton, and a stream of emissaries sent by Leicester softened the Queen's wrath. In part this was accomplished by the Earl's shameless shifting of blame onto Davison's shoulders. Even then it took a threat of resignation from Burghley to get the Queen to agree that Leicester should for the time being remain Governor-General. There was one last hiccup of royal protest before letters were finally sent off in early April. Raleigh could now write that Leicester was once again the Queen's "sweet Robyn."[20]

The storm seemed to have abated and the English ministers could get on to the main problems of war, but it proved a mere false armistice. Suddenly, barely a month later, Walsingham wrote a despairing note conveying the Queen's renewed and angry demand that the Earl resign his Netherlands office. The Queen gave no reasons and furiously refused to hear objections; the Secretary conjectured that there were new negotiations with Parma. The Queen followed this up with directions that Heneage and Leicester confer with the Dutch on how to abolish the title without impugning the latter's military authority. Heneage was roundly rebuked, in the best royal manner, for having dared to use his own judgment in the matter. The Earl in desperation asked for his revocation, promising in the meantime to renounce the title so soon as Heneage could rise from his sick-bed to join him. Burghley in vain exerted his best efforts to reverse the Queen's decree; he declared the matter "more cumbersome and severe" than "any whatsoever since I was a counsellor." The letter ends on a note of utter weariness. Yet in the end the matter was allowed to drop

[20] Bruce, *Correspondence of Dudley*, 95-103, 117-26, 165-67, 168-71, 188-90, 193-99, 204-5; *CSPF*, XX, 371-72, 446, 450-52, 500, 510-11.

once again and when Heneage returned home in June he was favorably received.[21]

It was a disturbing episode, for it revealed how little trust and how little freedom of action the Queen was disposed to give her commander in the Low Countries, even though he was her long-time favorite and confidant. Her treatment of him mingled considerations of public policy with her own personal resentments. Jealousy of his wife was one factor; more important was her almost perverse determination publicly to humiliate him, to undermine his independent reputation, and to flaunt to the world the fact that he was her servant, her creature. As the future would demonstrate, she had gone far in destroying Leicester's own self-confidence. The public policy considerations were more alarming still. The core of them was Elizabeth's half-hidden determination to pursue some kind of negotiation with Parma. What lay behind that was her profound distaste for the involvement in the Low Countries and her restless desire to escape by whatever means from these entangling bonds.

The row over Leicester's governorship reverberated into the late spring, but long before it died down the Earl was enmeshed in the multiple problems which were thrust upon him the moment he set foot on shore. They arose from his divergent roles as supreme commander, general in the field, and political leader in the provinces; they are closely intertwined with one another, but for purposes of analysis they can be sorted out into military and civilian categories. More narrowly, one can distinguish between Leicester's problems as a military administrator and as a general. He found on his arrival a ready-made army, sent over the summer before under Norris' command. There was also a skeleton organization for finance and supply. But the novelty of the whole enterprise, English lack of experience, and the absence of any pre-existent military administration faced the Earl with a series of baffling difficulties.[22]

[21] Bruce, *Correspondence of Dudley*, 239-40, 241-43, 259, 262-64, 266-68, 306; *CSPF*, XX, 585-86, 629-30, 636-37, 654-56, 657-58, 670-71, 677-78.
[22] For detailed discussion, see Cruickshank, *Elizabeth's Army*, esp. chaps. 8 and 9.

The Earl was well aware that the entourage which accompanied him was more of a court than a military headquarters and aware too of his own ignorance of military matters. To make up for this deficiency he had intended that a veteran soldier whom he trusted, Sir William Pelham, should assist him. As he put it, this man bore "love to my house who might always have converse of me" and could provide military expertise at the highest level. But here the Earl was thwarted by the Queen. Pelham was in debt to the Crown; she would not permit him to go to the Low Countries without paying his debts. Leicester filled up letter after letter with desperate pleas for Pelham's dispatch. In a rare moment of humor he wrote that the Dutch had heard so much of the man "as almost they believe in him." But the repeated efforts of Burghley were in vain; the Queen would not budge for months; it was not until late July 1586 that Pelham finally arrived to take up his appointment as marshall of the Earl's forces.[23]

The vacuum at the top level of the English command might have been filled by Sir John Norris, the experienced and much admired commander of the English forces in States service, who was appointed Colonel-General of Foot by Leicester.[24] But, as we shall see, Leicester and Norris were soon acrimoniously quarrelling, although they managed to collaborate in the campaigns of summer 1586.

The Earl's army was already on the scene when he arrived, but it was not up to treaty strength. Nor was it made up of very satisfactory soldiers. Many, the Earl complained, were householders, married men and not fit of body; Digges, the muster-master, wrote in March that half the troops who came over at the end of the previous summer were "dead, gone, or wasted" and many others sick. Leicester had already estimated in January that he needed at least 1,500 men to fill up his ranks. But the Queen refused to allow any new levies and even forbade recruiting except for forces which the States would pay.

[23] BL, Harl. Ms. 6993, f. 129; *ibid.* 285, f. 239; Cotton Ms., Galba C XI 143-44; Bruce, *Correspondence of Dudley,* 28, 37, 45, 55-56, 78-79, 132, 370-71.

[24] CSPF, XX, 322.

It was not until April that she lifted the ban on volunteers and allowed a small levy of 300 men in the North. During the next few weeks about 2,000—perhaps more—arrived, although without equipment, before the Queen again suspended recruitment in May.[25]

Since it was so difficult to obtain English soldiers, it was proposed that men be obtained from Ireland and from Scotland. The Irish troops would be recruited from bands being discharged there; the Scots were to come under the command of the Master of Gray. The Queen blew hot and cold on these proposals, but was firm on one matter—that she should pay none of the costs for them. Sir William Stanley went off to Ireland; negotiations with Gray continued for many months. The Scottish contingent (some 2,400) arrived at the end of the summer after the Queen reluctantly provided £2,000 for travel. But Stanley's efforts were not, so far as the evidence goes, successful. Nevertheless, at the height of the campaigning season Leicester had some 11,000 to 12,000 English foot at his disposal (including those in States service). Untrained and without equipment, they were not immediately usable in the field, but—at least on paper—the home authorities, albeit somewhat fitfully, provided Leicester with the quotas of foot promised by the treaty plus a flow of volunteers for the States service. But if quantity was maintained, the same could not be said for quality. Leicester complained that of those who arrived after many delays in late July, at least 2,500 were unfurnished. And the desertion problem was acute, one out of six of those who crossed, the Earl thought. There was a round-up of some 200 deserters found at the seacoast. The Earl hanged many, although as he grimly writes, "they could have been content all to have been hanged rather than tarry." The veterans, he declared, were such "old ragged rogues," for all the world "like dead men" that their very appearance frightened the newcomers.[26]

[25] *Ibid.*, 437; Bruce, *Correspondence of Dudley*, 73, 86, 181, 187, 206, 230, 250, 259, 272, 374. If coat and conduct money were paid directly to the soldier, he was likely to desert on the spot.

[26] Bruce, *Correspondence of Dudley*, 26, 93, 179, 185-86, 230, 237

At the root of Leicester's difficulties in putting together a viable army lay the problem of money. Sir John Neale, in a valuable article, has skillfully elucidated much of the detail of Leicester's finances in the two periods of his service overseas. He describes for us the cumbrous and inherently inefficient military fiscal system. A Treasurer at War (in this case Richard Huddleston, an uncle of Norris) was appointed when the troops were first sent over in 1585, to whom large lump sum payments were spasmodically made by the Treasury; they varied from around £10,000 to as much as £30,000 in a single payment. It was his responsibility to supply funds to the disbursing officers, victuallers, armorers, and, above all, captains of companies. It was to the last that the largest sums were paid out. Nominally "pay" was disbursed only at a muster—i.e., a formal assembly of all men in the company. At this time company records were to be presented with full account of all "defalcations," expenditures for arms, clothes, victuals, etc., made by the company commander, and for which he should receive credit. In fact such a formal occasion was rare; normally the treasurer made periodic "prests," loans to the captains, who could make advances to their men against muster-day. Arrangements of such a kind, informal and irregular, were an encouragement to slackness; above all, they were an encouragement to captains to fill their own pockets. Their companies were seldom at full strength, but it was obviously to their profit to report as large a number of soldiers as possible. It was also to their advantage to delay muster-days as long as possible and a great temptation to hold the sums of money prested to them for their own use.

Huddleston had received an initial payment of £17,000 in July on his appointment. He had another £10,000 in October, and Leicester took £20,000 with him in December. These sums, as all others issued to them, were charges against an annual allocation of £126,000, which was the Queen's financial

(for Irish); 185-86, 220, 291, 348, 396, 402 (for Scots); see also *CSPF*, XX, 304. For desertions and numbers in service, see Bruce, *Correspondence of Dudley*, 338-39, 374, 398.

commitment under the Treaty of Nonsuch for the support of her forces in the Netherlands. (Her total expenses were to be repaid at the conclusion of peace.)[27]

Leicester had hardly set foot in the Low Countries before his financial woes commenced; they were never to cease until the end of his term of office. First of all there was the endemic shortage of money. Funds were sent over in chests from England, including the sum the Earl brought with him on landing (which was supposed to total £20,000, although the treasurer insisted he had but £14,000 and the Earl could account for only £16,000). By February all money on hand was exhausted and no more came from England until April. When, in March, the Earl had hurriedly to assemble a force to relieve Grave, he had to borrow £4,000 from the Merchant-Adventurers at Middleburg. On the arrival of the next installment in April it was found insufficient to cover the accumulated debts of the Earl. In May there was another Merchant-Adventurer loan of £5,000, and Leicester wrote home that it was only this money which staved off a dangerous mutiny. In July he complained that a promised £32,000 had shrunk to a mere £10,000 on arrival, with the same amount promised for August. No wonder 500 men had run away in two days, he lamented. And so the story continued up to the Earl's departure for home in November.[28]

To Leicester's steady litany of demands for money, the response from home was nervously apologetic. In March Walsingham, announcing the dispatch of funds (the first since December), warned Leicester not to look for any more since the "sparing humor" was gaining on the Queen. In June Burghley commented on the royal unwillingness to send money to the Low Countries, but the Lord Treasurer sought to ease the problem to some degree by exchange arrangements

---

[27] J. E. Neale, "Elizabeth and the Netherlands, 1586-7," *English Historical Review* 45 (1930), 373-96; reprinted in *Essays in Elizabethan History* (1958); see also BL, Cotton, Mss., Galba D I f. 120 (for Privy Seal issues, 1585-87) and D I 268-73, 280-82; *CSPF*, XIX, 635.

[28] Bruce, *Correspondence of Dudley*, 87, 190, 236, 260, 271, 338, 365; *CSPF*, XX, 413, 673.

with the Merchant-Adventurers which would obviate the need for shipping specie. In July the Secretary reported that "by the malicious practices of the ill-affected" murmurs against the war were heard from the people "so as it is thought meet for a time to stay the making of any new levies, either of men or money." A few days later Burghley excused the slowness of funds on the grounds that the Merchant-Adventurers apologized for delays in transmitting money; the Merchant-Adventurers had drawn back after the bad news of the fall of Grave and Venlo. From Leicester's point of view the provision of money had been slow, irregular—indeed unpredictable—and grudging. The threat of mutiny by unpaid troops hung continually over his head, while his capacity to move swiftly against an alert and active enemy was impeded by the uncertainties of finding money.[29]

But if Leicester had some grounds for complaining that he was not adequately supplied from England, his mistress on her side had cause for dissatisfaction. As she saw it, her money was being spent recklessly and extravagantly, with no real effort to keep within the alloted budget of £126,000. As early as March 1586 Walsingham noted the Queen's discontent with Huddleston's accounts while the treasurer in turn was complaining that Leicester paid out wages without having taken a muster and also was paying English troops in the States service. This latter charge the Earl denied, in his turn blaming Huddleston. These circumstances certainly encouraged the Queen's niggardliness in providing more money for Leicester's needs. By June Burghley bluntly wrote "we cannot by any account find what is due, either now or until any time past . . ." and a few weeks later Sir Thomas Shirley was made joint treasurer with Huddleston, with the intention of straightening out the mess. By then criticism of Huddleston's methods of accounting was clamorous.[30]

Leicester's own role in this financial imbroglio was an ambiguous one. Early on, he was a critic of the treasurer; in Jan-

[29] Bruce, *Correspondence of Dudley*, 191, 293-94, 345, 357.
[30] *CSPF*, XX, 587; *ibid.*, XXI(ii), 82-83; Bruce, *Correspondence of Dudley*, 191, 293-94.

uary he was complaining that Huddleston could not produce accounts for his disbursements. By summer the Earl was in full cry after the Treasurer at War. Urging the latter's recall, he wrote, "I see there be no assurance to keep money from disbursing," and declared he would not be responsible for any certificate Huddleston sent in. He extended his accusations, which hinted at more than mere inefficiency, to the captains, especially to Norris. He suggested that they were in collusion with the treasurer, signing whatever he put before them, in return for prests of money, which they could pocket themselves. Instead of using the money to feed or clothe their men, they borrowed locally from the Dutch townsmen for day-to-day costs and allowed the debts to run indefinitely.[31]

But Leicester himself came under fire for financial irresponsibility, and the Queen listened to his critics. They charged him with extravagance in provisioning, with failure to see that the men actually received their pay, and with asking for more troops than he could pay. In addition the Earl was accused of paying the Queen's money for the support of States troops. He defended himself as well as he could, arraigning the system itself. He could not, he argued, make it work when money came so slowly and irregularly from England and without proper muster rolls. He ascribed his high costs in the field to the necessity of using only English troops (no Dutch being available). But the Queen was disturbed enough to appoint the additional treasurer, Shirley, in July although at the same time she defended both Huddleston and the captains.[32]

Clearly the financing of the expedition was muddled in such a way as to satisfy neither the Queen nor her general—nor, most of all, the unlucky soldiers serving in field or garrison. The system itself was certainly a bad one in that it encouraged corruption and slackness. The chances of private profit were high, and neither the mores of Elizabeth's civil servants nor of mercenary officers discouraged such benefits. Neale, in his study of the finances of this expedition, looking at it from the

[31] Bruce, *Correspondence of Dudley*, 68, 260, 265, 298, 325; *CSPF*, XX, 680; BL, Add. Ms. 14,028, ff. 90-93.
[32] *CSPF*, XXI(ii), 94, 189-97.

royal point of view, blamed Leicester severely. Certainly the Earl must share a considerable measure of blame; he seems never to have made any real effort to master the fiscal administration or to keep track of the Queen's funds. Faced with the obvious facts of failure, he shrugged off responsibility onto the treasurer and captains, seeming to assume that he had no obligation to attempt remedies for the faults. On the other hand, one need not accept—as Neale does—the innocence of the treasurer and the captains. The former took a percentage on prests; many of the latter saw themselves as military entrepreneurs as much as soldiers of the Queen. Leicester's worst fault lay in his refusal to attack the central abuses of the system, but then Burghley, the Lord Treasurer, showed only the mildest interest in reforming an administrative system for which he was officially responsible.

The Queen was understandably worried about the squandering of her scant resources, but she seems to have concentrated so exclusively on the trees of economy as to lose sight of the woods of war. She seemed almost to forget that her money was being risked on a military venture with its recurrent emergencies. Her fits of miserliness bore heavily on the shoulders of generals in the field.

All things considered, it is surprising that Leicester was able to mount a campaign marked by some modest successes in the summer season of 1586. The immediate military problem he had to deal with was how to halt the systematic capture of one town after another by Parma. The prime deficiency of the Dutch in previous years had been the lack of a field army; without this they could do little or nothing to hinder the Spanish commander when he sat down before a city; given such freedom of action, it was only a matter of time before he starved or stormed it. Norris had bluntly pointed out the need for a field army before Leicester left England and the Earl was to echo the argument when he arrived on the scene. "We must erect a camp [field army] to bridle this liberty of the enemy or else he will keep a war this twenty years." But the Queen, ever counting her pennies, wanted no risks to be taken which might cost money and repeatedly commanded her general to stand on a defensive war, which meant essentially keeping all the forces in garrison. Nevertheless, the circumstances of war gave the English commanders their chance to act. In early May Leicester set out with a field force and marched up the Rhine; it was here that enemy action threatened. If the Earl could clear this area of enemy forces, he would reopen the river to traffic from Germany to the Dutch ports. In a series of moves he cleared the whole of the Betuwe (the island between the Rhine and Meuse) of enemy fortifications. But the town of Grave was under siege by Parma and hard-pressed, so later in the month Leicester borrowed £5,000 at Middleburg in order to head a force to relieve it. He was too late and in the first days of June the town fell to Parma. The Duke swept on into Guelderland to assault Venlo, and although Williams and the Dutch commander, Schenk, made a bold attempt to relieve the town, they failed, and before the end of June it too had yielded. These defeats badly shook the Earl's reputation among the Dutch. It jarred Leicester himself into urging the Queen to take over the sovereignty of the Low Countries as the only means by which Parma could be halted. And this in turn frightened the Queen with the prospect of perpetual war and increased costs.[33]

Nevertheless, the Earl was able to recoup some of his prestige by a successful surprise attack on Axel in Flanders in early July. After a pause, a force was again put into the field in August, commanded by Norris and sent to relieve Berck. This operation was successful when Doesburg was taken in early September. The campaign ended with a series of skirmishes around Zutphen which were made famous by the death of Sir Philip Sidney and which ended with the withdrawal of the Spanish from their sconce outside Zutphen and with Parma's retreat from the area. The town, although still in Spanish hands, was surrounded by English garrisons in various towns and forts which encircled it. It was not an inglorious conclu-

---

[33] *Ibid.*, XX, 84, 617, 666, 673; *ibid.*, XXI(ii), 18; Bruce, *Correspondence of Dudley*, 13, 64-5, 72, 126, 131, 284, 322, 340-41.

sion to the season of fighting. In 1586 for the first time in several years the Spaniards had chalked up only minor conquests and insignificant advances of their lines into rebel territory.[34]

Yet, in spite of the limited successes of his military operations, the Earl faced the end of his campaigning season with a deepening sense of failure. Even at the time of his appointment in the previous autumn he had had, as we saw, profound doubts as to the seriousness of the Queen's intentions. These doubts had been borne out by events. But without doubt the most scarring experience was the outburst of contemptuous fury with which the Queen greeted his assumption of the governor-generalship. She kept him on tenterhooks for six weary months over this issue. The public humiliation which she forced on him with the loss of standing both at home and in Holland chilled his sense of self-confidence and made him hauntingly aware that at any moment the royal support on which he so desperately depended might be pulled away, leaving him again in the lurch. The series of his letters which survive for the year 1586 are very revealing of the Earl's steady loss of confidence. Rambling, sometimes incoherent, but surprisingly candid, they are filled with nervous self-justification, and with a growing paranoia, sometimes rising to a hysterical pitch. His fellow-officers, his servants, the Dutch leaders, courtiers at home, are all seen as betraying him or intriguing against him.

As early as April, the Earl fired off two frantic letters to Burghley and Walsingham, full of the rumors which were flying about the Low Countries to the effect that he was of little account at home and that the Queen had never trusted him, that she would send him no more funds, and that he was simply being used to make a diversion until she could work out a peace with Parma. In May in a very rhetorical letter to the Queen the Earl expressed his despair at accomplishing anything and asked to return home. And in a similar mood he declared himself to Walsingham, "I think you all mean me a forlorn man as you set me in the forlorn hope." Self-pity

[34] *CSPF*, XXI(ii), 75-77, 127, 146-47; Bruce, *Correspondence of Dudley*, 337; Camden, *Annals*, 330.

dominated later letters—"how those are most cherished that any [way] can use me worst." "I see all men have friends but myself." In a spasm of suspicion the Earl began to wonder if even Burghley was intriguing against him. Less emotionally he wrote in September, warning that the States would yield no more contributions until they were reassured that they could really rely on the Queen. "I have signified my own opinion in these causes both to Her Majesty and the Council but never hearing what she resolves upon touching the proceedings with these countries and knowing these advices of mine not to concur with her intention at my being, I dare not wade further in that cause."[35]

Leicester was prone to outbursts of self-pity, but he was not wrong in sensing the Queen's diminishing confidence in him. A candid letter from Court in September reported that the subject of Leicester's recall was under discussion. "Such as desire the good of that state do hold that question affirmatively, but such as do not love him (who are the larger number) do maintain the negative." The writer of this letter was Thomas Wilkes, who had in the summer been sent over on an investigatory mission, with a gently chiding letter from the Queen rebuking Leicester for his quarrels with the Dutch leaders and with his own officers. In September Wilkes was sent again with far more extensive instructions which included the reversal of several of Leicester's main decisions. The Earl was to be recalled—on the pretense that he was needed at home—and Wilkes was to replace Killigrew on the Council of State. Leicester took the royal criticisms hard and wished "he were dead rather than have such discomfortable words" from the Queen. It was not until late November that Leicester sailed, but during the preceding weeks power was slipping out of his hands.[36]

One of the gravamen against the Earl which had eroded the Queen's confidence in his abilities was his unhappy relations with the most experienced and probably the most able of his

[35] Bruce, *Correspondence of Dudley*, 214-19, 290, 379, 393, 395; *CSPF*, XX, 525, 677-79; *ibid.*, XXI(ii), 163.

[36] *CSPF*, XXI(ii), 94, 163-64, 168-69, 174-75, 187-88, 189.

officers, Sir John Norris. This commander had served for years under the States as their principal English officer and he had a distinguished reputation as a field commander. He was in charge of the forces sent over by the Queen in 1585 until Leicester's arrival. Leicester was to speak of him as a long-time protégé "brought up by me and preferred by me chiefly to all his former charges especially in this country," and in January appointed him Colonel-General of Foot. But the Earl was complaining of Norris' behavior as early as April 1586 after a mutiny of Norris' troops at Utrecht. Walsingham's comments on the colonel are revealing. The Secretary believed Norris was egged on by Leicester's enemies at home. He added, "I would to God that with his valor and courage he carried the mind and reputation of a religious soldier." But instead he conducted himself with a licentious and corrupt government in which neither religion nor policy could flourish. Clearly Norris was no favorite of the Puritans.[37]

As the campaign season drew near, relations between the two men worsened. In May there was a quarrel over precedence between Norris and Leicester's stepson, Essex (General of the Horse), and at the same time a falling out over the appointment of the foot captains. The Earl was accused of partiality for his kin and was said to be in the hands of a clique composed of North, Cavendish, and Digby. Norris' advice on military measures was neglected and in July the quarrel between the two men reached its peak. Leicester's letters became shrill with indignation; Norris was "right the late Earl of Sussex son," a dissembler full of malice and craft; the Earl clamored for his recall. Norris, on his side, poured out his grievances to Burghley. Things were made worse when the colonel quarreled with Leicester's protégé, Pelham, while his brother, Edward, was challenged to a duel by Count Hohenlohe, the principal States commander, after a drunken brawl. And then, quite suddenly in September, there was a reconciliation. "Mr. Norris is a most valiant soldier surely and all are now perfect good friends here," so wrote Leicester. And when

[37] *Ibid.*, XX, 159-60, 163-64, 322, 439, 591-92; BL, Add. Ms. 48,116, f. 76; BL, Harl. Ms. 285, f. 149; Bruce, *Correspondence of Dudley*, 222.

the Earl left, it was Norris, to his surprise, who took command of the English forces. Until the last minute it was Pelham (the Earl's choice) who was scheduled for this office.[38]

The history of Leicester's uneasy relations with Norris and with others of the older captains is another indication of his unsure hand. He veered between commendations of the colonel and vituperative accusation, between demands for his recall and "all good friends here." No doubt there was much tension between the veteran professional and the gentleman amateur and it is significant that Leicester went to great trouble to bring in Pelham from Ireland as his principal military advisor rather than making use of the long-time resident expert. It is clear that Norris had a strong interest at Court (not only with Burghley but in the Queen's old friendship for his family) and that in Court and Council it was the colonel rather than the Earl who was taken more seriously.

Wilkes's arrival in the Low Countries as the new member of the Council of State and Leicester's departure initiated a new phase in England's Low Countries enterprise; it also brought to a boil a series of issues which had been simmering for some months past. They concerned the worsening relations between the English government and the States. The treaty of Nonsuch had left some awkwardly unsettled questions. Even after the Queen agreed to increase her forces so as to comprehend garrisons for Brill and Flushing (1,400 men additional), she balked at paying their wages although she finally gave in on this. When Leicester arrived, there was a short honeymoon season, marked, of course, by the appointment of the Earl as Governor-General. The Queen's own action marred this harmony when she delivered a stinging rebuke to the States-General for their action. The Earl's loss of prestige told on events and in April he was writing despondently of a loss of the States affection. Pallavicino, writing from Germany, "what was not safe to write from Holland," thought Leicester had bitten off more than he could chew; the Earl was surrounded

[38] *CSPF*, XX, 591-92, 666-69; *ibid.*, XXI(ii), 47-48, 87, 92-93, 115-17, 137, 208, 232-33, 234; Bruce, *Correspondence of Dudley*, 301, 391, 405, 430.

by mediocrities, military and civil, and by the faction-ridden States of the two provinces. The Italian grimly predicted trouble to come. He was certainly right in suggesting that Leicester would run into problems with the factions within the States.[39]

In his relations with the Dutch, the Earl was to show the same ineptness he displayed in dealing with his own countrymen. He gave his confidence too soon and too easily to those who first had his ear and then threw himself with partisan fervor into supporting them. He was quick not only to take offense but to jump to the worst conclusions about the motives of his opponents. He took his own dignities rather too seriously and was consequently oversensitive to any slight upon them. He never understood the ambiguities and subtleties of Netherlands political institutions. He rather simplistically saw the parties as mere copies of those he knew at home and hence fell all too easily into the arms of the extreme Calvinists. Lastly he continued, not very discreetly, to hanker after a real English takeover with the Queen installed as sovereign. These defects not only led him into conflict with the Netherlands leaders but also placed him athwart the Queen's own considered policy.

When Leicester first arrived, he summed up the leading personalities in terms of their pro-English or pro-French activities. Among the former, the most prominent was Paul Buys, former Advocate of Holland, who had lost his office for his pro-English stance. And indeed the name of Buys (representing Utrecht) had figured very frequently in the embassy which negotiated the alliance. But before February was out, the Earl declared Buys to be a "dissembler, an atheist, and a practicer to make himself rich and great." These denunciations were repeated in the summer with the more specific allegation that Buys was spreading rumors about Leicester's loss of favor at home and that he was dealing with the Papists. In July Buys was arrested in Utrecht (although without Leicester's assent). In previous month, the Utrecht authorities had offered Leicester supreme power in the province, threatening, if he

[39] *CSPF*, XX, 516.

did not accept, to refuse the authority of the States-General.[40]

At the same time that Leicester was embroiling himself in the factional quarrels of Utrecht, his relations with the States moved towards a general crisis. In June the Queen had written a scolding letter to the States, blaming them for not paying their share of costs and for not obeying Leicester's orders. She acknowledged that she had had overtures from Parma and had not rejected them, but insisted that she would look after Dutch interests. At about the same time Leicester was spelling out his grievances against the Dutch. Dutch morale was low since the loss of Grave and Venlo and this was giving leverage to Leicester's enemies, particularly to Buys, who alienated both Hohenlohe and Count Maurice from the English and was persuading them to think of a Danish protectorship in lieu of an English.

In a meeting of 22 July the States, whose irritation had been building up, poured out their grievances against the English. They complained of the failure to hold joint musters so that the actual wages bills could be determined; they objected to the creation of a new council of finance without their approval, and more angrily still to the appointment of Ringout as finance minister. He was a former servant of Alva, a bankrupt, and he deserved prison rather than office. There was also the problem of the embargo on trade with the enemy imposed by Leicester in April, which, the Dutch asserted, only resulted in this valuable trade's passing to the English, French, and Scots while their own tax-paying capacity was destroyed.[41]

Leicester, as always inclined to take an extreme view, saw these discontents as nothing less than an assault on his authority and an attempt to wrest sovereignty for the States. It was all tied up in his mind with Buys's intrigues. The only solution, he repeatedly urged, was for the Queen to take over the sovereignty of the provinces herself.[42]

[40] *Ibid.*, XXI(ii), 17-18, 33, 38, 87, 122-23; Bruce, *Correspondence of Dudley*, 74, 130, 216, 291, 303, 310-11, 352, 364.

[41] *CSPF*, XX, 36, 37; *ibid.*, XXI(ii), 15-17, 88-92, 100, 155-157.

[42] *CSPF*, XXI(ii), 106; Bruce, *Correspondence of Dudley*, 362-63, 393, 409, 410.

The Queen reacted coolly to these heated allegations of the Earl. In July she wrote him a friendly "dear Robin" letter, unusually terse and straightforward for her.[43] In it gently but firmly she urged him to patch up matters with Hohenlohe and Maurice as well as with Norris and the other veteran captains, and to bring his financial affairs into some better order. Without saying so directly, she gave him to understand that she thought that not all the right was on his side. She also warned him, about the same time, not to meddle in religion and to leave those Papists who were not pro-Spanish alone. In August she went a good deal further and wrote directly to the States-General, specifically denying any desire to take over the supreme power in the provinces. By September she had committed herself to a series of changes which were all directly or indirectly reflections on Leicester's policies.

The main heads of the States' grievances were summed up in a document drawn up just before Leicester's departure.[44] Some of them dealt with problems of Anglo-Dutch military cooperation: the Dutch wanted the Queen's contingent of 1,000 cavalry brought up to full strength; they asked for the better disciplining of the English soldiers; they demanded a better payment for frontier towns (a crisis was even then brewing at Deventer); and they wanted the Earl to reduce his levies of foreign troops in the States pay. To all these demands Leicester conceded, implicitly acknowledging the justice of the charges.

Other matters touched on the internal government of the provinces. The Dutch insisted that no governors of towns be appointed without their participation; on the vexed question of Utrecht they wanted the long-standing union of that province with Holland reestablished, with Count Maurice (already Stadhouder of Holland) to hold the same post in the other province. But some of these demands rose to grander constitutional questions. The States made the classic demand of parliamentary bodies that there be no impositions without their consent. They also claimed that people had been de-

[43] *CSPF*, XXI(ii), 94.   [44] *Ibid.*, 221-23.

prived of justice (a reference to Buys and the burghers of Utrecht), summoned before Council and dealt with contrary to the custom of the land. On these issues the Earl was not so yielding; he either denied the request or reserved it for further consideration.

Leicester's departure was a deeply unsettling event for the Low Countries. He left the Council of State, of which Count Maurice was a member, in charge of civil government but with no power to change the principal officers. Wilkes replaced Killigrew as an English member, but Clerk was left in office. The English forces were left in the charge of Norris, who, however, complained that the frontier garrisons under Sir William Stanley and Rowland Yorke were exempt from his jurisdiction. At the same time the States dispatched an embassy to the Queen to ask her to increase her forces by 6,000 men (1,000 horse and 5,000 foot) and to lend them £60,000 for a field army. They hoped on their part to add 200,000fl. a year for three years; with the Queen's forces they hoped to field an army some 20,000 strong, enough to challenge Parma seriously. But they insisted that there be no peace negotiations with Parma and that the Union of Utrecht be inviolate (i.e., that England not countenance the autonomists of Utrecht).[45]

But while the envoys were at the English Court, other events transpired at home. Before the end of November the English command began receiving alarming reports from Deventer, where Sir William Stanley, hero of the late campaign, commanded an English garrison. He had so distinguished himself in the actions of early fall that Leicester had bestowed an annuity of 100 marks on him. The citizens of Deventer complained that Stanley was tyrannizing them, and a stream of correspondence passed back and forth between Norris and Wilkes, at one end, and Stanley, at the other. Stanley defended himself and countered with the complaint that his men had had no pay in six months. Rumors of negotiations between Stanley and the Spaniards flew around in December and January; the money was finally sent to pay his men, but the

[45] *Ibid.*, 227, 228-30, 234-35; BL, Cotton Mss., Galba C XI ff. 111-13.

choice was already made: on 19 January, Stanley and Yorke betrayed Deventer to Parma and entered the Spanish service.[46]

This event was a heavy blow to English prestige and more particularly to Leicester's since both Stanley and Yorke had been appointed at his insistence against the warnings of others. And it served to trigger a series of definitive moves among the Dutch leadership which would have very far-reaching consequences. We have seen how in the previous summer Leicester claimed that there was a conspiracy to wrest power from him and to vest it in the States-General. Although there was an element of the paranoid in this attitude, there was also some ground for it. The Dutch had entered into the English alliance at a moment of desperation when they seemed about to be overwhelmed by the Spanish. Following the strategy set by the Prince of Orange, they had sought a new sovereign, first at Paris and then in London; rejected by both the monarchs whom they approached, they had settled for a second-best solution—Elizabeth's protectoral role. But many of the Dutch leaders continued to believe that their salvation lay in the imposition of a strong monarchical power over their chaotic localism. It was this impulse that led the States-General to offer Leicester the governor-generalship upon his arrival. The Earl himself, frustrated by the choking complexities which he faced at every turn, came to share the view that only monarchical power could save the Low Countries, and we have seen how he pressed this view, quite without avail, on the Queen. But by now a counterforce had emerged within the Dutch ranks. Disillusionment with Leicester's ineptitude, deep distrust of the Queen's intentions, and resentments between the Dutch and English soldiery helped to arouse what might be termed a "nationalist" response. At last the notion that the Netherlands themselves, rather than some imported potentate, might mount the leadership necessary to repel the Spaniards, began to take root.

The idea drew its sustenance from the States of Holland and from the Hollanders in the States-General, most particularly

[46] *CSPF*, XXI(ii), 186, 241-42, 287, 326-27, 330-32.

from the man whose name now begins to appear in English correspondence—Oldenbarnevelt. He was able to shape a party by exploiting the most potent loyalty in the provinces—that felt for the house of Orange. He worked closely with the young Count Maurice and with the Count Hohenlohe, general of the forces and brother-in-law of Maurice. A kind of coup took place in late January, when the States of Holland proclaimed Count Maurice Captain-General of Holland, Zealand, and Friesland, with Hohenlohe as his lieutenant. It was also resolved that the principal captains and officers were to be natives and the burgomasters to be approved by "His Excellency of Nassau."[47]

This action took place in an atmosphere of distrust and disagreement. Early in the month the provinces had refused to pay up the latest assessment of the States-General for English volunteers' wages, saying they had already fulfilled their obligations. (This assessment was to be counted as the final installment of the moneys due in 1586, and the provinces insisted they had already filled those quotas. Their commitment to pay ended with the old year.) Moreover, many towns now refused to accept the English garrisons quartered in them, and the unlucky soldiers were driven to pillage the countryside to stay alive. At almost the same time, Wilkes wrote that no garrisons (except Flushing and Brill) had received pay since September. A provocation of a different kind came when the States-General deliberately flouted Leicester's authority by releasing Paul Buys, and he was soon to be seen in the Council of State.[48]

The situation was summed up by Gilpin, the English Secretary to the Council of State, who wrote that "these Hollanders would incorporate and rule all, so as authority, commandment, trade, traffic, gains, quietness, and what they would else should be theirs and all used as their instruments to serve their turns." Gilpin also referred to the passionate speech of Olden-

[47] BL, Add. Ms. 48,129, no pagin.; "Certain summary notes," etc., BL, Cotton Mss., Galba C XI 70-71; *CSPF*, XXI(ii), 317, 334-35.

[48] Hajo Brugmans, ed., *Correspondentie van Robert Dudley . . . 1585-1588* (3 vols., Utrecht, 1931), II, 19; BL, Egerton Ms. 1694, ff. 81-82, 83-84, 87-88; *CSPF*, XX(ii), 333-35, 371-72.

barnvelt in the States-General. And the States themselves, in an ill-tempered letter to Leicester which gave great offense, rehearsing again their grievances against him, ended by saying that since Deventer they felt compelled to take control. Next they assailed Leicester's authority and judgment over the question of grain licenses.[49]

The mission in London had to report complete failure in its efforts to secure more soldiers and a loan from the Queen; she denied them both and took the opportunity to deliver a few "hard speeches . . . as charging them with breach of promise, baseness of mind and other things. . . ." The mission departed in ill humor. Ill will against the English troops grew; most of their captains were absent on home leave; and the soldiers were quite out of control. Worse still, an alarming polarization seemed about to take place in the provinces. Hohenlohe was moving to seize control of garrison towns, and rumors flew about that Count Maurice and the States were recruiting men for their service. The States-General renewed the commission of the Council of State for two months only, but with the proviso that they were not to be bound by acts of Leicester restricting their powers. The States of Holland also issued a proclamation placing all soldiers in the province under the sole direction of Count Maurice and Hohenlohe. Russell, the governor at Flushing, could write that levies were being raised in Holland and Zealand in the name of the States and in Utrecht in Leicester's name. The latter province was in fact in virtual rebellion against the authority of The Hague.[50]

A memorial brought over by Roger Williams sketched out an elaborate plot by the disaffected Dutch, led by Oldenbarnvelt, St. Aldegonde, and Orange's confidant, Villiers, to use Maurice as a stalking horse; once he was established as governor of Holland, Zealand, and Utrecht his rank would make it impossible for an English nobleman to be placed over him.

---

[49] Brugmans, *Correspondentie*, II, 69-72, 76-78; *CSPF*, XXI(ii), 334-35, 346-47; BL, Add. Ms. 48,014, f. 307.

[50] Brugmans, *Correspondentie*, II, 104-5; *CSPF*, XXI(ii), 358, 359, 363, 377, 378.

This scheme involved plots for the conquest of Utrecht, but more immediately for gaining control of all revenue, of all important offices, and of all garrisons; many of these goals had already been achieved.[51]

In early March, Maurice was solemnly proclaimed Governor-General of Holland, Zealand, and Friesland. A few days later, when Wilkes complained of the derogation of Leicester's authority, he was roundly told by Oldenbarnvelt that the States were the sovereign power and the Earl but their servant. In the meantime, the Orangist party made a determined effort to seize control of key garrisons, but at Gorcum, Dordrecht, and especially in North Holland and in Zealand, they were resisted by Dutch commanders who refused to give up their posts, which they held at Leicester's appointment.[52]

At Utrecht in the meantime there had been a kind of declaration of independence from Holland. Before his departure, Leicester had tried to force VanDeventer on Utrecht as its burgomaster. Then the situation had been complicated by a local quarrel which pitted the Protestant clergy and the nobles against a party of citizens. Hohenlohe backed the former, and by January VanDeventer was clamoring for military support from the English. Norris was in fact on hand in the city, and in spite of the anti-English intrigues of Count Nieuwenaar, the Governor, kept the place in the hands of the pro-Leicester party.[53]

In the meantime at the English Court, Leicester had been very favorably received by the Queen on his return. He could triumphantly write, "I have had a most gracious welcome at Her Majesty's hands as ever I had since I was born," and added that the Queen "shall be satisfied of all my doings, I doubt not." The Earl's magnetic effect on the Queen was proportionate to his distance from Court and when he returned

[51] *CSPF*, XXI(ii), 381; BL, Cotton Mss., Galba C XI 193-94.

[52] *CSPF*, XXI(ii), 387-88, 407-9, 414-15, 421, 423-24; Brugmans, *Correspondentie*, II, 145-51.

[53] *CSPF*, XXI(ii), 283-84, 308, 325; Brugmans, *Correspondentie*, II, 268; BL, Egerton Ms. 1694, f. 91.

from overseas speedily reacquired its accustomed potency. However, it did not suffice to move the Queen's unshakable refusal to give the Dutch any larger quantity of aid. Nor was she disposed to omit a thorough accounting from the Earl for all his activities while overseas. Her relentless demands for details left him bruised and sore, resentful that a great officer should be held accountable for such sordid minutiae. Leicester and his ailing brother, Warwick, withdrew to Bath to recuperate.[54]

As English authority and prestige disintegrated in the provinces, the Englishmen there made frantic appeals for the Earl's return as the only means of restoring the situation. Rumors of all kinds flew about—that the Queen was negotiating with Spain or even that she knew in advance of Stanley's treason at Deventer. The unfortunate Wilkes was soon caught between two fires, the States on one side and the Earl on the other. Leicester early on persuaded himself that Wilkes—like Davison a year earlier—was not adequately defending his interests, and the frantic envoy was soon begging Burghley and Hatton for protection against his superior's wrath. The other principal English officer in Holland—Norris—was full of bitterness against the Earl and refused any reconciliation. He was engaged in discharging enough under-strength companies of the Queen to provide the necessary surplus to fill up the remainder. But there were now no more than 3,000 Queen's soldiers left, and these were six months in arrears in their wages. The colonel, disgusted with an impossible task, asked for recall and replacement by someone acceptable to Leicester.[55]

The Queen and her councillors, bombarded with bad news from across the Channel, finally took action when in early March Lord Buckhurst (a new appointee to the Privy Council) was ordered to cross to Holland with a brief to investigate and to conciliate. The instructions had a strong pro-Leicester bias and were haughtily critical of the States actions, particu-

[54] *CSPF*, XXI(ii), 257; PRO, SP 12/198/19.
[55] *CSPF*, XXI(ii), 332-33, 412, 419-20; BL, Add. Ms. 48,116, ff. 52-79; BL, Add. Ms. 48,014, ff. 460-61; BL, Egerton Ms. 1694, ff. 101-2.

larly of the offending letter of 4 February and of the subsequent flouting of Leicester's authority in one actual instance after another. The threat of English withdrawal was to be held over their guilty heads.[56]

Privately, he was to seek answers to questions about internal conditions in the provinces, the state of public opinion, and also the condition of the Queen's own forces. There was a hint in these latter clauses that the Queen distrusted existing channels of information. Presumably Leicester regarded the Buckhurst appointment favorably; at least he had put forward the latter's name as long ago as July as a fit man "to come over, who shall see plainly that all shall be true I write or advertise." In the Low Countries there was little enthusiasm for the mission; Wilkes and VanDeventer both declared it to be a dangerous waste of time which would allow the Spaniards to advance. Both were urgent in feeling that Leicester himself must return at once. The English colonel, Morgan, was more forthright; he declared that now was the time to strike. The Earl should come now and refuse to negotiate with the States. "Now is the time to make the law in this country as pleases you and those which doth counsel Your Excellency to the contrary . . . are not true men to the action of God's religion and Her Majesty and her country."[57]

These were the terribly difficult circumstances under which Buckhurst entered on his mission. His first moves upon landing at the end of March were pacific and conciliatory. He got in touch with the pro-English commanders, but he also saw Maurice and Hohenlohe and within ten days was able to report a general reconciliation; apologies and explanations flowed; those old rivals Hohenlohe and Norris embraced. But Wilkes, reporting this happy news to Walsingham, more soberly warned that actions must follow words; the enemy were on the move at a moment when the States authorities were

---

[56] *CSPF*, XXI(ii), 400-3, 411-12; BL, Harl. Ms. 285, ff. 284-92; BL, Add. Ms. 48,084, ff. 56-60.

[57] *CSPF*, XXI(ii), 411-12, 421, 424, 432; Bruce, *Correspondence of Dudley*, 378; BL, Cotton Mss., Galba C XI 256-57.

discredited and Leicester absent; the Earl must return promptly. The first news that Parma might be closing in on Sluys
had come in mid-March.[58]

The demand for Leicester's return was echoed in many
quarters during the next few months, but the decision lay in
the hands of the Queen and for weeks she hesitated uncertainly, pulled in opposing directions. Vast amounts of her
treasure had been poured out in the Low Countries with little
to show; the States, sullen and quarrelsome, balked at any
commands she gave them and yet sought even more of her
money and men. The negotiations with Parma, which had
dragged on for a year or more, at last began to show some
promise of results. More and more the Queen turned longingly to the hopes of a negotiated peace. Yet she was willing to
allow Drake to set sail for Iberian waters, albeit under crip-
pling restrictions on his freedom of action.[59]

The official instructions laid down for Buckhurst reflected
these pressures. At the end of May he proposed to the States
a reduction in their forces which would eliminate any need
for additional English funds; they were to pay over the money
this saved to Dutch nominees of Leicester. The proposal was
justified on the grounds that Parma was now very weak because of lack of victuals. Buckhurst was also under orders to
press the Dutch leaders to concessions which might ease the
peace negotiations. He was to "seek out good patriots who
do not wish the continuance of the war," urging on them the
impossibility of finding means, either at home or in England,
to continue the struggle. And a little later he was given the
awkward task of telling the States that the Queen was about
to enter negotiations with Parma; he was to assure them that
she would seek honorable terms for them, the restoration of
their ancient liberties, and release from foreign control. When
Buckhurst delayed relaying her instructions, anxiously hinting
at difficulties of implementation, the Queen testily scolded him,

---

[58] BL, Cotton Mss., Galba C XI 318-19; BL, Add. Ms. 14,028, ff. 87-
89; BL, Add. Ms. 48,116, f. 54; *CSPF*, XXI(ii), 413-14; *ibid.*, XXI(iii),
10, 14, 15, 19.

[59] *CSPF*, XXI(iii), 91; BL, Cotton Mss., Galba C XI 11 Apr. 1587.

"O, weigh deeplier this matter than with so shallow a judgment to imperil the cause, impair my honor and shame yourself."[60]

But apart from his official tasks, difficult enough to carry out, Buckhurst found himself entangled in the thorn-patch of personal quarrels, compelled to "please the particular humors of private men or rest subject to sinister informations against himself." Leicester came more and more to view the whole scene in a very personal light, and the wounds to his ego produced repeated cries of anguish. There were the various humiliations of the winter, but they were overshadowed by the allegation put about by Hohenlohe that the Earl had sought to kill him. This raised the favorite's pitch of indignation to one of shrill hysteria. And it soon spilled over onto Buckhurst, who was accused of betraying the Earl's interest and character. Leicester's suspicion of Buckhurst rapidly increased, and the unfortunate envoy found himself under the same cloud of disapproval as Secretary Wilkes. Nor did he fare any better in attempting to reconcile Norris to the Governor-General. The Dutch very much wanted to retain the expert services of the colonel, but the latter held that his commander-in-chief regarded him as "a fool, a coward, and a hinderer of all services." Leicester was steady in pressing for Norris' recall (and replacement by Pelham) as a condition of his return. Buckhurst found that there was little he could do to reduce the animosity which Hohenlohe in particular felt towards the English governor or to quiet the internecine quarrels among the English leaders.[61]

But slowly circumstances drove the Queen to a decision on Leicester's return. By early June, Parma had about completed the blockade of Sluys, the vital port on the lower Scheldt, and the Dutch had set up a field force under Maurice to relieve the town. By now the Queen had finally decided to dispatch Leicester once again. This decision had not been arrived at easily; Wilkes had forthrightly opposed Leicester's return as like-

[60] *CSPF*, XXI(iii), 41-42, 48-50, 79, 83, 95.

[61] *Ibid.*, 37-40, 69-70, 74, 93, 99; BL, Add. Ms. 48,127, ff. 1-14; BL, Add. Ms. 19,398, ff. 77-78.

ly to be disastrous, and Buckhurst had tentatively sketched out a scheme of government to be adopted if the Earl did not return. The Earl angrily asserted that such a scheme was merely a blind for Buckhurst's own ambitions to take his place. Buckhurst indignantly denied any such ambitions, but to Walsingham he confided his doubts that the Earl could successfully master the headstrong States.[62]

Leicester had blown hot and cold about a return. Writing from Bath in April, in a perfect passion of self-pity, he had asked Walsingham to procure his discharge from the Low Countries assignment, if such a favor could be obtained for "so outcast a person." Later, in a calmer mood, he expressed his willingness to take up the burden again; but he needed at least £10,000 from the Crown. When the Queen offered to make a loan only on the condition of repayment within the year, the Earl declared his heart more than half broken, and asked Walsingham to press for his release from the office. A month later he was still insisting on the need for a full loan and for an immediate supply of £3,000. The Queen was finally willing to lend £6,000, to be repaid within two years; Leicester proposed as assurance his leases of the sweet wines and of alienation fines.[63]

The Earl's public instructions were issued on 20 June. He was to insist on full authority over fiscal matters and power to issue edicts with penal force. Ironically—after her fury of the previous year—the Queen was content that Leicester should have the absolute authority which the States had then bestowed on him. (Buckhurst was at this very time solemnly warning the Queen against any move to assert Leicester's supreme authority; the jealousy of the States-General, which regarded itself as successor to Philip, was so great that only a popular rising could give the Earl power.)[64]

[62] *CSPF*, XXI(iii), 40, 79, 86-88, 94, 100-1; BL, Cotton Mss., Galba D I ff. 49-50, 58, 104-10.

[63] BL, Harl. Ms. 287, f. 22; *CSPF*, XXI(iii), 20-21, 69-70; *Hatfield*, III, 265. For Leicester's mortgage, see PRO, SP 15/30/24 April 1587. Ultimate foreclosures on his lands amounted to £28,000.

[64] *CSPF*, XXI(iii), 121-23; BL, Cotton Mss., Galba C XI 60-62.

The Queen had also given way so far as to make a £15,000 loan to the States (they had asked for £50,000). But the sting in the instructions lay in the clauses which commanded the Earl to press very hard to incline the States towards peace. He was to emphasize the heavy burdens that war entailed, the poor chances at success, and, if necessary, to threaten a separate English peace. Count Maurice and Hohenlohe were to be given private assurances that their interests would be protected.

Leicester was accompanied by reinforcements of 3,000 foot and a supply of money for pay. He was enthusiastically received at his first landing in late June and met by Maurice, but the skies very quickly clouded over and within a few days his letters sounded an all-too-familiar note. They rang with complaints against Buckhurst, Wilkes, Norris, and the Dutch leaders. The States-General's open disrespect was much marked and wondered at; no man of his standing had been so dealt with as he was by Wilkes and Norris for a hundred years. Wilkes indeed soon found himself in the Fleet prison, and Norris was summoned before the Privy Council, while Buckhurst was confined to his house. Hohenlohe refused to see or to serve under Leicester, and remained sulking in his tent at Gertruydenburg. The Treasurer, Shirley, reported that of the £30,000 he brought over with him (presumably in May) only £3,000 remained by 15 July; £8,000 had been spent before he left England; the Merchants-Adventurers were refusing a loan. Leicester wrote that the £26,000 he brought with him was similarly diminished to about £3,000; the States refused to find money because they believed that the Queen was about to desert them. A month of such ill-tempered wrangling ended with the fall of Sluys. Leicester heaped the blame on Buckhurst and Wilkes and their Dutch confederates and on the States. Norris he pursued with unrelenting animosity, comparing him again with the late Sussex and declaring that he would have lost his head in Henry VIII's time for such behavior.[65]

[65] *CSPF*, XXI(iii), 128-29, 151-54, 170-72, 174-75, 186-87, 188, 189-90, 195-96, 196-97, 199-200, 206-8, 213-15, 232-33; BL, Harl. Ms. 287,

What followed the fall of Sluys was pretty much anticlimax. There was no hope of putting an army in the field this year and most of the Earl's efforts were expended in continuing skirmishes with the States-General. He demanded control of finances and freedom from limitations of his power to collect taxes. And in September the States-General did formally re-affirm his authority as Governor-General under the terms orig-inally stated, but it was a hollow victory since they chose to interpret this as a delegation of power by them. None of these exchanges were very meaningful since the central issue be-tween the Dutch and English governments was now the peace negotiations with Parma, which are discussed at length below. After smouldering damply for a year, the negotiations had sud-denly fired up in early summer and, as we have seen, Leicester had been instructed to press the States to join in them. But he had rather cravenly evaded this instruction and not until the end of the summer was it rather obliquely reported to the States-General. Rumors of the negotiations abounded every-where in the provinces, and Leicester learned of their progress through unofficial channels before any letters from Court ar-rived to confirm them. To make things worse, Oldenbarnevelt secured copies of Leicester's original instructions of June, which made it clear that the Queen contemplated negotiations with Parma even before the Earl returned. Many now believed that the treaty was already signed, including the cession of the cautionary towns to Spain. At home too the Earl's prestige had been shaken and the possibilities of peace seemed more than ever alluring to the Queen. "I never saw Her Majesty's dispo-sition so unfit for war as at present," wrote an informant from Court.[66]

Leicester by now was a tired, sick, and desperate man, and in early September he was reminding Burghley of the Queen's

f. 32; BL, Add. Ms. 14,028, ff. 94-99; BL, Cotton Mss., Galba D I ff. 139-41, 227-29.

[66] *CSPF*, XXI(iii), 230-32, 234-35, 244-46, 272, 285, 302-10; BL, Cotton Mss., Galba D I ff. 230-31, 244-46, 268-73; *ibid.*, D III ff. 10-13; BL, Harl. Ms. 287, f. 41; *ibid.*, 6994, ff. 88-89; BL, Add. Ms. 48,129, no foliation.

promise that he should not stay more than three months. He asked for a replacement (recommending Lord Admiral Howard), to arrive not later than the end of October. Elizabeth had in fact already decided on his return but wished not to act so suddenly as to give the appearance of abandoning the Low Countries. The Earl's actions from this time on were merely rear-guard maneuvers, enlivened by some final skirmishes with Hohenlohe and by a more serious effort to leave an English party established behind him. But in fact Leicester had lost control over all the States forces in Holland and Zealand, and the English forces were concentrated in the cautionary towns, Ostend, and Utrecht. Pro-English forces existed only in the rural provinces (Overyssel and East Friesland) and in a few scattered garrisons in North Holland. The Dutch leaders had by now effectually established a regime which stood on its own feet, ignoring—indeed flouting—any authority which the English general claimed.[67]

Leicester made his unlamented departure at the beginning of December (the States forbore to send a delegation to bid him farewell). The entourage of hopeful dependents who had thought to make their fortunes in the enterprise were scattered in disappointment—Pelham to death; Bingham back to Connaught, and North back to his Cambridgeshire estates. Lord Willoughby was left to take on the command of the English forces, but with express prohibition against interference in political matters. Only Robert Sidney and Sir William Russell remained at their garrison posts, still looking to the Earl as their patron.[68]

Leicester's second return from the Low Countries was, if anything, more ignominious than his first. He had failed at the one central military task he was sent to perform: the relief of Sluys. His credit with the Dutch, once so great, was so dissipated that, as one correspondent wrote, the States object

---

[67] *CSPF*, XXI(iii), 302-7, 330-31, 346-47, 355-57, 367-68, 371-73, 399-401, 427-29; BL, Cotton Mss., Galba D III ff. 62-64, 139.

[68] BL, Cotton Mss., Galba D III ff. 233-34, 289-90; BL, Add. Ms. 14,028, ff. 70-71; *CSPF*, XXI(iii), 319, 388, 433, 452; *ibid.*, XXI(iv), 399-400.

seemed to be to tire out the Earl and "make him drop this morsel." Certainly they succeeded, for the Earl went home full of anger at the States and thoroughly convinced that he was the victim of disloyalty and of self-regarding greediness on every hand.[69]

Certainly the purposes envisaged when the Treaty of Nonsuch was drawn up in the summer of 1585 were not realized. Leicester had not provided that stirring and effective leadership for which so many Dutchmen had longed and which the glittering English milord had seemed to promise. The Spanish advance had been slowed, although not halted, but no one ascribed that to the skill of Leicester or to English valor. Leicester had totally failed to deal with that problem—to recur again in succeeding centuries—of coordinating the actions of an English expeditionary force with those of a continental ally within a comprehensive strategy. Nor had he succeeded in rearing any structure of mutual confidence between Englishmen and Dutchmen; if anything, their suspicions were deeper and more bitter in 1587 than two years earlier.

In fact, the conditions on which the alliance had initially been built were fast changing, and one cannot avoid the feeling that during Leicester's second tour of duty the eyes of all the principal actors were turning away from the immediate events in the Low Countries to other horizons. It was the Spanish advance in the Low Countries and the perilous disorganization of their defense which had shaped the treaty of Nonsuch. In the two years following, the momentum of Parma's advance, which had swept him to the high-water mark of Antwerp, began to ebb. The attention of his royal master was being drawn elsewhere; from early 1587, at least, Spanish energies were being channelled more and more into preparations for the *impresa d'Inglaterra*. And at the same time Philip was concentrating more and more attention on the worsening crisis in France, where the Catholic League sought to reduce Henry III to their control and thereby to bar Henry of Navarre from the French throne. The English, in turn, were in-

[69] See Leicester's defense of his actions in BL, Cotton Mss., Galba D III 257-60; *CSPF*, XXI(iii), 285.

creasingly preoccupied with the possibility of invasion, and Drake's two expeditions—to the Indies and to the Iberian coasts—were a vigorous response. At home the preparation of defense and the accumulation of materiel became more and more important.

And in the Low Countries, as suggested above, a new leadership was emerging which sought to control the destinies of the provinces by their own efforts and through their own institutions. Leicester noted rather irritably the growing—to him, irrational—confidence that the Dutch could stand on their own feet, that England needed them as much as they needed her. It would be pressing too far into the future to see the events of 1585-1587 as the beginning of the "Dutch Republic," but certainly the wresting of power from the Earl and his nominees by the Oldenbarnvelt-Nassau combination in 1586 and 1587 was the first success of this new leadership. At least one shrewd English observer, Wilkes, had observed something of the true nature of Dutch society and politics.[70] Writing at the time of Leicester's return, the Secretary pointed out that the real rulers were the *vroetschap*, the chief burghers, from whom the local magistracies and the States were recruited. They feared the Earl and would bitterly oppose him; those who argued that he could rouse the commonalty against them were wrong. The magistrate class had too tight a hold for that, as Orange had realized; he had carefully trimmed his sails so as to collaborate closely with these natural leaders of Dutch society. What was emerging by late 1587 was a regime built on just this kind of collaboration between the Nassaus and the regent class led by Oldenbarnvelt. Even Leicester, before he left, realized the power of the regents, although he saw Maurice and Hohenlohe as stalking horses for, rather than as collaborators with, the States of Holland and Zealand. With a growing self-confidence, with an expanding wealth (noticed by all observers), and with the opportunity offered by the pause in the Spanish drive, they had the chance to find their own feet, to establish a regime which would not be a mere

[70] *CSPF*, XXI(iii), 162-66; BL, Harl. Ms. 285, f. 294, and Cotton Mss., Galba C XI 149-50, D I 151-59, D III 190-92.

protégé of some foreign sovereign, an updated replay of Charles V's era. What this spelled out for Anglo-Dutch relations was the necessity for a military collaboration between two governments rather than the maternal solicitude of a powerful protectress for a feeble ward.

Leicester's resignation of his Low Countries post in December 1587 led to an almost immediate improvement in Anglo-Dutch relations. Once his prickly *amour-propre* was removed from the scene, both English and Dutch officials could take steps to put their relationships on a better grounding. The Queen, increasingly preoccupied with the approaching Spanish threat and forced to spend money on her sea forces, wished to economize in the Low Countries and was amenable to any suggestion which accomplished this. Such a policy meant the liquidation of what remained of Leicester's establishment in the Low Countries.[71]

Initially, things ran on in their old ruts; the Queen wrote letters backing the recalcitrant magistracy of Utrecht and the obstinate governor of North Holland, Sonoy. Willoughby complained in familiar terms of the increasing power of the Nassau party. In January an act of the States-General reorganized the executive slightly by vesting power in a Council of State which, with the English general and the English counsellors, was to have authority; Killigrew saw this as a deliberate snub to Leicester.[72]

One result of these moves was a quarrel between Russell, the governor of Flushing and an admitted dependent of the Earl, and Maurice over control of the island of Walcheren. Another was an effort by the States to oust Sonoy, the Leicestrian governor of North Holland. The States-General and Prince Maurice stood firm against all protests from London. There was a confrontation of wills for a short time, but each side displayed signals of reconciliation and finally in late March the Queen yielded and told Sonoy (from whom Leicester's resignation was still a secret) to make terms; similar advice was given to the other recalcitrant captains, and signifi-

[71] *CSPF*, XXI(iv), 412-13.   [72] *Ibid.*, 20, 21-22, 33-34, 34-35.

cantly John Norris was to be sent on a mission of conciliation. Leicester's resignation, which had been executed in December 1587, was now officially proclaimed by the States and their act, vesting power in a Council of State, made public.[73]

From then on, the English retreat was steady. England now badly needed active support from its allies; it was imperative that Dutch ships take action to blockade the Low Countries coasts so as to prevent Parma's making any move to meet a fleet coming from Spain; Maurice was willing to perform his part of this bargain, but hinted rather strongly that he could not guarantee his sailors' loyalty if English opposition to his house continued. The Queen reemphasized her desire for conciliation in the Low Countries and forbade any more dabbling in the internal affairs of the provinces. There was grumbling, but to no avail, from the deserted partisans of the Earl, who now found themselves helpless before the assertion of Nassau power. Willoughby, who still regarded Leicester as his patron, gradually adapted to the new situation and sensibly argued that an ambassador be credited to what was now essentially an ally rather than a dependent. In October, a month after the Earl's death, a coup at Utrecht wiped out the last contingent of the pro-Leicester Low Countries adherents. The liquidation of the late governor's schemes was complete. More important were the strong footings now laid for effective cooperation between the two independent allies—the Queen and the States. Elizabeth had come to recognize the coming of age of the new Dutch regime.[74]

MORE IMMEDIATELY, relations between the English Crown and the States were deeply disturbed by the train of negotiations with Parma set in motion by Elizabeth. The beginnings of this effort of the Queen can be dated back to the very first months of alliance. When Leicester set off in December 1585, he wrote to Walsingham, "I perceive by your message your peace with Spain will go fast on, but this is not the way." Early in the

[73] *Ibid.*, 51, 61, 94-95, 115-16, 132-34, 139-40, 204, 232, 247, 253.
[74] *Ibid.*, 277, 358-59, 501-2; *ibid.*, XX, 224-25.

new year, Leicester heard the first of repeated rumors of peace negotiations between England and Parma. He got some solid information from Burghley at the end of March. Behind the rumors there was a basis of fact. There were stirrings in both London and Antwerp for the throwing out of peace feelers. At the English Court the main mover was Croft, the Comptroller of the Household, who had in Mendoza's time been the Ambassador's main source of information and who had always pressed a pro-Spanish line. In Belgium it was Champagny, the Catholic nobleman who had played a large part in the States government in the late 1570's and who had been at one stage its representative in England. Although a confidant of Parma's, he was the last vestige of the old noble opposition to Spanish domination.[75]

The agents who were used by both sides were merchants who still kept open some limited contacts between Antwerp and London. In May 1586, after a series of verbal messages passing through several intermediaries, Croft dealt directly with Andreas deLoo, a Dutch merchant in London, and he was to play a leading role in the months to come. Croft had made Hatton, Cobham, Mildmay, and two other (unnamed) councillors privy to his dealings by then, as well as Burghley. DeLoo went off in May orally instructed to seek an interview with Parma. Another merchant, Graffini, left at the same time, without the blessing of Burghley; his mission was made known to Walsingham and Leicester by the Queen, but apparently they did not know of the more prestigious deLoo mission. The activities of both deLoo and Graffini were public knowledge in the rebel provinces within a few weeks.[76]

It was not until well into June that deLoo saw Parma, who in the meantime had received Graffini and sent him back to London, accompanied by Croft's relative, Bodenham, with a message. DeLoo's message was largely a defense of Elizabeth's policy in the Low Countries but indicated a willingness to lis-

[75] CSPF, XX, 192; Bruce, Correspondence of Dudley, 200.
[76] See CSPF, XXI(ii), 143-44, for short history of these negotiations up to August 1586; see also CSPF, XXI(iv), 145-46; Bruce, Correspondence of Dudley, 200, 231, 289-90.

ten to any agent whom Parma accredited. The upshot of this flurry of criss-crossing messages was a letter from the Queen herself in July to the Prince of Parma, crisply and firmly reiterating her aims—her safety and her neighbors' freedom from misery and slavery—but expressing her willingness to hear any reasonable terms which safeguarded these goals.[77]

This letter brought about a halt in further communications. Not until October did Parma reply (through deLoo); he expressed indignation at the Queen's position but left a loophole by saying that all he asked of her was the assurance that, if the Prince sent an emissary, he would be received. DeLoo worked hard to reestablish a contact and finally was able to deliver a message from Burghley to Parma in December. He was to say that the Queen wished to see Spanish authority reestablished in the Low Countries but only after the removal of foreign troops and the restoration of the ancient privileges of the provinces.[78]

By this time the States were thoroughly upset by the repeated rumors of these negotiations, confirmed to some extent by the Queen's own message to them through Heneage, admitting that she had received overtures to which, as a sensible ruler, she would listen. Rumors of these negotiations were widespread; they were openly discussed at Paris and used as an argument to persuade Henry III to break with England. They were current as far away as Copenhagen. At the beginning of 1587 the States expressed very vigorously their opposition to any negotiations with Spain. But the Queen kept open her lines of communication. In March there was an exchange; deLoo presented Parma with a statement of the Queen's demands: she would not press the toleration issue further than the King could concede in conscience and honor. She proposed oblivion for all past disputes between England and Spain in the Indies, Portugal, or elsewhere; reimbursement of her expenditures in the Low Countries; the removal of foreign troops (at least to frontier garrisons); and a general amnesty with the restoration of native officials to offices—and, finally,

---

[77] BL, Add. Ms. 22,563, f. 23; *CSPF*, XXI(ii), 45, 56-59, 78-80.
[78] *CSPF*, XXI(ii), 202, 276.

no Inquisition. Parma at about the same time, through Champagny, let Croft know that he could not negotiate on the question of religion and could not send an agent to England, but would be willing to send one to a neutral place to meet agents of the Queen.[79]

The Queen was disappointed by Parma's reservation of the religious issue but, as we saw above, she did move to press the States to join in the negotiation, using the Pacification of Ghent as a basis for discussion. Parma seemed to make some slight concession on religion in the next round of exchanges and the Prince talked of nominating commissioners and urged the Queen to do the same.[80]

The siege of Sluys belied Parma's stated desire for a truce (to be agreed upon after the commissioners met), but its loss heightened Elizabeth's eagerness for peace, and by the end of July 1587 Croft could report a slate of English envoys to be sent, and deLoo responded with a similar list from Parma. On 3 September Burghley drafted instructions for the mission, but the Queen hesitated about actually dispatching it. She did, however, continue to press the indignant States (who complained that the names of the commissioners were common knowledge in the Low Countries) and wrote of peace by Michaelmas. She seemed to believe in the sincerity of Philip and Parma. The Duke became increasingly skeptical of the Queen's intentions and returned to the field to lead his army. At home even Walsingham urged Leicester to dispose the hearts of the Netherlanders to give ear to a peace, "seeing that both we and they are so inapt for war." The Queen sought to blame the delay on the States and declared that if Parma would agree to the meeting and to a cessation of arms during discussions, she would send off her representatives without a day's delay. On 3 November instructions were finally issued to the Queen's commissioners; they were to proceed to Ostend, there to negotiate cessation of arms, and, that done, go on to

[79] *Ibid.*, XXI(i), 304; *ibid.*, XXI(ii), 16-17, 320-21, 343-45, 428-29, 435-37; BL, Cotton Mss., Galba C XI 114-18.
[80] *CSPF*, XXI(i), 369; *ibid.*, XXI(iii), 27-29, 41-42, 53-55, 161-62.

Bourbourg to treat of peace. At the same time, Dr. John Herbert was sent to the States to press them to join the Bourbourg conference. But the actual meeting hung fire as the English tried desperately to find out more about Spanish naval preparations. The Brussels authorities continued to give bland assurances that they knew nothing of the "Armada," that the English commissioners would be welcome, and that negotiations for a cease-fire would be the first item on the agenda. So things stood at the end of 1587.[81]

English commissioners had been appointed, but matters stuck at that point until a proposal from Champagny at the end of January 1588 to discuss a meeting place set things in motion again. In February the English commissioners made ready for departure and instructions were drawn up by Burghley. The mission was headed by the Earl of Derby, accompanied by Lord Cobham, Comptroller Croft, Sir Amyas Paulet (now a Privy Councillor), and Dr. Valentine Dale. Both Dale and Paulet had served as ambassadors at Paris.[82]

The gist of their instructions was to seek a general cease-fire, including a halt in Spanish naval preparations, but, failing that, a local armistice for the English-held towns. As to the substance of the treaty, they should aim at restoring relations as they were between Henry VIII and Charles V. Croft, the original sponsor of the whole effort and the most optimistic of the envoys, envisaged the general restoration of the ancient amity and a balancing off of individual claims at a later session. It was nearly the end of February before the commissioners actually crossed to Ostend, but they found no delegation awaiting them and, when they were able to contact the Duke, found him willing to concede virtually nothing. There was deadlock over the place of meeting, the English holding out for Ostend (in Dutch hands with an English garrison), the Spanish for

---

[81] *Ibid.*, XXI(iii), 215-17, 243-44, 287-89, 318-19, 347, 365-67, 375-76, 398, 399, 414-17, 439, 457-58; PRO, SP 12/202/56, 12/203/37, 12/204/44; BL, Cotton Mss., Galba D I 244-46; D II, ff. 3, 4, 6-9; D III, ff. 10-13, 145-52; BL, Add. Ms. 48,084, ff. 62-64.
[82] *CSPF*, XXI(iv), 25, 43-45; PRO, SP 12/208/69.

some place in their territories. It took a month to sort this out and come to an arrangement for assembling at a place near Nieuport. Parma now balked at any armistice other than a merely local one with the English garrisons, and to this the Queen agreed. Then the Duke made further difficulties over the place. By now Cobham and Dale were becoming very skeptical of Parma's intentions and the former asked for revocation. Croft then took the ball in his own hands and went off for a private and unauthorized interview with the Duke, proposing to the latter a restoration of the *status quo ante*, Holland and Zealand being granted such toleration as the King could square with his conscience. The Duke was skeptical of Croft's powers and through Champagny suggested the appointment of Buckhurst (an idea which may have been put in his head by Croft, who had been clamoring for the same appointment). The Queen indeed repudiated the Comptroller's rash effort, but Dale was now able (early May) to report the appearance of a Spanish commission of adequate scope, including the making of an armistice for the four garrison towns only, renounceable on six days' notice. The Queen backed away to a demand for an armistice covering England and Scotland as well, and she abandoned even this a little later. Spain would not even yield a cessation (4 June) except for the four towns, thus leaving her free to move against England.[83]

Still the Queen pressed on with the negotiation, and at a conference at Burghley's on 10 June it was resolved to abandon any attempt at a truce but to continue with the treaty. They were to seek free exercise of religion for ten years, the removal of foreigners from the provinces, and the restoration of the ancient order of government. A note by Burghley of the same date restates pretty much the same terms; the best conditions for peace would be the restoration of the old liberties and freedom of conscience publicly exercised, plus repayment of

---

[83] *CSPF*, XXI(iv), 96-98, 130-31, 171-72, 206-7, 211-12, 256-58, 264-65, 295-96, 311-12, 314-15, 322-25, 329-31, 338-39, 348-49, 350-51, 363-64, 368-70, 386-88, 439-40, 456-58, 461-62; BL, Add. Ms. 22,563, ff. 26-27.

the Queen's outlays. The Queen's instructions of 14 June reduced the period of toleration to two years (with further extensions to be referred to the States-General). But in fact the commissioners at Bourbourg were still sparring over the preliminary question of a truce. Finally, in July, the Queen gave in so far as to command Dale to see the Duke privately and to tax him with the assertion in Cardinal Allen's recent book proclaiming a holy war by the Pope and Spain to overthrow the Queen. The Duke solemnly denied all knowledge of such a book. This was too much even for the Queen, and she indignantly ordered her envoys to ask for a plain declaration from the Duke that he had no direction from Philip and the Pope to invade her realm and depose her. Her somewhat inconsistent second demand was that Parma promise not to move against England during the time of treaty or for twenty days thereafter. This instruction was written on 17 July (OS), by which time the Armada was nearing the English coast. A week later, with the actual arrival of the Spanish fleet, the Queen finally revoked her commissioners.[84]

To the modern historian, aware not only of later events but also privy to Spanish intentions, this whole episode has a whiff of Lewis Carroll about it. By the time the commissioners set off, Spanish preparations at home and in the Low Countries were far advanced and by April the Queen expected a Spanish fleet to sail a month later.[85] Yet she persistently kept the parley alive when the commissioners themselves absolutely despaired; it was the Queen, usually so tough and unrelenting a diplomat, tenaciously struggling for every slight advantage, who calmly gave away one bargaining point after another, reducing the whole treaty to a kind of parody.

In seeking to understand the situation, we need to remember first of all the very imperfect state of English intelligence; there had been so many false alarms in the past of Spanish fleets which had proved to be mere phantoms. Secondly, the

---

[84] *CSPF*, XXI(iv), 103-4, 471-74, 485-88, 494-95; *ibid.*, XXII, 32-38, 51-54, 81.

[85] *Ibid.*, XXI(iv), 254.

Queen may still have believed what she told Dutch deputies in February that Philip's losses at war, on the seas and in the Indies, plus his advancing age, would be sufficient inducement to bring him to the peace table.[86] This seems to have been the Queen's conception of Drake's recent exploits—warning shots loud enough to dissuade the Catholic King from the endless demands of continuing war. Thirdly, the Queen—and Burghley—would have settled for a peace which gave precious little to the revolted provinces. The terms they were discussing as acceptable to them in the spring of 1588 would have turned back the clock to 1550 (with the modification of a short-term toleration for the Protestants of Holland and Zealand). Their ideas of a satisfactory peace were almost identical with the proposals which they had put forward well over a decade earlier in the first years of the insurrection. The repeated and vehement statements by the States-General and by the provincial states—that compromise over religion, and thereby any restoration of Philip's authority, was totally ruled out—had fallen on deaf ears. It may have been that discouragement born of the last two years' experience and the pessimistic prophecies of the disappointed Leicesterians had convinced the English leaders that the provinces had no option but a virtual capitulation.[87]

Finally, there had always been a hope that Parma might break with his royal master and collaborate with the Flemish magnates in casting off Spanish control. This belief had rested on the assumption that Farnese resented the rejection of his claims to the Portuguese throne. These were the vainest of dreams; yet it is true that, as late as March, Parma was urging on Philip a peace with England, emphasizing his doubts about the whole Armada strategy and the inadequacy of his own resources. By May, however, he had bowed to the royal will and accepted the task of spinning out the negotiations simply in order to win time, not to come to a settlement. At any rate, it does seem certain that until well into the summer the Queen—and possibly the Lord Treasurer—continued to hope that the

[86] *Ibid.*, 118-20; BL, Cotton Mss., Galba C XI 79-81.
[87] See Walsingham's views in BL, Add. Ms. 48,127, f. 101.

negotiations would yield a real compromise which could bring the misery of wasteful war to an end.

AFTER THE DEATH of Anjou, the gap between English and French policy steadily widened. France now faced a succession crisis and Henry III was under ever-stronger pressure from the Guises and from the new Catholic League to suppress the Huguenots and their leader, the heir, Henry of Navarre. As we have seen, their influence was decisive in his rejection of the States offer of sovereignty in the spring of 1585, and their links with Spain grew stronger all the time.

England's response was two-pronged. On the one hand, there was continuing, although obviously ineffective, pressure on the French King to maintain his alliance with England and its corollary—freedom of worship for the Huguenots. Elizabeth went so far as to offer Henry aid against the Guises and their foreign backers; Sir Thomas Leighton was sent off on a special mission to urge this. His response was evasive, and indeed the Queen was already acting on her own to aid Navarre, who had sent a desperate call for a common effort against a common foe. In April 1585 the Queen in characteristic fashion dredged up a well-worn precedent and wrote to Duke Casimir, seeking to employ his services once again. He replied favorably but estimated his total costs would ‘be £100,000. In the meantime the King had thrown himself into Guise's hands and war had broken out. The Queen with her usual financial caution was ready to lend 100,000 crowns in Bremen, provided the German princes made a contribution. But matters hung fire; the English envoy in Germany, Willoughby, got a cold reception at the Danish and German princely courts. In December Condé himself came to England, but it was not until February 1586 that the Queen finally agreed to lend £15,000 (half of what the Huguenots asked for). Stafford, in Paris, thought the money would be better expended on direct subsidies to the Huguenot forces in the field and apparently got a small amount out of the Queen for this purpose. In the meantime the English Ambassador and the French Council continued their tug of war, the first seeking to pull the King away from the Catholic party, the councillors seeking to persuade him to break the alliance with England.[88]

Negotiations with Casimir and with the German princes dragged on inconclusively. Casimir blew hot and then cold, asking for more money before he would move so that Palavicino, the English agent, had to leave the Palatinate without an agreement. The court of Navarre failed to provide its share of the money altogether and the Queen had to raise her contribution (but only on condition of German funds being added); even then Casimir again hesitated before finally taking the plunge. It was money ill-spent; Casimir, after one or two more attempts to blackmail the Queen, took so long to mobilize that it was October before he joined the Huguenots on the Loire. Within a month he had capitulated to royal forces, and French Protestant affairs were in the most terrible confusion. Early in 1588 Condé died and there were fears that Navarre would convert. The Queen refused to find any more money for the Protestants. Strafford, in his post-mortem of the reiters' capitulation emphasized the King's continuing hate for the League and the need to keep open a line to him. The King himself wished the Queen to persuade Navarre to a conversion, an act which would cut the ground out from underneath the League. The Queen responded by a last desperate effort to nerve up the feeble Henry when she sent Leighton once again in June of 1588 with a ringing exhortation to play the part of a king by declaring Guise a traitor. Parma, she declared, was too weak to intervene. It was to no avail and, as the Armada approached the English coast, France was quite firmly in the grip of the Catholic and pro-Spanish Guises. The last ghostly hope of an Anglo-French combination, for nearly two decades a great object of Elizabethan policy, faded away at the moment of supreme danger.[89]

[88] *CSPF*, XIX, 393-97, 400-1, 408-10, 434-35, 447-48, 584-85, 588-89; *ibid.*, XX, 119, 194-95, 216-17, 238, 251-53, 255-57, 377-78, 417-19, 429-31, 462-63, 491-92, 554.

[89] *Ibid.*, XX, 514-16, 595-96, 675-76, 695-96; *ibid.*, XXI(i), 81-82, 111-12, 134-45, 282, 396, 428, 478-83, 519-28, 573-77, 633-36.

In this last phase of relations with Henry III Elizabeth had played a familiar set of cards—repeated efforts at alliance, on the one hand, meager subsidies for German mercenaries, on the other. The first was of no avail because events in France were quite beyond any leverage England could hope to exercise, while Henry III was equally helpless in the face of the Guisan party.

CHAPTER 15

ENGLAND AND

SCOTLAND, 1572-1588

INCREASINGLY, in the years after 1572, the attention of the English government was focussed on events across the Channel, and relations with the continental powers became the major theme of English policy. These new preoccupations overshadowed but by no means eclipsed the familiar long-term problems of Anglo-Scottish relations. During the years after 1572 that relationship was shaped in large part by events within the smaller kingdom, but, not surprisingly, these events often intersected the activities of the continental powers. In the 1570's Scottish affairs were more or less isolated from those of the Continent. This interval of relative quiet ended at the close of the decade with the arrival of Eṣmé D'Aubigny, James's French cousin, and the ensuing fall of the pro-English and strongly Protestant Regent Morton. From then until the eve of the Armada, Scottish affairs were extremely fluid, and the English government had to wage an unrelenting diplomatic campaign to checkmate French and Spanish efforts at intervention in Scotland. They were able to keep the struggle at a diplomatic level, although there was constant fear that it would escalate into a more violent form. In these years they had to learn how to deal with a new protagonist, the young James VI. From the beginning of the 1580's he began to assert his royal will; it was an uphill struggle for him with frequent setbacks. More than once it was English influence which checked his initiatives. But little by little he won a grudging respect from the English Court. Their own urgencies drove them to an accommodation with him, albeit on the most ungenerous terms. James, on his side, learned to accept present humiliations as a necessary sacrifice for the glittering future which lay before him in the succession to the English Crown. To understand these events we need to turn back to the year 1572.

THE DEATHS of Norfolk and Northumberland in that summer were the final acts in the complex of events which had begun with the intrigue to marry Mary to the Duke and ended with the unravelling of the Ridolfi plot. But in Scotland itself there remained a major piece of unfinished business. There the Castle of Edinburgh was still held in Queen Mary's name against the divided and feeble government of the Regent Mar. The "Castillians" were strongly based in the fortress and hoped to hold out long enough for French aid to reach them. The Regent's government lacked the means—in men, money, and arms—to besiege the Castle effectively, and their hold over the country at large was uncertain; both the Hamiltons and the Gordons held menacingly aloof.

The dangers to England were obvious enough as Burghley, in one of his comprehensive surveys, pointed out. As long as there was a live center of disaffection in Scotland, France and the Papacy would seek to assist the Marian party there; Mary herself would bend every effort to escape. France could not abandon her easily; pride, the maintenance of the old alliance, Guisan pressure, and fear that Spain would become Mary's patron all combined to keep French interest in Scotland alive. Hence an English intervention might all too easily provoke a French move—and just in these months the two countries were in the final stages of negotiating an alliance.[1]

Hence Elizabeth had to opt for a temporizing policy. A joint Anglo-French mission was to seek a truce to hold until

[1] *CSPSc*, IV, 160-62, 183-84.

the controversy as to who was rightful sovereign was dealt with by the rulers of England and France. At the same time the Queen offered the Castillians a guarantee of their rights in any settlement they accepted. The discovery of a plot between Mary's partisans and the Duke of Alva quickened French apprehensions about Spanish designs on Scotland and thereby strengthened Anglo-French cooperation. This policy was not wholeheartedly backed in the Council; Burghley, writing in April 1572, grumbled that the Queen, by forbearing direct aid to James's supporters and allowing their enemies to stand, achieved nothing—neither was the one any better nor the other any worse. The whole achievement—the labors and charges—of the last thirteen years might be lost.[2]

The upshot of this somewhat hesitant policy was a fragile truce signed at the end of July 1572. The Castillians had conceded very little: they would acknowledge the King's authority but not the Regent's, and they would continue to hold the Castle. In fact they were becoming desperate for lack of food and the truce was their best hope that somehow they could hang on until they had help from France.[3]

Events disappointed what were at best slender hopes. St. Bartholomew strengthened the hands of the Englishmen who were urging Elizabeth to destroy any possible Catholic foothold in Britain. Negotiations continued desultorily, but the death of the Regent Mar in early November and his replacement by the Protestant hard-liner, Morton, ended any prospect of agreement, and early in the new year the truce was broken. In February, Secretary Smith pressed the Queen to give the Regent military aid to reduce the Castle. Although Elizabeth characteristically proposed a letter which would accomplish the same end without any charge, she was finally convinced that she should send the required aid. The French were now preoccupied at home and unlikely to be able to intervene. Morton had been able to secure the formal submission of the Gordons and Hamiltons to James, and all was now clear for a final blow at the Castillians. Even after the commission to

[2] *Ibid.*, 165-67, 197-98, 207, 233-39, 272-74.
[3] *Ibid.*, 291.

Drury, the English commander, was drafted, Burghley hoped to negotiate, but Killigrew, in Edinburgh, resolutely declared that he would walk barefoot to Rome rather than take such a course. In April the Castle was summoned, and a month later (28 May), after heavy bombardment by English cannon, the starving garrison yielded. Of the two Marian leaders, one, Maitland, died of natural causes within a few days; the other, Grange, was hanged. The distractions of the French civil strife had delivered England from a threatening situation. The happy relationship which had been attained for a fleeting moment under the Moray regency seemed at last, after four turbulent years, to have been recovered. Scotland was in the control of a Protestant and pro-English government, dependent on English favor and support. That cooperation, on the basis of a common religion, which Burghley had heralded in the first year of the Queen's reign, now seemed to be realized.[4]

As early as June 1573, the Regent Morton called for the renewal of the amity established after the expulsion of the French; more particularly, he pushed forward a proposal for a league to maintain religion against the Council of Trent, offering the assistance of Scottish forces in case England were invaded. There is no indication that Elizabeth responded to these initiatives. They were repeated in slightly different form in January 1574, when Morton urged a larger alliance of all the "Christian princes and states who are professors of the true religion" under Elizabeth's leadership, aimed especially at the relief of the Prince of Orange and the Low Countries Protestants. In fact, there was by then no English resident at Edinburgh, Killigrew having left in October 1573, and he did not return until May of the next year.[5]

Killigrew's instructions when he went northwards again are a guide to the Queen's policy towards Scotland. He was to make careful inquiry as to any French intrigues in the country, especially any plot for spiriting away the young King. To Morton's overtures for a league, he was to give vaguely favorable answers, referring to the Queen's negotiations with Count

[4] *Ibid.*, 393-95, 443-44, 452, 488-89, 495-98, 514, 518-19, 571-72.
[5] *Ibid.*, 592-94, 638-39, 660-61.

Casimir, but stalling on any specific measures. While promising aid in case of necessity, he was to evade the Regent's requests for money, particularly for pensions, palming him off with a promise to write to the Queen.[6]

Killigrew's mission was a brief one; he was recalled in August 1574, having done little business. In several letters, there are hints of "a great matter" afoot. It is possible this was a plan for conveying James into England—a favorite scheme of the English government, but nothing came of it. There were also discussions, at the Queen's direction, of a project for returning Mary to Scotland for safekeeping. Walsingham, who conveyed the royal instructions, thoroughly disapproved of the scheme—"no less dangerous for him to accept . . . than to us to offer"—and strongly hinted that Killigrew should ensure its rejection. In addition to these bits of business, the English Ambassador mediated a quarrel between the Regent and the Earl of Argyll (a candidate for the regency, should Morton disappear) and also dealt with that great northern potentate, the Earl of Huntly. The Queen's policy was to hold the Regent politely at arm's length, giving him nothing more than fair words. This maintained her credit as an impartial arbiter among the rival Scottish factions, committed to no one of them rather than assuming the role of patron of a particular partisan regime. Killigrew disapproved of this policy, as did Walsingham. They would have preferred a league with the Regent and a system of pensions for the principal nobles. Pensions would come cheap, no more than £2,000 a year. And Scottish opinion, Killigrew warned, was chilling. The Scots felt that Elizabeth had used them at a time when she was endangered by events in France and now ignored them. He went on to warn that their dependence on England was by no means automatic; they were being wooed by the French and were willing to listen.[7]

But the Queen was unmoved by these representations, and, after Killigrew's return, relations drifted on in the same in-

[6] *Ibid.*, 663-64.
[7] *Ibid.*, 668, 678-79; *CSPSc*, V, 1-2, 5-7, 25, 27-28, 33, 34-35.

definite way. They were ruffled in 1575 by suspicions as to the pro-French sympathies of the Regent. Leicester and Walsingham, both admirers of Morton, became worried that he had been won over by the French, and the Queen was seriously enough disturbed to send Killigrew northwards once again in what was becoming an annual spring pilgrimage. Significantly, he was told this time to leave his Secretary, William Davison, behind as the Queen's agent. Killigrew was to soothe the Regent's feelings, excusing the Queen's long delay in responding to his proposals for a league, at the same time gently rejecting them, although assuring the Regent of her determination to protect Scotland. But the Ambassador was also to spy out the land and, if he found Morton too deeply alienated to be recovered, he was to find other allies among the Scots.[8]

Before Killigrew reached Edinburgh, a storm had blown up on the Borders, where the English wardens Forster and Russell had been captured by their Scottish counterpart and carried off prisoners to the Regent at Dalkeith. The Queen was very angry, took a high line, and insisted that the Regent meet with Huntingdon, the President of the Council in the North, to apologize. The matter was settled by early autumn and Morton declared to Huntingdon that he was Regent only to protect the Queen's interests, and Killigrew was able to return, as usual, at the end of the summer.[9]

There followed a long hiatus in formal diplomatic relations. Robert Bowes, the Treasurer of Berwick, relayed Scottish news to the Court, and there were occasional letters between the Regent and the English Queen or her ministers. There was little for Bowes to report for a long time. It was not until July 1577 that he warned of a confederation among Atholl, Ruthven, and Lindsay which was hostile to Morton; in October he was urging a mediatory mission to settle the differences between the Regent and his opponents. The Queen responded by appointing Bowes himself to this task in December and followed this up by sending the more senior Randolph

[8] *CSPSc*, V, 83, 112-13, 116-18, 118-19, 152-54.
[9] *Ibid.*, 165-75, 188-90, 190-95.

to join him in January 1578. His instructions are interesting since he was first to work for a reconciliation between Morton and his enemies, Argyll and Atholl. But if the Regent proved recalcitrant, the Ambassador was to make it plain that the Queen, fearing foreign intervention, would join with his enemies against the Regent. She dribbled out £2,000 for Randolph to use as "pensions" to those best-affected to her service. As a carrot to use with the Regent, the ambassadors were authorized to revive the proposals of 1573 for a league, although doing it in such a way as to make it seem a Scots initiative.[10]

Their mission came too late. Their first report home described the ill temper felt towards Morton; a few days later the Regent had fallen and the twelve-year-old King announced that he was assuming the government of the realm himself. The angry outburst from London which followed reveals a great deal of Elizabeth's own view of her relations with Scotland. Expressing her astonished displeasure at the dismissal of Morton, she insisted that no innovations should take place without her prior knowledge. Morton had taken the regency at her persuasion—and against his own will—and if Atholl and Angus had grievances against him, they should have been directed to the Queen, who had sent her agents specifically to mediate between them and the Regent. But tacitly yielding to the present situation, the Queen urged the young King to use Morton as his principal counsellor, since in her view he was too young to govern alone. For the moment there was a fragile coalition in Scotland which embraced both Morton and his rivals.[11]

The new Scottish regime hastened to respond by sending an agent to London. He was authorized to revive the old schemes for an alliance of mutual protection and a general religious league, but his real business was to find out what the state of affairs was among England, France, and the Low Countries, and whether war was in the offing. The new turn of affairs in Scotland coincided with the swing of English policy away from intervention in the Low Countries and the first recovery of

[10] *Ibid.*, 244-45, 252, 268-70.
[11] *Ibid.*, 275, 276, 279-80, 297-300, 316.

Spanish fortunes there with Don John's victory at Gembloux in January 1578.[12]

Elizabeth countered the Scottish initiatives with a generally favorable answer by accepting their proposals for alliance, but on condition that she receive a virtual veto on all foreign policy, and particularly on any marriage for the young King. The discussions went nowhere.[13]

From the initial fall of Morton in the spring of 1578 until the winter of 1580-1581 Scottish affairs remained in a dangerously fluid state. The former Regent made a partial recovery of power by joining a coalition with his enemies, but this fell apart in the summer of 1578, when Atholl and Argyll stayed at Edinburgh, denouncing the authority of the Parliament sitting at Stirling. Actual resort to arms was averted only by the intervention of the English ambassador, Bowes, who patched up a reconciliation. In May 1579 there was a new flare-up when Morton and Angus overthrew the Hamiltons, but they did not recover power at Court.[14]

A sudden change of direction took place with the arrival in September 1579 of a new actor on the Scottish scene. This was Esmé Stuart, Sieur D'Aubigny, a Lennox cousin of the King's, born and reared in France. His arrival was almost certainly no accident. As long ago as the summer of 1578, there had been rumors of his coming. He was accompanied to his ship at Dieppe by the Duke of Guise. His progress in the King's affections was very rapid. By October it was said he could be the second in the realm if he chose to conform to the reformed religion; the French Ambassador was already predicting his promotion to the earldom of Lennox and to the succession to the Scottish Crown after James. This undistinguished man was to prove the first in that series of favorites to whom James in the course of his life gave his entire confidence.[15]

Morton wavered uncertainly between cooperation with the new favorite and open opposition. In March 1580 D'Aubigny was created Earl of Lennox and given custody of the key for-

---

[12] *Ibid.*, 297-300.   [13] *Ibid.*, 309-13.
[14] *Ibid.*, 316-20; Camden, *Annals*, 229-30.
[15] *CSPSc*, V, 314, 354-57; PRO, Baschet, 29 Oct. 1579.

tress of Dumbarton. By April, Bowes was warning of a coming storm in Scotland which might destroy Morton altogether, and before the end of the month reported that the Earl would seek military support from the Queen. The alarmed English Court instructed Bowes to proceed to Edinburgh and to pull every string he could to weaken the new Earl of Lennox, stirring up the rival lords and the clergy, who were to be warned that D'Aubigny was a Guisan agent. Lennox himself announced his conversion to Protestantism and asserted his pro-English sympathies. All Bowes's efforts were to be diplomatic in character, and all that he had in the way of resources was a derisory £500. He did what he could, but Morton and his allies would not move without overt English aid. Bowes's attempts to reconcile the rival lords did not come to much, and he returned to Berwick. Bowes bluntly told his masters that unless the Queen gave Morton stronger backing, the Earl would have to make terms with his enemies.[16]

The Queen finally brought herself to write to Morton, but in such vague terms that the Earl came to despair of any meaningful assistance from her. Elizabeth's actions merely served to illustrate the proverb about barn doors and stolen horses. Morton's complaint that the Queen's actions served only to gain time was shared by Walsingham. The Earl now sought to make the best terms he could with the favorite, convinced that Elizabeth left him no alternative.[17]

The Queen in late August changed her tack and ordered Bowes to return to Edinburgh, to demand an audience of the King and Council from which D'Aubigny was to be excluded. He was to warn them that the favorite sought to admit the French and to overthrow religion, and to demand his dismissal—or at least his removal from the command of Dumbarton. But a supplementary instruction took much of the punch out of the earlier one by making it clear that Bowes was to persuade rather than to threaten and not to suggest the use of force until the Queen was convinced of its necessity.

[16] *CSPSc*, V, 334 (misdated 1579; should be 1580), 384-85, 386-88, 392-94, 394-96, 399-400, 400-402, 431-32, 441-44, 444-45, 449-51.
[17] *Ibid.*, 55-56, 469-70, 470-71, 480-81.

One weapon he was allowed to use was the hint—to be given privately—that the English Parliament might cut off James's rights in the succession.[18]

Bowes did what he was told, demanded audience, and then refused to give his message from the Queen unless Lennox absented himself. The Scottish Court in turn refused permission. There was deadlock for a time until James sent a messenger to England; this device served to prolong discussion, although it solved nothing. In fact, Lennox's position steadily strengthened through the fall, while that of Morton weakened. As early as September, Hunsdon, the governor at Berwick, had given the latter up as too weak a reed to lean on. Bowes had had some talk with Lord Ruthven, who was willing to act in the English interest but only if the Queen were willing to counter Lennox influence by the direct promotion of a marriage candidate.[19]

In November the Queen proposed to send her cousin, Hunsdon, to Edinburgh with somewhat milder instructions; rather than attack Lennox head-on, he was to press for reconciliation among all the lords. Only if this failed was Hunsdon to seek to build a pro-English party. But the whole train of events was cut short by the arrest of Morton on the last day of 1580.[20]

There followed six months of desperate maneuvers by the English in an effort to save the Earl. The English strategy was a traditional one. A pro-English party would be encouraged to raise its standards, with the promise of armed aid if necessary. It was a recipe used many times before, and the man sent to organize this strategy was the veteran Randolph. Hunsdon was issued a commission as captain of the English forces and Lord President Huntingdon set about levying 2,000 foot and 500 horse in his province. But early hopes of strong opposition to Lennox began to dim as early as February, and Randolph rather desperately suggested that it would be better to win over the favorite. He tried as best he could to build an opposition around the Earl of Angus. The more he labored, the more he feared. Invasion might only result in the flight of the

[18] *Ibid.*, 492-94, 495, 497.   [19] *Ibid.*, 499, 500-503, 514-16, 525-29.
[20] *Ibid.*, 569.

King to France, or to the fastnesses of Argyll; to scorch the countryside would only make enemies; and conquest was out of the question. In early March the Scottish Court got wind of these intrigues and ordered the detention of Angus.[21]

The Scots, on their side, suggested a conference of commissioners, a move which Bowes forecast would alienate any lingering loyalties to England among the dissident nobles. Throughout these weeks, Randolph, the man on the scene, was consistently more pessimistic than Hunsdon and Bowes at Berwick or Walsingham in London. The two former continued to urge armed action, while Randolph declared that after the discovery of the Angus plot, the negotiation was at an end, and that Elizabeth should accede to the Scots proposal for a conference of commissioners. Shortly afterwards, an attempt was made on Randolph's life, and the frightened envoy retired to Berwick. The Queen, torn between these two counsels, agreed at one time to a commission and then a few days later yielded to proposals for an advance over the border. This was a short-lived resolve, and four days later she ordered the disbanding of the forces assembled on the border.

The next two months were passed in desultory maneuvers; the Scots sent an unacceptable envoy, who was turned back at the border, while the English watched helplessly the judicial proceedings against the Earl of Morton. They ended with his execution in early June 1581, and the subsequent flight of Angus to England. The triumph of Lennox and his supporters was complete.[22]

The English Council had never wavered in the opinion put forward by Burghley in the previous September—that Lennox would break the friendship with England, bring about a French marriage, and in the end lead the young King to make a claim on the English throne. This would be a greater risk than his mother's attempt nearly two decades earlier, for his succession would end the nightmare of uncertainty; he would draw all discontented persons to support him; and the Scots

21 *Ibid.*, 572-74, 575, 584-85, 591-92, 606, 613, 619-20.
22 *Ibid.*, 623-24, 646-50, 655-56, 679-80, 681-83, 689-97; *ibid.*, VI, 14-23.

themselves had acquired—in the Low Countries and at home —far greater military skills. Nevertheless, Lennox was for the time being master of the situation, and Scottish policy, which had been safely insulated from extra-insular influences since 1573, was now quite out of English control. How had this come about?[23]

In part, the failure stemmed from the very strategy which the Queen had consistently followed since 1573. While backing the Regent Morton in a general way, she had refused to make him her particular protégé; by retaining her character as an impartial arbiter, who could act as mediator in a crisis— as in August 1578—she had kept all the Scottish lords to some extent on her leading strings. This policy had influenced her attitude towards Morton as his power began to wane, and up until the arrival of D'Aubigny it had not worked badly. His rivals were not radically anti-English, and the Queen was prepared to live with any Scottish regime which was not openly hostile.

But the rise of D'Aubigny altered the very frame of politics. His power did not rest on family or regional lordship, nor on combinations with other like magnates, but solely on the monarch's favor. Admittedly, the affection of the boy-king was a fragile base, for James was by no means master of the Scottish political world, but for the moment it sufficed. English intervention no longer involved merely an exercise in faction politics, of the kind so tediously familiar for a decade past. There now existed once again a royal will which had to be persuaded or constrained. Both English and Scottish politicians would have to learn how to deal with this phenomenon. For the time being, the situation was extremely unpredictable; no one had quite yet learned his cues.

Many of Elizabeth's ministers wished to use force, as they had done in 1559, in 1569 (after the murder of the Regent Moray), and again in 1573 at Edinburgh Castle. But there were many new factors in the situation at the end of the 1570's. There was now a major continental crisis, forced on

[23] *Ibid.*, V, 504.

England by events in the Low Countries. The fall of Morton from the Regency coincided with the first stage of this prolonged episode, and his final disappearance from the stage came just at the time when Elizabeth was making her supreme effort to secure a French alliance. It was also overshadowed by the growing menace of Spain, manifest in the two expeditions to Ireland, in 1579 and in 1580. These circumstances posed awkward problems. The fall of Morton had opened possibilities for revived French intervention in Scotland and the Guises—if not Henry III—took advantage of it. Somehow the French had to be denied any renewal of their influence in the North and yet won to alliance with the English. The Queen's worries about these incompatible desiderata show up in her repeated references to the Scottish problem in the trying months when she was urging Anjou to visit England.[24]

In any case, the arrest of Morton at the end of 1580 left English policy towards Scotland in a shambles. The all-powerful favorite was the dominant influence on the young King. Although the English councillors were convinced that Lennox was the instrument of the Guises who would reverse Scottish policy, revive the power of Mary and of the Catholics, and destroy the reformed religion, it is not clear that they were altogether justified in their fears. There certainly was correspondence with Guise, and some modest supplies of munitions reached James VI from his French cousin. But Lennox tried to keep open his other options as well. He wrote to Leicester in an attempt to persuade the English that he wished to maintain amity with them; he professed publicly the Protestant faith and attempted to build a party among the Presbyterian clergy. Certainly he does not seem, on the evidence, to have been either a strong personality or a skilled intriguer. His sole asset seems to have been his capacity for captivating the fancy of the young King just at the moment when James first asserted his independence as a monarch.[25]

[24] PRO, Baschet, 16 June, 26 July, 30 July 1579; *CSPF*, XV, 277.

[25] *CSPSc*, VI, 47-50, 51-52, 52-53, 54; David Calderwood, *History of the Church of Scotland* (Edinburgh, 1704), 89.

Lennox' rise to power had been more or less paralleled by the ascent of another adventurer—Captain James Stewart, a younger son of the Lord Ochiltree, who had returned from military service against the Spaniards in the Low Countries in 1579 and, catching the royal eye, had been rewarded with a series of promotions. Among other offices he held that of tutor to the mad Earl of Arran, who was head of the Hamilton house and a very distant cousin. He was able to parlay this post into an actual grant of the earldom of Arran, by two patents in April and October 1581. During the final attack on Morton, he was hand in glove with Lennox, but, victory won, the victors soon began to eye each other jealously. Already in October 1581 the English agent being sent northwards was instructed to try to widen the rift between Lennox and Arran, and by December Lennox was seeking the King's support against Arran.[26]

In the meantime, the English were buying time by a three-cornered negotiation among Elizabeth, James, and Mary Stuart. Mary took the initiative by proposing an association between James and her as joint sovereigns; in further discussion with Robert Beale, sent by Elizabeth to interview her, she offered—once legally re-established as queen—to relinquish her rights to her son. The English government was prepared to listen, partly as a ploy for continuing diplomatic discussions with Scotland, partly out of real fear that Mary might win protectors from abroad. If Mary were willing—as she asserted she was—to recede to an entirely passive role, they were willing to give her some kind of nominal voice in Scottish affairs and to allow her somewhat more freedom and comfort in England, where she would continue to reside. All this filled up the time while the English government watchfully waited for a break in Scottish politics.[27]

Lennox, in addition to his uneasy relations with Arran, was at odds with the Presbyterian clergy, thanks to a clumsy effort to appoint a protégé of his to the archbishopric of Glasgow. By June 1582 his nominee had been excommunicated by the

[26] *CSPSc*, VI, 42-43, 60-62, 93-94, 104-6.
[27] *Ibid.*, 55-56, 63-72, 74-77, 77-82, 85-89, 100-104, 106-7, 116-19.

presbyteries of Glasgow and Edinburgh, and the Duke himself was threatened with the same fate. Lennox in desperation declared his willingness to swear loyalty to the existing religion of state. But, before this matter went further, a coalition of discontented lords, headed by Ruthven, had already acted, seizing the person of the King and detaining both Lennox and Arran. It was a classical move in Scottish politics, all too unhappily familiar. Just how much the English knew in advance is not certain, but money was certainly being paid over to the conspirators, and Angus returned under English auspices. Lennox lingered on for a few months, hoping for some turn in his fortunes. The French Ambassador in London, regretfully reporting the fall of the favorite, admitted that there was nothing short of war which would enable France to help him and, since that was not to be thought of, nothing more than words could be summoned to his aid. English pressure was brought to bear, and the Duke actually departed, via England, at the very end of 1582.[28]

This was cause for satisfaction at the English Court, but there was still reason for much concern.[29] Lennox himself had gone, but he had left behind an anti-English party of some strength while the would-be pro-English element was disorganized. They looked to the Queen for financial and moral support and, unless she was willing to grant it, she could not expect their support. The next year was largely consumed in an attempt to create a viable English party and to recover some effective control over the Scottish King. Even though his evil counsellor had gone, he was restive and little disposed to settle into the role of an English dependent. The happy days when a pro-English regent, needful of English backing, could be counted on to be duly regardful of English interests had ended.

The first phase of Anglo-Scottish relations in this awkward era was a contest with the French; Henry III was represented

[28] Calderwood, *History*, 126, 127, 129-30; *CSPSc*, VI, 184-85; PRO, Baschet, 13 and 14 Sept. 1582.

[29] *CSPSc*, VI, 230.

by a resident at Edinburgh and Fénélon, the Ambassador at London, had requested and received permission to go north. He encountered the Duke of Lennox in northern England as the latter travelled into exile. He dealt with James at length, pressing his mother's claims to some kind of association and— so the English ambassadors feared—offering James a French pension. The English agents—Bowes and Davison—had at their disposal £1,000, which they had paid out as wages for the guards which the Ruthven conspirators placed around James. They had promised an additional 2,000 marks. Typically, Elizabeth balked at this last sum, and the unlucky ambassadors had to beg for it, only to have it disallowed.[30]

Discussions on policy continued at the English Court. The Council boldly proposed to their mistress that she budget £10,000 a year for Scotland, half for the King, the balance to go to the leading nobles and the ministers of the Kirk. The Queen was quick to quash any rash expenditure of her money. What her hopes were are summed up in a memorandum of May. The Queen was willing to lend on adequate security but not to give money to James. But in return he must submit himself to her direction in all matters touching the foreign relations of Scotland, his marriage, and the appointment of his principal officers; he was really being asked to accept tutelage at Elizabeth's hands.[31]

James's ambassadors sent to England in the spring on special mission returned empty-handed, except for the vague half-promise of a pension of 10,000 crowns. The death of Lennox in France eased English fears of his return with French backing. Negotiations were also pursued with Mary through these months. They envisaged Mary's retirement from active politics, but a retirement preceded by a temporary association with James and a Scottish political settlement covering the issues and personalities of the past two decades, in which Mary would play an active role. Elizabeth expressed interest in such an arrangement, and Mary was profuse in asserting her desire

[30] *Ibid.*, 254-56, 257-60, 274-84, 288-89, 295-96, 299-300, 300-302.
[31] *Ibid.*, 316-17, 456-58.

to withdraw altogether from politics. The negotiations, whatever else was intended, served to put some pressure on the young King.[32]

But the initiative remained with James. In June he summoned a convention at St. Andrews and, when it met in early July, James broke away entirely from the tutelage imposed upon him by Ruthven, and within a short time Arran re-emerged into the limelight, sharing it this time with yet another adventurer, Colonel William Stuart. The Queen was angry and disturbed by this manifestation of James's independence but uncertain how to counter it. By the end of July, Bowes was anxiously writing to England, reporting the ruin of the pro-English party and urging the dispatch of some eminent English figure to re-establish it. Even before his letter reached London, instructions were being drawn up for Walsingham, who was to be sent to Edinburgh. The Secretary was extremely reluctant to go. His instructions were in the best Elizabethan high style, cast as a condescending lecture from a wise and experienced princess to an untutored neophyte. After plentiful reflections on the conduct of princes, the Queen came down to cases—an act of oblivion for all actions since 1572, English supervision of James's foreign relations, particularly with France, and English approval of his appointments. In return he was offered a pension—calculated to be the same as Elizabeth or Mary had had from their father—but with some hopes of an augmentation. James's hopes for the return of the Lennox lands in England were altogether dashed. Walsingham's own views were that the risks from France were now slight (Henry III having warned off Guise) and that the Queen could keep James in hand by stirring up his own subjects, if necessary.[33]

Walsingham's interviews with the King could not have gone worse. James, not unreasonably—"with a kind of jollity"—urged that he was an absolute king and entitled to the same freedom of action in controlling his subjects as Elizabeth.

[32] *Ibid.*, 467-69, 472-73, 482-83, 484-86, 487-88, 496, 498.

[33] *Ibid.*, 508, 522-24, 531-33, 535-36, 545-48, 569, 572-75, 577, 589; Calderwood, *History*, 141.

Walsingham condescendingly replied that "his young years could not so well judge what appertained to matters of government as the necessity of his estate required" and that he might think himself happy to have "a prince so careful of him as [Elizabeth] was to give him good and sound advice." The Secretary finished off by asserting that England could get along very well without Scotland and would do so if James did not mend his ways.[34]

Walsingham's assessment of the young King in his report to Elizabeth was in much the same vein. The Queen was right in her judgment of him; he was ungrateful and would take the first opportunity to turn upon her. This pride and contempt of Elizabeth grew from the advice of his mother, who encouraged him to believe that he had a strong party in England and hope of Spanish and Papal assistance. Walsingham foresaw the King's following Mary's persuasion. Nothing could be done to change the policy of the King of Scots, and Walsingham proposed that some plot be laid to bridle him. On his return he was busily engaged in trying to lay the foundations of such an intrigue. But all this came to little; the Secretary returned home in September, but before the end of the year the pro-English lords were totally scattered, some in exile, others in restraint, while Arran was in full command of power. The year closed with a coolly polite letter from James to the Queen expressing his continued good will and congratulating her on her recent escape (the Throckmorton plot).[35]

This high-handed English behavior reflected English assessments of the Scottish situation. James, as they saw it, was an unreliable and potentially dangerous neighbor who would bear close watching, but, for the time being, he need not be feared. The French, as their own ambassador admitted, were quite incapable of armed intervention or financial subvention, so James could be left to stew in his own juice. It was not an entirely satisfactory situation from the English point of view, but one which could be lived with for the present.[36]

---

[34] *CSPSc*, VI, 603-6, 608-9.
[35] *Ibid.*, 611-13, 618, 622-23, 626, 647-49, 668-70, 682-83.
[36] *CSPSc*, VII, 15-16.

This stalemate lasted for several months, but by March 1585 another plot was afoot, with the aim of seizing the King's person and unseating the current favorite, Arran. Bowes, the English agent at Berwick, was well aware of what was going forward. In the end the conspiracy turned out to be a very damp squib; Gowry was arrested before the uprising began and, although the remaining lords, led by Angus, Mar, and Glamis seized Stirling, they could not hold onto it. The English were unable to fulfill the promises, which apparently Bowes had made, of armed assistance. The best the Queen could do was to send off Davison on an embassy, instructed to back the lords at Stirling, while Bowes was given £2,000 to use for their aid. But before Davison made his journey northwards, all was over; by the end of April the rebels had made their appearance at Wark, asking asylum—repeating a performance drearily familiar over the past few years. English credit at Edinburgh was now very low indeed, and the Queen suffered the humiliation of asking Mary Stuart to use her influence in behalf of the exiled lords and of permitting the French Ambassador to go northwards to act as mediator.[37]

The following months were a period of uncertain drift. The proposed mediation by an agent of Mary Stuart and the French Ambassador failed because the Scottish Queen pitched her demands too high. Elizabeth instead sent the faithful Davison once more. France was seriously considering intervention in the Low Countries, the English Court believed, and were thus seeking an entente with England, which meant that the probabilities of either French or Spanish meddling in Scotland were reduced. In the meantime, Arran threw out feelers to Hunsdon, at Berwick, and the Queen allowed her cousin to respond cautiously to this approach. Discussions with Mary Stuart were also initiated so that various lines were kept open to Scotland and Leicester had a separate chain of communication. The faint hope that the obstinate constable of Edinburgh Castle might hold out against the Crown and afford a nucleus for action was extinguished just after the Queen had grudg-

[37] *Ibid.*, 40-42, 65-67, 70-72, 89-92, 92-93, 95, 108-9, 121.

ingly allowed a tiny subsidy for this purpose. Arran was now more firmly in control than ever when he finally went to meet Hunsdon at Berwick for an exploratory talk. Nothing came of this conference, and Elizabeth was reduced to stipulating only that the exiled lords receive the income from their estates.[38]

In August 1584 the Scottish regime sent south an agent—the Master of Gray—with instructions to take a strong stand about English support for the rebels but a conciliatory attitude towards any proposals for a league. Attitudes towards the new ambassador varied at the English Court: Davison and probably Leicester distrusted him; Hunsdon, on the other hand, rebuked Walsingham and Burghley for their distrust of the King and Arran and urged a sympathetic hearing for the Master of Gray.[39]

Negotiations were still kept up with the Queen of Scots, and even Walsingham came around to the opinion that some real trial should be made of her offers since he now believed that she had influence over her son. He must have seen, a few weeks later, an intercepted letter written by Mary at this juncture, which changed his mind. In it she expressed her despair as to any good result in the treaty with Elizabeth and urged that the Pope and Philip get on with their designs as swiftly as possible.[40]

In the meantime, the Master of Gray arrived in England, where he was patronized by Hunsdon but still opposed by Leicester and Walsingham. The latter was very much in King James's bad books. The new Ambassador continued on to Court, where he was coldly received; he was certainly in touch with Mary, although his loyalty to her must remain a question in doubt. Discussions with Mary continued and elaborate sets of proposals were exchanged, but presumably the English government by its control of the Scottish Queen's correspondence could gauge all too accurately the degree of her sincerity. Still,

[38] *Ibid.*, 141-42, 144-45, 171-72, 187-88, 191-92, 199-202, 212-15, 229-30, 238, 255-56, 276-79, 282-83.
[39] *Ibid.*, 306, 317-18, 328-30.   [40] *Ibid.*, 360, 368-69.

with no effective leverage at the Scottish Court, they had to make the best of what they had at their disposal. Elizabeth had to retreat yet another step in her dealings with James by agreeing to order the Scottish exiled lords to leave the Border counties. Mary was allowed to send an agent into Scotland (accompanied by an English official), but she was told that the state of English opinion after the revelations of the Parry plot made impossible any present treaty. The growing strength of the Guises in the French Court gave the English cause for concern and strengthened the need for a close surveillance of Mary. She was shifted from Shrewsbury's care to that of Sir Amyas Paulet, whom the Scottish Queen feared as a radical Protestant.[41]

By April 1585 the threatening state of England's overseas relations made some more satisfactory arrangement with Scotland a necessity, and Edward Wotton was dispatched to Scotland with concrete proposals for an alliance which would comprehend not only James but other Protestant princes and—more tempting—the offer of a pension for the King. The sum to be offered, not specified in the extant documents, was evidently to be small, too small, Walsingham thought, to do much good. The Secretary was certain that events would force his mistress to raise her bid. Wotton was also to broach the problem of James's marriage, with either a Danish princess or the Lady Arbella Stuart, the candidates favored at London. James's initial reactions were civilly hopeful. By early June a draft treaty was being circulated, which would tie Scotland tightly to English policy, limiting Scottish freedom to conclude any other alliance, and giving Elizabeth veto over James's marriage. But the size of the pension had not even been broached as yet. Wotton was also dealing with a group of Scots lords who were conspiring against Arran.[42]

Wotton sent hopeful reports of his progress, but suddenly all was upset when the young Lord Russell, son of Bedford, was killed in a Border skirmish. The English had a moral

[41] *Ibid.*, 392-93, 401-2, 405-6, 425, 456-58, 500, 513-14, 596-98, 602.
[42] *Ibid.*, 611-14, 648-49, 653-54, 661, 662-64, 682-83; *ibid.*, VIII, 2-3, 42-43.

advantage as a result of this episode which they used with moderation. There followed a confused sequence of events as the English sought reliable Scottish collaborators in the task of overthrowing Arran. Wotton, fearing for his safety, returned, with the Queen's permission, to Berwick. The usual remedy for Scottish political ailments was now tried again— a conspiracy of violence, led from across the Border by the exiled lords. They entered Scotland in October and by early November had won control of the Court and overthrown Arran. When Elizabeth's new emissary, William Knollys, arrived, James spoke of the recent rebels with absolute affection.[43]

This precarious equilibrium was upset once again with the arrival of a new French ambassador in Scotland in January 1586. Elizabeth promptly dispatched the veteran Randolph as a counter-move, but empowered him to offer the bait of alliance and of pension if satisfaction was given for the Russell murder. The English envoy arrived at a time when Scottish politics were entering an important new phase in which the King was effectively ruler for the first time, relying heavily on the services of a small group of bureaucrats, led by Secretary Maitland and the Master of Glamis. For the first time James was out from under the shadow of some clique of nobles or of an individual favorite. The first lineaments of a stable, modestly efficient, centralized royal government began to emerge.[44]

In these circumstances Randolph found his task less difficult than he had anticipated. Progress was made in negotiations; in March 1586 the King declared his general intention to conclude it. Elizabeth now made a characteristically stingy offer of a £4,000 pension (less by £1,000 than the sum first bruited); the war in Ireland was blamed for the modest size of the sum offered and the rather feeble excuse that Walsingham had misunderstood French crowns for English ones was

[43] *CSPSc*, VIII, 42, 79-80, 127, 131, 141-45, 150, 156-57.

[44] *Ibid.*, 187-88, 207-9, 215-16. See Maurice Lee, *John Maitland of Thirlestane*, etc. (Princeton, 1959), for a general account of this development.

used to account for the reduction from £5,000 to £4,000. James, understandably disappointed, nevertheless accepted the Queen's offer in early May. He had second thoughts when he contemplated the size of his pension, and the Queen's insistence that it was just what Henry VIII allowed her and Mary in their youth hardly solaced him. He may have been more gratified by a letter from Elizabeth promising that she would allow nothing to be done to impugn any title that James had to the succession.[45]

An embassy was readied, led by the Earl of Rutland, assisted by Lord Evers and Randolph. Their instructions were to proclaim the purposes of the league as defense against the Catholic alliance, led by the Pope and Philip and backed by Guise. Great pressures were brought to bear on James by the French Ambassador and by the pro-French Scots politicians to refuse the alliance, and the balance swayed uncertainly backward and forward through the early summer. But at last, on 5 July, the commissioners for both sides, meeting on the Border, signed the preliminary instruments. Randolph was recalled, his work done. Scottish soldiers poured over to the Low Countries for a few months, and there was much correspondence about a force to be led by the Master of Gray, but in the end the Queen, uncertain of her purposes in the Low Countries, cancelled the proposed expedition and halted the flow of volunteers from Scotland.[46]

But hardly had the new amity been established when the last episode in the life of Mary Stuart threw its grim shadow across these fair new prospects. There is no need to detail the lengthy exchanges between James and Elizabeth over this painfully embarrassing issue. The central elements in the situation are simple. Both sovereigns were under tremendous public pressure, Elizabeth to execute the hated Queen of Scots; James to rescue, and then avenge, his mother. Elizabeth, after the execution, was anxious to wring from James some acknowledgment that she was personally innocent of Mary's

[45] *Ibid.*, 249-53, 254-55, 302, 370, 414-15.

[46] *Ibid.*, 415-16, 422, 440-42, 485, 506-9; *CSPSc*, IX, 19; Rymer, *Foedera*, XV, 805.

death. Initially all this meant that the English government refused to give heed to Scottish representations, and the Scottish King consequently had to make war-like noises. But in fact the King was quite determined not to go to war over the issue. He had no illusions about French or Spanish support, and his eyes were firmly fixed on the glittering prize of the English Crown. After a few weeks of blustering, it did not prove too difficult to find the necessary face-saving formulas. The Davison affair served admirably the needs of both sides. The Queen shifted all responsibility to the shoulders of her unlucky second Secretary. James, while continuing to deplore his mother's execution, could gradually accept Elizabeth's version of events and thus avoid open rupture. The English were also willing to give James strong assurances on the one issue which troubled him far more deeply than Mary's death. He feared that the circumstances of her condemnation might impugn his inherited claim to the English throne; the English were willing to give strong reassurance that this was not the case. And so the crisis, factitious in its dimensions, gradually faded out; relations returned to the smoother path already laid out in the previous year.[47]

By the time the Spanish menace became real, relations between the two Courts had settled back into reasonable amity. The English remained suspicious of James's motives, at times almost to the point of paranoia. James gave them some basis for concern by a policy of flirtation with the Scottish Catholics (and indirectly with Spain), in an effort to squeeze more concessions out of England in her hour of necessity. They were successful in frightening the English agent in Edinburgh into the offer of an extra £1,000 a year, funds for a royal bodyguard and Border forces, and an English dukedom. All this took place while the Armada was actually off the English coast. Its rapid dispersal transformed the scene; Elizabeth coolly repudiated her agent's offer and James was left without anything to show for his efforts. He accepted this as part of the normal give-and-take of a relationship which, although far

[47] *CSPSc*, IX, 224-25, 285, 324, 331-32, 393-97, 400-401, 491-94, 553-55, 579-80.

from easy, was now settling down. James would do his best to exploit any opportunity which came his way, but he had no delusions about Spain's interest in him.[48]

The years between Morton's loss of power, at the end of the 1570's, and the coming of the Armada were difficult and to some extent dangerous ones in Anglo-Scottish relations. In the previous twenty years Elizabeth's policy towards Scotland resembled that of Victoria's government towards Asian or African potentates on their colonial frontiers. The objectives of the nineteenth century were to keep the native states under firm British control without incurring the costs or the risks of annexation. So the Elizabethan government viewed its northern neighbor as a state whose political climate was always unstable and whose weather patterns were unpredictable. A friendly regime such as that of Morton was given a modicum of support, but care was taken not to offend other faction leaders who might supplant this Regent. An unfriendly regime, such as D'Aubigny's, could be displaced by a little discreet aid to his rivals. What was desired was a government in Scotland too weak to pursue an independent policy of its own abroad yet strong enough to maintain basic order at home. Such a strategy worked somewhat clumsily but adequately while James was a minor.

But the almost forgotten spectacle of an adult male seated on the Scottish throne gradually made such a line of action outdated and unusable. James first manifested a will of his own by choosing a favorite; this move could be countered by traditional methods—patronizing a *coup d'état* by rival nobles. But it did not solve the long-term problem of dealing with a willful and increasingly restless monarch pushing his own interests and less vulnerable than a Regent, the mere head of an unstable faction. It was perhaps the good luck of both monarchs, English and Scottish, that James had enough leverage to force the English to pay attention to his demands, but not enough to embark seriously on a continental alliance. France was certainly eager to intervene in Scotland. Henry III

[48] *Ibid.*, 561-72, 496-502, 588-89; Lee, *John Maitland of Thirlestane*, 167-69 (quoting David Willson, *King James VI and I*, 80), 170-72.

sought to embarrass the English; the Duke of Guise had higher hopes of bringing his cousin into the Catholic camp. Spain shared the latter's hopes, at least for a time, intriguing to use the mother's influence on the son. But, as the English ministers, in their hectoring way, kept pressing on James, neither of the continental powers was free to act and, even if they had been, their motives were far from disinterested, and they sought only to make use of him for their own purposes.[49] Moreover, an entanglement with continental—and Catholic— powers would forfeit James the confidence of the English Protestants, on whom all his hopes of the succession depended.

Experience and the young King's native shrewdness taught him the soundness of this somewhat harsh analysis, and by the mid-1580's James was willing to accept the role of dependence upon England which conditions imposed on him. He did not cease to press for every advantage possible, but he did this within the framework of a working relationship with Elizabeth. She, on her side, brought herself, grudgingly, to concede to James the barest minimum of what he sought; he was to be a very junior partner in the firm, but at least enough was yielded to shore up the young King's self-respect and to give him some sense of leverage. It was done with the worst possible grace by the English Court; at the best, the young ruler was outrageously patronized, at the worst, mercilessly bullied; and neither the Queen nor her senior ministers bothered to conceal their contempt for him. James perhaps is owed more credit than he often receives for his patient endurance of circumstance.

[49] *CSPSc*, IX, 496-502, 542-46, 561-72.

PART III

THE SETTING OF POLITICS:
COURT AND PARLIAMENT

CHAPTER 16

THE POLITICIANS

The Elizabethan political system was at once simple and complex—simple in external structure and its underlying rationale, but complex and variable in operation. Its mechanics were those of a solar system; the Queen, the prime mover, gave motion and vitality to all the satellite members. The largest and most visible of these—the greater planets—were the dozen or so Privy Councillors, who moved in regular and calculable relationships to the sovereign and to one another. But there was also a great multitude of smaller bodies, varying in size, revolving around this sun—the courtiers. They formed a society of service and of privilege; some of them performed real functions in the royal household, particularly within the elite body of the Chamber, those in immediate and regular attendance on the sovereign. Others were sinecurists, rendering their service by deputy. Outside the formal ranks of the Household there was a throng of catechumens, attendant in the outer chamber. These would-be courtiers, as yet lacking preferment, strove by unremitting attendance and by arduous solicitation to obtain an official footing within the magic circle.

Each man's place in the system was measured by his distance from the sovereign and by the reflection of royal favor, great or small, with which he shone in this political constellation. But the solar analogy breaks down when one seeks to analyze the operation of the system. Each Privy Councillor stood in a particular relationship to his royal mistress, and this measured his importance, but he was also a member of a collective body of great importance. The Privy Council formed a small, compact, and omnicompetent committee which was at once the central administrative board of a busy government and the consultative organ for the royal executive. Its membership was exceptionally stable; its functions well defined; its routines well established. This stands in marked contrast to the French system, for instance, with its multiple councils, numerous secretaries and intendants, and its bewildering criss-cross of responsibilities and of functions. The Elizabethan Privy Council included every major political figure and all the major administrators of the government; it centralized the whole process of decision-making, both in domestic and in foreign affairs—with the possible exception of ecclesiastical policy. It gave to English political life a stability and predictability which was notably lacking at Paris; it was free of the tensions of rivalry and of the harrowing insecurity which characterized the Court of Madrid.

In such a system, the political role of the courtiers was proportionally diminished; those who were excluded from the inner circle of the Privy Council were denied any major role in power-brokering or decision-making. Nevertheless, the career of a courtier was worth the candle. The direct stipend was small, but the perquisites were considerable; more important, their stations, at the doors of power, gave them strategic advantages of great value. They were able to hinder or to help the thronging candidates for royal favor in their approach to the throne, or to those closest to the sovereign. The opportunities for personal profit were obvious and often substantial.

The courtiers were a link with the larger aristocratic world of the counties. This world was, of course, linked to the Court through official ties: the corps of JP's scattered across the realm worked under the general direction and supervision of the Council, implementing policies conceived and decreed from the center. This made for constant and busy relations between the country magnates and those of the Court.

But the country had its own local politics, more absorbing and more important still. The endless struggle for place and power—to advance to new positions or to secure old ones—was the very staple of aristocratic political life. It was a politics inextricably linked to the Court, for local offices, so often the key to victory in county politics, were largely in royal gift. And in the end the ultimate arbiter in all such struggles was the Crown. In such a situation, a brother or cousin in the Household or the Chamber was invaluable in opening up access to one of the great Court magnates and thence to Council or Crown. No small part of the Council's business was the adjudication of such disputes; the sorting out and smoothing over of these aristocratic rivalries was an essential part of the nation's politics.

At irregular intervals, these local politicians were brought together on the national stage of Parliament. They came laden with their own local concerns and interests and regarded Parliament, as their medieval predecessors had, as a great court where at least some of their grievances would be remedied. But they also came to Westminster holding strong views on many topics of wider import—the succession, the marriage, and, above all, religion. Stimulated by leaders from their own ranks into assertions of opinion and of desire, an otherwise shadowy national political community suddenly took form, a desert plant of swift growth and short life-span, which vanished with the royal decree of dissolution. Yet, as the years went on, the frequency of parliamentary meetings and the intensity of the life manifest in these sessions gave a protean character to English politics which began to blur the traditional lines of the system.

The center and focus of politics was always, unmistakably, the Queen herself. In her the theory and practice of divine-right monarchy coincided; the formal splendors of majesty were congruent with the brute facts of political decision. But what set her off from most of the contemporary royal colleagues was the absence of conventional royal ambitions. She had little of her grandfather's interest in strengthening and

433

extending royal power within the realm; she shared none of her father's expansionist dreams; and she was quite indifferent to the intense ideological passions of her sister. She eschewed a brilliant foreign marriage such as her sister or her cousin of Scotland made, and in the end put aside all hopes of matrimony. Yet, however lacking in conventional royal drives she might be, Elizabeth's instinct to power was of the strongest. Monarchy was no toy to her, as it was to the last Valois princes. She pursued the pleasures of Court life with undiminished zest, but there was never any weakening in her relentless control over every significant decision of state.

Moreover, she was guided in her exercise of power by certain deep-lying convictions. She has sometimes been contrasted with her successor as a thoroughgoing pragmatist, who let actions speak louder than words, while he, with his dominie's lectures on kingship, only managed to demonstrate the gap between theory and practice. But in fact Elizabeth was quite articulate about her conceptions of kingly office, and gave voice to them on frequent parliamentary occasions. The tone was certainly more fortunate than James's; the rhetoric was richer and had about it an air of solemn enunciation of truth rather than a didactic explication of doctrine. But the dogmas were no less firmly asserted.

The psychological advantages of this stance were numerous. It fitted, of course, into the larger role of sovereign, as Elizabeth played it. It was essential to the royal myth that the monarch should be above mere personal or partisan ambition, that her purview should always be the widest possible, embracing the whole interest of the commonwealth, god-like in its olympian detachment. The political nation at large was kept in a state of mingled awe and delight by this royal performance, while the inner circle of ministers and courtiers were also kept in a very satisfactory kind of subordination. By emphasizing the contrast between an infallible royal judgment and the flawed efforts of even the most experienced and trusted councillors, the Queen kept her servants continually off-balance, always in a humbled and apologetic posture *vis à vis* their mighty mistress. There was also the additional advantage that any imperfections in the actual governance of the realm could be ascribed to the failures of her subordinates; such virtues as they had were merely pale reflections of the royal glory. And would-be critics from outside the Court circle (Puritans and Catholics, most obviously) were silenced before they opened their mouths, since criticism was so easily equated with disloyalty.

All this was invaluable in establishing an unassailable defensive stratagem for a woman ruler in a traditionally male role. It was equally effective in cementing those habits of deference and of obedience to constituted authority on which the Tudor state—so lacking in instruments of coercion—rested its foundations. But there nevertheless remained the problem of fitting these solemn splendors into the more mundane necessities of policy-making and execution in a workaday world.

It was here that the Council complemented the Queen. It was her custom when hard-pressed by events to turn to that body with a formal request for their advice. But beyond these formal occasions there was a steady upward flow of informal advice and persuasions from individual Councillors to the Queen. Some of it was solicited by her; much of it was pressed upon her; but it is quite clear that she accepted and probably expected this kind of conciliar activity. There was, of course, no guarantee that she would accept the advice given or act as her advisors wished; she was careful to reserve every possible freedom of action. Nevertheless, the result was a working relationship which ensured a flow of information and of ideas, which kept the Queen from being isolated, and which gave the minister a sense of being more than a mere servitor.

Individual relations were defined by the Queen's estimate of her servant, but also by the ambitions and personalities of the Councillors themselves. The men who made up the Council in the Queen's middle years, from the 1570's to the 1590's, were of the Queen's own choosing; those Councillors she had inherited from her predecessors had largely passed from the scene. She needed to choose well, for her own conservatism was such that, once chosen, a minister was hardly ever discarded. She disliked new faces; even someone who had blotted his copy-book as badly as Arundel was allowed to return to the Council after a period of confinement for his share in the Norfolk plot. He continued to turn up spasmodically at meetings to his death in 1580. But death, from time to time, forced on the Queen the choice of new Councillors.

Three deaths in 1572—Norfolk on the block, Winchester and Howard in their beds—led to a flurry of new appointments at the beginning of the decade.[1] Sussex, just returned from his Northern Presidency, was admitted to the Council and promoted to Howard's old post of Lord Chamberlain. Cecil, promoted to the peerage, resigned his secretaryship in order to accept the Treasurership. In his place two new Secretaries (both former ambassadors in Paris) were sworn in, Smith in 1571 and Walsingham in 1573, and both, of course, Privy Councillors.[2] Shrewsbury had been sworn to the board in 1571, but his was a nominal appointment since his duties as warder of Mary Stuart kept him permanently away from Court. A second nobleman entered the Council in 1573— Leicester's older brother, the Earl of Warwick, Master of the Ordnance since 1559.[3] And a second member of the Dudley circle was admitted when Sir Henry Sidney (Lord President of Wales and Lord Deputy of Ireland) took his seat in 1575.[4] But his appointment, like Shrewsbury's, was largely nominal, since Sidney returned immediately to Ireland as Lord Deputy (until 1578), and even after his return he was an infrequent attender.

In the second half of the decade, additional changes occurred. Smith died in 1577, to be succeeded as Secretary by Dr. Thomas Wilson; Lord Keeper Bacon died in 1579 and was replaced by Sir Thomas Bromley as Lord Chancellor. More important than these replacements of officials was the nomination of the new favorite, Sir Christopher Hatton, to the Council in November 1577. Within the same week, Lord Hunsdon, Governor of Berwick and a Boleyn cousin, was sworn to the

---

[1] Howard died in January 1573, but he had resigned earlier.
[2] See MacCaffrey, *Shaping*, 443-49, for these changes.
[3] *APC*, VIII, 134. [4] *Ibid.*, IX, 11.

board.[5] Three more veterans disappeared in the early 1580's, two peers, Sussex (1583) and Lincoln (1585), and Sadler, Chancellor of the Duchy in 1587. Their replacements included two nobles, Lord Admiral Howard (son of the late Chamberlain and another distant royal cousin) and Derby, in 1584 and 1585.[6] In the next year (significantly while Leicester was overseas) the Queen appointed three new councillors in one go, Buckhurst, yet another Boleyn cousin (and son of a late Privy Councillor); Cobham, a Kentish magnate and long-time Warden of the Cinque Ports; and, most important of all, John Whitgift, Archbishop of Canterbury, the first cleric to sit since Mary's time.[7] The next round of change would come with the successive deaths of Leicester (1588), Warwick and Mildmay (1589), Walsingham (1590), and Chancellor Hatton (1591).

The tendency to restrict the Council to a limited and familiar circle is clear enough. Most of the new Councillors were either family connections of the Queen (Howard, Hunsdon, Buckhurst) or high-ranking officials whose previous service had brought them to the periphery of the inner circle (Walsingham, Cobham, Warwick, Smith, Sidney). Of the remainder, two (Wilson and Bromley) were professional civil servants, promoted to higher rank; two more (Derby and Shrewsbury) were regional magnates, appointed to a merely nominal membership. Hatton and Whitgift were the two obvious outsiders, admitted for very special—and different—reasons, one as royal favorite and the other to carry out a particular task for which he was uniquely fitted. Of all these appointees, Hatton alone had failed to serve an onerous apprenticeship.

How far can we sort the Councillors into distinctive categories? It is tempting to classify them under party labels, either ideological or personal, but quite misleading to do so. Of course, individual members had partisan commitments, but it is important to remember that the Council was more often an

[5] *Ibid.*, X, 85, 89, for Wilson, Hatton and Hunsdon; for Bromley, see *ibid.*, XI, 68.

[6] *Complete Peerage* (13 vols., 1910-40), IX, 783 (s.v. "Charles [Howard]"); *ibid.*, IV, 211 (s.v. "Henry [Stanley]").

[7] *CSPF*, XX, 352-53.

administrative rather than a policy-making committee; it should not be seen as the forerunner of a modern cabinet, hammering out a collectively agreed common policy. It was only occasionally that the Queen sought formal advice on some policy matter, and even then it was not a matter of majority-minority reports but rather of informal individual polling to ascertain the opinion of each Councillor.

It is more to the point to classify the Councillors by a variety of different but overlapping criteria. Leicester and Hatton, for instance, although opposed on religious questions, had in common the fact that both were favorites, a position which much influenced their political behavior and separated them from their other colleagues. The Boleyn cousins, Hunsdon, Knollys, and Buckhurst, probably owed their councillorships to their kinship to Elizabeth and in this sense can be linked, yet their political opinions were widely different. Leicester, Warwick, and Sidney constituted a family group of more coherence (to which Knollys was linked after his daughter married Leicester); he shared their left-wing Protestantism. There were other, weaker, family links. Hunsdon was father-in-law of the younger Howard; Walsingham was the brother-in-law of Mildmay and became linked to the Dudleys when his daughter married Sir Philip Sidney. In 1589 Cobham's daughter married Burghley's younger son, Robert.

A more useful and more significant way of sorting out the Councillors is by examining their personal ambitions. One can make a rough three-fold division which suggests the varying thrust of these ambitions and the role which each Councillor conceived himself as filling. The first and smallest group distinguished by these criteria is that of the politicians, that is, those men who consciously and consistently sought to shape policy and to share in decision-making at the highest level. It is a short list; Burghley, Leicester, Walsingham, and Hatton fill it out. These men pursued personal advantage, profitable office, monopolies, or land, but in each case larger public ambitions played a major role. Walsingham was certainly the most single-minded ideologue in the group. In Burghley's case, personal ambition seems gradually to have overshadowed public ambition, while Leicester's career moved in the opposite direction. Only Hatton managed to blend the two aspects of his career in a harmonious balance.

The second category—that of the courtiers—was both larger and more ambiguous. In general, these were men whose ambitions were more narrowly personal, although some, like Knollys, held strong ideological views. The royal cousins—Hunsdon, Knollys, Buckhurst, and Howard of Effingham—constituted a special sub-group.[8] None of them, except possibly Buckhurst, possessed much in the way of land; they were dependent on the Queen's bounty, and especially on the profits of office. This dependence served to circumscribe their behavior and mute whatever larger or more impersonal views they might hold. A second sub-group was that composed of the earls of ancient descent—Sussex, Lincoln, Derby, and Shrewsbury. The latter two played a very insignificant role in Council. They were all men of less pushing ambition than their arriviste colleagues; their status was hereditary, their consequence established, and, in the case of the last two, extended to a whole region. None of them was a man of strong ideological bent. The two more active ones, Sussex and Lincoln, saw their conciliar role in a rather old-fashioned way; they regarded themselves as simple servants of the Crown, bound to give the best and most disinterested advice possible and loyally to execute the royal will.

The third category—the bureaucrats—was limited to Mildmay, Sadler, Wilson, and Bromley. They were appointed as experts; their status more nearly approximated that of the modern under-secretary. They confined their attentions to departmental business, for the most part, although Mildmay proved to be an excellent parliamentarian and was a devout, although not especially militant, left-wing Protestant. Characteristically, none of these men—Mildmay and Sadler, in particular—were frequent attenders at Council.

The politicians, because of their individual importance, re-

[8] For Howard, see Robert W. Kenny, *Elizabeth's Admiral: The Political Career of Charles Howard, Earl of Nottingham, 1536-1624* (Baltimore, 1970), 63-87, 213-16.

quire our more particular attention—first in a rapid survey of their careers, and then in more detailed analysis of each individual. The most assiduous and restless politician in the realm was Robert Dudley, Earl of Leicester. Although he did not hold an administrative post of first importance—he was Master of the Horse from 1558 to 1587 and Lord Steward of the Household from 1584 to his death—he was a regular attender at Council and indeed had his finger in every pie. Along with Burghley, and later Hatton, he belonged to an inner circle of power close to the Queen herself. In the early years of the reign he had hoped to be the royal consort, and as that vision faded he cast about for other roles. He intrigued with the Howards—and indirectly with the Queen of Scots—against Cecil and escaped from that foolhardy episode with better luck than he deserved, thanks to the Queen's indulgent regard for him. But even before that venture he had cast himself in a more serious part—that of patron-general to the left-wing Protestants. Leicester's influence on ecclesiastical appointments went back to the earliest days of the reign; his patronage of individual left-wingers had become more and more conspicuous in the later 1560's and continued into the next decade. As they came into open conflict with the establishment, individual clerics found that they could count on his intervention in their behalf, even though he declined to follow them in their rapidly developing radicalism.

But from 1572 onwards Leicester became increasingly drawn away from domestic Protestantism to the larger international concerns of the reformed religion. More and more he was consumed by the ambition to play a grand role on this international stage. Most immediately he pressed Elizabeth to intervene in the Low Countries; in 1577 he seemed to be within reach of his ambitions. England would assume the protection of the States-General and Leicester would lead a crusading army of Protestant Englishmen to the succor of their co-religionists on the Continent. This cup did not reach his lips, and he had to wait another restless decade before finally setting out across the North Sea at the head of a great expeditionary force. By that time some of his interest in the English evangelicals and much of his influence as their protector had waned. Rival influences, above all those of Archbishop Whitgift and his conciliar ally, Hatton, had altered the scene at Court. Leicester was to win few laurels in the Netherlands and to see his vaulting ambitions to be a Protestant hero go aglimmering. Yet he returned to England to draw again on his almost illimitable credit with the Queen and in the last months of his life to play a prominent although somewhat empty part in the military preparations against the Spaniards.

No other Elizabethan politician made such a conspicuously public display of his ambitions nor aimed at such extensive goals. Burghley's interest in policy was broader than Leicester's since it extended beyond religious to economic and social matters, and his key departmental responsibilities gave him a strategic administrative position of great advantage. There were very few areas where Burghley did not have interest, knowledge, and influence. But, at least in the 1570's and 1580's, these interests were discreet and low-keyed, and much of the time the Lord Treasurer remained warily noncommittal, an elder statesman before his time, as Conyers Read has observed, and something of an enigma to the historian.

Hatton, as we shall see below, was a different story. From his first rise to prominence in the early 1570's he steadily went forward, advancing his own career as the Queen showered favors on him, but also emerging as a policy-maker and as a major statesman. Walsingham, on the other hand, was the one wholehearted ideologue in the Council. Although not without personal ambition, almost all of his energies were poured into the effort to promote English intervention on behalf of the beleaguered continental Protestants, Dutch or French.

But to turn back to Leicester: the scope of his ambitions gave him, to posterity as to contemporaries, a peculiar interest. For he comes closer to something resembling a party leader than any other Elizabethan politician, at least before the uneasy decade of the 1590's. There can be no doubt that Leicester made the most of the royal favor in establishing himself as a grand "patronage secretary" through whom men were able to obtain place and privilege from the Crown. The earliest opportunity to exploit the possibilities of patronage came at the very opening of the reign, when the defection of the Marian prelates suddenly created a large-scale need for new appointees. Dudley seems to have been particularly shrewd in seizing the opportunity. No less than six of the first generation bishops counted him as their patron and promoter; so did an additional four of later appointment.[9] There were also half a dozen deans who were his appointees, as well as a cluster of academic dignitaries at both universities. So far as the evidence goes, there was no other Councillor, not even Burghley, who played a comparable role in the earlier ecclesiastical appointments.

There was a second important area in which Leicester's influence was equally apparent. England had no diplomatic corps as such at the beginning of Elizabeth's reign, and the elimination of the clerical appointees who had traditionally carried out ambassadorial missions dried up the pool previously used. There still remained a small group of civil lawyers whose background was useful and from them several important appointments were made—including Thomas Wilson and Valentine Dale—but it was also necessary to draw on the services of courtiers with no particular professional skills. These appointments were made in a rather casual way; language skills or past contacts abroad presumably influenced particular choices; so did the backing of a powerful patron. Gradually in this *ad hoc* way a corps of experienced—if not expert—diplomats came into being. Two of the most conspicuous in the early years of the reign were Henry Killigrew and Thomas Randolph, both of whom gravitated into Leicester's ambit; Killigrew very clearly became his protégé. After 1572 the need for such personnel rapidly increased, with a constant stream of special missions to the Low Countries and Germany. Conyers Read pointed out that virtually all the men selected for these missions were drawn from the Leicester circle and were adherents of left-wing Protestantism.[10] Among the most con-

[9] Wood, *Letters*, xxi-xxii.
[10] Conyers Read, "Walsingham and Burghley in Queen Elizabeth's Privy Council," *English Historical Review* 28 (1913), 34-58.

spicuous were William Davison, Robert Beale, Edward Horsey, and the Earl's nephew, Sir Philip Sidney. Many of them served on several missions and became familiar figures to the Netherlands leaders in the busy years from 1577 onwards. Davison ultimately rose to be Second Secretary while Beale was appointed Clerk to the Privy Council as early as 1572. It is significant that the Earl's influence with the Queen seems to have been pretty well limited to the *ad hoc* missions to the Low Countries; only occasionally was one of his protégés sent to Paris, and the succession of resident ambassadors at that Court seem not to have been familiars of the Earl.

Apart from these well-defined groups, Leicester exercised a general and somewhat miscellaneous patronage. All over the kingdom were individuals who signed themselves as his "servant" or were so regarded by others. Some were prominent gentlemen such as Edward Horsey, Captain of the Isle of Wight, or Henry Killigrew, Teller of the Exchequer, or John Norris, the eminent soldier. Others were country gentlemen and others yet too obscure to leave any sure evidence of identification. Every great magnate wove his network of clientage about him, and Leicester was by no means singular in his. We cannot accurately count his dependents—or those of other noblemen—but it is a fair guess that his list was probably the longest.

Not all of Leicester's dependents were individuals; many were corporations; the boroughs of Bristol, Andover, Reading, Abingdon, New Windsor, Kings Lynn, and Great Yarmouth all counted him as their high steward.[11] So did the chapter of Norwich Cathedral and the University of Cambridge. He was Recorder of Maldon and Chancellor of Oxford University. Most of these bodies paid him a small fee each year and counted on him to back them in their quarrels or their ambitions, especially when they had to seek the favors of the Crown to settle the former or to achieve the latter. Here again there was nothing unusual in the Earl's role except the large number of corporations who looked to his protection.

Patronage of this kind often opened the door to another

[11] J. E. Neale, *The Elizabethan House of Commons* (1949), 210.

kind of intervention—in the selection of burgesses in Parliament. Neale has uncovered ample evidence that Leicester played this game with as much zest as his fellow-councillors or peers. He reckons that in the Parliament of 1584 Leicester may have nominated seven members.[12] But, beyond the bare fact of nomination, there is no proof that the Earl made any serious effort to manipulate these men on the floor of the Commons or even to build the kind of coherent parliamentary connection which the second Earl of Bedford may have constructed earlier in the reign.

In short, there is plenty of evidence that Leicester had an extensive clientage of men who received favors from him, looked to him for protection and advancement, and were in some sense his protégés. Most of them shared common ideological commitments as adherents of the advanced evangelical party at home or as champions of the Protestant internationale abroad. But what did it all amount to? Did they in any sense constitute an organized faction? What services were they expected to render the Earl? Were they an instrument which Leicester could use for his own political, or personal, ends? To answer these queries, one really has to raise the more basic question as to what function such a party might serve in the Elizabethan political world.

The answer surely is that in the normal course of politics it would have none. This was not a court like that of the Valois, where violence or the threat of it were constant factors, where organized faction could be used to shoulder aside a rival or to bully the Crown. The Queen had asserted beyond any question her unshakable control of political movement. She had made it perfectly clear—especially since the abortive Norfolk intrigue of 1569—that she would tolerate no such actions in her court. Rivalries there were—Cecil and Dudley; Leicester and Sussex—but the rivals had to live in common civility under the watchful eye of their mistress, in reluctant cooperation within the Council. The Queen kept herself above all these factions, bestowing her favors where and when she pleased; she might be persuaded, but she would certainly not be co-

[12] *Ibid.,* 211-12.

erced. So the use of faction within the Court to destroy a competitor or to put pressure on the Crown was outside the rules of the game. And indeed, after his somewhat half-hearted participation in the scheme of 1569, there is no evidence that Leicester ever again contemplated breaking the rules.

But politics might not always be normal; the game might come to a halt if the ever-looming spectre of Elizabeth's death turned into awful reality. If the Queen had died at any time before 1587, there would almost certainly have been civil war.[13] The candidacy of the Scottish Queen would have sprung to life; just as surely, her opponents would have risked everything to prevent her succession. But they had no agreed alternate; in their eyes, James VI was a young man of uncertain and untrustworthy character. Burghley, at least, as is clear from his abortive parliamentary bill of 1585, would have preferred a conciliar regency with the power to choose the next sovereign vested in it and Parliament.[14] In such a situation a devoted following which might be turned into an armed force would have been an invaluable asset. Quite possibly some such notion floated in Leicester's head, but there is no surviving evidence to indicate that he took any practical steps in this direction. It was too uncertain a contingency to allow for easy planning.

Leicester, in short, does not fit into any of the convenient and familiar pigeon-holes of political classification. He was not an old-fashioned regional magnate of diluted fifteenth-century vintage (like Shrewsbury and Derby); nor a noble courtier such as Howard of Effingham or his rival Sussex; nor yet a forerunner of seventeenth-century party leaders, mingling ideology and patronage in various proportions. He was first of all a favorite; the passions of the early 1560's had long since cooled, but "Robin" remained an indispensable member of the small circle of familiar faces which provided the Queen with the psychological stability imperative to her continued well-being. Even the Earl's liaison with Lady Sheffield and his marriage to Lettice Knollys failed to weaken the ties which linked

[13] See Cardinal Allen's comments in *True Defense*, 238-39.
[14] Neale II, 44-45.

Elizabeth and Robert Dudley. She could scold, bully, and humiliate him, but to the end of his life he never forfeited her deepest trust in him. Even after his conspicuous failure in the Low Countries, he was summoned home to take up a leading post in the defense of the realm.

Leicester's position as favorite meant, among other things, that he had the royal ear; that he could recommend and in practice nominate to ecclesiastical, civil, and military posts; that he could secure pardons; that he could influence decisions in Star Chamber, Council, or even the common law courts. He used this power for various ends. The corps of amateur diplomats who served in the Low Countries provided him with information, and with contacts which enabled him to forward the international Protestant cause to which he gave his allegiance and through which he hoped to realize his dearest ambitions. His military protégés in the English volunteer forces in Flanders served the same purpose. His ecclesiastical appointments were perhaps a trifle more altruistic; they served the advancement of the evangelical Protestantism in which he believed. That his personal life was not a model of Puritan rectitude does not mean that his devotion to religion was merely superficial or expedient. His more general following perhaps served to some extent to provide the consequence and status which came somewhat more easily to peers with ancient regional loyalties to support them—such as the Talbots or the Stanleys. At any rate, such displays of the Earl's influence with the Queen affirmed publicly the extent and reality of his political greatness.

Once, however, Leicester did mobilize at least some of his following for an organized campaign to influence a major policy decision. The evidence is incomplete, but it does look as if in 1579 the Earl and his allies played a calculated game in exciting public opinion against the Anjou match. If we can believe Spenser in the *Shepheardes Calender*, there was deep anguish, indeed something approaching despair, in the circle around the favorite.[15] Grindal's suspension in the previous

[15] See McLane, *Spenser's Shepheardes Calender*, esp. chap. 4.

year spelled finis to their hopes of a reformist ecclesiastical establishment. The Queen's new posture in foreign policy damped their hopes of a forward policy in the Netherlands. Above all, there was the spectre of a foreign and Catholic husband who would stand closest to the Queen and whose presence was intensely feared by the favorite and by the whole radical Protestant movement at Court and in the country. Stubbs's pamphlet, the sermons preached against the match, Spenser's effort in the *Shepheardes Calender*—all form part of a grand design to checkmate the Queen's plans. There were other factors at play which influenced the final outcome, but there can be little doubt of the importance of Leicester's campaign in checking the Queen's wayward impulses to matrimony.

But in general it cannot be said that Leicester's extensive following served to bring him much political gain. His most serious and long-lived ambition after 1570 was to forge a great Protestant alliance and to lead a force to the relief of the beleaguered Dutch. Yet all his elaborate efforts to build an Anglo-Dutch alliance—or rather an English protectorship—vanished in a trice when the Queen suddenly turned away in 1578 from her tentative negotiations with the States General to a determined wooing of the French Court. During the years that followed, Leicester had to submit to the royal will and to collaborate in the making of a foreign policy for which he had but limited sympathy. When England did finally intervene in 1585, it was the sheer force of events rather than the efforts of Leicester and his allies which brought about the Treaty of Nonsuch. And when the Earl took up the role of Protestant champion in the Low Countries, it was only to suffer humiliating failure. Ironically, one factor in his failure was his quarrels with some of the very men whose careers he had advanced—most notably Norris and Davison.

Nor, in the long run, was the Earl much more successful at home. The evangelical clergy whom he patronized proved to be increasingly embarrassing protégés as they moved steadily to the left, into positions too far out for the protecting wings of the Earl's influence. The radicalizing of the younger generation of evangelical clergy made them unfit candidates for promotion in the Queen's eyes and robbed Leicester of the pool from which he had been able to recruit new nominees.

At the same time, the emergence of a strong and opinionated Primate who stood well with the Queen had edged him out from his place as chief patron of ecclesiastical appointments. By the end of his career, Leicester still retained his place as Elizabeth's favorite, but his following, always an amorphous and somewhat diverse group of men, was fairly well dispersed. Most of the ecclesiastics were dead by then; so was the stalwart Horsey; others, like Randolph, were old men; and others yet, like Davison or Norris, were now ranked by the Earl among his enemies. Of the few younger protégés the Earl had gathered around him, the most famous, his nephew, lay dead on Zutphen field. Only in a vague way was his stepson, Essex, the inheritor of his mantle.

The other two great political figures—Burghley and Hatton—stand in striking contrast to the flamboyant Earl. Of the two, however, Hatton's position more resembles that of Dudley, and I shall deal with him first before turning to Burghley. It is a baffling career to understand, in large part because its early stages are so shrouded in obscurity. He was, like Leicester, a favorite; yet, having said that, one has to go on to point out the striking difference in their careers. The Earl began as a suitor for the royal hand, and the possibilities of a Dudley marriage rocked the Court to its very foundations. And, even when those possibilities faded away, the recklessness of the Earl's behavior, his flirtations with the Catholics at one stage and later his involvement with the Howard marriage scheme and with the plot against Cecil, confirmed the view held in many conservative quarters that Dudley was an unstable and dangerous man. His more staid behavior after 1570 never quite extinguished the earlier image. That venomous publication, *Leycester's Commonwealth* (1584), might well win a prize for sheer scurrility even among the choice political polemic of the sixteenth century. Nevertheless, it reflects something of the intense hostility which the favorite engendered in many quarters. Some considerable residue of heat lingered on in the very sober and respectable pages of Camden, who almost certainly echoed Cecilian views of Dudley.

But Hatton's career fitted none of these patterns. Although it was his graceful dancing and handsome figure which first caught the Queen's eye, there was never the slightest hint of matrimony, and indeed relatively little gossip of intimacy between the two. Although he was less than a decade younger than the Queen and Leicester, these years were sufficient to make a subtle but essential difference in Hatton's relationship with his mistress. By 1564, when his appointment as a Gentleman Pensioner[16] first made him visible in the Court, the Queen was thirty-one to his twenty-three and the relationship was always to have something of the air of an older woman's fascination for a younger admirer. The famous love letters which still survive heighten the impression of the curiously artificial form in which the relationship was cast. Hatton remains throughout the smitten youth, dazzled and overpowered by the charms of his more mature mistress, living only for the slightest token of her favorable regard, daring to hope for nothing more.

Whatever the inward realities of this complex relationship, the outward form of it profoundly influenced Hatton's public career. It meant that he made his entrée into public life under much more unfavorable conditions than any other Elizabethan political figure. By the time he arrived, Burghley and Leicester had been in high politics for twenty years; Walsingham and Smith had entered the Council after the seasoning experience of the Paris embassy; all of the others had had some political apprenticeship. But Hatton came on the scene the perfect amateur, recommended solely by the Queen's favor, bestowed, as contemporaries mockingly pointed out, because of his skill at dancing.

He had, so far as we can make out, no sponsor in the Council and no political or family connections. Dudley, whatever the uncertainties of his early career under the Queen, was the scion of a great political family and by inheritance a member of the highest social and political order. Of the other Council-

[16] Hatton, *Memoirs*, 6.

lors, those who did not possess of themselves such high rank and standing as Sussex, Lincoln, or Shrewsbury had enjoyed the patronage of some greater politician and in many cases a family connection with some incumbent Councillor. But Hatton had none of these advantages; the Queen's favor counted for much, but he was astute enough to understand that she expected him to work for his keep and to earn any further promotions. He must have understood, too, the jealousy he excited, particularly in the breast of Leicester; in 1573, when he was so sick that he had to retire to Spa for a cure, an attempt was made to put forward the Earl's friend and dependent, Edward Dyer, in the hope that his charms might supersede those of Hatton.[17]

Under these circumstances Hatton adopted a very cautious and wary strategy. Since his only advantage consisted in the royal regard, he had to trim his sails very closely to that favoring wind and to make his career as the faithful executor of the royal will and pleasure. It is hardly surprising that his first appearance in public affairs was as the bearer of a secret message from the sovereign to the speaker in the Parliament of 1572. She was demanding, against the will of the House, an immediate second reading of the bill touching the Queen of Scots. There is an undated letter, which could refer either to this Parliament or to its predecessor of 1571 in which Hatton took a seat for the first time.[18] In it he complains of being blamed for the unpopular courses pursued by the Crown in regard to Mary, Norfolk, and religious legislation. So it is as the Queen's agent in checking the inclinations of the House that Hatton makes his Parliamentary debut. Such a role necessarily pushed him into an anti-Puritan stance, and already by 1573 he was marked down in extremist circles as an enemy to true religion. He became the target of the mad zealot, Burchett, who nearly killed the unlucky John Hawkins under the impression that he was the "Papist" Hatton. This was a year after Hatton's first important promotion; in 1572 in the musical chairs which accompanied Burghley's elevation to the

[17] Lodge, *Illustrations*, II, 18.
[18] Neale I, 283; Hatton, *Memoirs*, 21.

Treasurership, he replaced Knollys as Captain of the Guard, a dignified Household office and one which kept him close to the Queen.[19] There is little evidence of his political activities in the immediately following years, although much of his social. But he obviously won an increasing measure of royal approval.

There were generous grants of land, including Corfe Castle and the estates attached to it, and an annuity of £400 for life. Royal backing enabled Hatton to force Ely House from the unwilling hands of Bishop Cox. But elevation to the highest political level came in 1577, when Hatton was knighted (along with Walsingham and Heneage), made Vice Chamberlain of the Household, and, most important of all, admitted to the Privy Council.[20] Thenceforth he was a member of the innermost circle of power, sharing with Burghley, Leicester, and Walsingham access to all correspondence, particularly foreign dispatches, and joining with them in constant consultation about the greatest business of state.

Hatton's appointment came at a crucial moment in the course of English policy. Only a few weeks before he entered the Council, the Queen, after a seeming conversion to the policy of intervention in the Low Countries, pressed by Leicester and Walsingham, had suddenly backed away and in the next few months she would move steadily towards the alternative of collaboration—alliance, even marriage—with the French Court. This was a bitter disappointment to Leicester, who had counted on commanding the expeditionary force for the succor of the reformed cause. At almost the same time, Grindal's disgrace widened the breach between Elizabeth and those who had hoped for moderate reform in the Church and marked the beginning of a new phase of ecclesiastical history.

How far there was a direct connection between Hatton's appointment and these evidences of a shift in general policy, we can only speculate. But the role which he chose to play now that he had arrived at the highest levels surely reflected at least the domestic situation. We have seen that he had already a reputation as an opponent of the reformers; his actions

[19] Hatton, *Memoirs*, 13.   [20] *Ibid.*, 36, 38-39.

now confirmed their suspicions. Already before he entered the Council he seems to have succeeded in his first effort at exercising ecclesiastical patronage. John Aylmer was promoted to the see of London in 1576; his correspondence with Hatton leaves little doubt that he regarded the favorite as his patron and indeed the promoter of his appointment. It was a doubly important connection since, with Grindal's suspension, the Bishop of London stood in as a kind of acting Primate and president of the ecclesiastical commission. As we have seen elsewhere, Aylmer readily assumed the task of enforcing conformity and thus his patron was more than ever identified as the Puritans' foe. We catch a glimpse of Hatton and Aylmer in 1579 arranging for a strong sermon against Stubbs's book and seeking to sway public opinion to the Duke of Anjou.[21]

Hatton's patronage of Aylmer proved only the first act in a long collaboration with the conformist leaders within the establishment. Sometime in these years he took as his chaplain Richard Bancroft, and when Whitgift was translated from Worcester to Canterbury, he would find his firmest protector (and later conciliar ally) in Hatton, and their alliance would last for the lifetime of the favorite.[22]

In the light of these developments, it is tempting to ticket Hatton as a counterpart to Leicester—patron of conformity against the protector of the Puritans. But the analogy would be misleading. Leicester had taken up his stand because of a personal ideological commitment to the reformers' cause. He had self-consciously assumed a public and in a sense a national position and one known to be opposed to the Queen's own religious sympathies. His strategy had been to promote the appointment of sympathetic divines and to defend individual preachers who got into hot water by their outspoken advocacy of change.

Hatton's behavior had been shaped on a very different mold. He had taken up his position, not out of ideological conviction or personal belief, but as a calculated political strategy. Heavily dependent on the royal favor, he saw the defense of the

[21] *Ibid.*, 55-56, 58-59, 132-34.
[22] Paule, *Whitgift*, 36-37; Hatton, *Memoirs*, 371-72, 379-80.

prerogative and the suppression of nonconformity as his logical posture. Unlike the Earl, he had worked largely behind the scenes in administrative or conciliar collaboration with Aylmer and, later, Whitgift. And with the latter his relationship was much more that of a powerful ally than that of a patron. His public advocacy of the establishment was limited to its defense in Parliament against the great assaults launched in 1584-1585 and 1586-1587.[23] He remained throughout his career the courtier-official, working within the narrow ambits of Court and Council, relying on his favor with the Queen and his conciliar allies, a striking contrast to the popular and public stance of the older favorite. Indeed, in spite of the mere eight years in age which separates them, they seem almost to belong to different generations.

Yet one must not imply more of a rivalry than in fact existed. As we have seen, in many areas Leicester and Hatton cooperated harmoniously and easily, while their rivalry over religious policy was perhaps dulled by the differing rhythms of their careers. Leicester's role as a patron of ecclesiastics was already fading when Hatton came on the Council; he would continue to defend individual Puritans for the balance of his career, but it was increasingly a rear-guard action rather than a head-on battle. More and more, the Earl's energies were consumed in overseas matters.

But many contemporaries accounted Hatton to be more than anti-Puritan; rumor had it that he was a secret Catholic. The existing evidence for this belief is all of the most shady kind, *Leycester's Commonwealth*, or the report of exiled recusants. Slightly more to the point, is a remark of Camden.[24] Commenting on the "tart and sharp" proclamation against priests in 1591, he says the Catholics blamed Burghley "wherein yet they commended Sir Christopher Hatton, as a man more inclinable to their side, who was of opinion, that in matters of religion neither fire nor sword was to be used." This only suggests a tolerant and mild attitude towards religious contention, and there is no solid evidence for ascribing Catholic belief to Hatton.

[23] See below, 484.   [24] Camden, *Annals*, 458.

On the other hand, it is quite evident that Hatton went out of his way to help individual Catholics. Early in his career he was a friend to the Duke of Norfolk and later to his son, the Earl of Arundel, and his brother, Henry Howard, both of whom intrigued against the regime. Henry Howard, along with his friend, Charles Arundel, was involved in the addle-pated scheme to convert the Earl of Oxford and to use him in conspiracy with foreign powers. Charles Arundel was probably the author of *Leycester's Commonwealth* and eventually had to flee into exile. Both Howard and Arundel at different points of their career found themselves under arrest; both sought and received help from Hatton.[25]

However, Catholics were not the only victims of religious contention who sought Hatton's assistance. Grindal twice sought the Vice-Chamberlain's help in regaining the royal favor; so did John Stubbs in prison in 1579, and the Protestant publicist, Thomas Norton. Philip Sidney plainly regarded Hatton as a friend at the time of his famous quarrel with Oxford.[26]

What seems probable is that Hatton, as a man of great influence with the Queen, was constantly sought after by suitors of all ranks and persuasions and that he was impartial in the distribution of his favors. In part it may have been a mild and pacific temper, such as Camden's comment implies; in part, it was no doubt a politic calculation that credit in more than one bank might be useful in the future. Certainly Hatton gives the impression of a politician who sought to have as few enemies as possible and who burned no more bridges than he had to. The underlying core of consistency is not partisanship nor ideology but a measured cooperation with the royal will. He never forgot that Elizabeth's favor was his original stock-in-trade; unlike Leicester, he made no effort to add assets of another character. He was content to remain the servant and instrument of his royal mistress.

Hatton proved to be a man of surprisingly many talents.

[25] J. A. Bossy, "English Catholics and the French Marriage, 1577-81," *Recusant History* (Bognor Regis, Arundel Press), 5 (1959-60), 2-16; Hatton, *Memoirs*, 116-17, 137-39, 169, 180-81, 265, 368-69, 376-77.

[26] Hatton, *Memoirs*, 52-53, 118-19, 128-29, 141-43, 234-35.

The Queen astonished everyone when she appointed him Lord Chancellor in 1587, but his conduct in an office normally the preserve of experienced lawyers more than justified her judgment. He was equally skillful on the floor of the House of Commons, where he did yeoman service in the years when the Crown badly needed defenders of its ecclesiastical policy. Hatton was in many ways the odd-man-out of Elizabethan politics. Lacking a patron to launch him, seemingly without professional skills or administrative expertise, a latecomer in the race, he yet enjoyed a career of exceptionally smooth and unhindered advancement and of solid political achievement. An irenic man in a court rent by political passion and by unappeased ambition, he made remarkably few recorded enemies and died in the fullness of honors.

The absence of information casts an air of mystery over much of Hatton's career. Burghley's is better documented than that of any other Tudor statesman, yet he remains, particularly in the decades under examination, a curiously enigmatic figure. The weightiest and most honored of the royal Councillors, a man of European fame—the great Lord Burghley—he seems, on the evidence, to have played a singularly passive role in the great events of Elizabeth's middle years. In the first decade of the reign, Cecil had taken the lead in bold and sometimes risky ventures and had proved more skillful than any other minister in persuading the Queen to back him. In Scotland in 1559-1560 and in the Spanish treasure episode at the end of the decade he had demonstrated imagination, daring, coolness, and great diplomatic resource. In 1568-1569 he had turned back a determined assault on his position in the government and received the most gratifying evidence of his sovereign's confidence. In 1571 and 1572 he was raised to the peerage (the only Councillor, other than the royal cousins, Hunsdon and Buckhurst, to receive such promotion) and to the high office of Lord Treasurer.

Yet almost from the moment of his elevation Burghley seems to have deliberately withdrawn from center-stage, and in the great decisions which had to be made during the next twenty years it is often very difficult to ascertain what he counselled. When we do have his views, they meticulously add up pros and cons so as to leave the scale in perfect balance.

He worked diligently although rather unimaginatively at his departmental tasks as Treasurer. He kept a careful eye on the Queen's resources, and it is pretty clear that no grant that diminished the royal income passed easily through his hands. The correspondence of the other courtiers is full of their anxiety lest their "books" not pass his watchful scrutiny. He kept in close touch with the localities, worried over the appointment of JP's, played uncle in the family quarrels of the aristocracy, and from his post in the Wards kept a tight hand on the fatherless scions of the greater houses. Like Leicester, he sought high stewardships and the nomination of parliamentary burgesses as well as intervening in the county elections of Northampton and Hertfordshire. He conscientiously supervised the affairs of Cambridge University and kept a finger in the ecclesiastical pie. Pretty certainly Burghley was the dynamo which kept the routine business of government running smoothly and effectively. And on one great issue of policy—the treatment of the English Catholics—he was as determined and vigorous as ever. He remained their resolute and vigilant foe, particularly of the missionary movement based on Douay and Rheims.

But on past performance one would have expected a great deal more in the way of active leadership on the great issues of foreign policy. As has been said, it is not easy to determine where Burghley stood on these questions. He was always active in negotiation, fully informed, and fecund in perceptive analysis. But, pressed for an opinion, he was always judiciously noncommittal. He favored the Queen's marriage—in principle; he thought the Duke of Anjou might do—if the Queen so willed it. The risks of war with Spain were great; so were those of abandoning the Low Countries to their fate. The daring Cecil of the 1560's, willing to risk all when his keen sight sees the dangers ahead, is now a monument of caution and indecision, seemingly paralyzed by the very complexities which he skillfully deploys on paper. It was only in the final negotiations with Parma in 1587-1588 that Burghley stepped forward to take a lead. And this may give us a glimpse of the man behind the mask. These negotiations were a desperate last bid to maintain peace. In the past, Cecil had been prepared to take great risks, but he had always struggled hard to avoid war. It may be that he all too keenly sensed that now, in the 1580's, war was unavoidable—a war which he feared would be disastrous for his country and for the regime which he had played so large a role in building. The aging Burghley seems to have taken on more and more the outlook and temperament of his mistress—shuddering away from the endless chances of war and seeking at all costs somehow to preserve England from involvement in the Continent's frightening turbulence.

It was true that Burghley now had much to lose; he had won through to the great magnate status which must have been his fondest hope. He lavished money and care on the great houses he had built at Stamford and Theobalds; he sought noble alliances for his children and pushed the careers of his sons. He played the great seigneur in Northamptonshire, Lincolnshire, and Hertfordshire. He had not lost his keenness of vision or his interest, but the old crisp decisiveness and boldness were gone. No doubt age had something to do with it, but perhaps more important still was his genuine bafflement at the intractability of the problems which he all too clearly saw before him. In any case, England's elder statesman, her most perceptive politician, remained curiously withdrawn and inactive in the years when his talents were most demanded.

THESE WERE the personnel of high politics. They—with the Queen—made the decisions in the 1570's and 1580's. We have said something about their personal characteristics and their ambitions. We know that they acted under the dual pressures of events external to the kingdom and under the restless stirrings within the gentry and clergy within the realm. What was the resulting mixture which characterized high politics in the years between St. Bartholomew and the Armada?

The contrast with earlier decades is obvious. In the years after Henry's death the national leaders had had to face the dangerous discontents of an angry peasantry, which seemed to shake the very foundations of English society at the end of the 1540's. Those agitations had now faded away without trace. In the 1550's open revolt against the foreign policy of the Crown had flared dangerously, and in the first decade of Elizabeth's reign rivalries within Council and Court had threatened stability. At the end of the 1560's major Court intrigues were linked with another bout of rebellion. This was all damped down now and showed itself only in the faintest occasional glow of the coals.

This decay of factionalism was reflected in the behavior of the Council. In the 1560's the great issue of the succession (and its attendant problems) had tended to polarize that body around the two rivals, Dudley and Cecil. The issues of the 1570's—those of foreign policy—had a different effect. There were varying views in the Council as to the right course of action in the Low Countries; Leicester and Walsingham were strong and persistent lobbyists for intervention, at least up to the Anjou match. But disagreements seem to have taken on a more impersonal tone and to have focussed on differences of opinion rather than on personalities. The Anjou match placed a severe strain on the Councillors. No one behaved with entire consistency, except perhaps Sussex, who steadily pressed for the match. Leicester tried to reconcile his desire to appear as France's friend with his basic fear of the match; Hatton tried to square his loyalty to the Queen with his own dislike of Anjou. Burghley never let slip his mask of judicious neutrality. After that crisis was past, the Council seems—with the insignificant exception of Croft—to have closed ranks and to have acted with general unanimity in support of the Queen's initiatives in the early 1580's. When the final decision came in 1585, as far as we can tell, there was a consensus behind the approval of the Treaty of Nonsuch. Only Burghley, as is suggested above, may have had his private reservations.

On domestic religious matters there was more of a polarization between Leicester and Hatton, the rival patrons, particularly as the latter rose to the highest eminence. But the important thing is that, however much opposed on this issue, the two men found it quite possible to collaborate intimately and steadily in support of common foreign policy goals. Indeed, the Council of these decades was a strikingly successful political institution. It contained within its flexible bounds a cluster of strong and competitive personalities who found it possible to disagree on some fundamental issues while at the same time cooperating effectively on others where they shared common views. The Queen's ability to hold together and to make use of this group of talented but jealously competitive rivals was one of her greatest political achievements.

Yet it was events rather than men which dominated the activities of this body. Sovereign and Councillors alike were constantly forced to react to new developments over which they had little or no control; increasingly they were left in a position where they could not take initiatives. The Queen was temperamentally comfortable in such a situation; but Leicester and, above all, Walsingham lived in constant frustration. This was most obvious in foreign policy. With the breakdown of Spanish government in the Netherlands, particularly after 1576, and the increasing anarchy in France, England found herself in the uncomfortable and dangerous neighborhood of two great powder factories, in both of which uncontrolled fires and explosions raged. It was not only England's inability to influence developments in these countries but the unpredictable sequence of events which kept English statesmen continuously on edge. At home the pressure of events was less relentless. The problems of Protestant and of Catholic dissent built up at an uneven and somewhat spasmodic pace, although here again the initiatives were largely in the hands of the zealots on both sides who pressed singlemindedly on in pursuit of their transcendent goals, with little regard for the susceptibilities of more worldly minded politicians.

But chaotic and bewildering as the sequence of events was to contemporaries, they do fall, in historical perspective, into some rough patterns. From 1572 to about 1577, men's attention was drawn largely to the scene abroad—to Holland and to France. It was a time of tension and of worry for Englishmen, but also a time when the possibilities of movement were very slight. The outcome of events in either of the other countries was so obscurely uncertain as to discourage any action whatsoever. Elizabeth's ill-conceived conspiracy with Anjou in 1576 nearly ended in deep embarrassment—if not danger—for England.

The log-jam broke about 1576-1577 with the Spanish fury at Antwerp and the ensuing collapse of Spanish government in the seventeen provinces. Leicester and Walsingham now had a freer hand to press their policy of intervention and, as we have seen above, it looked as though they might persuade the Queen to their way of thinking. Her sudden decision to drop this policy and to turn towards France marked not only a sharp turn in English foreign policy but also a significant shift in the English leadership. During most of the 1570's the Queen had played a somewhat passive role, allowing the Councillors to propose policy and accepting or rejecting—usually the latter—what they urged on her. Now she took matters very firmly in her own hand, and for the next several very crucial years it was she who called the tune while the ministers danced to it. Down to the collapse of Anjou in the Low Countries in 1583-1584, the initiatives were royal ones; the Queen worked hard and consistently to push through the active alliance with France which she had chosen as her preferred strategy. That it failed was in part her responsibility, although intractable circumstance had more to do with it. In the final phase which led up to the Treaty of Nonsuch, the Queen seems again to have lapsed into a kind of passivity, and it was the force of events which drove her at last—reluctantly—to intervention, and war. The depth of her reluctance was displayed all too patently in her treatment of Leicester in 1586 and 1587 and in her persistent attempts to come to terms with the Spaniards, at whatever cost to her allies or to the Protestant cause.

The domestic religious crisis moved at a different rhythm, although here too the late 1570's proved to be the turning-point. The pace was set by the reformers themselves, particularly by Cartwright and his radical colleagues, both by their pamphlets and by their program for action at local levels. But the timing of the royal reaction—the Queen's angry prohibition on the prophesyings—was accidental, touched off not so much by any specific move of the reformers but possibly by some chance side-blow of local rivalries. The change of policy which followed came more slowly and not as a result of royal initiative. Aylmer and Hatton labored on rather uncertainly, with only a modicum of royal support; it was Whitgift's arrival that signalled the real change of direction. And here the initiative was plainly the Primate's; the Queen's backing was firm but largely tacit, expressed openly only in the parliamentary crisis of 1586.

The effect of these changes on individual careers varied directly with the ambitions of each Councillor. Leicester's (and Walsingham's) were therefore most affected since theirs were the grandest ambitions among the politicians. Leicester's decline—which aroused the lamentations of Spenser as early as 1579—was a relative but significant one. First of all, he lost the command of extensive ecclesiastical patronage which he had enjoyed since the beginning of the reign. Secondly, he had to share personal and political favor with Christopher Hatton as well as with Burghley. As far as we can see, this did not lead to an open or bitter competition; they found it possible to rub on together in reasonable amity, but it did diminish Leicester's share of the pie. The Earl did at last realize his dream of leading an English army overseas, but there was a taste of ashes in his mouth even before he left, prophetic indications of the failure which followed. Perhaps the pomps of his lieutenancy in the Armada summer made some amends to him in the last weeks of his life.

The counterpoint to Leicester's gradual decline was the rise of Hatton—and of Whitgift. For the younger favorite these were golden years: favor heaped on favor, the rise to the splendors of the Chancellorship, the success of his episcopal collaborator. But it was a career that succeeded because Hatton's ambitions were so closely adjusted to the motions of the royal will. With his sights set substantially lower than the Earl's, there were fewer chances for disappointment. As for Burghley, little seems to have changed one way or the other. He had already won the great prizes of office, power, and status; he was busy consolidating a family position which would outlast his own lifetime. He had set himself, so far as we can see, no larger goals than the defense of the regime which he had helped to bring into being. He rejoiced in the destruction of its great enemy, the Queen of Scots, but he looked with only lukewarm enthusiasm on the alliance with the Dutch and the great effort of the war, in his eyes probably nothing more than a necessary evil.

CHAPTER 17

PARLIAMENT

ORDINARILY the great business of state was done within the Council Chamber or within the Queen's audience room; the sovereign and her Councillors were obviously the permanent elements in the politics and the administration of the kingdom and the locus of all important decisions. But periodically the small world of the Court was inflated for a few weeks or months by the addition of some four hundred country gentlemen and about fifty peers. The Privy Councillors, in their capacities as members of one house or the other, took their seats in the appropriate chamber, and during the session the center of political gravity moved temporarily to the parliamentary arena. There were ten Parliaments in Elizabeth's reign, meeting in sixteen sessions; five of these fell in the years 1571 to 1589, inclusive.

Parliament was an ancient institution which had acquired its formal structure over a century earlier and had become a well-established part of English constitutional machinery. Its membership and its internal organization had been settled before the Tudors arrived on the throne; so had the qualifications of the electorate. In all these structured respects the English Parliament was a far more mature institution than its Scottish or French counterparts. Its functions were also more clearly defined than theirs, but not nearly so sharply as its structure, and indeed the functions of Parliament—particularly of the House of Commons—were undergoing steady alteration, especially from the 1530's onwards. Parliament was not yet the central arena of politics, that is, the place where the ultimate struggle for power and place was fought out; that was still the Court, more narrowly the Council. Nevertheless, most of the great issues dealt with in preceding chapters—the aspirations of the Puritans, the recalcitrance of the Catholics, even, as time went on, some of the problems of foreign policy —were steadily spilling over into the Houses. Their agenda was growing, in no small part because of initiatives by members of the lower chamber. And not only were the Houses more busily and more variously involved, but this very activity went far to change the character of the parliamentary institution itself. The fundamental nature of Parliament had never been spelled out in formal terms but rested on an accumulation of understandings shared by Crown, Lords, and Commons alike. These understandings, these assumptions, had grown up in response to the successive and varying grievances of generations. They reflected the tacit acceptance of Parliament as the place where the pressing needs, the unresolved problems, and the exacerbated frictions of English society could be aired and, in some measure, dealt with.

In the forty-five years of Elizabeth's reign the conventions which governed the conduct of parliamentary business were in constant flux, as were the functions which shaped those conventions. The basic relationship of the Crown to the Houses— their formal "constitutional" relationship—remained unaltered, as did most of the formal routines which controlled the conduct of daily business. The royal prerogatives of summons and dismissal remained intact, but Crown control of agenda and of debate became less and less effective. By the latter years of the reign, there was a perceptible weakening of the royal grasp on parliamentary business. The framework of understandings which remained was so brittle that it would not stand much strain and could be kept intact only by the most sensitive care. To understand how this lessening of royal control came about, we need to look more carefully at contemporary views of what Parliament's business properly consisted.

But to do that it is necessary to turn back in time, at least a generation before Elizabeth's accession.

In the past—at least in the Yorkist and early Tudor past—the immediate occasion for summoning Parliament and the government's prime motive in so doing was the need for money: taxes required for emergencies, almost always war or the threat of war. But the Crown's ministers also looked forward on these occasions to a round of law-making, in which most of the public statutes would be of their devising. But the prime consideration was the raising of money. At the first meeting of the 1529 Parliament—the historic Long Parliament of the Reformation—a new note was struck in Chancellor More's traditional speech to the Houses.[1] He had nothing to say about money, but much to say about the decay of old laws "by long continuance of time and mutation of things very insufficient and unperfect" and of "new enormities" sprung up "for which no law was yet made to reform the same." More's cloudy rhetoric pointed the way to the opening of a new epoch in parliamentary history, for the next decade was to see a host of new statutes enrolled on the books. Guided by Thomas Cromwell's strong hand, Parliament moved into a range of activities which, if not wholly new, were hugely expanded. Religion formed the most striking category, but these years also saw the first development of a system of relief for the poor and a host of other initiatives, some abortive, which aimed at the material betterment of the social and economic order. The impulse lost much of its strength at the fall of the minister, but the concerns of Parliament as a law-making body were permanently enlarged.

What did the term "law-making" signify in its Tudor, and particularly in its Elizabethan, context? We need to turn to contemporary pronouncements. There is a useful clue in Lord Keeper Bacon's speech at the opening of the 1571 Parliament.[2] Speaking in an admonitory vein, he told the Commons from the Queen that they "should do well to meddle with no mat-

---

[1] Edward Hall, *Chronicle* (1809), 764.
[2] BL, Cotton Mss., Titus F I, f. 135.

ters of state but such as should be proposed unto them and to occupy themselves in other matters concerning the commonwealth." The terms were commonplace ones to Elizabethans, but commonplaces serve the historian well.

Matters of state—which the Commons were to discuss only at the royal invitation—were self-evident to Bacon's audience: war, peace, all foreign relations, royal marriage, the succession, and, for the Queen, most certainly, religion. Commonwealth matters were no less obvious in their nature and were indeed, supply apart, the business which normally commanded most of the attention of Parliament and bore most fruit in the statute book.

They recalled the most primitive of parliamentary functions —grievance-bearing. The prime business of the medieval Commons was to bring before the King for redress the accumulated grievances of the country, large and small, general and local. Long since, the bare bones of fourteenth-century petition had been fleshed out in the fifteenth- and sixteenth-century form of statute. By this process the most frequently recurring categories of grievance had been absorbed into the permanent agenda of government, had become matters of policy. For the grievances which knight and burgess brought up to Westminster were of as much concern to Tudor sovereigns and their ministers as they were to the bearers themselves. The great quotidian business of late medieval government was the maintenance of public order, in the largest sense of that term. Unredressed grievance was the tinder which might ignite the flickering fires of riot or even the roaring blaze of outright rebellion. In the endless task of protecting the social order, allaying discontent, reducing friction, suppressing violence, the Crown had constantly to solicit the support of the landed aristocrats; on their shoulders, as Justices of the Peace, lay the whole burden of execution. But they were equally necessary as collaborators at the precedent stage of law-making. As the men on the spot who knew the social and economic facts of the countryside, they could advise most wisely and helpfully as to the strategies of legislation and of implementation. Above all, they would, when they returned home, be the men charged with carrying out the very statutes which they had assisted to frame and to which they had given assent. They would extract a price, as the legislative history of the Statute of Artificers illustrates;[3] they would be as hard-headed and as hard-nosed as any latter-day log-roller in the Congress of the United States in shaping the exact form of the act. But the initiation and general formulation of national legislation was something left to the Queen's Councillors.

Commonwealth business had been much augmented by the spate of new and far-reaching legislative reform which was inaugurated by Thomas Cromwell in the 1530's. None of his successors was so fertile in ideas, but the impulse he had given did not die out, as the legislative history of later Tudor decades bears witness. Most apparent is the great procession of statutes which between 1530 and 1560 fundamentally reordered the national life by recasting the national religion. But these enactments are fairly paralleled by the landmark statutes which sought, in varying ways, to meet the needs of a society strained by tremendous demographic pressures which affected the whole fabric of the economy and social order.[4]

Cromwell and his successors were quick to learn that the enhanced activity of Parliament required sustained and careful management. Even in Henry's time, it took all the skill of his minister to ease through the Houses the great statutes of the Reformation as well as other major items in the legislative program of the 1530's. The Edwardian Parliaments seem to have been responsive to the lead given by the young King's ministers (except for Somerset's program of agrarian reform).[5]

[3] S. T. Bindoff, "The Making of the Statute of Artficers," in *Elizabethan Government and Society*, ed. S. T. Bindoff, Joel Hurstfield, and C. H. Williams (1961), 56-94.

[4] For these paragraphs I rely on S. E. Lehmberg, *The Reformation Parliament, 1529-1536* (1970) and his *Later Parliaments of Henry VIII, 1536-1547* (1977); and on G. R. Elton's *Reform and Reformation: England, 1509-1558* (Cambridge, Mass., 1977) and *Reform and Renewal* (1973).

[5] W. K. Jordan, *Edward VI: The Young King* (1968), chaps. 6, 10; M. L. Bush, *The Government Policy of Protector Somerset* (Montreal, 1975), chaps. 3, 4.

Mary's Parliaments balked from time to time, and a deter-mined minority in the Lower House obstructed the royal will on more than one occasion.[6] In the first Parliament of her suc-cessor—which was to enact the last of the Reformation statutes —there was a muted but intense struggle of wills between the sovereign and members of both Houses, radical Protestant in the lower, Catholic in the upper.[7] The government's intentions were initially thwarted—by conservatives in the Lords, less certainly (for the record is dismayingly incomplete and hard to read) by radicals in the Commons. It took time and man-agement to isolate the bishops, to bring over the conservative lay peers and to satisfy the clamors of the left-wingers in the Lower House. It may be that the final settlement represents a compromise between the Crown and the latter.

The unique circumstances of 1559 were not to recur for an-other eighty years; not until the meeting of the Long Parlia-ment would the opportunity to reorganize the national reli-gious establishment be again open. Contemporaries could hardly know this, but they had no intention of retreating from the new ground which had been thrown open to them by the two reformer kings. As they saw it, the national religion was a topic permanently annexed to the agenda of all Parliaments, for discussion and for action.

PARLIAMENT was always opened by a speech given by the Lord Chancellor, speaking for the sovereign, which laid out the rea-sons for the summons. The speeches form a useful starting-point for examining relations between the Queen and her Parliaments in the first decades of her reign. The task of mak-ing these "speeches from the throne" fell to Lord Keeper Bacon. His prose style is laborious and learned, but has a cer-tain stately authenticity. His orations in 1563, in 1566, and in

[6] David Loades, *The Reign of Mary Tudor* (1979), *passim*.
[7] The classical account of this Parliament is J. E. Neale's in Neale I, 51-84, and "The Elizabethan Acts of Supremacy and Uniformity," in *English Historical Review* 65 (1950), 304-32. For a penetrating cri-tique, see Norman L. Jones, "Faith by Statute: The Politics of Religion in the Parliament of 1559," Cambridge University Ph.D. thesis, 1977.

1571 illuminate very fully the Crown's approach to these assemblies.[8] In 1563 he divided his speech formally under two heads—religion and "policy." In 1571, more prolix, he declared "the causes [for summons] to be chiefly two, the one to establish or dissolve laws as best shall serve for the good governance of the realm, the other so to consider for the Crown and state as it may be best preserved in the time of peace and best defended in the time of war, according to the honor due it." In both speeches the Lord Keeper touched on ecclesiastical issues. In 1563 he warned against divergence in doctrine and bewailed the neglect of rites and ceremonies and the consequent lack of attendance at Common Prayer. In 1571 he called on his associates to consider whether the ecclesiastical laws for the discipline of the Church were sufficient, but then, having said so much, backed away by insisting that any initiative for statute must come from "my lords the bishops to whom the execution thereof specially pertains."

As to the temporal laws the Lord Keeper spoke in both instances even more generally. It is worth quoting in full his 1571 comments: ". . . you are to examine whether any of them already made be sharp or too far overburthenous to the subjects or whether any of them be too soft and too loose and so over perilous to the state." Further "you are to examine the want and superfluity of laws; you are to look whether there be too many laws for anything which breedeth so many doubts that the subject sometime is to seek how to observe them and the councillors how to give advice concerning them."

After these somewhat cloudy counsels, the Lord Keeper broached the question of supply. Beginning on a high note, he asserted that the rule of reason dictated that extraordinary expenses should be met by extraordinary revenue. Then, more concretely, he listed the benefits that the Queen's reign had brought—"the reforming and setting at liberty of God's holy Word among us," a decade of peace and finally the clemency and mercy which had kept the Queen's hands free of blood. Under the heading "necessity" he reviewed recent events—the

---

[8] BL, Cotton Mss, Titus F I, f. 123ff. for 1571 speech; Neale I, 186.

Northern Rebellion, Irish unrest, costly convoys for merchant shipping, the decay of revenue in the wake of the Spanish embargo. The Queen had not indulged herself in the pleasures and pomps of royalty; she had spent sparingly on buildings and no more than necessary for the grandeur of her Court. He called for their generous support. In 1563 the tone had been similar; then brief references to the campaigns in Scotland and in France served to justify the request for money.

These were characteristic performances of the earlier Elizabethan Parliaments. They could hardly be called statements of legislative intent, for they were, rather, eulogies of the government, well-larded with commonplaces, patronizing and self-satisfied in tone, designed to impress, indeed to over-awe rather than to inform. Bacon was explicit in 1571 in his assumption that the subsidy would be passed without discussion, and briskly condescending in his brief explanation of the reasons why they should contribute. His speech was a formality which hardly bothered even to defend the government's record; it certainly did not invite debate on high policy. All this emphasizes how wide was the gap between the business of Council and the business of Parliament in the "constitutional" theory entertained by the Queen and her ministers. The latter, when it met, was kept carefully at arm's length as far as the great business of state went. The purpose of the summons was above all to provide money, and to do this with minimum fuss. Nothing was said to the MP's about the government's future intentions; all they heard was a minimal account of those past actions which had occasioned the accumulation of debt.

Up to a point, this patronizing attitude of the Crown reflected the realities of the Crown-Parliament relationship. Parliament was duly deferential, expected the Crown and its ministers to take the lead, and with some coaxing and a little bullying could usually be induced to follow the path marked out for it. Nevertheless, even in the early years of Elizabeth's reign a certain restlessness was showing itself in the Commons, most patently on the subjects of religious reform and of the marriage/succession issue. Topics like these showed up the ambiguities of that border land between "matters of state" and "commonwealth matters." A subtle historical chemistry was blurring the line which Bacon wanted to make so sharply distinct. His monitory speech to the Parliament of 1571 reflected the troublesome behavior of its predecessor in 1566, when members had pressed the Queen remorselessly on her marriage and on the succession, and then had gone on to compound their sins by introducing a series of religious reform bills. Such matters as these—along with all aspects of foreign relations—were, for Elizabeth, parts of her prerogative for which she was answerable to no earthly authority. She was willing, as she allowed Bacon to say, to invite their consideration of matters of state, but she was adamant in denying them any rights to be consulted. But in fact, even as early as the 1560's, sovereign and subjects were so far out of phase on this central "constitutional" question that only repeated and self-conscious assertions of the royal will served to check parliamentary aggressiveness.

As the relations of Crown and Parliament developed in these years, three kinds of disharmony became visible. From at least 1571 onwards the Commons displayed an increasing disposition to intervene in the passage of government-sponsored social or economic legislation, often insisting on major amendments. Secondly—a different kind of problem—there was the embarrassing eagerness of MP's to outrun the government's intentions in legislation for which it had sought parliamentary cooperation. This occurred both in the passage of anti-Catholic statutes and in the vexed question of the Queen of Scots. Last—and most dramatic—were the efforts of groups in the Commons to push through legislation that was explicitly disapproved by the Queen. These efforts were devoted to changing the religious settlement.

The interference of Commons in more or less routine legislation sponsored by the government began as early as the 1563 Parliament. Two great measures, Artificers and the first Poor Law, were before the House. Thanks to Professor Bindoff's brilliant reconstruction[9] of the former's legislative history, we

---

[9] Bindoff, "Statute of Artificers," 56-94.

can now see how very far the House went in rewriting the original piece of legislation that came before them; the second seemingly passed more easily, although this may only reflect the lack of records; we know how often and how radically it would be revised in the next forty years. Cecil's bill for compulsory fish days was debated at length and passed only with some difficulty. And the Commons attempted to initiate on its own measures on the irritating issue of purveyance, only to meet with a royal veto.[10]

The Parliament of 1566 was preoccupied with the succession problem and with the first attempts to initiate religious reforms from the floor of the House, but in 1571 there was renewed friction over routine legislation. Debate on a motion for the subsidy suddenly opened the floodgates of resentment, and there tumbled out one after another a whole catalogue of grievances—the issuance of "licenses," i.e., grants of privilege contrary to statute; the use of public funds in the hands of royal collectors for their own advantage; purveyance; abuses in the Exchequer over respite of homage and the writ *quo titulo*. They all have a familiar ring to students of Stuart history. This rush of indignation took practical form in a committee "for motions of griefs and petitions." The pressures were strong enough to extract a rather vague promise from the Queen that she would be more careful with licenses, a placatory speech from the Comptroller of the Household on purveyance, and a statute dealing with the liability of receivers of Crown revenue. Bills dealing with Exchequer abuses and limiting lawyers' fees did not run the full course.[11]

In 1576 the government put forward a bill for regulation of apparel, a favorite subject of Tudor administrators, only to run into unexpected opposition in the Commons. Some disapproved the bill altogether; others raised the delicate constitutional issues of proclamations. This measure seemed to give a royal proclamation the force of law, a dangerous precedent for a future when a less gracious sovereign might reign. There was, in addition, much criticism of the penalties attached, as

[10] Neale I, 114-15, 122.   [11] *Ibid.*, 218-21, 223-35.

too severe. The upshot was that no legislation on this subject passed. A bill regulating justices of the forests was also sunk by Commons opposition and, after a prolonged quarrel, a Lords bill for restoring Lord Stourton in blood foundered over the Commons objections to one of its clauses.[12]

In the Parliament of 1584 there were even more severe setbacks for the government. A bill, explicitly approved in advance by the Queen, concerning fraudulent conveyances, was offered; its main provision was a transfer of jurisdiction from Common Law courts to Star Chamber. There was an explosion of anger in the Lower House, and not all the big guns the ministers could bring up were sufficient to pass it in the original form. When it became statute, it was shorn of all provisions for Star Chamber intervention. Cecil's pet Wednesday fish-day statute also failed of renewal, even after the Lord Treasurer's most urgent efforts. Two bills sponsored by the Court of Wards for improvement of the royal revenue went down to defeat; so did two more designed to tighten the censorship. It was a record massacre of government legislation.[13]

The Post-Armada session of 1589 raised similar issues. This time there were attempts by members of the House, acting with the officials concerned, to remedy the abuses in Exchequer which had been the subject of complaint in 1571 and which the Queen had then promised to reform. This time a bill satisfactory to the Exchequer officials, including Mildmay, went through the House and was sent up to the Lords, but the Queen's old objection that it trespassed on her prerogative was to prove its death warrant. A bill to reform purveyors, quite carefully and responsibly drafted from the floor of the House, was sent to the Upper House. There the Queen intervened directly and made explicit her objections to these intrusions on her prerogative. However—an interesting foreshadowing of the monopolies episode in 1601—she back-tracked far enough to promise a special committee on reform of purveyance, which was to include four MP's. A similar commission may have been set up on exchequer problems.[14]

[12] Ibid., 354-58.   [13] Neale II, 84-90.   [14] Ibid., 207-15.

In 1581 there was a revealing difference of opinion between Crown and Commons. The ministers brought in a sedition bill which would have widely extended the scope of penalties for slandering the sovereign contained in a Marian statute of 1554-1555. It was under the provisions of this Marian act that John Stubbs had been prosecuted for his pamphlet, a procedure criticized in responsible legal circles at the time. No doubt many MP's saw the government's new measure as aimed at Puritans as much as at Catholics. The result was a much softened bill which among its other provisions repealed the original 1554 statute. This was no doubt a disappointment for the government, but significantly it did not result in a royal veto.[15]

These successive defeats—or major revisions—of government legislation by the House of Commons bear strong witness to the steady erosion of the Crown's moral authority, particularly over the Lower House. More and more, members expected to be treated as full-fledged partners in the legislative process— in those areas which touched directly on their own interests or added to their responsibilities as magistrates. They were no longer content to follow where the Councillors led; they were prepared to pit their knowledge and experience against that of the royal ministers and to expect that legislation would be amended appropriately.

The history of this erosion is quite plain; yet the reasons for the decay of royal authority are not so readily apparent. There was no solvent, such as the religious passions which led to the repeated attempts at ecclesiastical reform. There is no evidence of any emergent political or constitutional doctrine, although fragments of received wisdom were trotted out from time to time in the course of debate as sanctions for proposed actions. The sense of respect for common-law procedures and the vaguer notion that they are a bulwark of Englishmen's liberties peep out occasionally. But much of the protest over the provisions of individual bills seems to rest on common-sense propositions about justice and fair play. There is also apparent a growing distaste for the government's paternalism, for its bland assumption that it always knew what was best

[15] Neale I, 393-97.

for its subjects. What we are witnessing is one of those not uncommon instances in which an ancient and unchallenged authority melts away invisibly, not because of any outrageous abuses or crying injustices, not because of the appearance of some bold and exciting new political theory, but because of a mysterious loss of charisma. The magic aura which had given royal leadership uncontested authority was beginning to fade around the edges. It was only by a self-conscious and elaborately theatrical effort that Queen Elizabeth, by sheer force of personality, propped up the fabric of royal leadership through her lifetime. Without her extraordinary combination of talents, the process might well have gone much further than it did.

Interference in the shaping of ordinary legislation was one aspect of the changing relations between the Crown and Parliament; imperceptibly it drove Councillors—and their royal mistress—towards a clumsy but workable cooperation with the Lower House. But beyond this the government was being forced into an unwelcome dependence upon parliamentary good will by the sheer force of circumstance.

The first major instance of such a circumstance arose in 1571. Fresh legislation was needed to deal with the threat to the government's security raised by the rebellion of 1569 and by the Papal bull of 1570, storm-signals of renewed Catholic hostility. The ministers, particularly, desired a new and stronger treasons act (modelled on Henry VIII's of 1534), and the Crown's learned counsel accordingly had drafted such a bill. It would become treason to imagine the death of the Queen, to question her right to the throne, or to assert that she was a heretic, schismatic, or tyrant. When it came before the Commons, that House, abounding in Protestant zeal and resolved to protect not only the Queen but also their religion, sought to improve on the measure by drawing in the question of the succession. Active pressure on Elizabeth to marry or to declare the succession had dwindled away, but there was the keenest concern in all Protestant circles to defeat any efforts of the Queen of Scots. Hence a clause was added to the bill which would have made a traitor of anyone claiming title to the Crown during Elizabeth's life or refusing to acknowledge her as lawful sovereign. Significantly, the penalty would extend to the child of any such person—i.e., to the young James VI. It would also be made treason to affirm that the Queen and Parliament could not determine the succession by statute.

This embarrassing example of over-kill forced Queen, Lords, and Commons into a long and complex negotiation to sort out the muddle and to produce legislation which did not prejudge the succession and yet added to the royal security. The Queen had her way in the removal of the succession clause, but she had to tolerate the provision by which Parliament could settle the succession. A major piece of government legislation had to be reshaped under the pressure of the anti-Marian sentiments of the House, and much energy and time had to be expended in a much more careful management of the Commons.[16]

But this drama was to have yet another act. Hardly had the Parliament of 1571 been dissolved than the Ridolfi plot was uncovered, with the consequent condemnation of the Duke of Norfolk and the revelation of Mary's new iniquities. The Queen may have been reluctant to summon Parliament at all, but the pressure from her ministers, anxious to discredit Mary and to bring Norfolk finally to the block, was too much for her. The Lord Keeper told the assembled Houses that they were there because existing laws were inadequate to protect the Queen against the dangers now revealed. It was another instance when high politics rather than fiscal pressures led to the summons of Parliament. But no government draft bill was brought forward; instead, Thomas Wilbraham, attorney of the Wards and prosecuting attorney against Norfolk, was put up to recite Mary's (and the Duke's) ill-doings at great length, taking the story back to 1559, with the quartering of the royal arms, and ending with a full account of Ridolfi's activities. The Houses were given their head, and a joint committee of Lords and Commons went about preparing bills. Two were produced, one attainting Mary of high treason and subjecting her to its penalties; the second disabled her from succeeding Elizabeth. The Queen indicated her pleasure that they proceed only with the second.

[16] *Ibid.*, 226-34.

What followed was a long and disorderly debate, ranging widely but always coming back to two themes—the clamorous demand for Norfolk's death in accordance with the judgment already pronounced by the Lords, and, secondly, the inadequacy of the single act against Mary which the Queen was prepared to allow. The Commons had the satisfaction of success in the first of these efforts when Norfolk went to his doom early in June. They labored long and loquaciously over the act against Mary, loading the measure with every possible clause for disabling Mary Stuart and discouraging her supporters; at the same time they constantly lamented that all such labor was in vain; what was needed was the execution of the Scottish Queen. They had little reward for their pains; at the conclusion of Parliament, Elizabeth took refuge in a characteristic evasion by declining either to approve or disapprove the measure.[17]

It is not easy to know what to make of this assembly. The government's intentions are far from clear; the Houses were given no cue by the Crown and allowed an uncommon degree of freedom in shaping the legislation against Mary, even though in the end the Queen declined to give it effect. It is possible that the Councillors had different hopes from the Queen. Many of them wanted the death of Norfolk, and the clamor from the House certainly proved an effective weapon to pressure the Queen into signing the death warrant. And perhaps the Queen herself was not sorry to be relieved of some of the burden of decision.

Her hopes and intentions as to the Queen of Scots are far from clear. We can hardly suppose that she really wanted an attainder and certainly not any definitive judgment on the succession. In the end, the muddled uncertainty in which matters were left was pretty much to the Queen's taste. The terrible force of popular hatred for the Stuart Queen was given full vent; the official revelations of the Ridolfi plot (portrayed as another episode in a long history of subversion) deepened the stains on Mary's character by exhibiting her as a plotter with foreign princes—and with the Pope—aiming at nothing

[17] *Ibid.*, 241-90; MacCaffrey, *Shaping*, 429-37.

less than foreign invasion. In short, the Queen of Scots was thoroughly discredited in English eyes and the possibility of her organizing an English party virtually wiped out. A strong case was also established—for use at home and abroad—for the continued detention of Mary Stuart. Parliament had been used, not as an instrument of legislation, but as a vehicle for mobilizing public opinion and as a political weapon against Elizabeth's rival.

Contention over Mary emerged again—more than a decade later—as a major problem, but in the interval other issues would duplicate the embarrassments which arose when parliamentary enthusiasm outran governmental intentions. Embarrassments of this kind recurred in 1581, when the ministers sought new repressive legislation. They were mostly concerned with measures to control the activities of the missionary priests. This was a popular cause with the Commons and there was no need to doubt the enthusiastic response of the House. They were given freedom to go ahead on their own in drafting appropriate legislation, and a joint committee of both Houses set to work immediately. Once again, as with Mary of Scotland's case, the Houses galloped far ahead of the government's intentions. The Queen was resolute to keep such a measure within narrow bounds, avoiding any hint of persecution for religion's sake and striking primarily at the active agents of Rome, the priests, rather than at the lay Catholic population. Parliament, as might have been expected, produced a draft measure of great severity—not to say savagery—which aimed at nothing less than the extermination of the Catholic population if its provisions were actually enforced. It would become treason not only to reconcile an Englishman to Rome but also to be reconciled. Royal intervention gradually softened the legislation so that it was the civil offense of conversion for the purpose of withdrawing subjects from their natural obedience rather than the merely religious offense of changing one's faith which was punishable. The government had been able to rein in the extreme anti-Catholic impulses of the Houses and yet secure their cooperation in producing a viable statute.[18]

[18] Neale I, 382-91; Walker, "Recusants," chap. 3, *passim*.

In 1584 Parliament, called on to produce major legislation under great pressure, once again outran the wishes of the Queen. This time the issues were more delicate than in 1581 and disagreement ran deeper. Earlier in the year, the Council had devised the novel scheme of the Bond of Association, an instrument signed by thousands of Englishmen all over the country, binding them by oath never to accept any claimant to the throne in whose name an attempt had been made on Elizabeth's life. The signers were bound to hunt such a person to death. The provisions extended to the heirs of such a claimant, should they take up the claim. In short, lynch law was to be applied both to Mary and to James in the event Elizabeth was murdered in a Catholic, Stuart-backed conspiracy. The extreme terms of the Association were embarrassing to the government since zealous Protestants declared they could not conscientiously accept a statute which commanded less than they had already sworn to do.[19]

In this instance the Queen and the Lord Treasurer were also at odds since Burghley went to the trouble of drawing up another draft, like that of 1563, for dealing with the aftermath of an assassination. It would have provided that Parliament and Council together would exercise supreme power during the interregnum—and choose the new monarch. So low was the stock of James VI in the most responsible English political circles. The Queen, however, would have none of such a scheme; aside from her determination that the succession question should not be broached, she was anxious to secure the good will of the Scottish monarch as England lurched nearer to open war with Spain. To satisfy Elizabeth as well as the over-excited gentlemen at Westminster required delicate handling, but once again it was achieved, in a statute which would serve to try the Queen of Scots in 1586 and yet leave her son's rights unimpeached.

Professor Neale justly pays tribute to the skill the Queen showed in her management of Parliament in these crucial sessions. But it is also important to note the growing dependence of the Crown on Parliament for the most necessary kinds of

[19] Neale II, 33-37, 44-54.

legislation. It meant that clear-cut distinction between prerogative and commonwealth matters so dear to the Queen's heart
was gradually fading under the force of irresistible circumstance.

The last Parliament to meet before the coming of the Armada, that of 1586-1587, was an extraordinary occasion. To
some extent it reenacted the events of 1572; once again the
central—indeed the only—question was the fate of Mary Stuart. This time the Lord Chancellor told Parliament that they
were called, neither to pass laws nor to grant a subsidy, but
merely to advise on the Queen of Scots. She had already been
tried for her share in the Babington conspiracy and stood con-
victed by the special court which had heard the case. Pressure
on the Queen to carry out the sentence of death was intense,
and there can be little doubt that this Parliament met more at
the Councillors' desire than at the Queen's and that they intended to use it to put maximum pressure on their mistress to
execute the Queen of Scots.

Consequently, the history of this Parliament's first session
was dominated by one issue. It was not a question of legislation but of the mobilization of a parliamentary opinion so
strong that the Queen could not evade it. There is no need to
recount the story of these weeks of maneuver; the intention
of the Houses was plain enough from the beginning, and no
effort was spared in preparing argument and petition. The
Queen could not possibly doubt what was the unanimous will
of her great Council of the realm. Yet her answer, although
gracious in tone, was as evasive as ever, and Parliament had
nothing immediate to show for its efforts except the formal
publication of the sentence against Mary. But the combined
pressure of the Houses must have contributed to the signing
of the warrant, the act which at last enabled the Council to
work its will on Mary—with how much or how little of Elizabeth's approval we can only guess. But once again Parliament
had been used as an instrument for arousing public sentiment
and using that sentiment as a lever against the Queen. It had
been a case of Parliament and Council working together
against the Crown.[20]

[20] *Ibid.*, 103-44.

Between the first session of fall 1586 and the second, which opened on 15 February 1587, the Queen of Scots had gone to her fate. The Houses' attention could now be drawn to another, even more momentous, matter. Since the previous Parliament had met, England had gone to war. Drake had sailed on his great sweep of the Iberian coasts and of the Indies; Leicester had taken his army to the Netherlands; and now there was every reason to suppose that a Spanish fleet was preparing against England. Money was of course needed and Parliament would be asked to provide. But this was by no means the first time that the subject of English foreign relations had been raised with the MP's by the Crown's ministers. As early as 1576 the ministers' agenda for the Commons included such an item. The Parliament of that year was summoned not because of some immediate need for money or for new legislation—as in 1571 and 1572.[21] It was the troubled condition of Europe which made the Councillors apprehensive of the future and they wanted to persuade the House to provide funds, not for the payment of accumulated past debts or for a looming emergency, but as a reserve to be laid by against future contingencies. It meant a new kind of approach to the members.

In 1576 Parliament was meeting on a prorogation, so there was no oration by the Lord Keeper, but the keynote speech was given by Sir Walter Mildmay, Chancellor of the Exchequer, who was to become—along with Sir Christopher Hatton —a kind of leader of the House for some years to come. Mildmay's speech struck a new note, persuasive, almost deferential, quite unlike the ponderous condescensions of Bacon.[22] "That in the beginning of this meeting such matters as be of importance may be thought on I am bold of your favors to move you of one that in my opinion is both of moment and necessity to the end that if you likewise find the same to be so you may commit it further to the consideration of such as you shall think convenient."

Mildmay sought to direct the business of the House but he did it by taking the House into his—and the Queen's—confi-

---

[21] Neale I, 346-48. [22] BL, Sloane Ms. 326, ff. 1-6.

dence rather than by a pompous lecture from on high, the style favored by Lord Keeper Bacon. The speech was divided into three parts: how the Queen found the realm, how she restored it, and where the realm stood now. The historical exposition was fully fleshed out, a contrast to the cursory references used by Bacon. It began with a condemnation of Mary's reign, and her reestablishment of Catholicism, "a wicked time and wicked ministers to bring to pass so wretched and wicked an act." There was a deliberate linking of Spanish dominance and Popery, "a strange nation [brought] to press our necks again into the yoke." The war which ensued with France and Scotland was no "quarrel of our own but to help them forward to their great advantage and our great loss and shame." These were the causes of the great debt the Queen inherited.

Mildmay then went on to celebrate the Queen's own achievements: the restoration of the Gospel, at great risk since it incurred the enmity of her neighbors; good relations with Scotland, in the past so "tickle," now steady as in no former age. The Leith expedition and the capture of Edinburgh Castle along with the Northern Rebellion had all cost heavily, but the Queen—and here was her singular achievement—had cleared away not only these debts but the accumulated inheritance from her predecessors, going back to the last years of her father. Her credit was now the best in Europe. This paean of praise closed on a traditional, but important, note: "how the justice of the realm is preserved and ministered to her people by Her Majesty's political and just government . . . that justice which is the bond of all common wealth do so tie and link together all degrees of persons within this land as there is suffered here no violence, none oppression, no respect of persons in judgment but *ius equabile* used to all indifferently."

Why, then, in "our blessed time of peace that we enjoy of the goodness of God through the ministry of Her Majesty," when all debts were cleared off, should the Queen be asking her subjects for more money? The weather might be calm now but wise mariners prepare for future bad weather and "these storms which are so bitter and so boisterous in other countries may reach us also before they be ended." Let us not forget the hatred borne us by our religious adversaries, he went on, both for our profession of faith and because England is a refuge for the persecuted.

Mildmay continued on a more prosaic note, listing one by one the purposes for which money had been spent, emphasizing the economy of a Queen who eschewed the expenses of mere pleasure and who thrust aside the temptation to which her predecessors had yielded—debasement of the coinage. He came to a conclusion by rehearsing the major items of recurring expenditure and by a reminder of the inflation of prices which was now universally felt.

It is worth noting so much of this long speech, for it marks a subtle movement in the government's attitude towards Parliament and it provided a model for future use. Parliament was being treated with an unaccustomed measure of frankness and more nearly as a partner, entitled to some fullness of explanation. Mildmay was doing more than merely catalogue events; he was expounding a coherent policy which deserved their support. Parliament responded with a subsidy and two-tenths and fifteenths.

When this same Parliament met again, for its third session, in 1581 Mildmay once again gave the House a lead.[23] Picking up the religious theme, he identified Elizabeth's defense of the Gospel as the root of "that implacable malice of the Pope and his confederates" who seek to bring her realm "again into thraldom." Since their last meeting he had new, confirmatory, evidence to add to the old story of the Northern Rebellion and the bull of 1570. The two successive expeditions to Ireland were plain indications of the Pope's malice and that of his auxiliaries. "Note from whence the last invasion into Ireland came, of what country the ships and of what nation the most part of the soldiers were and by the direction of whose ministers they received their victuals and furniture."

The Queen had suppressed these attempts, but there would be more: "there is but a piece of the storm over and . . . the great part of the tempest remaineth behind and is like to fall on us." Mildmay summed up all the active forces at work—

[23] *Ibid.*, ff. 19ff.

the Pope's own malice, the directives of Trent, and the support that the Pope had from the Catholic powers, who longed to see "the sparks of the flames that have been so terrible in other countries" flying over into England to kindle as great a fire here. Ireland, he argued, must be held, both for simple geographical-strategical reasons and because of England's mission to plant religion and justice in that island.

Lastly, in spite of the preaching of the Gospel and a regime of unexampled mildness, Mildmay reported that there were among the Queen's subjects recalcitrants who not only refused obedience to her laws but who actively accepted the ministrations of Rome. The lenity of time and mildness of the laws were no longer adequate for such offenders; more strait and severe laws were required. The passing of such laws and the provision of money to build the defenses of the country were Parliament's business. Let them be generous; the Queen had spent twice as much money of her own revenues as she had received in parliamentary subsidies. Once again, Parliament responded with a subsidy and two-tenths and fifteenths.

When Parliament met again in 1584, Mildmay must have pulled out his old notes from earlier sessions, for the two speeches (November 1584 and February 1585) go over much familiar ground, but with even stronger emphasis on Papal enmity and the threats of invasion which this posed.[24] He updated this line of argument by including the Campion trial, Allen's book, and the missionary colleges. He also, for the first time, singled out James of Scotland for mention, largely to praise the Queen's maternal care for that young sovereign. He ended with a plea for laws to control the Catholics, "those malicious, raging runagates, the Jesuits and priests" and for more money for military purposes. Even more emphasis was laid on the inflation of prices, all costs in this age far surmounting the times before.

In the November session, Mildmay was followed by Hatton.[25] The interest in the Vice-Chamberlain's speech lies in his open attack on the King of Spain. Philip's contemptuous treat-

[24] *Ibid.*, ff. 71ff., 82ff.
[25] Fitzwilliam of Milton Mss., f. 5.

ment of English envoys, his protection of the northern exiles, and Mendoza's intrigues (particularly the Throckmorton plot) with Mary Stuart were all retailed, and it was plainly said that "the King of Spain coupleth himself in league with the Pope against the Queen our mistress giving his word to join with him in any action against England." Parliament once more yielded the customary subsidy with two-tenths and fifteenths.

These speeches along with their predecessors in the previous Parliaments go beyond the rather perfunctory apologias of earlier years and move towards a systematic exposition of a foreign policy which self-consciously involves the nation in the defense not only of its safety but also of the true religion. Much is made by Mildmay of the blessings of the Gospel enjoyed under the present Queen, and a black picture is painted of the Marian regime, mingling religious with nationalist themes and linking Papistry with a foreign domination. Willy-nilly, foreign policy is being transformed from an arcane preserve of the Crown into a topic of wide public concern.

The historian must take note of the fact that this presentation of foreign relations in Parliament diverged rather widely from the actual line of policy being pursued by the government in its day-to-day dealings with foreign states. But one should not dismiss the ministers' speeches as mere window-dressing. In a complex and clumsy way, the conduct of England's relations with her neighbors was becoming an activity which included not only the normal diplomatic interplay between court and court but also an appeal to a formed public opinion. Mildmay and Hatton were beginning the task of forming the raw materials of inarticulate prejudice and voiceless intuitions into something like a national myth.

This change of direction on the part of government did not mark a conversion to some new constitutional doctrine but simply reflected the grim realities of a darkening political situation at home and abroad. By 1581 French power and the resistance in the Low Countries, the buffers on which England had been able to rely, were perceptibly ebbing. Spain, her power immensely augmented by her recent acquisitions, could no longer be counted on to remain neutral towards England. Within the realm the Catholic renascence was steadily gathering strength. The government needed money to hold Ireland, for the navy, and for strengthening England's land defenses, and in a larger sense it needed the active approval and enthusiastic support of its people.

THE FEARS which had agitated the ministers in earlier Parliaments and which they had sought to communicate to their fellow-MP's became dread realities by the meeting of February 1587. English soldiers were fighting the Spanish in the Netherlands, while English sailors harassed the coasts of King Philip's dominions. It was almost certain knowledge that a great invasion fleet was preparing against England. Money—much money—would be needed as well as the wholehearted support of the nation. The task of rousing the Commons to back the government was assigned to Sir Christopher Hatton, who was instructed by the Queen to inform the House of certain impending dangers. The Vice-Chamberlain's speech on this occasion was a long one—perhaps as much as two hours—and important in the history of Crown-Parliament relations, for Hatton went into great detail in explaining the causes of the war and in defending royal policy over the past decades. More important—and more novel—he took great pains to explain present and impending actions in the Low Countries and to sketch out the government's general plans for meeting the emergency of attack.[26]

Interestingly, the first section of the speech said little or nothing about the Low Countries. The whole thrust of Hatton's speech drove home a central and now familiar argument. England was the victim of a long-standing conspiracy of the Catholic powers, grouped around the Pope. Present events were merely the culmination of these deep-laid plans. A familiar recital of events followed—the Northern Rebellion, the bull of 1570, the expeditions to Ireland in 1579 and 1580, the recent conspiracies with the Queen of Scots—all pointed to the focus of enmity: Rome. The impending dangers proceeded "of an-

[26] D'Ewes, *Journals*, 408-10.

cient malice," and their principal root was the Papally inspired agreement among the Catholic princes, following on Trent, to "extirp the Christian religion (which they term heresy)."

Spain was seen as the instrument of this policy; Philip had comforted the Queen's enemies, had charged her (falsely) with aiding the Low Countries rebels and (again falsely) with abetting Drake's first voyage. Her efforts to secure his good will were brusquely rejected. The Queen, it was asserted, had not only forbidden English participation in the Netherlands but had punished captains who went over there. As to Drake, Elizabeth knew nothing of his intentions in 1577 and had promptly seized the booty when he returned. Don Antonio had been entertained because he was an anointed king who was merely given the honors due his rank.

The actions in the Low Countries were introduced into the speech only when Hatton came to explain what defense the Queen proposed against the threatening invasion from Spain. The first step was assistance to the States. Here the argument shifted somewhat as Hatton moved to justify the alliance. He urged the ancient leagues between England and Burgundy, leagues which were "people to people" rather than "prince to prince" in nature and cemented by much intercourse, commercial and personal, which had created a special relationship. The Spanish had treated the provinces abominably, "setting tyrants over them to use them like dogs." Their purpose "was to bring the Low Countries into a Monarchal seat and then *vae nobis*." And at that point the argument shifted ground again. "Necessity of safety" moved the Queen to act to preserve her own dominions, but also to keep open trade. (The notes from committee discussion go further and suggest that Spanish control of the Low Countries would literally strangle English trade.) Finally, reason of state was brought forward again: "it may not be suffered that a Neighbor should grow too strong." The princes of Italy had practiced such a prudent policy; so had Henry VII when he sought to preserve Brittany from French domination. But then, in closing, the Vice-Chamberlain returned to his first tune, "that the great grief is religion and . . . all godly ones are bound to defend it."

It was a very skillful performance, playing on old fears of international Catholicism, representing England as a long-intended victim, and portraying the coming struggle as a grand-scale religious struggle between the forces of righteousness and those of ancient superstition. But at the same time great care was taken to justify the expensive campaign in the Low Countries, with particular emphasis on the threat of Spanish domination and the throttling of English trade. Lofty ideological goals were tied to the pragmatic needs of trade and national security.

In committee discussion and in further debate on the floor, much was said about the latter theme. Hatton (in a second speech on the floor) painted a frightening picture of what would follow if the Low Countries were neglected.[27] England would lose her dominion over the Narrow Seas. There would pass to the hands of the mighty monarch "that all the world cannot now give him, *scilicet*, navigation." And in the same passage he foresaw an England stifled in her own traffic and suffocating in her own unsold commodities. The trouble which he took to defend the Low Countries' expedition, both as morally justifiable and strategically imperative, may well reflect the uncertainties of a House not altogether happy about the costs and the risks of overseas war. One member at least, Sir Harry Knevett, doubted that the Dutch could be trusted; they would simply use the English to serve their own turn. And the more Puritan-minded members tended to react by chasing the hare of home-grown Papists, to them more threatening than continental Papistry.

But the most important consequence of Hatton's initial speech was a determined effort to pressure the Queen into accepting the sovereignty of the provinces. The offer had been made more than once by the leaders of the Low Countries, and Leicester's assumption of the Governor-Generalship in 1586, which had so enraged his mistress, was probably meant to tug English policy from mere protection to actual sovereignty. Hence the parliamentary maneuver in the same direc-

<hr />

[27] BL, Harl. Ms. 6845, ff. 34-39; Neale II, 179 for Hatton's speech and other comments.

tion was a bold move and one made in the face of known royal disapproval. The thrust of the arguments used in committee was that only full sovereignty would make the alliance a workable one and lead to the desired victory over the Spaniards. What the committee proposed was to lure the Queen into the new commitment with the bait of a "benevolence." This special tax—to be levied over and above the subsidy— would fall only on wealthier subjects. But it was to be promised to the Queen for as many years as necessary—if she would take on the sovereignty of Holland and Zealand. The matter was discussed thoroughly in committee, and at least two papers were prepared, one a petition of the House, the other a speech to be made by the Speaker Puckering.[28] What is even more striking is that the backers of this move included Hatton himself, Sir Walter Mildmay, and Sir Francis Knollys, as well as a number of weighty MP's. This was no left-field play by the radical fringe but a strategy planned by the star players. There are plenty of signs of hesitation; they were quite aware that they were assuming an unfamiliar and risky role—the vale dictating to the hill, as one put it—and not all of them were equally venturesome. Puckering's speech would have done no more than offer an alternative to the Queen but would have tied the benevolence to her acceptance of the sovereignty. In the end their nerve failed and the matter was not pressed. But this does not diminish the importance of the episode. The interventionist party in the Council—and note that Hatton here is very much on the same side as Leicester—was certain enough of its goals to be prepared to risk the royal wrath; the Queen was to be mollified by the offer of the benevolence. Nevertheless, it would have put that wary courtier, Hatton, the willing instrument of the royal will, and the cautiously reserved bureaucrat, Mildmay, on the same side as the reckless Job Throckmorton, who had just been put in the Tower by royal command for a long speech advocating—in most indiscreet terms—much the same policy. The episode is a measure

[28] For this whole episode, see Neale II, 166-67, 176-83. The sources are in D'Ewes, *Journals*, 408-10, and BL, Harl. Ms. 7188, ff. 89-103; *ibid.*, 6845, ff. 30-42.

of the importance which parliamentary action had come to assume in the minds of the most practiced and most astute politicians in the Council.

The episode also casts a great deal of light on the winding intricacies of Elizabethan policy-making. The outward image of monarchy was one of monolithic stability and of self-confident decisiveness. In fact, as the record reveals to us, there was inner tension and considerable diversity of viewpoint and even contradiction among the policy-makers. The public view to which Parliament and the larger public were treated blended the spectacle of a great ideological struggle: England, the defender of the true Gospel versus the Babylonish tyrant of Rome, with the more mundane vision of a contest for trade and dominion in the North Sea. Elizabeth's own conception differed widely; she had moved only with the greatest reluctance to war and was now struggling desperately to limit herself to a short-term intervention, lasting only long enough to bring the contending parties to the negotiating table. Already she and Burghley were putting out feelers to Parma for a compromise peace and bullying the States to accept whatever she could get for them. In this operation she was quite willing to sacrifice Dutch Protestant interests if it would bring about peace. Elizabeth was astute enough to realize that parliamentary backing for the military offensive was necessary to give authenticity to her diplomatic moves. For this purpose she was prepared to make a show of candor in order to coax the Commons into a subsidy. If she could bring Spain to a compromise settlement, the rhetorical stage-setting could be returned to storage.

Her Councillors did for the most part believe in what they told the House of Commons. Yet they too were not entirely ingenuous, for the goals which Hatton and his friends sought to realize had another end in view besides the preservation of the Gospel faith. Half-hidden in their arguments supporting English sovereignty over the provinces was a nakedly expansionist ambition. By moving from protection to sovereignty, the Queen would shift from short-term intervention in the Low Countries to permanent dominion. It was an act of annexation which they were pressing on their mistress, one which would create anew an English empire on the continent. How conscious they were of these long-term consequences is hard to say; there is little direct argument on behalf of such a move. But the logic of their argument is plainly to be seen. Only by becoming the Queen's subjects would the Netherlanders attain the discipline and cohesion which would give them victory.

So England lurched into war, moved by a complexity of conflicting fears and hopes. The sovereign clutched at every straw in her desperate efforts to disentangle herself from the struggle altogether. Yet she allowed her ministers to raise the terrible spectre of an anti-Protestant crusade aimed directly and particularly at England. Among them there were those who fervently believed in that menace, while others mingled their fears of the Catholic threat with their half-conscious dreams of empire, political and commercial, beyond the North Sea. How these mingled visions of the present would shape the future, only time could tell.

THE AGGRESSIVE INSISTENCE of the House of Commons on interfering in the passage of government bills had been irksome to the Crown and to its ministers, but it had proved possible to work out compromises for at least some important measures. The Commons' tendency to outpace government intentions on legislation on which ministers and MP's agreed in principle had been embarrassing from time to time, but here again they had been able to work out satisfactory arrangements and to push through necessary statutes. But there was a third area of friction between Crown and Parliament not so susceptible of compromise. From 1566 onwards, almost every session of Parliament had been marked by determined attempts to alter—and finally to destroy—the settlement of 1559. The Queen had been outspoken in her displeasure and had not hesitated to use her prerogative powers to halt these attempts, even to the extent of imprisoning recalcitrant members. Yet, in spite of these explicit royal actions, the reformist spokesmen had obstinately continued to bring forward again and again in each successive session yet another version of their program for change.

This determination to press on at all costs—banging their heads against a stone wall—baffles the modern observer. The Puritan agitators in the House of Commons were not political novices; the most important of them sat repeatedly in a succession of Parliaments; they had Court connections and opportunity for knowing something of what was going on. They certainly knew the Queen's mind; their loyalty to her was fervent. How, then, are we to account for their insistence in pushing a politically hopeless enterprise and one so patently irritating to the soverign?

The answer is not simple. First of all, much of this agitation was essentially apolitical in character. The most vehement and the most articulate of these men—a Job Throckmorton or a Peter Wentworth—were primarily idealists, or, if one prefers, zealots. And one catches in their words the accents of a certain innocence, the innocence of the wholehearted believer, the totally committed, of the man whose tenets of faith are so self-evidently true—and so persuasive to action—that one has but to hear to be convinced and to act. If they could only catch the ear of the Queen, she could not fail to be persuaded by the infallible proofs they offered her. It would take many rebuffs to discourage a faith so lively and so ingenuous as this.

Not all were so innocently ardent as this; others, more worldly-wise although no less committed, such as Sir Francis Knollys, were unremitting in their efforts but more acutely aware of the limits of the possible. These men would have been content with a more modest program of change, within the general framework of 1559. But even they were slow to realize that the Queen would not be budged so much as one iota from the position she had taken up. She, on her side, could never comprehend the genuine idealism of the reformers; they, on theirs, could not grasp the fundamental secularity of her mind. But beyond these illusions of the zealous, which afflicted even familiars of the Court circle, there were other causes for this seeming political myopia. One must allow for the distance which separated "Court" and "country." In spite of personal and familial links which bound many country families to courtiers and kept some channel of communication open, most of what went on at Court was known only to a very limited circle. There was no network of communication which disseminated information or ideas easily. Consequently, the average country gentleman who came up to Westminster for a parliamentary session lived in a world whose horizons were surprisingly different from those of the courtier. He was by no means without opinions, especially on the subject of religion, and he listened responsively to speakers who excited his feelings on such topics. It was such primitive Protestants as these —anti-clerical and anti-Roman, contemptuous of clerical pretensions and easily moved to vote against them—who made up the bulk of the majorities which cheerfully voted for so many of the Puritans' parliamentary proposals. Their response was simple and straightforward, an expression of deep-felt biases, but not a politically calculating action. They rushed in cheerfully where courtiers feared to tread.

But these are only partial explanations; one needs to look to the larger dimensions of Elizabethan political culture to achieve a better understanding of the legislators' role in government. In a sense it is inappropriate to discuss "parliamentary politics" at all in the Elizabethan setting. The term lends a spurious air of modernity which is dangerously misleading, for it contains in it the implicit assumption of a national political community. In fact, late Tudor England had not yet achieved an integrated political culture on a national scale. Politics was the business of the much smaller world of the Court, indeed even more narrowly of the Council. And this microcosm took its being from that sole person, its prime mover, the Queen. It was her "mere will and motion" which powered the whole system. It was she who granted admission to the magic circle, and the role that one played there was determined directly by his relationship with the sovereign lady. The inner dynamics of this world were not contests of ideas but the rivalry of men. The Puritans were able to obtain protection and patronage at Court because the favorite had taken up their cause; interventionist foreign policy was urged on the

Queen because of Leicester's ambitions to play the Protestant hero on the continental stage. The Puritans were in the end crushed—at least in part—because a new favorite, Hatton, found it to his advantage to oppose them. In such a setting, the making of policy is the activity of a limited elite and its history linked to the history of Court politics.

What, then, were the relations between the two political worlds of Court and Parliament? The permanent, ongoing world of the Court was marked by a remarkable degree of stability. Its members, lifetime appointees, served out long careers, terminated only by death. Their relationships with the Queen were established and predictable; so were their views on public matters. Sober continuity was the keynote in this political establishment. Parliament, on the other hand, was comet-like in relation to this sedate solar system, with the important difference that its appearances were irregular and unpredictable. Its personnel, although overlapping from one session to another, was ever changing; more important, it had no real leadership. Individual men held the House for a moment by their eloquence, but there was not even the embryonic kind of leadership cadre which began to show its uncertain shape in Stuart Parliaments. What continuity there was arose from issues, not from men. The familiar topics—succession, marriage, the Queen of Scots, above all, religion—echoed from one Parliament to another, as well as the less dramatic business of commonwealth legislation. These questions were the staple of every meeting, but the order of business, the sequence of debate and of legislation, remained helter-skelter, at the mercy of random circumstance. The House behaved like an unruly horse, likely to bolt in any direction at the slightest start.

Yet in spite of its erratic life-rhythm and its untidy habits of business, the House came to make a greater impress on public life than for many generations past. The contrast with the reasonably biddable Parliaments of the Queen's father's time is obvious. From being very much a junior partner waiting obediently for directive signals from above, it was moving uncertainly towards a position more nearly resembling that of a partner. In some measure this new vitality arose from efforts within the House itself; it also sprang from the growing habit of collaboration with leading Councillors which drew the two political worlds, at least for the moment, onto a common track. But, most important, the lower House was neither a vehicle for magnate rivalries, as it had been sometimes in the fourteenth and fifteenth centuries, nor an arena into which the partisan squabbles of conciliar faction spilled over, as in Jacobean and Caroline times. So far as the record goes, it is hard to see any evidence of systematic magnate manipulation of the Lower House. Councillors did indeed intervene in parliamentary elections on behalf of relatives or friends, but there is no visible indication—with the possible exception of the Earl of Bedford—that they sought to use this patronage to press particular legislation or significantly to influence the behavior of the House. Sympathies, personal ties, shared aspirations there certainly were, but no evidence of an attempt to turn to fuse these into conscious political action within Parliament. Conciliar politics and parliamentary politics were drawn together, but by collaborative rather than by manipulative strategies.

Instances of this collaboration are numerous and date from very early in the reign. In the 1560's Councillors and Commons shared an eager interest in the marriage/succession problem and joined in pressing their views on the Queen. This question fell into the background later on, or rather, was transformed by the presence of that sinister claimant to the throne, the Scottish Queen. Her fate was the subject of debate in two Parliaments of the early 1570's and of two more in the next decade. The role of Parliament in these questions varied; their petitions for marriage and determination of the succession were made much against the Queen's will, but on the subject of the Queen of Scots Elizabeth was more ambivalent. She was at least willing to allow discussion, although hardly disposed to take the advice offered. In all these cases there were groups of Councillors and of MP's with common views, and the difficulties of cooperation were largely tactical ones, above all, of reining in Commons enthusiasm within terms which might have some chance of royal acceptance. The immediate results of these collaborative efforts were somewhat disappointing. The Queen did not marry, nor appoint a successor, nor—for two decades—would she cut off Mary's head. But there was measurable effect; there can be little doubt that parliamentary pressure contributed to the execution of Norfolk in 1572 and to the signing of the death warrant in 1587.

The most interesting episode in this collaboration occurred in the Parliament of 1586 in the effort, spearheaded by Hatton, to cajole the Queen into accepting the sovereignty of the United Provinces with the bait of a benevolence over and above the subsidy. The enterprise was aborted, but the boldness of the scheme, the participation of the favorite, the detailed discussion of tactics, are all signs of the precocious growth of novel political conceptions. Had it been carried through, this scheme would have taken Parliament into the very *arcana imperii* of the Tudor monarchy, and not only as a petitioner but as a would-be bargainer.

But the most time-consuming of the great policy questions which agitated the Elizabethan House of Commons was religious reform, and here, significantly enough, the initiatives seem all to have come from within the Lower House, from a clique of MP's working together (and collaborating with Puritan divines) but quite independent of any overt magnate direction. The reformers did have friends in high places, but their benevolence was pretty much limited to the protection of individual dissenters; they were not prepared to sponsor reform legislation. Hence the Puritans' parliamentary campaign for reform remained very largely a House of Commons enterprise promoted by members of their own.

THESE ARE DECADES of rapid and far-reaching changes within the parliamentary institution; how are we to characterize them? It would be all too easy to see Elizabethan parliamentary history as mere prologue to the constitutional struggles of the next century; for us there are premonitory signs of things to come. But contemporaries had no such range of vision. To them Parliament still seemed what it had been for some generations, a body at once petitionary and consultative.

The members came up to Westminster bearing the grievances of their constituents, although cast now as bills rather than as petitions. Some of these were private bills for the particular needs of a locality, but others might very well be incorporated in some larger piece of national legislation. On a whole range of legislation—all those measures which were regulative of the economy or of the social order or remedial to the procedures of the common law—they expected governmental initiative, but they also expected and received the right to criticize and to amend. But they had also come, since Henry VIII's time, to expect to hear something of the grander issues of state as well. In these matters they thought of themselves either as auditors, or as petitioners respectfully urging on the Queen their worries and their hopes as to her marriage, the succession, or religion. On some questions, such as the treatment of the Queen of Scots, they were prepared with much more specific recommendations. But in this second area they hoped only to be listened to; they were prepared to abide in patience the Queen's rejection of their proposals; the right of decision was undeniably hers.

Nevertheless, the expanding role and the rising expectations of the Commons led to ambiguities and to frictions. The House had reached a stage where it was invited by the government to give its advice on matters of national concern and, in some measure, to share in framing the requisite legislation. This was a very delicate stage, for the newly aroused expectations of the Commons tended all too easily to outrun the limits which the Crown's ministers wished to set. Once the Commons was invited to give its advice it would be a short step to offering it unasked. Very quickly the Commons were trespassing into the sacred enclosure of the prerogative. This led to continual skirmishes between Crown and House over the latter's right to discuss, let alone to legislate on, sensitive topics.

Below this level of overt friction which manifested itself whenever Parliament met, there were changes in the deeply-lying levels of public consciousness. If there was yet no real national political community, there was an embryonic public opinion on national questions which was growing apace throughout the Queen's reign and which was fumblingly seeking means of articulation. On religious issues the protagonists on each side turned to print, to pamphlet warfare, but on more straightforwardly political questions the only forum that seemed appropriate was the floor of the House of Commons. But it is essential to understand that the goal of the orators who made themselves heard there was not really legislative; they did not expect to control policy-making, to force the Queen to accept their bidding. They wanted to air as fully and as eloquently as possible their views, and they hoped to persuade the Queen. If she declined to heed their urging on one occasion, it was quite appropriate to renew it on the next. But, however frustrated they might be by her obstinate deafness to their pleas, they never, on any occasion, moved to the next logical step—that of questioning her authority, or that of her servants, as their seventeenth-century successors would soon do. The Elizabethan parliamentary debates were on the immediate substantive issues of the day, not on "constitutional" questions, on the right ordering of state power.

One caveat has to be entered here: the Puritan reformers are clearly an exception to this generalization. They were seeking something more fundamental than a mere redress of grievances. As they saw their mission, they had a charge from above, laid down in the prescriptions of the New Testament. The reordering of ecclesiastical government was a necessity laid upon them by the Deity's specific directions. It was not the redistribution of power but the absolute precondition for the saving of men's souls which moved them. Hence they felt compelled—no matter how many times they were rebuffed—to return to the charge and to renew their urgings upon Parliament and sovereign. The favorable response they received from the House reflected a general sympathy with their Protestant ideals rather than a wholehearted agreement with their whole platform. It is important to note that when in 1586 the extreme Puritan program was urged on Commons, Hatton's powerful counteroffensive, in which he appealed both to instincts of order and of property, served to pull the House back from its first impulse of support for the radicals.

Parliament by 1590 was something different from what it had been thirty years earlier, something a good deal more than a merely petitionary or tax-granting body, something more than an advisory Council waiting to be asked its opinion. The Commons were beginning to offer, unsolicited, their own opinions, not only on "commonwealth" matters but on "matters of state" as well, on anything which was a matter of public concern. But they were far from being a conscious competitor for power with the Crown and far from being a systematic critic, a perpetual grand jury, forever prepared to bring in another indictment. There was clearly a good deal of new wine being poured into old and increasingly fragile bottles. There was perhaps a sense of discomfort, but fundamentally there was still awesome regard for the Crown, respect for its chosen councillors, and a predisposition to cooperate wholeheartedly in the doing of the commonwealth's business. The loose and rather clumsy ties which bound Crown and Parliament together were strained here and there and the strains were growing, but the system was still a healthy and a workable one.

CONCLUSION

I~ A~ EARLIER STUDY I sought to understand the making of the
Elizabethan regime. Elizabeth came to the throne under unpropitious circumstances and immediately had to face a series
of dangers which menaced not only the stability but the very
survival of the new government. By 1572 the regime had
passed successfully through a testing period marked by
threats both from without the realm and within the ranks of
the Court. All the crises had been triumphantly surmounted,
and the regime rested firmly on the enthusiastic loyalty of the
political classes; its own internal affairs were in good order;
the Queen's unchallenged leadership was backed by a united
and an efficient corps of councillors and ministers.

This second study, taking up at that point in Elizabethan
history, has examined the functioning of the regime during
the middle years of the reign, a time when the English leadership was buffeted by a series of events, foreign and domestic,
which tested its abilities to the utmost. During these years adverse circumstances worsened most of the problems which
these events created, and the later 1580's found the country
engaged in a war in which the stakes were the very survival
of the regime and indeed of English independence. The preceding chapters have examined these developments in some
detail. As we look retrospectively and comprehensively at
them, what conclusions can be drawn from these years of bitter struggle? What balance of judgment can be struck in an
assessment of the English leadership and of its making of
policy?

Such a judgment cannot be made without attempting to understand what goals the English leaders set themselves in these
years. There was no articulated program which they set before
themselves, but their intentions can be deciphered without
much difficulty from their actions. A spectrum of differing,
but not widely divergent, positions is visible. At one end
stood the Queen, a resolute conservative whose goals were

summed up in her famous motto: *semper eadem*. Quite without the usual ambitions of her kind, Elizabeth's natural instinct was to avoid any initiatives, never on her own to set in motion any waves of change. Pressured by men and by events, she was resolved to yield as little as possible. But her conservatism was neither blind nor insensitive; keenly alert to the currents in motion all around her, she sought constantly to divert them or, if that were not possible, to minimize their pressures upon her and her affairs. Consequently her policy was usually a reactive one, responding to events as they unfolded.

Over against this royal immobility stood the activism of the radical Protestants. In its simplest terms, their program was one of active patronage of evangelical zeal at home and vigorous encouragement of Protestant movements abroad. Most of the royal Councillors were ranged somewhere between these two extremes, a good deal more sympathetic to reformers' views than the Queen, but more cautious in their commitments, more open to the accommodations which circumstances forced on them.

Under the pressure of events, as we have seen, both the Queen and the Protestant enthusiasts had to compromise with events, and in practice found it fairly easy to work together in a loose although not frictionless harness.

Indeed, in assessing the Elizabethan regime at work, one must immediately take note of the unity of purpose, at once flexible and enduring, of the inner leadership. Its members were men of far-reaching ambition, who, nevertheless, subordinated their individual aspirations to the needs of the state and to the will of the sovereign. Naturally competitive, they submitted to the bonds of collegiality within the Council. Decisions were made collectively and carried out loyally. The disagreements and rivalries within the Council are mere trifles when set against the breathless disorder of the Valois Court, where personal ambitions ran riot and shattered every effort to achieve unity of purpose and action or even basic civil order. The steadiness and continuity of the English regime is in sharp contrast not only to the topsy-turvy confusions of the

French situation but also to the slippery insecurities in Philip's suspicion-ridden court at the Escurial.

The unity of the English leaders provided a strong nucleus for the whole political order of England. It steadied the local aristocracies of the counties and confirmed them in habits of obedience and of responsibility. Across the Channel both the King of France and the Spanish government in the Low Countries were struggling with the restless ambitions of an untamed aristocracy, with a problem that England had left behind a century earlier. In the island kingdom, aristocratic turbulence, so formidable in the fifteenth century, was now merely a memory; the last ripples of such opposition to royal authority had troubled the surface of politics in the Pilgrimage of Grace and again, more faintly, in 1569. They served only to demonstrate that magnate ambitions and aristocratic unruliness were a spent force. And the absence of such a force in the English political world effectively foredoomed efforts towards a Catholic political renascence, since it meant that one of the vital ingredients for such an alliance of nobles and religious malcontents as shook Scotland in the 1550's, France after 1560, and the Low Countries in the same years was now altogether missing in England. Hence all but the lunatic fringe of the English gentry was innoculated against the infection of foreign conspiracy. Even the Catholic gentry, with a few notable exceptions, is to be included in this immune population. And the confidence of the ruling classes in their sovereign and her Council meant that when the testing-time of war came —indeed even before hostilities commenced—there was steady support for the herculean effort which the nation was called upon to make.

To have achieved such vital and solid support was an immense achievement, but when one turns to the making of policy and to the actual conduct of affairs both at home and abroad, the picture is obviously a much more checkered one. To attain some view of it, one must begin by separating out foreign policy from domestic. As was suggested above, the regime was divided between a sovereign who wished to avoid commitments of any kind at all and activist ministers who wanted her to take the lead in championing Protestantism in every theater of action. Circumstances in the early 1570's favored the Queen's position. Rebellion in the Low Countries flickered so fitfully that even the left-wingers had to admit that there was little room for more than an official neutrality which was bent so far as possible in favor of the rebels. In France, so long as the opposition was solely religious in character, the Queen was prepared to do no more than keep the fires of discontent alight. But when the broader-based coalition of Protestants and politiques, including the Montmorencys and Alençon, tempted the Queen to a more far-reaching intervention, she was stirred to unwonted interest. Casting aside much of her usual inertia, Elizabeth encouraged the activities of the dissident coalition in such a way as might have led her to major involvement in French internal affairs. She might have found herself bogged down in a commitment from which it would have been impossible to withdraw, too demanding for her capacities but too dangerous to abandon. What she might have done had events favored her we cannot say; it may be that chance—and the mediating skills of the Queen Mother Catherine—saved the Queen of England from a grave misjudgment, from her own worst instincts.

At this point the sudden collapse of Spanish power in the Low Countries of its own weight transformed the scene and forced the Queen and her ministers to a series of testing decisions. The Queen's own conservative goal, consistently pursued through all these years, the restoration of the *status quo ante* of Charles V's time, now seemed within reach. Those of her ministers who dreamed of a Protestant regime across the North Sea could now hope for its realization. But clearly the outcome of events in the Netherlands would be decisively shaped by English action. The Queen could no longer procrastinate; she was driven to an active role, one which she took up without hesitation. It was her will which determined English policy for the next half dozen years. As we know, she rejected, after some hesitation, the direct intervention which Walsingham and Leicester pressed upon her, in favor of the more indirect strategy of alliance with France. Initially this was to be cemented by her marriage to Anjou. The rift which this opened within the English governing circles served to cast light on the nature of the regime.

First and most obvious is the sudden intrusion of the Queen's own personal impulses into high politics. The flare-up of her matrimonial ambitions reveals a middle-aged spinster snatching at her last opportunity for marriage. It would not be a marriage for love—as a Dudley match would have been in 1561—but it would be a splendid marital alliance as well as a great diplomatic accomplishment. With England and France linked, Spain could be decisively checked in the Low Countries and balanced off in the larger equation of the European community.

The shipwreck of the Queen's matrimonial plans illuminated the limits of her power within her own realm. She could have made the marriage but only at the cost of rupturing the amity which bound together the inner world of the Elizabethan Court and which by extension ensured stability to the whole English political order. However little the Queen liked it, a weighty mass of her greater subjects were so passionately committed to the Protestant faith that they could not tolerate the risk of a Papist husband for their monarch. Moreover, these religious loyalties were hardly to be distinguished from a deep-rooted xenophobia, nourished by the experience of Mary's reign, which could not abide the prospect of an alien ruler on the English throne. The Queen, however much she may have been tempted by the delights of matrimony, never lost her footing on the solid ground of English political reality. She saw that the Anjou match would risk too many solid assets and would erode the assured and comfortable routines which buoyed up her own sense of security and her control of her own world.

The fading out of the marital venture left the English leaders to face the weakness of the hand they had to play in the great game of international politics. Their constant assumption was that England could not stand alone against the might of Spain. In 1576, alliance with the new States regime had been rejected, certainly because of its demonstrated disunity and probably because of the royal distaste for rebels against constituted authority. Now, in 1581, alliance was being sought with a French state shaken by endemic civil war, one in which the monarchy could no longer master the factions within the kingdom, let alone carry out such an active foreign policy as England proposed. But even had this been possible, England was in no position to persuade the French to the advantages of such an alliance, for her ministers could not bring the Valois to believe in the honesty of English intentions. Elizabeth's personal diplomacy, based on a shameless opportunism, had succeeded handsomely in situations where the prolongation of an unresolved tension was the goal, but now, when clearcut decision and resolute commitment were required, she faltered badly. The contrast between the unrelenting logic of the English arguments for actions against the overweening power of a Spanish Crown which threatened to dominate all Europe and the feeble evasions with which Elizabeth met every French demand for concrete commitments of men, money, ships, or arms stand in pitiful and revealing contrast. A virtuoso in the fine arts of diplomatic intercourse, Elizabeth could not measure up when the realization of her own clearly defined goals required bold risk-taking. Her failure of nerve at this crisis of affairs left no alternative but the very second-best strategy of backing Anjou. Here wishful thinking blinded the royal vision, when to the eyes of lesser mortals the Duke's failure was patent.

In sum, the argument has been that Elizabeth's decision to reject cooperation with the States in 1577 rested on plausible and well-grounded arguments as to the internal weakness of that regime, while the alternative policy which she pursued—alliance with France—was fundamentally misconceived. The first and major error was the failure to perceive how far French royal power had disintegrated under the stresses of religious civil war. The English vision of France was an anachronistic one, lagging well behind historical reality. Beyond that, the strategy of alliance was also misconceived. Alliance would have been possible, if at all, only by forging the indissoluble bond of a royal marriage. That proved impossible without endangering the whole fabric of English political life. Alliance without matrimony foundered on well-grounded French skepticism of Elizabeth's willingness to take any real risks. The failure of the French alliance made real the worst nightmares of the English leaders—the prospect of solitary confrontation with the Hapsburg power. Now the rift between London and Madrid had been widened and deepened almost beyond measure; alliance with the great power of France had gone glimmering, while the alternate alliance, with the Low Countries States, had been disastrously devalued by the mounting successes of Parma.

To turn from foreign to domestic concerns in these years brings to view a very different landscape. The vexing difficulties which the English leadership faced in the shaping of a satisfactory new religious order for the nation were of a profoundly serious nature, but they did not risk the security or the survival of the regime itself. As in foreign affairs, there was a range of differing goals as between the Queen and her Councillors. She was adamantly opposed to any movement away from the norms established in the first year of the reign —the Acts of Supremacy and of Uniformity and the Injunctions issued in the same summer. By the early 1570's her Councillors were men resolutely set against Rome and its ways, and most of them favored, in varying degrees, continuing changes in a Protestant and evangelical direction. They found it difficult to accept the Queen's unyielding conservatism and did not hesitate in obstructing her policy by patronizing Puritan divines and by encouraging disobedience to the measures which the bishops, under royal instruction, tried to enforce on the clergy. And the prelates themselves were for the most part only half-hearted in their measures of enforcement.

The problem became more acute when, from 1570 on, the evangelical protest became shriller and more intense and was articulated in an alternative platform of Church government. The reaction of the English leadership over the next dozen or so years, fumblingly uncertain, is in sharp contrast to its relative unity of purpose in foreign policy. Once again the key to understanding lies in the sovereign herself. The Queen's own deep-rooted secularity made her quite tone-deaf to the claimant aspirations of her devouter subjects. The consequences of her insensitivity were several. The persuasions of her Councillors in favor of a more flexible attitude towards the moderate evangelical went unheard, and many of them ultimately swelled the ranks of the irreconcilables. The Queen's refusal to listen to the reasoned case which Archbishop Grindal made in behalf of the prophesyings choked off all hope of the kinds of modest adaptations which would have satisfied the great bulk of the discontented evangelicals. The Queen's ultimate support for Whitgift's primacy was less an acceptance of his vision of an Erastian Church than approval of a strong authoritarian personality who would, at last, enforce the uniformity after which she so ardently hankered. The new Primate moved with great speed to reveal his policy and to enforce it. The angry buzz of protest which it aroused left him unmoved, secure in his own beliefs and in the royal favor. What success would attend his policy was left for the future to reveal, but it was clear that for the first time since 1559 a strong hand sought to impose a clearcut policy on the still malleable forms of the English reformed Church.

In the almost two decades under consideration, the English leadership had been severely tested. Under the unyielding pressure of threatening events, the Queen had unfalteringly maintained her unquestioned command of English policy and of English politics, and her Councillors had rallied loyally behind her. A mistress of the diplomatic art, the Queen had not measured up to the demands of grand strategy. The goals she set herself were reasonable and relevant, but the means she proposed to use did not square with the realities of European life in the 1580's. The Queen's judgment of men and events, so just and so acute when it dealt with the English scene, went badly awry when she turned her attention to the world beyond her borders. Here her misjudgments denied her the objective she had set before herself and her ministers. After 1585, the Queen and her subjects had to live with the consequences of those misjudgments; the next decade and a half would reveal what those consequences were.

BIBLIOGRAPHY

ABBREVIATIONS

APC   *Acts of the Privy Council*
BL   British Library
CSPD   *Calendar of State Papers, Domestic*
CSPF   *Calendar of State Papers, Foreign*
CSPSc   *Calendar of State Papers Relating to Scotland*
CSPSp   *Calendar of State Papers Spanish*
KL, *Huguenots* Kervyn de Lettenhove, *Les Huguenots*
KL, *Relations* Kervyn de Lettenhove and Gilliodts-Van
                 Severen, *Relations politiques*
PRO   Public Record Office

MANUSCRIPTS

British Library
  Additional Manuscripts 4,149; 14,028; 22,473; 22,563; 26,473;
    28,571; 29,546; 48,064; 48,084; 48,116; 48,127; 48,129.
  Cotton Mss.: Galba C XI, D I and III; Titus F I
  Egerton Ms. 1694
  Harleian Mss. 285, 287, 3845, 6994
  Lansdowne Mss. 25, 27, 28, 396
  Sloane Ms. 326
Longleat House
  Dudley Papers
Northamptonshire Record Office
  Fitzwilliam of Milton Mss.
Public Record Office
  Baschet Transcripts
  State Papers 12

PRINTED SOURCES

Allen, William. *A True, Sincere, and Modest Defense of English Catholics*, etc. (1583). Edited, with *The Execution of*

Justice in England, by William Cecil, by Robert M. King-don. Ithaca: Cornell University Press, 1965.

Bruce, John, ed. *Correspondence of Robert Dudley, Earl of Leycester . . . 1585 and 1586.* Camden Soc. 27 (1844).

Brugmans, Hajo, ed. *Correspondentie van Robert Dudley . . . 1585-1588.* 3 vols. Werken van het hist. Genootschap, 3rd ser., nos. 56-58. Utrecht, 1931.

Calendar of Letters and State Papers Relating to English Af-fairs . . . Principally in the Archives of Simancas. Edited by Martin A. S. Hume. 4 vols. London, 1892-1899.

Calendar of State Papers, Domestic Series, of the Reigns of Edward VI, Mary, Elizabeth, etc. Edited by Robert Lemon, et al. 12 vols. London, 1856-1872.

Calendar of State Papers, Foreign Series, of the Reign of Eliz-abeth, etc. Edited by Joseph Stevenson et al. London, 1863+.

Calendar of State Papers Relating to Scotland and Mary, Queen of Scots, 1547-1603. Edited by Joseph Bain et al. 13 vols. London, 1898-1969.

Camden, William. *Annals of Queen Elizabeth.* London, 1675.

Cardwell, Edward. *Documentary Annals of the Reformed Church of England*, etc. 2 vols. Oxford, 1839, 1844.

Cecil, William. *The Execution of Justice in England*, etc. London, 1583. Edited, with William Allen's *True Defense*, by Robert M. Kingdon. Ithaca: Cornell University Press, 1965.

A Collection of Original Letters from the Bishop to the Privy Council, 1564, etc. Edited by Mary Bateson. Camden Society n.s. 53 (1895): *Miscellany IX*.

A Collection of Scarce and Valuable Tracts . . . of the Late Lord Somers. 2nd ed. Edited by Walter Scott. Vol. I, Lon-don, 1809.

Collinson, Patrick, ed. *See* Wood, Thomas.

A Compleat Journal of the Votes, Speeches and Debates, Both of the House of Lords and House of Commons throughout the Whole Reign of Queen Elizabeth, etc. Collected by Si-monds D'Ewes. London, 1693; reprint, Wilmington, Del., and London: Scholarly Resources, 1974.

A Complete Collection of State Trials. Compiled by William Cobbett, T. B. Howell, et al. 42 vols. London, 1816-1898.

Digges Dudley. *The Compleat Ambassador,* etc. London, 1655.

A Discoverie of the Treasons Practiced and Attempted against the Queene's Majesty and the Realme, by Francis Throckmorton, etc. London, 1584. Reprinted in *Harleian Miscellany,* with annotations and notes by Oldys and Park. Vol. III. London, 1809.

Documents concerning English Voyages to the Spanish Main, 1569-1580. Edited by I. A. Wright. Hakluyt Soc., 2nd ser. 71. London, 1932.

Dudley, Robert. *See* Bruce, John; Brugmans, Hajo.

Fénélon, Bertrand de Salignac, Seigneur de la Mothe. *Correspondance diplomatique.* 7 vols. Paris and London, 1838-1840.

Frere, W. H., ed. *Visitation Articles and Injunctions.* Alcuin Club Collections 16, vol. 3. London, 1910.

———, and Douglas, C. E., eds. *Puritan Manifestoes: A Study of the Origin of the Puritan Revolt,* etc. 1907. New ed., with preface by Norman Sykes. London: S.P.C.K., 1954.

Fuller, Thomas. *Church History.* 6 parts. London, 1655.

Furnivall, F. J., and Morfill, W. R., eds. *Ballads from Manuscripts.* 2 vols. Ballad Society. London, 1868-1873.

Gachard, G. P. *Correspondance de Philippe II sur les affaires des Pays-Bas.* Vol. 3. Brussels, 1858.

Gee, Henry, and Hardy, W. J., compilers. *Documents Illustrative of English Church History.* London, 1896.

Grindal, Edward. *Remains.* Edited by William Nicholson. Parker Society. Cambridge, 1843.

Hakluyt, Richard. *The Principal Navigations,* etc. Edited by Walter Raleigh. 12 vols. Hakluyt Soc., extra series. Glasgow, 1903-1905.

Hall, Edward. *The Union of the Two Noble and Illustre Families York and Lancaster,* etc. 1542. New edition, as Hall's *Chronicle,* by Henry Ellis. London, 1809.

Hatton, Christopher. *See* Nicolas, Sir [Nicholas] Harris.

Haynes, Samuel, and Murdin, William, eds. *Collection of State Papers . . . Left by William Cecil, Lord Burghley*, etc. 2 vols. London, 1740. 1759.

Historical Manuscripts Commission. *Calendar of the Manuscripts of the . . . Marquis of Salisbury . . . at Hatfield House*, etc. Part II, London, 1888; Part III, London, 1889.

Holinshed, Raphael. *Chronicles of England, Scotland, and Ireland*. 3 vols. [London], 1587.

Jewel, John. *An Apology or Answer in Defence of the Church of England*, etc. London, 1562.

Kervyn de Lettenhove, J. M. B. C. *Les Huguenots et les Gueux . . . (1560-1585)*. 6 vols. Bruges, 1883-1885.

———, and Gilliodts-Van Severen, L. *Relations politiques des Pays-Bas de l'Angleterre, sous le règne de Philippe II*. 11 vols. Brussels, 1888-1900.

Lehmberg, S. E. "Archbishop Grindal and the Prophesyings." *Historical Magazine of the Protestant Episcopal Church* 34 (1965), 87-145.

Lodge, Edmund. *Illustrations of British History*, etc. 2nd ed. 3 vols. London, 1838.

Nicolas, Sir [Nicholas] Harris. *Memoirs of the Life and Times of Sir Christopher Hatton*, etc. London, 1847.

Papers Relating to the Navy during the Spanish War, 1585-1587. Edited by Julian S. Corbett. Navy Records Society 11. London, 1898.

Parker, Matthew. *Correspondence . . . from A.D. 1535, to . . . 1575*. Edited by John Bruce and T. T. Perowne. Parker Society. Cambridge, 1853; reprint, New York: Johnson Reprint, 1968.

Paule, George. *The Life of . . . J. Whitgift, the Most Reverend and Religious Prelate*. London, 1612.

Rymer, T. *Foedera*. 20 vols. London, 1704-1732.

Salignac, Bertrand de, *see* Fénélon, Seigneur de La Mothe.

Sandys, Edwin. *Sermons*. Parker Society. Cambridge, 1842.

The Seconde Parte of a Register. Edited by A. Peel. 2 vols. Cambridge, 1915.

Sir Fulke Greville's Life of Sir Philip Sidney, . . . 1652. Introduction by Nowell Smith. Oxford: Clarendon Press, 1907.

Statutes of the Realm. Edited by A. Luders et al. 11 vols. London, 1810-1828.

Strype, John. *Annals of the Reformation.* 4 vols. Oxford, 1820-1840.

——. *The History of the Life and Acts of . . . Edmund Grindal.* Oxford, 1821.

——. *The Life and Acts of John Whitgift.* 3 vols. Oxford, 1822.

——. *Life and Acts of Matthew Parker.* 3 vols. Oxford, 1821.

——. *Life of John Aylmer.* Oxford, 1821.

Stubbs, John. *The Discoverie of a Gaping Gulf,* etc. 1579. Edited by Lloyd E. Berry. Charlottesville: University Press of Virginia, 1968.

A Treatise of Treasons against Queen Elizabeth and the Crown of England. [Antwerp], 1572.

Tudor Royal Proclamations. Edited by Paul L. Hughes and James F. Larkin, C.X.V. 3 vols. New Haven and London: Yale University Press, 1964-1969.

Walton, Izaak. *Life of Richard Hooker.* London, 1665.

Whitgift, John. *Works.* Edited by John Ayre. 3 vols. Parker Society. Cambridge, 1851-1853.

Wood, Thomas. *Letters of Thomas Wood, Puritan, 1566-1577.* Edited by Patrick Collinson. *Bulletin of the Institute of Historical Research,* special supplement 5. University of London: Athlone Press, 1960.

Secondary Works

Andrews, K. R. "The Aims of Drake's Expedition of 1577-1580." *American Historical Review* 73, no. 3 (February 1968), 724-741.

Bindoff, S. T. "The Making of the Statute of Artificers." In *Elizabethan Government and Society,* 56-94. Edited by S. T. Bindoff, Joel Hurstfield, and C. H. Williams. London: Athlone Press, 1961.

Birt, Henry Norbert. *The Elizabethan Religious Settlement: A Study of Contemporary Documents.* London: George Bell, 1907.

Black, J. B. "Queen Elizabeth, the Sea Beggars, and the Capture of Brille, 1572." *English Historical Review* 46 (1931), 30-47.

Bossy, J. A. "English Catholics and the French Marriage, 1577-81." *Recusant History* 5 (Bognor Regis: Arundel Press, 1959-60), 2-16.

Bush, M. L. *The Government Policy of Protector Somerset.* London: Arnold, 1975.

Calderwood, David. *The True History of the Church of Scotland.* Edinburgh, 1704.

Church and Society in England: Henry VIII to James I. Edited by Felicity Heal and Rosemary O'Day. London and Hamden, Conn.: Archon, 1977.

Clancy, Thomas H. *Papist Pamphleteers: The Allen-Persons Party and the Political Thought of the Counter-Reformation in England, 1572-1615.* Chicago: Loyola University Press, 1964.

Collinson, Patrick. *The Elizabethan Puritan Movement.* Berkeley: University of California Press, 1967.

Continuity and Change: Personnel and Administration of the Church in England, 1500-1642. Edited by Rosemary O'Day and Felicity Heal. Leicester University Press, 1976.

Corbett, Julian S. *Drake and the Tudor Navy,* etc. 2 vols. London, 1898.

Cross, Claire. *Puritan Earl: The Life of Henry Hastings . . . 1536-1595.* London: Macmillan, 1966.

Cruickshank, C. G. *Elizabeth's Army.* 2nd ed. Oxford: Clarendon Press, 1966.

Dawley, Powel Mills. *John Whitgift and the English Reformation.* New York: Scribner's, 1954.

Dixon, Richard W. *History of the Church of England.* 6 vols. Oxford, 1878-1902.

Elton, G. R. *Reform and Reformation: England 1509-1558.* Cambridge, Mass.: Harvard University Press, 1978.

―――. *Reform and Renewal: Thomas Cromwell and the Common Weal.* Cambridge University Press, 1973.

Essen, Léon van der. *Alexandre Farnèse, . . . (1545-1592),* etc. 5 vols. Brussels, 1933-1937.

Gee, Henry. *The Elizabethan Clergy and the Settlement of Religion, 1558-1564.* Oxford, 1898.

Haller, William. *The Elect Nation: The Meaning and Relevance of Foxe's Book of Martyrs.* New York: Harper & Row, 1963.

Haugaard, William P. *Elizabeth and the English Reformation: The Struggle for a Stable Settlement of Religion.* Cambridge University Press, 1968.

Heal, Felicity. "The Bishops and the Act of Exchange of 1559." *Historical Journal* 17 (1974), 227-246.

————. "The Bishops of Ely and Their Diocese during the Reformation Period: c. 1515-1600." Ph.D. dissertation, Cambridge University, 1972.

Hughes, Philip. *The Reformation in England.* 3 vols. New York: Macmillan, 1951-1954.

Jones, Frank. *The Life of Martin Frobisher,* etc. London, 1878.

Jones, Norman L. "Faith by Statute: The Politics of Religion in the Parliament of 1559." Ph.D. thesis, Cambridge University, 1977.

Jordan, W. K. *Edward VI: The Young King. The Protectorship of the Duke of Somerset.* London: George Allen & Unwin, 1968.

Kenny, Robert W. *Elizabeth's Admiral: The Political Career of Charles Howard, Earl of Nottingham, 1536-1624.* Baltimore and London: Johns Hopkins University Press, 1970.

Lee, Maurice, Jr. *John Maitland of Thirlestane and the Foundation of the Stuart Despotism in Scotland.* Princeton University Press, 1959.

Lehmberg, Stanford E. *The Later Parliaments of Henry VIII, 1536-1547.* Cambridge University Press, 1977.

————. *The Reformation Parliament, 1529-1536.* Cambridge University Press, 1970.

Loades, D. M. *The Reign of Mary Tudor: Government and Religions in England, 1553-1558.* London: St. Martin's Press, 1979.

MacCaffrey, Wallace T. "The Anjou Match and the Making of Elizabethan Foreign Policy." In *Essays Presented to Professor Joel Hurstfield,* 59-75. Leicester University Press, 1979.

MacCaffrey, Wallace T. (*cont.*) *The Shaping of the Elizabethan Regime*. Princeton University Press, 1968.

McGrath, Patrick. *Papists and Puritans under Elizabeth I.* London and New York: Walker, 1967.

McLane, Paul E. *Spenser's "Shepheardes Calender."* Notre Dame, Ind.: University Press, 1961.

Manning, Roger B. *Religion and Society in Elizabethan Sussex: A Study of the Enforcement of the Religious Settlement, 1558-1603*. Leicester University Press, 1969.

Meyer, Arnold Oskar. *England and the Catholic Church under Queen Elizabeth*. Translated by Rev. M. R. McKee. London, 1915. Reissued, with new introduction by John Bossy. London: Routledge and Kegan Paul, 1967.

Neale, J. E. "Elizabeth and the Netherlands, 1586-7." *English Historical Review* 45 (1930), 373-96. Reprinted in *Essays in Elizabethan History*. London: Jonathan Cape, 1958.

———. *Elizabeth I and Her Parliaments, 1559-1581*. London: Jonathan Cape, 1953.

———. *Elizabeth I and Her Parliaments, 1584-1601*. London: Jonathan Cape, 1957.

———. "The Elizabethan Acts of Supremacy and Uniformity." *English Historical Review* 65 (1950), 304-332.

———. *The Elizabethan House of Commons*. London: Jonathan Cape, 1949.

A New History of Ireland. Edited by T. W. Moody, F. X. Martin, and F. J. Byrne. Vol. III. *Early Modern Ireland, 1534-1691*. Oxford: Clarendon Press, 1976.

Pollen, J. H. *The English Catholics in the Reign of Queen Elizabeth: A Study of Their Politics, Civil Life and Government*. London: Longmans, Green, 1920.

———. "The Politics of English Catholics during the Reign of Queen Elizabeth." Pt. 3: "Revival of Spiritual Life and of Political Aspirations, 1580-1582." *The Month* 99 (1902), 290-305.

Read, Conyers. *Lord Burghley and Queen Elizabeth*. London: Jonathan Cape, 1960.

———. *Mr Secretary Walsingham and the Policy of Queen*

Elizabeth. 3 vols. Cambridge, Mass.: Harvard University Press, and Oxford: Clarendon Press, 1925.

———. "Walsingham and Burghley in Queen Elizabeth's Privy Council." *English Historical Review* 28 (1913), 34-58.

Reid, R. R. *The King's Council in the North.* London: Longmans, Green, 1921; republished, 1975.

Scarisbrick, J. J. *Henry VIII.* London: Eyre & Spottiswoode, 1968.

Seaver, Paul. "Community Control and Puritan Politics in Elizabethan Suffolk." *Albion* 9 (1977), 316-336.

Sheils, William. "Some Problems of Government in a New Diocese: The Bishop and the Puritans in the Diocese of Peterborough, 1560-1630." In *Continuity and Change: Personnel and Administration of the Church in England, 1500-1642,* 167-187. Edited by Rosemary O'Day and Felicity Heal. Leicester University Press, 1976.

Smith, A. Hassell. *County and Court: Government and Politics in Norfolk, 1558-1603.* Oxford: Clarendon Press, 1974.

Smith, Alan G. R. *Servant of the Cecils: The Life of Sir Michael Hickes, 1543-1612.* Totowa, N.J.: Rowan and Littlefield, 1977.

Stone, Lawrence. *The University in Society.* 2 vols. Princeton University Press, 1974.

Taylor, E.G.R. "The Missing Draft Project of Drake's Voyage of 1577-80." *Geographical Journal* 75 (1930), 46-70.

———. "More Light on Drake: 1577-80." *Mariner's Mirror* 16 (1930), 134-147.

Törne, P. O. de. *Don Juan d'Autriche et les projets de conquête de l'Angleterre . . . 1568-1578.* 2 vols. Helsingfors, 1915, 1928.

Usher, Roland. *The Rise and Fall of the High Commission.* Oxford: Clarendon Press, 1913.

Walker, F. X. "The Implementation of the Elizabethan Statutes against Recusants, 1581-1603." Ph.D. thesis, University of London, 1961.

Williamson, James A. *Hawkins of Plymouth,* etc. London: Adair and Charles Black, 1949.

Wilson, Charles. *Queen Elizabeth and the Revolt of the Netherlands*. London: Macmillan, 1970.

Wilson, Elkin, C. *England's Eliza*. 1939; reprint, New York: Octagon, 1966.

Wright, Thomas. *Queen Elizabeth and Her Times*. 2 vols. London, 1838.

Yates, Frances A. *Astraea: The Imperial Theme in the Sixteenth Century*. London and Boston: Routledge and Kegan Paul, 1975.

INDEX